PRIVATE CLIENT: WILLS, TRUSTS AND ESTATE PLANNING

PRIVATE CLIENT: WILLS, TRUSTS AND ESTATE PLANNING

Helen Cousal MA (Cantab), Solicitor

Lesley King LLB, Dip Crim (Cantab), Solicitor

Published by

College of Law Publishing,
Braboeuf Manor, Portsmouth Road, St Catherines, Guildford GU3 1HA

British Library Cataloguing-in-Publication Data
A catalogue record for this book is available from the British Library.

ISBN 978 1 907624 28 5

Typeset by Style Photosetting Ltd, Mayfield, East Sussex
Printed in Great Britain by Ashford Colour Press Ltd, Gosport, Hampshire

Preface

The aim of this book is to provide a comprehensive introduction to the legal and taxation implications arising from estate planning work for clients within the private client department of a solicitor's practice. At the beginning of **Chapter 1**, there is reference to the problem of definition of private client. In view of this it has been necessary, but difficult, to define the scope of the text, although the subtitle to this book has helped to a considerable extent.

We have had the benefit of helpful, and often long, discussions with many practitioners, from whose suggestions we hope to have arrived at a consensus. However, we remain aware that the private client department of a London firm is often very different from a provincial practice. We should like to express our appreciation to the many busy private client partners who have so willingly provided their advice and suggestions, and their time, in relation to the content of this book.

This book is written primarily to complement the Legal Practice Course elective, Private Client, but it is hoped it will provide a useful introduction to others interested in this type of work. Students studying for this elective will have already completed the compulsory part of the Legal Practice Course; there are, therefore, some references to that course and to other LPC Guides.

The permission to reproduce a number of precedent forms and clauses from the following publications is acknowledged with thanks: *Practical Trust Precedents* (Sweet & Maxwell); *Practical Will Precedents* (Sweet & Maxwell) (permission obtained from Withers); and White, *Post-Death Rearrangements: Practice and Precedents*, 5th edn (Sweet & Maxwell, 1995).

For brevity, we have used the masculine pronoun throughout to include the feminine. The law is stated as at 20 October 2010.

Throughout, we have endeavoured to provide the principal statutory references to enable further research to be made into a topic where this is required. In a subject as broad-based as Private Client (even as interpreted within this book), there are many relevant textbooks and precedent books to which a student or practitioner may wish to refer; these include:

Lasting and Enduring Powers of Attorney

Cretney & Lush on Lasting and Enduring Powers of Attorney, 6th edn (Jordans, 2009)

Trust Law

Parker and Mellows, *The Modern Law of Trusts*, 9th edn (Sweet & Maxwell, 2008)
Hanbury and Martin, *Modern Equity*, 18th edn (Sweet & Maxwell, 2009)

Precedents

Practical Will Precedents (Sweet & Maxwell)
Practical Trust Precedents (Sweet & Maxwell)
Encyclopaedia of Forms and Precedents (LexisNexis), Trusts and Settlements

Estate and Tax Planning

Estate Planning (Tolley)
Tax Planning (Tolley)
Taxation of UK Trusts (Tolley)

Wills and Probate

Barlow, King and King, *Wills, Administration and Taxation: A Practical Guide*, 9th edn (Sweet & Maxwell, 2008)
Williams on Wills, 9th edn (Butterworths, 2009)

Revenue Law

Revenue Law: Principles and Practice, 28th edn (Tottel, 2010)
Dymond's Capital Taxes (Sweet & Maxwell)

HELEN COUSAL and LESLEY KING
The College of Law

Contents

Table of Cases

Table of Statutes

Table of Statutory Instruments and Practice Rules

Table of Abbreviations

The following abbreviations are used throughout this book.

A & M	accumulation and maintenance
AEA 1925	Administration of Estates Act 1925
AEA 1971	Administration of Estates Act 1971
AIM	Alternative Investment Market
AVCs	additional voluntary contributions
BMT	trust for bereaved minors
BYP	trust for bereaved young persons
CGT	capital gains tax
COB Rules	Solicitors' Financial Services (Conduct of Business) Rules 2001
CPA 2004	Civil Partnership Act 2004
EPA	enduring power of attorney
EPAA 1985	Enduring Powers of Attorney Act 1985
FA	Finance Act
FSA	Financial Services Authority
FSAVCs	free-standing additional voluntary contributions
FSMA 2000	Financial Services and Markets Act 2000
ICTA 1988	Income and Corporation Taxes Act 1988
IHT	inheritance tax
IHTA 1984	Inheritance Tax Act 1984
IPDI	immediate post-death interest
ISAs	Individual Savings Accounts
ITA 2007	Income Tax Act 2007
ITEPA 2003	Income Tax (Earnings and Pensions) Act 2003
ITTOIA 2005	Income Tax (Trading and Other Income) Act 2005
LCT	lifetime chargeable transfer
LPA	lasting power of attorney
LPA 1925	Law of Property Act 1925
MCA 2005	Mental Capacity Act 2005
OEIC	open-ended investment company
PAA	Perpetuities and Accumulations Act
PEP	personal equity plan
PET	potentially exempt transfer
PHI	permanent health insurance
PR	personal representative
RAO 2001	Financial Services and Markets Act 2000 (Regulated Activities) Order 2001
RPI	retail price index
SERPS	State Earnings-Related Pension Scheme
SLA 1925	Settled Land Act 1925
TA 1925	Trustee Act 1925
TA 2000	Trustee Act 2000
TCGA 1992	Taxation of Chargeable Gains Act 1992
TESSAs	Tax Exempt Special Savings Accounts
TIA	Trustee Investments Act 1961
TLATA 1996	Trusts of Land and Appointment of Trustees Act 1996
VTA 1958	Variation of Trusts Act 1958

Chapter 1
Private Client

1.1 What is private client work?

Lord Denning, in *Griffiths v JP Harrison (Watford) Ltd* [1962] 1 All ER 909, HL, said, 'We can recognise a "trade" when we see it. ... But we are hard pressed to define it'. In that case, he was considering whether an activity was a trading activity. He might have said much the same thing had he been considering 'private client work'.

At its broadest, private client work may be said to include all work except commercial work, although even commercial work has a private client dimension. At its narrowest, it will generally be taken to exclude such topics as conveyancing, family law, litigation and employment law, leaving a residual category of personal taxation, wills, probate and trust work.

Some firms, generally the larger firms, have separate departments with partners and assistant solicitors who concentrate exclusively on serving the needs of their private clients. Smaller firms often have a number of partners and assistant solicitors who do private client work but not necessarily within a separate department. These firms will not usually define this work as private client work as such. If asked, they would probably see it as covering most of the firm's clients except the purely commercial clients. In recent years, some large practices have developed a policy of concentrating on commercial work and referring any private client work to other firms specialising in that area.

The subtitle to this book, 'Wills, Trusts and Estate Planning', describes, and places a limit on, the scope of the book. Therefore, it covers private client work in the narrow sense. Other aspects of private client work as more broadly defined are the subject of other books in this series.

Extensive discussion with City of London firms, provincial city firms and many other firms with private client departments has confirmed that the main emphasis of their work within the private client department is 'estate planning'. This emphasis has led to an equivalent main theme for this LPC Guide.

1.2 Private client work and the compulsory subjects of the Legal Practice Course

1.2.1 Probate and estate administration

The study of private client work follows naturally from a study of probate, estate administration and related succession issues. Many of the topics introduced in the LPC Guide, **Legal Foundations**, for example lifetime gifts and the use of annual tax exemptions, are developed further. Many new topics and ideas for estate planning are also introduced. In some cases, reference is made to particular aspects of other LPC Guides. It will be necessary to re-read some of the material contained in those books.

1.2.2   Revenue law

The three principal taxes applicable to private individuals are relevant to this area of work. The principles of these taxes are set out in the LPC Guides, *Legal Foundations* and *Business Law and Practice*.

1.2.3   Financial services

Estate planning for clients will inevitably involve a consideration of financial planning, particularly in relation to investments. For example, clients may want advice in relation to their existing shares, or as to what investments they should make in the immediate future.

In some cases, a solicitor may become involved in other investment activity for a client. After giving advice, the solicitor may follow this up by making arrangements for the client to acquire (or sell) investments. In some cases, the solicitor may even be prepared to manage a client's investment portfolio. However, this is less likely since the Financial Services and Markets Act 2000 (FSMA 2000) increased the regulatory burden on firms involved in such work.

Not all solicitors' firms will wish to carry out investment business for clients, even though they undertake a substantial amount of private client work. Many practitioners prefer to 'hive off' the financial aspects of a client's business to specialist independent financial advisers leaving the solicitor to concentrate on the purely legal aspects of the work. However, some of the larger firms, as well as many medium-sized or smaller firms, take the opposite approach. They see financial services work as potentially lucrative for the practice. Thus, using their existing client database as their prime source of investment business, firms which decide to become involved in financial services work may often set up a separate financial services department. This may be 'headed up' by a solicitor with the necessary expertise or by an individual brought into the firm for the purpose. Such a person would normally have qualifications and experience gained from working in the financial services industry. Departments of this type will work closely with the private client department but will also provide a support role for other areas of the practice. Firms need to decide whether they are prepared to comply with the requirements of FSMA 2000 and be regulated by the Financial Services Authority (FSA), or whether they wish to limit themselves to activities which can be carried out under the regulation of the Solicitors' Regulation Authority.

This book presupposes that the solicitor's firm has opted for regulation by the Solicitors' Regulation Authority. However, we will consider the nature of the various investment products available on the market, their similarities and differences and their suitability or otherwise for any particular client. Such a client, within the context of this book, may either be an individual or a trustee.

1.3   Ownership and disposition of assets

Private client work for any client will involve the solicitor in two separate, though closely related, matters.

1.3.1   Ownership of assets

The decision to acquire assets, for example the family home or investments, is for the client to make, although the solicitor may be asked to offer advice. Even where clients do not require advice as to the selection of particular assets, they may need advice on how family assets should be owned. The solicitor will frequently need to advise on the advantages and disadvantages of sole ownership or joint ownership (as joint tenants or as tenants in common) or whether to hold assets through a trust. Hence, this book deals with (inter alia):

(a)   financial planning; and

(b)   estate planning.

1.3.2 Disposition of assets

Clients who have substantial assets will want to consider how to pass them on to family members in the most tax-effective way. The options available are:

(a)   lifetime gifts: these may be outright gifts to individuals or into trusts; or

(b)   gifts by will: these may also be outright gifts to individuals or into trusts.

Chapter 2
Financial Planning

2.1 Planning the client's financial affairs

This chapter introduces some of the concepts which lie behind financial and investment planning advice for individual clients as part of their estate planning.

The object of financial planning is to maximise the wealth (capital and income) of an individual.

Financial planning is a continuing process. It requires the development of a strategy based on short- and long-term forward planning. Ideally, a plan, an investment strategy, should be developed for the client. Any immediate needs identified by the plan can be implemented at once. Longer-term planning can be given effect as the opportunities develop.

The range of financial planning and investment opportunities available to private clients is very wide. In view of this, the key to successful advice to clients lies in:

(a) knowing all the circumstances of the particular client; and

(b) devising a financial and investment plan which is appropriate to meet those circumstances.

2.1.1 Financial planning

Financial planning covers savings, for example in a bank or building society, investments, life assurance and pension arrangements, mortgages, school fee schemes (see **Appendix 2**) and tax planning generally (see **Chapter 4**).

2.1.2 Investment planning

Investment planning is one aspect of financial planning. In everyday use the phrase is understood as covering a wide range of investments from unit trusts, investment trusts, and other stocks and shares (see **Appendix 2**) to specialist items such as works of art, stamp collections and investment in woodlands. It is not confined to 'investments' as defined in the FSMA 2000 (see **2.2**).

2.1.3 Fees and commissions

It is, of course, usual for a solicitor to charge a client a fee for work done for the client.

Investment business often gives rise to payment of commission by the provider of the investment product. A solicitor who arranges an endowment policy for a client may be offered a commission from the life company. If, instead, the transaction is carried out through an authorised person, it may be agreed that the authorised person shares the commission he receives with the solicitor.

Receipt of fees and commissions requires consideration of the Solicitor's Code of Conduct 2007 and the general principle that there must be no conflict of interest between the solicitor and the client.

Rule 1 sets out the core duties of a solicitor. These include the duty to act with integrity and in the best interests of the client, together with the duty not to allow the solicitor's independence to be compromised. Rule 3.01 requires the solicitor to refrain from acting if there is a significant risk that the solicitor's duty to act in the best interests of the client may conflict with the solicitor's own interests.

This does not prevent receipt of commission. However, placing a client's business with the company which pays the biggest commission may be in the solicitor's best interest, not the client's. A breach of Rule 1 and Rule 3 would occur.

Rule 2.06 – The solicitor must account to the client for any commission received if more than £20 unless the client, in full knowledge of the amount or basis of calculation of the commission, agrees that the solicitor should retain the commission.

Commissions for investment business will frequently exceed £20. Even where the commission is less than £20, a firm which wants to stay within the Financial Services (Scope) Rules 2001 provisions will have to account for it (see **2.2**).

Rule 9.03 – Solicitors who recommend that a client use a particular firm must do so in good faith, judging what is in the client's best interests.

The guidance to Rule 9 emphasises that all referral arrangements are subject to the general requirements of the Solicitors' Code of Conduct 2007 as well as the particular requirements of Rule 9.

It is not normally in a client's best interests to be referred to a firm which only offers products from one source. Rule 9.03(5) therefore provides that a solicitor who refers a client to a firm, agency or business that can only offer products from one source, must notify the client in writing of this limitation.

Rule 9.03(6) states: 'If a client is likely to need an endowment policy, or similar life insurance with an investment element, you must refer them only to an independent intermediary authorised to give investment advice.'

'Independent intermediary' has never been a defined term. However, in July 2009 the SRA issued guidance stating its view that 'independent intermediary' has the same meaning as the Financial Services Authority gives to 'independent financial advisers'. An independent financial adviser is an adviser who is able to advise on products from across the whole of the market *and* offers the consumer the option of paying fees. Advisers who advise from across the whole of the market but do not offer the option of paying fees will not be able to call themselves 'independent'.

The guidance was issued because some aggressive financial institutions were said to have been promoting themselves as eligible to receive referrals from solicitors when they were not.

Independent intermediaries are different from multi-tied advisers (who are able to recommend the products of a limited selection of providers) and tied advisers (who can only advise on the products of one provider).

Fees or commission?

A solicitor has a choice:

(a)   to charge a fee for the work and account to the client for the entire commission received;

(b)   to charge a fee for the work but to offset this (with the client's agreement) with the commission received;

(c)   to retain the commission with the client's agreement in lieu of charging a fee.

There are advantages and disadvantages to each method. One particular point to note is that the amount charged, whether as fees or by way of commission, can always be challenged if not 'fair and reasonable' for the amount of work done (Solicitors' (Non-contentious Business) Remuneration Order 1994, SI 1994/2616).

As we will see at **2.2**, a solicitor who is not authorised to carry on regulated activities under FSMA 2000 will often use an authorised person to arrange investments for a client. This will exempt the solicitor from the need to obtain authorisation under the Act so long as he does not receive any pecuniary award or advantage for which he does not account to the client.

The Law Society's Professional Ethics Department stated that it believed that retaining commission with the consent of the client in accordance with Rule 2.06 amounted to accounting to the client. The FSA confirmed this. Note that all commission must be disclosed to the client, even commission of £20 or less.

2.2   The Financial Services and Markets Act 2000

The FSMA 2000, is discussed in the LPC Guide, **Legal Foundations**. Any solicitor who is involved in developing and implementing an investment strategy for a client must comply with the relevant provisions of FSMA 2000 and the Financial Services and Markets Act 2000 (Regulated Activities) Order 2001 (RAO 2001), SI 2001/544. Remember that carrying on a regulated activity without the necessary authorisation is a criminal offence under FSMA 2000, s 19.

Under FSMA 2000, firms carrying on regulated activities as defined by the RAO 2001 have to be regulated by the FSA.

However, Pt XX of FSMA 2000 makes special provision for professional firms which do not carry on mainstream investment business but which may carry on regulated activities in the course of other work such as probate and trusts. This enables solicitors to be treated as 'exempt professional firms' and to carry on 'exempt regulated activities' under the supervision of the Solicitors' Regulation Authority, which is a Designated Professional Body for this purpose.

In this book we deal with exempt professional firms but not with regulation by the FSA. Readers interested in obtaining authorisation from the FSA should consult a specialist text.

2.2.1   Regulation by the Solicitors' Regulation Authority

Designated Professional Bodies are required to make rules to ensure that their members only carry on regulated activities arising out of or complementary to the provision of professional services to the client. Solicitors are subject to the Solicitors' Financial Services (Scope) Rules 2001, which set out the scope of activities that solicitors can undertake within the Pt XX exemption. It is most important that solicitors do not stray outside the Scope Rules, as this is likely to amount to a criminal offence under FSMA 2000, s 19.

In the course of probate and trust work a firm will frequently perform services which fall within the definition of regulated activities in the RAO 2001. They need to ask the following questions:

(a)   Does the activity involve a specified investment?

(b)   Is the activity capable of being a regulated activity under the RAO 2001?

(c)   If so, does it fall within any of the exclusions in the RAO 2001?

(d)   If not, does it fall within the Scope Rules?

There is a further problem. The FSMA 2000 provides that any communication which amounts to an invitation or inducement to engage in an investment activity must be made (or in some cases approved) by an FSA-authorised person.

Solicitors regulated by the Solicitors' Regulation Authority must be careful not to breach this requirement. Communication can be oral or written. Almost anything a solicitor says or writes in connection with many transactions could be construed as a financial promotion. For example, a solicitor who advises executors to sell the deceased's shares could be inviting them to deal in investments.

Fortunately there is an exemption for 'one-off' communications, which will normally cover solicitors unless the communications are part of an organised marketing campaign.

2.2.1.1   Does the activity involve a specified investment?

Investments are specified in RAO 2001, arts 74–89. They include:

(a)   shares or stock;

(b)   debentures;

(c)   government securities;

(d)   unit trusts and open-ended investment companies (OEICS);

(e)   insurance contracts;

(f)   mortgages.

The following are not investments:

(a)   National Savings products such as National Savings Certificates, Premium Bonds, SAYE contracts;

(b)   bank and building society accounts;

(c)   cash ISAs.

2.2.1.2   Is the activity capable of being a regulated activity under the RAO 2001?

The activities are listed in RAO 2001 and usually the activity is expressed in relation to a particular type of investment, so it is the combination of activity plus particular investment which produces the regulated activity.

Some of the activities have particular exclusions associated with them which are dealt with below.

Regulated activities include:

(a)   dealing in shares as principal or agent;

(b)   advising on or arranging the acquisition or disposal of shares;

(c)   advising on or arranging the assignment of life policies;

(d)   arranging deals;

(e)   safeguarding and administering investments on behalf of clients;

(f)   managing investments.

Note: Advising means giving specific advice about a specific investment. Solicitors can give generic advice to a client without carrying on a regulated activity. For example, they can advise on the relative merits of buying shares as opposed to land.

2.2.1.3   Does the activity fall within any of the exclusions in the RAO 2001?

If the activity falls within one of the exclusions then the activity is not regulated and the firm will not be subject to the Scope Rules at all in connection with the activity. There are a number of exclusions. The most relevant to private client work are discussed below.

Articles 22, 29 and 33 – using an authorised person or introducing a client to an authorised person

A solicitor can:

(a)   Introduce a client to an authorised person with a view to the provision of independent advice (art 33).

The solicitor must do no more than introduce the client to the adviser. If the solicitor retains any sort of ongoing role (for example, acting as a channel of communication, discussing the matter with the client or explaining the meaning of certain terms) this will amount to more than mere 'introducing'.

(b)   Arrange deals for a client who enters into them with or through an authorised person:

(i)   on the advice of an authorised person, or

(ii)   where it is clear that the client, in his capacity as investor, is not seeking the advice of the solicitor (or if the client did seek it, the solicitor declined to give it and recommended that the client obtained advice from an authorised person) (art 29).

(c)   Enter into deals as agent for a client with or through an authorised person:

(i)   on the advice of an authorised person, or

(ii)   where it is clear that the client, in his capacity as investor, is not seeking the advice of the solicitor (or if the client did seek it, the solicitor declined to give it and recommended that the client obtained advice from an authorised person) (art 22).

In order to come within arts 29 or 22 the solicitor must not receive any pecuniary reward from anyone other than the client which is not accounted for to the client. In each case the solicitor must be careful not to comment on the advice of the authorised person in such a way that it amounts to separate advice coming from the solicitor.

This exclusion will not apply if the transaction involved is an insurance contract.

Article 66 – trustees

This exclusion relates to four functions which trustees or personal representatives (PRs) might perform in relation to investments. The exclusion does not apply if the solicitor trustee receives any additional remuneration on top of remuneration received for acting as trustee or PR. The trustee/PR is not regarded as receiving additional remuneration if he simply receives remuneration calculated on a time basis for time spent dealing with the investments. The four functions are:

(a)   *Arranging*. Arrangements made by a solicitor acting as trustee or PR will be excluded if for or with a view to a transaction which is made by:

(i)   him and any fellow trustees or PRs, acting in their capacity as PRs or trustees;

(ii)   a beneficiary under the trust, will or intestacy.

It is only available where the solicitor acts *as* trustee or PR and not where he acts *for* them. However, it is available where a member of the solicitor's firm carries out the activity on behalf of the solicitor trustee.

(b)   *Managing*. Managing investments as a trustee or PR is excluded. Again there must be no additional remuneration. This exclusion is not available if the solicitor holds himself out as providing a discretionary management service over and above that which a lay trustee would provide.

(c)   *Safeguarding*. There is an exclusion for safeguarding investments, but it is not available if the solicitor holds himself out as providing a discretionary management service over and above that which a lay trustee would provide. Again there must be no additional remuneration.

(d)   *Advising.* There is an exclusion where a solicitor who is a trustee or PR advises:

    (i)   a fellow trustee or PR for the purposes of the trust or estate; or

    (ii)   a beneficiary under the trust, will or intestacy concerning his interest in the trust fund or estate.

This exclusion does not apply to contracts of insurance.

Article 67 – necessary part of other professional services

There is an exclusion if the activity may reasonably be regarded as a necessary part of other services provided in the course of that profession or business. The exclusion does not apply if the service is remunerated separately from the other services. This simply means that the solicitor must not make a separate charge on the bill.

An example of reasonable necessity in connection with probate work would be arranging the sale of *all* assets to provide funds for payment of debts and inheritance tax. A decision as to *which* asset to sell to provide funds is unlikely to be 'necessary' as the solicitor can always go elsewhere for the advice.

This exclusion is unlikely to apply to insurance contracts.

2.2.1.4   Does it fall within the exemption for professional firms?

The exemption is contained in s 327 of the FSMA 2000. There are three main conditions.

Rule 4(b) – the manner of providing the service must be 'incidental to the provision' by the firm of professional services

To satisfy this condition the exempt regulated activities must not be a major part of the firm's practice. The FSA will consider whether the scale of regulated activity was in proportion to other professional services provided; whether the regulated activities were held out as separate services and the impression given through the firm's advertising of the way in which the firm provides the regulated activities.

In addition the regulated activity must be incidental to the particular client. A firm cannot carry out a regulated activity in isolation for a particular client. The professional service must be the primary service and any regulated activity should be subordinate to that professional service. Thus, in a probate matter where the client is the executor, advice given to a beneficiary will not satisfy the test.

Rule 4(c) – the firm must account to the client for any pecuniary reward or other advantage which the firm receives

If a firm receives commission or any other financial benefit from a third party because of acting for or giving advice to a client, the firm must account for the commission or benefit to the client. Accounting to the client does not mean simply telling the client that the firm will receive commission. It means that the commission or reward must be held to the order of the client. As we saw at **2.1.3**, The Law Society stated that solicitors will still account to the client if they have the client's informed consent to keeping the commission.

If the firm is charging the client on a fee basis, the firm can offset the commission against the firm's fees. The firm must send the client a bill or some other written notification of costs to comply with Solicitors' Accounts Rules 1998, Rule 19.

The requirement for informed consent will not be satisfied by the firm seeking a blanket consent in its terms of business to the keeping of unspecified commission.

The firm must be able to demonstrate that the client has given informed consent to any retention of the commission, having had full disclosure of the amount. The FSA's Perimeter

Guidance indicates that the firm should inform the client that, in effect, the commission belongs to the client.

The £20 de minimis provision contained in the Solicitor's Code of Conduct 2007, Rule 2.06 does not apply to a firm seeking to remain within the Scope provisions. Commissions of £20 or less arising out of regulated activities must be treated in the same way as commissions in excess of £20.

Rule 4(d) – the activity must not be on the list of activities prohibited from coming within Pt XX

Under the Financial Services and Markets Act 2000 (Professions) (Non-exempt Activities) Order 2001, SI 2001/1227, the Treasury has listed activities which cannot be provided within the Pt XX Designated Professional Body regime. The activities that are most relevant to solicitors are set out in the Solicitors' Financial Services (Scope) Rules 2001. They include:

(a)   market making and dealing in the same way as a stockbroker;

(b)   operating a regulated collective investment scheme;

(c)   advising a person to become a member of a particular Lloyd's syndicate;

(d)   managing a stakeholder pension scheme.

2.2.1.5   Insurance mediation

Clients may be interested in obtaining life assurance either as a personal investment or to provide funds for family members or to pay IHT. Private client practitioners must remember that the government extended the financial services legislation to comply with the Insurance Mediation Directive (2002/92/EC).

As a result of the amendments, any assistance given to a client to obtain insurance, even the introduction of a client to an insurance broker, will be a specified activity. The main exclusions do not apply to insurance contracts, so a solicitor who offers any assistance to a client in relation to insurance will commit a criminal offence unless covered by the exemption under s 327 of the FSMA 2000 for professional firms.

Assistance with the provision of insurance may be incidental, as described at **2.2.1.4**, and unremunerated, but there are additional requirements that must be complied with. The firm must appoint a compliance officer and be registered in the FSA Register.

2.2.2   The Conduct of Business Rules

If the firm carries out an exempt regulated activity it must comply with the Solicitors' Financial Services (Conduct of Business) Rules 2001 (COB Rules) as well as with the Scope requirements.

The COB Rules apply only when solicitors are carrying out an exempt regulated activity and not when the firm is doing something which does not amount to a regulated activity at all, say, using an authorised third party. However, it is safest to make sure that the firm always follows the COB Rules, as this will avoid any risk of accidental non-compliance. In any event, the Rules merely set out good practice.

Of particular relevance to private client departments are the following:

(a)   Rule 6 – The firm must keep records of all commissions received in respect of regulated activities and how that commission was dealt with.

(b)   Rule 7 – Where a firm safeguards and administers another's assets it must operate 'appropriate systems'. These should include the following:

    (i)   to register assets in the client's name;

    (ii)   to record all title documents held, and safeguard documents adequately;

(iii)   to maintain a central record of all documents of which it has custody;

(iv)   to check records against title documents at least once a year;

(v)   to report to clients at least once a year on title documents held.

2.3   Developing the investment strategy for clients

Although solicitors without special expertise will not be developing such a strategy, it is important to appreciate what professional investment advisers should be doing.

2.3.1   'Know your client'

When taking instructions in relation to any financial planning for clients, it is essential to 'know the client'.

There are two main aspects to this:

(a)   investigating, ie, ascertaining from the client all relevant personal and financial details; and

(b)   determining the suitability of investments, ie, only recommending investments suitable to the particular client.

2.3.2   The client's personal details

The information which should be obtained will include the following four major categories:

(a)   Personal details:

    (i)   name, address and occupation;

    (ii)   dates of birth and retirement;

    (iii)   whether single, married or in a civil partnership, divorced, or widow(ed);

    (iv)   whether employed, or self-employed.

(b)   Family details:

    (i)   spouse or civil partner (name and age);

    (ii)   children, grandchildren (names and ages).

(c)   Gifts previously made (including the amounts and whether outright or in trust).

(d)   Provision by any will (including the date of will).

The Money Laundering Regulations 2007 (which came into force on 15 December 2007) require solicitors to take measures to identify not merely clients but also 'beneficial owners' who are not clients. In the case of trusts, a beneficial owner for this purpose is defined in reg 6 as:

(a)   any individual who is entitled to a specified interest in at least 25% of the capital of the trust property; and

(b)   as respects other trusts, the class of persons in whose main interest the trust is set up or operates; and

(c)   any individual who has control over the trust.

2.3.3   The client's financial details

The financial details obtained from the client will generally concentrate on two broad areas:

(a)   the client's current assets and liabilities; and

(b)   the client's current income and expenditure.

Generally, there will be some 'signpost' or 'indicator' in the client's existing financial affairs which leads to the opportunity to provide financial planning advice. Some of these indicators are as follows.

A recent problem for many clients has been maintaining a reasonable income stream at a time when interest rates and yields on shares and bonds have been falling. This is a particular problem for trustees where there may be different classes of beneficiaries, some interested in income return and some in capital growth.

2.3.3.1 Savings predominantly on deposit in a bank or building society account

Savings in a bank or building society are relatively 'safe' and convenient in that the money can be withdrawn quickly (although some accounts do require up to 90 days' notice to be given unless interest is to be lost, see further **Appendix 2**). Interest payable is subject to income tax. The main danger in holding a lot of money in such an account is the loss of purchasing power because of inflation. Inflation is the investor's number one enemy. At 5% inflation, £100 today will be worth £95 next year. Money in excess of the state guarantee is at risk if the institution collapses.

Although it is prudent to hold some money in savings accounts as a ready source of money in case of emergency, clients should consider withdrawing some of it for investment elsewhere.

2.3.3.2 Investments all yielding high income returns

High income yields will be superficially attractive to the client, but there are features of such a return which indicate a review of the investment strategy, for example because:

(a)   high yields may be earned at the expense of high risk, ie, there may be a higher risk of losing the invested capital because of the nature of the investment. If so, it may be prudent to diversify the investment portfolio to an appropriate extent; and

(b)   high income indicates the probability of income tax rates of 50%. This may be alleviated by the transfer of some investments into the name of the client's spouse if he or she pays income tax at a lower rate, or by rearranging the investment portfolio into assets where the concentration is on capital growth rather than income yield.

2.3.3.3 No life assurance

For a consideration of the available types of life policy, see **Appendix 2**. Although premiums do not generally attract income tax relief, it is always prudent to use life policies as a method of saving to produce substantial sums of money on the occurrence of anticipated future events. Traditionally, these are the repayment of a mortgage, the retirement of the client and the death of a client. They can also be used to cover school fees.

2.3.3.4 No occupational pension scheme or personal pension

Ideally, anyone who is in work should be able to look forward to retirement in the knowledge that he will then benefit from a pension which provides an acceptable level of income. Payment of national insurance contributions during working life will ensure receipt of the State retirement pension. This is payable at State pension age. In some cases, a 'top up' pension will be payable as well, ie, the State earnings related pension. However, further 'top up' through an occupational pension scheme and/or a private pension is also desirable.

Occupational pension schemes

The absence of contributions by an employee to an occupational pension scheme should not necessarily be taken as meaning that the employee will not benefit from an occupational pension on retirement. These schemes may be offered by employers on a 'non-contributory' basis, ie, only the employer pays contributions. If approved by the Revenue, occupational pension schemes attract considerable tax advantages for employer and employee contributions and for the pension fund itself. Sadly, the increasing cost to employers of providing such schemes means that many are closing.

Personal pension schemes

Personal pension schemes are available to all, and are of particular importance to the self-employed and to employees who are either not offered an occupational pension scheme by their employers or who prefer not to join that pension scheme. If approved by the Revenue, these schemes also attract considerable tax advantages for contributions to the scheme as well as for the fund itself.

Stakeholder pension schemes

These became available on 6 April 2001 and are really a type of personal pension scheme. They are low cost and available to everyone, even those who are not in paid employment. They are much more flexible than traditional personal pension schemes, as contributors can contribute varying amounts and stop and restart contributions. Employed people can take the pension with them when they change jobs. They have substantial tax advantages as for every £1 contributed, the Revenue will contribute 25p even where the contributor is not a tax payer.

See **Appendix 2** for a more detailed discussion of pensions.

2.3.3.5   Assets held in the name of one spouse alone

The home, investments and other assets may, with advantage, be transferred into the joint ownership of spouses through the use of a joint tenancy or a tenancy in common. The various estate planning opportunities available to spouses are discussed in **Chapter 4**. It is frequently preferable to own as beneficial tenants in common rather than as beneficial joint tenants as this gives greater flexibility.

2.3.4   Suitability of investments for a particular client

The investment strategy for the client will reflect the information obtained from the client. Two particular factors will be the age of the client, and the client's existing investments and earnings.

2.3.4.1   The client's age

Younger clients, especially if married with children, may have little spare money beyond what is needed for everyday life, including mortgage payments. Because of the possibility of moving house and other changing circumstances, such clients should place any spare money in savings accounts whereby the income is reasonably high but the capital is relatively free from risk and can easily be recovered if needed. For example, high interest building society and bank deposit accounts provide safe, high returns. Should further money be available, a more complex strategy will be needed.

Middle-aged clients, with growing families, should begin planning for retirement and old age by improving their income and capital position as far as possible. They may, however, be burdened by the costs of school and university fees. So far as possible, they should try to fund pensions. Spare earnings and investment income should be invested to produce maximum capital growth.

Retirement-age clients, who no longer have mortgage and school fee commitments, may need to change the emphasis of their investment strategy from capital growth to income yield. Loss of earnings will need to be balanced as far as possible by investment yields and pension income. If a tax-free capital lump sum is withdrawn from the pension fund at retirement, this should be invested to improve the income position.

Elderly clients, often with low incomes, need to ensure that maximum advantage is taken of the increased levels of personal tax allowances – the age related allowances (see **Appendix 1**) – by holding high income yielding investments where possible. By s 851 of the Income Tax Act 2007 (ITA 2007), interest payable to depositors in banks and building societies is paid net of basic rate tax (20%). Non-tax payers can recover this tax if they submit an appropriate claim to the Revenue. However, if the client is not a tax payer, there is considerable advantage to be gained from holding money in a bank or building society because interest can be paid without deduction of basic rate tax at source. The elderly client will need to certify to the bank or building society that he is not a tax payer so that he can receive gross interest payments.

Planning the financial and other affairs of clients will become difficult where they are unable to take part in decision-making through loss of mental capacity. In order to overcome problems caused by loss of mental capacity, since 1985 individuals have been able to make enduring powers of attorney (EPAs) to appoint someone to deal with their property and affairs. From 1 October 2007, when the relevant provisions of the Mental Capacity Act 2005 came into force, it is no longer possible to make new EPAs. However, it is possible to make lasting powers of attorney (LPAs). It is appropriate for solicitors to recommend to clients that they make an LPA. The client may choose to appoint a member of the family, or perhaps the solicitor, to be his attorney.

Note that EPAs and LPAs should not be regarded as something reserved for elderly clients. People of any age can lose capacity as a result of accident or illness. They will then need someone to deal with their affairs for them. It is often convenient to raise the question of making an LPA at the same time as the client is making a new will or codicil. This is considered in detail in **Chapter 3**.

2.4 Portfolio planning

Every client is different, and each client will have different requirements. Excluding the buying of a house, a general plan for investments will probably be:

(a)   'ready cash' saved in a bank or building society;

(b)   protection through life assurance for the client and dependants;

(c)   pension; and

(d)   longer-term investments purchased with any spare cash.

2.4.1 High risk/low risk

Investments can be categorised as low, medium or high risk. Often the higher the return, the higher the risk. Each category might include the following.

Low risk

(a)   savings accounts in the bank or building society;

(b)   government stock ('gilts');

(c)   National Savings, for example National Savings premium bonds.

Medium risk

(a)   unit trusts;

(b)   investment trusts;

(c)   shares in public companies, ie, in blue chip 'equities';

(d)   loans to companies, financial institutions and local authorities.

High risk

(a)   shares in small public companies and in private companies;

(b)   'collectibles' such as works of art and stamp collections;

(c)   woodlands.

2.4.2   Short-term/longer-term

Short-term investments often mean 'savings', ie, short-term cash investments made for the purchase of a particular item such as a new car. Probably the bank or building society offers the best opportunity but interest rates may be low (and no capital growth).

Longer-term 'investment' depends on the client's available resources, personal likes and dislikes etc, and may include many of the investments in **Appendix 2**.

2.4.3   Capital growth/income yield

If the client has adequate income, he may prefer to invest for capital growth rather than for dividends or interest. Company shares are the most likely type of investment if capital growth is required, although companies showing good capital growth usually pay good dividends as well. In the last few years, it has proved unusually difficult to obtain capital growth.

If income yield is required, savings in higher rate bank and building society accounts may be sensible. So too may be investment in certain companies where the dividend record is good, or even government stocks ('gilts').

2.4.4   Income tax and capital gains tax

'Savings' producing an income and 'investments' producing both an income and capital growth will mean that both income tax and capital gains tax will affect the client. Some savings and investments are tax free and should always feature in the portfolio planning for clients who are, or who become because of the investment, tax payers. Examples include ISAs (see further **Appendix 2**).

2.5   Introduction to types of investment products

There are very many different types of investment product on the market. The term 'investment product' covers savings, ie, money deposited in a bank or building society, as well as stocks, shares, unit and investment trusts, ISAs, life policies, etc. All these products have different characteristics, uses and tax positions associated with them. They must be selected with care to suit the particular type of client.

The main categories of savings and investments producing tax-free income are detailed in **Appendix 2**. Where possible, a gross income should be obtained if the client is not a tax payer so as to avoid the need to obtain a refund of tax deducted at source from the Revenue. Some of these investments are free of capital gains tax as well as income tax.

Chapter 3

Enduring Powers of Attorney, Lasting Powers of Attorney and Living Wills

3.1 Introduction

3.1.1 Purpose of EPAs and LPAs

An ordinary power of attorney, whether granted under the Trustee Act 1925 (TA 1925) or as a short form power under the Powers of Attorney Act 1971, ceases to have effect when the donor of the power loses his mental capacity. This means that the attorney appointed by the power is no longer able to act just at the moment when the power is most needed.

The enduring power of attorney (EPA) was introduced by the Enduring Powers of Attorney Act 1985 (EPAA 1985) as a means of allowing the authority of the attorney to continue notwithstanding the intervening lack of mental capacity of the donor.

When the relevant provisions of the Mental Capacity Act 2005 (MCA 2005) came into force on 1 October 2007, the EPAA 1985 was repealed, and so it is no longer possible to create a new EPA. Instead a person can create a lasting power of attorney (LPA), which also allows the authority of an attorney to continue, despite the loss of mental capacity by the donor. However, EPAs created before 1 October 2007 (whether registered or not) will continue to be valid and operate in accordance with Sch 4 to the MCA 2005, which largely repeats the relevant provisions of the EPAA 1985.

It is necessary, therefore, to understand the rules applying to both LPAs and EPAs.

The Law Society has produced a practice note to assist solicitors advising on having an LPA, solicitors who act as attorneys under an LPA and solicitors dealing with EPAs.

3.1.2 Who should have an EPA or LPA?

It is appropriate for anyone to have an EPA or LPA. Loss of mental capacity can occur at any age as a result of accident or illness. However, although older clients might consider asking a solicitor about this, it is less likely that younger clients will do so. It is usual, therefore, for solicitors taking instructions for a will to suggest that the client also consider an LPA. Before 1 October 2007, many solicitors offered clients a 'package' of a will, an EPA and a 'living will', setting out their wishes with regard to medical treatment in the event of loss of mental capacity. Persons with an EPA may also wish to create a personal welfare LPA (see **3.4** below), as decisions as to welfare and medical treatment cannot be taken under an EPA.

Before 1 October 2007, EPAs were sometimes suggested where a donor was intending to be absent abroad for a given period of time. If the EPA was not restricted, it would be valid immediately upon execution and the attorney would be able to act during the donor's absence, thus using the EPA effectively as an ordinary power of attorney. It is less likely that LPAs will be suggested for this purpose as, unlike EPAs, they are effective only once registered, which involves paying a fee.

3.2   Enduring powers of attorney

3.2.1   What is an EPA?

An EPA is a power of attorney created (though not necessarily registered) before 1 October 2007, in accordance with the EPAA 1985. The donor must have been an adult with the appropriate mental capacity to make the EPA. This means that the donor must have understood the nature and effect of the power, ie that the attorney may assume authority over his affairs and that the power may continue if he becomes mentally incapable.

Once created, the EPA may continue despite the loss of mental capacity of the donor, but special duties then arise for the attorney (see **3.2.5** below). In particular, the attorney must apply to the Public Guardian to register the EPA. The Public Guardian is appointed by the Government to deal with various matters concerning people who lack mental capacity.

Any authority given by the EPA is limited to acts relating to the donor's property and financial affairs. The EPA may give the attorney general or specific authority to act on the donor's behalf. If general authority is given, this confers authority 'to do on behalf of the donor anything which the donor can lawfully do' (although there are statutory limitations on the ability to make gifts under an EPA). If specific authority is given, the authority is limited to the particular activity, for example, to contract to sell and execute a transfer of the donor's freehold property.

3.2.2   Who can be an attorney under an EPA?

A donor may appoint any adult as attorney, provided the attorney is not bankrupt, or a trust corporation. Under an EPA, one or more attorneys can be appointed. Where two or more are appointed, the donor must specify whether they are joint attorneys or joint and several attorneys. Failure to do so means that the EPA is invalid.

Joint attorneys must all act together; if one should die, become bankrupt or lose mental capacity, the power ceases to be effective. Joint powers provide protection for the donor but are inconvenient. Joint and several attorneys can act independently of the other or others. This may be convenient but could lead to lack of protection for the donor's property. A joint and several attorney can continue to act when a co-attorney has died or lost capacity.

3.2.3   Creation of an EPA

3.2.3.1   The Enduring Power of Attorney (Prescribed Form) Regulations 1990

An EPA is validly created only if the instrument complies with the following requirements:

(a)   The EPA is in the form prescribed in the 1990 Regulations. The Act provided that 'immaterial differences in form' can be ignored, thus making it possible for firms of solicitors to use their own form of EPA.

(b)   The EPA form incorporates the prescribed explanatory information together with all the relevant marginal notes. Part A of the form, entitled 'About using this form', must be included together with Parts B and C. The entire form must be explained to the donor of the power before it is signed.

(c)   The EPA must be executed in the prescribed manner by both the donor and the attorney, in each case in the presence of an independent witness. If the donor (or the attorney) is physically disabled then the EPA can be executed on his behalf, but in this case the signature must be made in the presence of two independent witnesses.

3.2.3.2   Postponing the attorney's authority to act

Once the EPA has been correctly executed, the attorney may act under its authority immediately and without further formality. The execution of the EPA does not deprive the donor of the ability to take decisions on his own behalf should he so wish; indeed, he can revoke the power at any time. However, if he is to act on his own behalf or revoke the power, he must retain sufficient mental capacity.

Some donors did not want the attorney to act until the donor had lost or was losing his capacity. In such cases the EPA was drafted to include an appropriate restriction on the attorney's authority. For example, the authority may be delayed until such time as the attorney believes that 'the donor either is, or is becoming, mentally incapable', ie the authority will arise at the same time as Sch 4 to the MCA 2005 places a duty on the attorney to register the EPA with the Public Guardian (see **3.2.5** below).

3.2.4 Authority under an EPA

Any authority given by the EPA is limited to acts relating to the donor's property and financial affairs. Thus, it can cover such transactions as buying and selling shares or a house on behalf of the donor. But even an EPA giving general authority is significantly limited. It does not cover such matters as where the donor should live, whether or not medical treatment should be given or withheld, or the execution of a will for the donor. This limitation on the authority of the attorney will not necessarily matter until such time as the donor of the power loses mental capacity. Decisions relating to matters not covered by the EPA must be taken by individuals and not by the attorney acting under the power. If the donor of the EPA does not have sufficient mental capacity to make a will, the Court of Protection may be asked to make a 'statutory will' on behalf of the donor. The MCA 2005 contains provisions for dealing with a person who lacks capacity to make decisions about other matters not covered by the EPA (see **3.3**).

Attorneys have limited authority to use the donor's property to make provision for others under paras 3(2) and (3) of Sch 4 to the MCA 2005 (previously s 3(4) and (5) of the EPAA 1985).

Paragraph 3(2) provides as follows:

> Subject to any conditions or restrictions contained in the instrument, an attorney under an enduring power, whether general or limited, may (without obtaining any consent) act under the power so as to benefit himself or other persons than the donor to the following extent but no further —
>
> (a) he may so act in relation to himself or in relation to any other person if the donor might be expected to provide for his or that person's needs respectively, and
>
> (b) he may do whatever the donor might be expected to do to meet those needs.

Thus, the attorney must ask three questions:

(i)   Is the provision required to meet a need?

(ii) Might the donor be expected to provide for this person's needs?

(iii) What would this particular donor have done to meet these needs?

Paragraph 3(3) provides as follows:

> Without prejudice to sub-paragraph (2) but subject to any conditions or restrictions contained in the instrument, an attorney under an enduring power, whether general or limited, may (without obtaining any consent) dispose of the property of the donor by way of gift to the following extent but no further—
>
> (a) he may make gifts of a seasonal nature or at a time, or on an anniversary, of a birth or marriage or the formation of a civil partnership, to persons (including himself) who are related to or connected with the donor, and
>
> (b) he may make gifts to any charity to whom the donor made or might be expected to make gifts,
>
> provided that the value of each gift is not unreasonable having regard to all the circumstances and in particular the size of the donor's estate.

The attorney can make gifts to charity at any time. Gifts to non-charities can be made only if they are seasonal (eg, at Christmas), or for a birthday or marriage. It is doubtful whether 'seasonal' extends to the end of one tax year and the beginning of another. Presents given for particular events such as christenings, engagements, graduations, barmitzvahs or confirmations are effectively excluded.

3.2.5 Registration of the EPA with the Public Guardian

3.2.5.1 Donor's mental incapacity

Unlike an ordinary power of attorney, an EPA is not revoked by the donor's subsequent loss of mental capacity. However, once the donor has become incapacitated the attorney is unable to act under the authority of the EPA until it has been registered. Under the EPAA 1985 registration was with the Court of Protection, but Sch 4 to the MCA 2005 provides that registration is to be with the Public Guardian from 1 October 2007. Schedule 4 imposes special duties on the attorney which arise once the attorney 'has reason to believe that the donor is or is becoming mentally incapable'.

3.2.5.2 Special duties

The attorney is required to notify the donor of the EPA and certain specified relatives of his intention to apply to the Public Guardian for registration of the EPA.

The specified relatives who must receive notification of intention to apply for registration of the EPA include:

(a)   the donor's spouse or civil partner;

(b)   the donor's children (including illegitimate children);

(c)   the donor's parents;

(d)   the donor's brothers and sisters, whether of the whole or half blood;

(e)   the widow, widower or surviving civil partner of a child of the donor;

(f)   the donor's grandchildren.

The list continues with further remoter categories of relatives.

The EPAA 1985 requires that three individuals be ascertained by working from the top of the list. All members of a particular category must be notified once any member of the category is counted to establish the minimum number of three. However, there is no requirement for the attorney to notify, inter alia:

(a)   a person who has not attained 18; or

(b)   himself, even if he is a specified relative, but he should be included when counting the number of relatives to notify.

Example

Adam is married with five adult children and a number of other surviving relatives. He has appointed his solicitor, Brian, to be his attorney. When Adam becomes incapable of managing his affairs, Brian must notify Adam's wife and all five children (plus Adam himself unless the court dispenses with this).

The Public Guardian has a general power of dispensation from the duty of notification. It can order dispensation if satisfied that it would be undesirable or impractical for the attorney to give notice, or if no useful purpose is likely to be achieved by it. However, clear medical evidence of detriment to health would be required before the court dispenses with notification to the donor.

3.2.5.3   Effect of registration

The registration of the EPA with the Public Guardian effectively revalidates the EPA and restores to the attorney the powers granted by the EPA. Once registered, the donor can no longer revoke, extend or restrict the extent of the EPA.

3.2.6   Effect of the Trustee Delegation Act 1999

Prior to the Trustee Delegation Act 1999 it was possible for trustees to delegate their powers by using an EPA (EPAA 1985, s 3(3)). Section 3(3) had been drafted in haste in response to the decision in *Walia and Others v Michael Naughten Ltd* [1985] 1 WLR 1115. There was a feeling that the section had gone too far. There were three main problems with it:

(a)   The delegation remained effective indefinitely, unlike a delegation under TA 1925, s 25 which could last for only 12 months.

(b)   Various safeguards present in TA 1925, s 25 were not present in EPAA 1985. The trustee did not have to give notice to the person entitled to appoint new trustees and was not liable for the acts of the delegate.

(c)   The delegation remained effective after the trustee lost capacity.

The Trustee Delegation Act 1999, s 5 therefore provides (subject to one important exception) that any delegation of trustee functions must comply with TA 1925, s 25, as substituted by s 5. The delegation cannot exceed 12 months; the trustee must give notice to any co-trustees and to any person able to appoint new trustees; and the trustee will remain liable for the acts of the attorney.

The exception is contained in s 1, which allows a person who is beneficially interested in land (or the proceeds of sale of land) to delegate trustee functions without complying with s 25. The appointment can, therefore, continue for more than 12 months.

The usefulness of the s 1 exception is to some extent eroded by s 7, which provides that where two trustees are required (for example, to give a good receipt for capital money), the requirement is not fulfilled by one person acting in two capacities, as a trustee and as an attorney of another trustee.

Example

H and W are co-owners of a house. H appoints W as his attorney under an EPA. He becomes mentally incapable and W registers the power. W wants to sell the house but she will not satisfy the requirement for two trustees. She can, however, appoint a further trustee under s 8.

3.3   Effect of the Mental Capacity Act 2005

The MCA 2005 contains a number of provisions of general application in relation to mental capacity.

Section 2 introduced a single test for capacity. It provides that:

(a)   a person lacks capacity *in relation to a matter* if at the material time he is unable to make a decision for himself in relation to the matter because of an impairment of or a disturbance in the functioning of the mind or brain;

(b)   it does not matter whether the disturbance is permanent or temporary.

Section 3 provides that a person is unable to make a decision for himself if he is unable to:

(a)   understand the information relevant to the decision; or

(b)   retain the information relevant to the decision; or

(c)   use the information relevant to the decision as part of the process of making the decision; or

(d)   communicate the decision (whether by talking, using sign language or any other means).

A person is not to be treated as unable to make a decision simply because he makes an unwise one. A person is not to be treated as unable to make a decision unless all practicable steps to help him to do so have been taken without success. The fact that a person is able to retain information relevant to the decision only for a short time does not prevent him being regarded as able to make the decision. The information relevant to making a decision includes information about the reasonably foreseeable consequences of:

(a)   deciding one way or another; or

(b)   failing to make the decision.

Section 1 provides, for the purposes of the Act, that a person is to be assumed to have capacity until the contrary is established on the balance of probabilities. It also states that anyone making a decision on behalf of a person who lacks capacity must act in the best interests of that person.

Part 2 of the MCA 2005 deals with the powers of the Court of Protection to make decisions on behalf of persons who lack capacity. The Act provides that if a person wishes to make decisions on behalf of a person who lacks capacity, he may do so informally in relation to many matters, particularly those involving personal welfare. However, for some decisions, including most decisions concerning property and financial affairs, it will be necessary to make an application to the Court of Protection (unless there is an effective EPA or LPA). The Court may empower a person to make a specific decision or may appoint a deputy or deputies to make decisions on an ongoing basis.

Section 42 of the MCA 2005 provides for the Lord Chancellor to issue a code or codes of practice giving guidance to persons with various duties and functions under the Act. Some types of person are obliged to have regard to the relevant code of practice when making decisions on behalf of another, including attorneys acting under an LPA.

The Act also provides for the creation of LPAs and the creation of advance decisions to refuse treatment.

3.4   Lasting powers of attorney

From 1 October 2007, when the relevant provisions of the MCA 2005 came into force, it is no longer possible to create an EPA (see **3.1**). Instead a person may create an LPA.

3.4.1   What is an LPA?

According to s 9 of the MCA 2005, under an LPA a person (the donor) is able to confer on the attorney(s) authority to make decisions about the donor's personal welfare and/or the donor's property and affairs, including authority to make such decisions in circumstances where the donor no longer has capacity (as defined in ss 2 and 3). There are two separate types of LPA: one allowing the appointment of attorneys to deal with decisions on property and affairs, and the other allowing the appointment of attorneys to deal with decisions on personal welfare. A person can choose to create both types of power or just one, and can appoint the same person or different people to act as an attorney under each power.

3.4.2   Who can be appointed as attorney?

Section 10 of the MCA 2005 provides that the attorney must be an individual over the age of 18, or, if the authority is only in relation to the donor's property and affairs, a trust corporation.

The donor may appoint more than one attorney, and may specify whether the appointment is joint, or joint and several. It is possible to provide that for some functions the attorneys must act jointly, and for other functions they may act jointly and severally. Although this would provide flexibility, it may cause difficulty for the attorney in using the power. An insitution such as a bank, when dealing with one of several attorneys, may refuse to comply with that attorney's instructions because it cannot assess if the circumstances are such that the attorney may act severally rather than jointly. If the donor does not specify, the appointment will be regarded as joint.

A bankrupt cannot act as an attorney in relation to the donor's property and affairs. However, if there are joint and several attorneys, the bankruptcy of one of the attorneys will not affect the validity of the appointment of the other non-bankrupt attorneys. A bankrupt can act as an attorney of a personal welfare LPA.

The donor may provide for a successor or substitute attorney to replace an attorney in certain circumstances, for example the death, loss of capacity or bankruptcy of the attorney.

3.4.3   Creation of an LPA

3.4.3.1   Prescribed form

Only an adult with capacity can create an LPA. It must be made in the form prescribed from time to time in regulations, and contain prescribed information, including:

(a)   that the donor has read and understood the prescribed information and intends to confer authority to make decisions in circumstances where he has no capacity;

(b)   who the donor wishes to be notified of any application for the registration of the LPA (up to a maximum of five), or that he wishes no one to be notified;

(c)   that the attorney has read and understood the prescribed information and understands his duty to act in the best interests of the donor;

(d)   a certificate, signed by a person of a 'prescribed description', as to the capacity of the donor. Where the donor indicates that no one is to be notified of any application for registration, it is necessary to supply two such certificates signed by different people.

The Lasting Powers of Attorney, Enduring Powers of Attorney and Public Guardian Regulations 2007 (SI 2007/1253) ('the Regulations') set out the format of each type of LPA. As a result of various extra features, the LPA is much longer than the EPA. The forms contain a considerable number of sections, and it is vital to complete the forms fully and correctly. An LPA may be refused registration if it contains any defect. In some cases the defect may be corrected simply on supplying further information, but if a new LPA is needed this will only be possible if the donor still has capacity to make one.

The length and complexity of the original LPA forms caused problems. As a result, the forms were redesigned to make them easier to use, and were renamed using terminology slightly different from that used in the MCA 2005. These forms came into effect on 1 October 2009.

3.4.3.2   Certificate of capacity

Paragraph 8 of the Regulations provides that the persons who may provide a certificate of capacity are:

(a)   a person chosen by the donor who has known the donor personally for at least two years immediately prior to the signing of the certificate;

(b)   a person chosen by the donor who, on account of his professional skills and expertise, reasonably considers that he is competent to make the judgments necessary to certify that the donor has sufficient capacity to make the LPA.

The Regulations give examples of the persons who might fall into the second category, and these include registered health care professionals, social workers, and barristers and solicitors. Note that persons in this category do not need to have known the donor for at least two years.

There are a number of persons listed in the Regulations who are not permitted to provide a certificate under either category. These include the intended attorney, or a person who is attorney under any other lasting or enduring power created by the donor, a business partner of an attorney, a family member of the donor or the donee, and those involved in running a care home in which the donor resides. 'Family member' is not defined in the Regulations or the MCA 2005. In *Re Kittle* [2010] WTLR 651 the Court of Protection ruled that a cousin was not a family member for this purpose.

The certificate provider must certify that in his opinion, at the time the donor makes the LPA:

(a)   the donor understands the purpose of this LPA and the scope of the authority conferred under it;

(b)   no fraud or undue pressure is being used to induce the donor to create the LPA; and

(c)   there is nothing else which would prevent an LPA from being created.

3.4.3.3 Execution

Paragraph 9 of the Regulations sets out detailed rules for the execution of the power, and states that a power must be executed in accordance with these.

The rules require that the donor must first read all the prescribed information, then 'as soon as reasonably practicable' after this the donor must complete part A of the power and sign it in the presence of a witness.

As soon as reasonably practicable after this the certificate provider must complete and sign part B of the power. Finally, as soon as reasonably practicable after this the attorney(s) must each read the prescribed information and then complete and sign part C of the power, in the presence of a witness.

The donor cannot be a witness, and the donee cannot be a witness other than for any other donee.

3.4.3.4 Registration

Unlike EPAs, which could come into operation as a power of attorney from the moment of execution, the LPA will not have any effect at all until it is registered with the Public Guardian.

There is no obligation to register the LPA once it has been executed. However, the donor or attorneys (or, where there are joint and several attorneys, any of them) may choose to do so at any time after the power has been executed. This will involve using a prescribed form and paying a fee. Whoever applies for registration must have first notified anyone named by the donor as a person to be notified in such circumstances.

Unlike EPAs, there is no obligation on the attorneys to register the power if the donor loses capacity, although if this does happen it is very likely that the attorney or attorneys would seek to register the power.

On receipt of an application for registration, the Public Guardian must notify:

(a)   the attorneys if the donor applied; or

(b)   the donor if the attorneys applied (and any attorneys who did not join in the application to register).

The donor, attorneys or the other persons notified can object to the registration on various grounds, but otherwise the Public Guardian will register the power and notify the donor and attorneys of this. The Public Guardian keeps a register of LPAs.

Once registered, the LPA is valid and may be used by the attorney(s), subject to any express restrictions in the LPA.

3.4.4 Authority under an LPA

An attorney making a decision under an LPA for a person who lacks capacity must act in the best interests of the donor, which means complying with MCA 2005, s 4, which sets out various matters to which the attorney must have regard. The attorney must also have regard to the relevant code of practice issued under s 42 of the MCA 2005.

3.4.4.1 Property and financial affairs LPA

(Previously known as a property and affairs LPA.)

An attorney who has authority in relation to the donor's property and financial affairs may act even though the donor has capacity (unless the power contains express restrictions preventing this).

The attorney cannot dispose of the donor's property by making gifts, unless in accordance with s 12. Section 12(2) provides that the attorney may make gifts:

(a) on customary occasions to persons (including the attorney) who are related to or connected with the donor; or

(b) to any charity to which the donor made or might have been expected to make gifts.

In either case the value of the gift must not be unreasonable in all the circumstances.

'Customary occasions' is defined in s 12(3) to mean:

(a) the occasion or anniversary of a birth, a marriage or the formation of a civil partnership; or

(b) any other occasion when presents are customarily given within families, or among friends or associates.

Unlike EPAs, therefore (see **3.2**), gifts to non-charities can be made other than at 'seasonal' times.

Under s 23(4), the court may authorise gifts not covered by s 12(2), eg a gift made for tax planning purposes.

3.4.4.2 Health and welfare LPA

(Previously known as a personal welfare LPA).

An attorney who has authority in relation to the donor's health and welfare may make decisions about the social and health care of the donor. Unlike the property and financial affairs LPA, the attorney of a health and welfare LPA can act only if the donor does not have capacity to make a particular decision. The MCA 2005 contains various restrictions on the attorney, eg the attorney cannot vote on behalf of the donor. The donor may also include express restrictions or conditions in the power, eg permitting the attorney to make decisions as to the social care of the donor but not health care. If the attorney is not expressly restricted then he may give or refuse consent to health care treatment; although if the decision involves the refusal of life-sustaining treatment, the attorney must have express authority in the LPA to make such a decision.

3.4.4.3 Comparison with EPAs

LPAs and EPAs are intended to deal with similar circumstances, but there are a number of differences between them. A selection of the main differences is set out below.

LPAs	EPAs
Created on or after 1 October 2007	Created before 1 October 2007
Two types – one for property and affairs and one for personal welfare	One type – only for property and affairs
Prescribed format for powers, requiring execution by donor, certificate provider and attorneys	Prescribed format for powers, requiring execution by donor and attorneys
Failure to specify if attorneys are joint or joint and several does not invalidate the power – attorneys treated as joint	Failure to specify if attorneys are joint or joint and several invalidates the power
Only effective on registration	Can operate from execution
No obligation for attorneys to register if donor loses capacity	Obligation for attorneys to register if donor loses capacity
Registration procedure includes notifying persons nominated by donor (if any)	Registration procedure includes notifying persons prescribed by statute
Attorneys may make gifts under a property and affairs LPA in limited circumstances: MCA 2005, s 12	Attorneys may make gifts in limited circumstances: MCA 2005, Sch 4, para 3(2) and (3)

3.5 Living wills and advance decisions to refuse treatment

3.5.1 Living wills

Living wills (also known as advance directives) are intended to allow individuals to specify the extent and nature of the medical treatment they would or would not find acceptable should they lose capacity in the future. The term 'living will' can be confusing since such documents have no connection with ordinary wills, but this term is probably too well established to change.

A mentally capable adult has no right to demand a particular treatment, but has the right to refuse any medical treatment (*Sidaway v Board of Governors of the Bethlem Royal Hospital and Maudsley Hospital and Others* [1985] AC 871).

The right to refuse treatment extends to a refusal made in advance. There are various cases which support advance directives.

After the Tony Bland case (arising from the Hillsborough stadium disaster), a *Practice Note (Persistent Vegetative State: Withdrawal of Treatment) (26 July 1996)* [1996] 4 All ER 766 was issued dealing with the procedure to be followed when an application is made to withdraw treatment from a person in a persistent vegetative state. It included the following statement:

> Previously expressed advance directions of the patient, in writing or otherwise, will be an important factor, and the High Court may determine the effect of advance directives as to future medical treatment.

In *Re T (Adult: Refusal of Treatment)* [1992] 2 FLR 458, the Court of Appeal said that an advance refusal is legally binding, provided:

(a)   the person making it had capacity at the time of making it;

(b)   a situation has arisen which was envisaged when the directive was made;

(c)   the person making it was not under any undue influence at the time the directive was made.

3.5.2 Advance decisions to refuse treatment

The MCA 2005 provides for an adult with capacity to make an advance decision to refuse specified medical treatment in future specified circumstances. Provided the provisions contained in the advance decision apply to the particular circumstances encountered by the persons supplying treatment, it will be as if the person had capacity to refuse the treatment, and those persons will not be liable for complying with the advance decision to refuse treatment. Such persons will also not be liable if they reasonably believe the advance decision to apply.

The advance decision can be revoked or modified by the person who made it at any time when he has capacity to do so. If a person who has made an advance decision later makes an LPA giving express authority to an attorney to make decisions on such matters, this LPA will supersede the advance decision.

It is not easy to draft effective advance decisions. It is difficult to anticipate the circumstances that may arise and make the direction sufficiently specific. In *Re B (Consent to Treatment: Capacity)* [2002] EWHC 429 (Fam), [2002] 1 FLR 1090, Ms B had made a living will but it was not appropriate to deal with the circumstances that arose. Doctors therefore ignored it.

Even if a person has written a perfectly effective advance decision, there is the further problem that an emergency doctor may give treatment before becoming aware of the existence of the advance decision.

An alternative approach is to give a personal welfare attorney power to accept or refuse life sustaining treatment.

Chapter 4
Estate Planning

4.1 Introduction

The object of estate planning is to pass on wealth to the desired objects as efficiently as possible.

Estate planning can range from advising on a will leaving everything to a spouse to complex 'off-shore' tax avoidance schemes. The majority of practitioners find that their cases fall somewhere between these extremes. The client offering the greatest scope for estate planning is wealthy and married, with children (and possibly grandchildren).

Civil partners

Note that since 5 December 2005, persons who have entered into a civil partnership are treated for tax purposes in the same way as married persons. For the sake of brevity this book will generally refer only to spouses and marriage, but it must be remembered that similar principles will apply to the parties to a civil partnership.

4.1.1 Estate planning

Estate planning is a combination of financial planning (see **Chapter 2**); lifetime giving, outright and/or into trusts (see **Chapter 5**); and will drafting (see **Chapter 11**). A Family Limited Partnership provides an alternative to a trust as a means of giving away assets to family members whilst retaining some element of control, and there has been more interest in this structure since changes were made to the way trusts are taxed in 2006. However, although the Family Limited Partnership may offer some tax advantages, it has disadvantages in terms of lack of flexibility and operational expense and we will not consider this arrangement further.

For clients with relatively limited means, it may only be possible to plan through a will, for example by leaving a legacy to the children to take advantage of the nil rate band, with the residue passing to the surviving spouse. Wealthy clients, however, should consider a combination of lifetime transfers and gifts by will. Where lifetime estate planning is contemplated, it is essential that consideration should also be given to a complementary will. If a client dies intestate, or leaves a will that does not take lifetime planning into account, unexpected claims can arise, such as, for example, from the Revenue for additional tax. There may be a claim in negligence against the solicitor by a surviving spouse or children who receive less than was intended.

4.1.2 Aims

The aims of a client are usually:

(a)   the provision of financial security for self and family; and

(b)   the avoidance of tax.

It is not always possible to achieve both objectives and many practitioners believe that tax savings should not be achieved at the expense of financial security.

Estate planning often involves a person giving away assets during his lifetime, perhaps to a spouse and/or children. Once the gift is made, it cannot be claimed back, for example if the parties subsequently divorce or the donor parent falls on hard times. If planning through a will, the will of the deceased spouse should not prejudice the standard of living of the survivor by leaving too much property away from that surviving spouse.

Whereas with basic tax planning through wills the intention is to limit the amount of inheritance tax (IHT) payable on a death, the tax planning element of lifetime estate planning is often as much concerned with avoiding capital gains tax (CGT) or minimising an income tax bill as it is with IHT. Because of the interaction of the taxes, clients may have to accept a small CGT bill as part of the cost of avoiding a large IHT bill, or a potential IHT charge for a considerable saving of CGT.

Example

James, who is divorced, has been told that to give away assets which are likely to increase in value is sound IHT planning. Accordingly, he plans to give his daughter his 10,000 shares in Widgets plc which have considerable growth potential. He hopes to reduce the IHT payable at death on his already large estate. Stockbrokers have advised that he will realise a gain of £20,000 if he gives the shares away now. There are no relevant reliefs which James can claim. He has made no other disposals in this tax year. James is a higher rate tax payer.

Compare the following:

Lifetime gift

(a)   CGT: chargeable gain of £9,900 (£20,000–£10,100 annual exemption) taxed at 28% = £2,772.

(b)   IHT, potentially exempt transfer (PET): even if death occurs within seven years, IHT will be calculated on the value of the shares at the date of the gift. The increase in value will occur in James's daughter's estate, not in his estate.

No lifetime gift: tax on death

(a)   CGT: none (tax-free uplift to value of shares at the date of death).

(b)   IHT: on value of the shares at death as part of James's estate attracting tax of up to 40%.

Where a client is contemplating estate planning, the solicitor must balance the cost of the legal work involved against the tax saving to ensure that the costs of the scheme do not outweigh the advantages. Making lifetime property transfers may give rise to an immediate tax bill which may make the proposal unattractive to the client even though it will save tax in the long run. Clients may also have to accept that the payment of some tax is inevitable (whether during their lifetime or on death) in order to ensure the best practical financial arrangements for the family.

The Law Society has issued a practice note (July 2009) giving advice to solicitors dealing with clients who wish to make lifetime gifts. It highlights, among other things, the need to advise fully on the benefits and risks of making such gifts.

In this chapter we consider estate planning by lifetime transfers. Estate planning through will trusts is dealt with in **Chapter 12**.

4.1.3 Some ground rules

When advising clients, solicitors should consider the following.

4.1.3.1 How much to give away?

Apart from the obvious – not too much – other factors to be taken into consideration are: ill health, separation or divorce, retirement, death of one of the parties to the marriage, and the effects of inflation on the purchasing power of income and on the value of retained capital. Any of these may suggest retaining more rather than less.

4.1.3.2 What to give away?

Where possible, assets likely to appreciate in value should be considered for lifetime giving. Shares in a private company will often rise substantially in value if the company is floated on the Stock Exchange. So too may the value of a painting following the death of the artist. Making the gift *before* the value increases ensures the growth occurs in the estate of the donee. It 'freezes the value' of the property (ie, a PET) at the value at the time of the gift, which will be relevant should death occur within seven years. A 'disposal' for CGT will occur, but the disposal consideration will be the market value at the date of the gift. Assets that qualify for tax exemptions or reliefs should also be considered, although there may be non-tax reasons for not giving those away.

4.1.3.3 How to give away?

Outright gifts are straightforward but are inflexible; if circumstances change, the property given away cannot be recovered. If the proposed donee is a minor, such a gift (if substantial) would not be sensible. The donor may come to regret making an outright gift; for example, the donee may become addicted to drugs, or may become mentally or physically handicapped. In either case, the money might be better held by trustees for the benefit of the donee.

4.1.3.4 Gifts into trust provide flexibility

Because unexpected events do occur, flexibility is an important part of planning, and therefore trusts are attractive. However, trusts require proper administration. Dealing with income and investment of trust funds, preparing trust accounts and making tax returns for the trust all cost time and money. These disadvantages must be weighed against the advantages of flexibility obtained by using a discretionary trust. So too must possible adverse change in tax law affecting trusts. Over recent years, such changes have made lifetime trusts less attractive to estate planners and their clients.

4.1.3.5 Don't let the tax tail wag the dog

The objective is to plan affairs so that the client's property is enjoyed by the beneficiaries (often the family) to the best advantage. In achieving this, tax avoidance is only one aspect.

4.2 Tax and estate planning

The following paragraphs contain some reminders of the basic rules relating to the taxation of individuals; many of these rules also apply to the taxation of trustees (see **Chapters 10** and **14**). The basic rules are covered in the LPC Guides, ***Legal Foundations*** and ***Business Law and Practice***. This chapter groups together all the points that are relevant when considering the various estate planning ideas put forward here. More complex tax law is explained in detail either here or in context.

4.3 Inheritance tax

The Inheritance Tax Act 1984 (IHTA 1984), s 7 provides that tax is charged in accordance with the table of rates in Sch 1 to the Act.

4.3.1 Rates of IHT chargeable on death

0% on the first £325,000 (nil rate band) from 6 April 2009.

40% on the balance.

The position is different where a person (S) dies on or after 9 October 2007, having survived a spouse or civil partner (F) (no matter when this first death occurred). In such a case, if F had unused nil rate band on his death, then the unused proportion of F's nil rate band may be claimed by S's estate on S's death. This is done by calculating the unused percentage of the nil rate band in force at the date of F's death. S's estate is then allowed to have the nil rate band that is in force at the date of S's death increased by the same percentage.

> **Example 1**
>
> Fred dies on 10 April 2007, when the nil rate band is £300,000. He leaves his whole estate (£500,000) to his civil partner, Stuart. There is no IHT to pay on Fred's death at this point as it is covered by the civil partner's exemption. Stuart dies on 19 September 2010, leaving his whole estate (£750,000) to his brother. As Fred used none of the nil rate band available at his death he had 100% unused, and this percentage can be claimed by Stuart's estate. When Stuart dies the nil rate band level has risen to £325,000, and so this can be increased by 100% to £650,000. The tax on Stuart's death would therefore be £650,000 @ 0% and £100,000 @ 40% = £40,000.

> **Example 2**
>
> If in Example 1 Fred had left £150,000 to his sister, and the rest to Stuart, it would have meant that he had used 50% of the £300,000 nil rate band in force at his death, and thus had 50% unused. On Stuart's death the nil rate band of £325,000 would be increased by 50% (£162,500) to a total of £487,500.

4.3.2 Rates of IHT for lifetime chargeable transfers

0% on the first £325,000 (nil rate band).

20% on the balance.

Many lifetime transfers are PETs, which become chargeable only if the donor dies within seven years. However, since 22 March 2006 the lifetime creation of all trusts, except for trusts for the disabled (see **5.2.4.1**), will be immediately chargeable. Inheritance tax must be reassessed at death rates if the settlor (the person creating the settlement) dies within the following seven years. Credit is given in the re-calculation for any tax already paid, ie, when the settlement was created.

> **Example 1**
>
> Helen gives property with a value of £371,000 to the trustees of her discretionary trust. There are no available exemptions and reliefs. The trustees agree to pay the IHT.
>
> | | | £ |
> |---|---|---:|
> | IHT at lifetime rates | £325,000 @ 0% = | nil |
> | | £46,000 @ 20% = | 9,200 |
>
> Helen, who is single, dies 14 months later – the IHT is reassessed.
>
> | | | £ |
> |---|---|---:|
> | IHT at death rates | £325,000 @ 0% = | nil |
> | | £46,000 @ 40% = | 18,400 |
> | | | 18,400 |
> | *Less:* IHT already paid at lifetime rates | | 9,200 |
> | Additional IHT as result of Helen's death | | 9,200 |

> If Helen, not the trustees, had agreed to pay the IHT when she created the settlement, the loss to her estate then would have included the IHT payable, ie, the legacies would be 'grossed up' when calculating the value transferred. This is considered further in **Chapter 5**.

Note that when calculating tax on lifetime transfers, at the time of the transfer, there is no increase in the nil rate band for a person who has survived a spouse with unused nil rate band. However, when the transferor dies, and there is a recalculation of the tax on the lifetime transfer, the increased nil rate band may be available.

Example 2

Simon's wife died five years ago with 100% unused nil rate band. In May 2010 Simon, who has made no previous transfers apart from using his annual exemption each April, gives £355,000 cash to the trustees of his discretionary trust. The trustees agree to pay the IHT.

| IHT at lifetime rates | £325,000 @ 0% = | nil |
| | £30,000 @ 20% = | £6,000 |

(Simon's nil rate band does not benefit at this point from any increase resulting from his wife's unused nil rate band, as this is a lifetime transfer.)

Simon dies ten months later – the IHT is reassessed. The nil rate band available to Simon on death is now increased by 100% (the proportion unused by his wife) to £650,000.

| IHT at death rates | £355,000 @ 0% = | nil |

There is no further tax to pay, but there is no repayment of the tax paid on the lifetime transfer.

(There is £295,000 nil rate band remaining which will be available for Simon's death estate.)

4.3.2.1 Tapering relief (IHTA 1984, s 7(4))

If a transferor dies more than three years after the date of a transfer, the full death rate of tax is reduced and only the following percentages are charged:

(a)   transfers within 3 to 4 years before death 80% of death charge;

(b)   transfers within 4 to 5 years before death 60% of death charge;

(c)   transfers within 5 to 6 years before death 40% of death charge;

(d)   transfers within 6 to 7 years before death 20% of death charge.

Notice that tapering relief is of no benefit if the transfer is within the nil rate band. This is because it operates to reduce the rate of tax charged. If the rate is nil, there can be no reduction.

Example 1

Ash dies in December 2010 with an estate of £500,000. Five-and-a-half years before this, Ash gave £125,000 to his son. Other than always using his annual exemption for IHT on 6 April each year, Ash made no lifetime transfers.

On Ash's death the PET to his son becomes chargeable, but as it is within the nil rate band there is no tax on the PET. Tapering relief is therefore irrelevant. The death estate will have a nil rate band available of £325,000 – £125,000 = £200,000.

In the case of transfers which were immediately chargeable to tax, the effect of tapering relief may be that no further tax is payable. The relief never results in a refund of tax already paid.

Example 2

Suppose in Example 1 in **4.3.2** above that Helen had died 6 years and 4 months after making the transfer.

> The effect of tapering relief is that only 20% of the tax at the full death rates is payable. The full death rate tax was £18,400 so only £3,680 is payable. The trustees have already paid £9,200. No further tax is payable but the trustees are not entitled to a refund.

4.3.3   Potentially exempt transfers (IHTA 1984, s 3A, as amended by FA 2006)

Potentially exempt transfers (PETs) are lifetime transfers made by an individual on or after 18 March 1986 which, apart from s 3A, are chargeable transfers. The following are PETs:

(a)   Gifts to other individuals, provided the donee's estate is increased or the property transferred becomes comprised in his estate.

(b)   Transfers to trustees of a trust for the disabled (IHTA 1984, s 89).

(c)   Transfers made on or after 22 March 2006 to trustees of a 'bereaved minor's trust' on the ending of an 'immediate post death interest' (IHTA 1984, s 3B) (see **Chapter 12**).

Some further transfers to trustees made before 22 March 2006 are also PETs:

(d)   Transfers to the trustees of an interest in possession settlement because the estate of the beneficiary with the life interest includes the property in which that interest subsists, ie, the settled property (IHTA 1984, ss 5 and 49).

(e)   Transfers to the trustees of an accumulation and maintenance trust (IHTA 1984, s 71).

Transfers to trustees are considered further in **Chapter 5**.

No charge arises at the time the PET is made and it is treated as fully exempt unless the transferor dies within the following seven years. There is no obligation on the transferor to notify the Revenue of the PET. Should the transferor die within the seven years following the PET, it becomes chargeable and is treated as if it had always been chargeable. It must be reported to the Revenue.

A transfer which is covered by an exemption is fully, not potentially, exempt.

4.3.4   Exemptions applying to lifetime transfers (IHTA 1984, ss 18–23)

(a)   Any property passing to a spouse (there is a limit of £55,000 on the exempt amount if the recipient spouse is non-UK domiciled – IHTA 1984, s 18(2) (see further **15.3**)).

(b)   Gifts to charity. Various ways of giving to charity are considered in **4.8**.

(c)   Small gifts. Gifts not exceeding £250 to any one person in any one year are exempt. Because of this limitation, it is not possible to combine the small gift exemption with another exemption, for example the annual exemption. The gift must be outright, not in trust.

(d)   Transfers of £3,000 per annum (any unused annual exemption can be carried forward one year).

Example

In Year 1, a donor makes his first ever gift of £1,000. The unused part of the annual exemption is carried forward to Year 2. In Year 2, he may give away £5,000 in exempt transfers. If the £2,000 carried forward from Year 1 is not used in Year 2, it is lost and may not be carried further forward.

A husband and wife who each use the annual exemption over a 25-year period could give their children a total of £156,000. By the simple use of an exemption, considerable estate planning for the parents could be achieved.

(e)   Gifts in consideration of marriage: up to £5,000 per parent of the couple (lesser amounts for other donors). The gift may be outright or into trust provided the beneficiaries do not include persons other than the couple or their issue (or spouses of their issue). It must be 'in contemplation' of a particular marriage, and should be so evidenced in writing.

(f) Normal expenditure out of income: if claimed (it is not given automatically), this exemption applies to a gift of cash that:

(i) is part of the normal expenditure of the donor;

(ii) taking one with another, is made out of income; and

(iii) after other such gifts, leaves the donor with sufficient income to maintain his usual standard of living.

It is a question of fact whether a gift qualifies for the exemption. What is 'normal expenditure' for one person is not necessarily so for another. Even though it is not one of a series of regular payments, a gift may none the less be 'normal' if there is evidence that payments of an ascertainable amount are likely to recur (see further *Bennett v Inland Revenue Commissioners* [1995] STC 54).

The exemption is most commonly used to fund the payment of premiums on policies of assurance written in trust, for example:

(i) an endowment policy written in trust by a parent in favour of a child on which the parent pays the annual premiums;

(ii) premiums on a policy written in trust to be used to fund a potential IHT liability should the donor die within seven years of a PET.

4.3.5 Valuation

4.3.5.1 Market value

The IHT legislation contains provisions relating to the valuation of property given away by a donor. The normal rule is that property is valued at 'the price [it] might reasonably be expected to fetch if sold on the open market at the time; but that price shall not be reduced on the grounds that the whole property is to be placed on the market at one and the same time'. Thus, it is not possible to argue for a reduced valuation because 'the market is flooded' where a lot of a similar type of property is available at once (IHTA 1984, s 160).

The 'open market rule' applies on a death, although changes in value of an estate caused by the death can be taken into account (IHTA 1984, s 171). For example, life policies which mature on death are valued at the maturity value (whereas if they are given away during lifetime the value transferred is generally the surrender value) and personal goodwill in a business is valued at a figure (usually lower) after allowing for the loss of the proprietor of the business.

4.3.5.2 Joint ownership of assets

Co-owners of land can discount the value of their respective shares to take into account the fact that it may be difficult to sell a share in co-owned property on the market; the purchaser will occupy the property with the other co-owner. A discount of 10%–15% is normal.

> **Example**
> Two brothers own a house equally. If the open market value of the house is £200,000, the value of a one-half share may be agreed by the Revenue to be £90,000.

Valuation of other jointly-owned assets does not attract such a discount. In these cases, the open market value is divided proportionately between the joint owners.

Where spouses are co-owners of land, a discount is not normally available. This is because of the related property rules (see **4.3.5.5**) which require each party's interest to be valued as a proportion of the whole.

4.3.5.3 Quoted shares

For IHT (as for CGT) the price is taken to be the price 'one quarter up' from the lower to the higher price for dealings on the day in question on the stock market. Thus, if a share is shown as 100p–104p for the day of dealing, the valuation would be 101p per share held by the donor.

4.3.5.4 Shares in unquoted companies

Shares in private/family companies are notoriously difficult to value; such a valuation is not an exact science. The principal reason for the difficulty is the lack of any real market. Final agreement of value may take many years of negotiation between the donor's valuers and the Revenue. Many factors will be relevant, including:

(a)   The success or otherwise of the company.

(b)   Other recent dealings in the shares (if any).

(c)   The number of shares as a percentage of the entire issued capital of the company:

- a 75% holding   can pass special resolutions;
- over 50% holding   can pass ordinary resolutions;
- 50% or less   a minority holding, with less voting influence (especially if small holding).

(d)   The existence of typical pre-emption rights in the company's articles of association requiring shares first to be offered to other shareholders. Here the lack of a market is the real problem. Nevertheless, the courts have over a long period held that shares must be valued on the assumption that the shares could be sold on the open market but that the purchaser will then himself become subject to the restrictions contained in the articles of association.

To reach agreement the Revenue will need from the company or its advisers much information, including:

(a)   a full description of the business carried on by the company;

(b)   the last three years' accounts of the company published before the date of valuation;

(c)   if minority holdings are to be valued, details of any restrictions on the transfer of shares;

(d)   if there are different classes of shares, a statement of the rights of each class, in particular those concerning voting, dividends and distributions on a liquidation of the company.

4.3.5.5 Related property (IHTA 1984, s 161)

Assets which make up a pair or set are worth more than the aggregate value of each item valued separately; for example, one of a pair of valuable earrings is not worth a lot on its own. The related property rules are designed to prevent tax payers who can make exempt transfers (eg spouses) avoiding IHT by dividing ownership of valuable assets between them. Section 161(1) provides 'where the value of any property comprised in a person's estate would be less than the appropriate proportion of the value of the aggregate of that and any related property, it shall be the appropriate proportion of the value of that aggregate'.

Example

Harriet has a 60% holding in H and T Ltd. She transfers half of this to her husband, so that they now each have a 30% holding. (This transfer is exempt for IHT and at no gain or loss for CGT purposes.) Taken separately, each holding is valued at £25,000, but together the controlling holding of 60% is valued at £75,000. Harriet considers giving her shareholding to their child, Rick. Under the related property rule, her shareholding would be valued as the appropriate proportion of the value of their total holding, ie, £75,000 ÷ 2 = £37,500.

If Harriet makes her gift, she will make a PET. If she dies within seven years the PET will have become a chargeable transfer. Business property relief at 100% will be available if Rick owns the shares when his mother dies.

4.3.6 Reliefs

4.3.6.1 Agricultural property relief (IHTA 1984, ss 115–124)

Agricultural property relief is given automatically for transfers of value of 'agricultural property'. 'Agricultural property' is defined as including agricultural land and pasture; and cottages, farm buildings and farmhouses together with the land occupied with them as are of a character appropriate to the property.

The Revenue is quick to argue that houses are not of a 'character appropriate' in an attempt to deny the relief.

The relief is given against the 'agricultural value' of the agricultural property. Agricultural value is defined as the value which would be the value of the property if the property were subject to a perpetual covenant prohibiting its use otherwise than as agricultural property. Thus, any value attributable to possible development or to mineral deposits under the land would not be eligible.

Agricultural property relief applies to property which was either:

(a)   occupied by the transferor for agriculture throughout the two years immediately before the transfer; or

(b)   owned by the transferor throughout the seven years immediately before the transfer (provided it was occupied by someone (the transferor or another) for agriculture throughout the seven-year period).

For these purposes, periods of occupation and ownership by a deceased spouse can be included.

100% relief

Available where the transferor had the right to vacant possession immediately before the transfer, or the right to obtain it within the next 12 months or, by concession (ESC F17), within 24 months from the date of the transfer. To encourage agricultural tenancies, this relief is also available where property is let on a tenancy starting on or after 1 September 1995 (FA 1995, s 155).

50% relief

Available on any other qualifying agricultural property.

> **Examples**
> Giles, who farmed Greenacre for 28 months, has just died. Agricultural property relief is available at 100% against the vacant possession value due to the owner occupation.
> Jim ceased farming Blackacre 10 years ago. He let the farm to his son, who has continued to farm it, and he retained the freehold reversion himself. Jim has just died. His PRs will be able to claim agricultural property relief at 50% against the tenanted value of the agricultural property.

Agricultural property in settlements

Subject to the time-limits, the relief can apply to agricultural property held by trustees. There is a distinction between trusts with and without a 'qualifying' interest in possession. A trust with a 'qualifying' interest in possession means a trust where the life tenant is deemed for IHT purposes to be entitled to the settled property, ie the agricultural property. Broadly, such trusts are those with an interest in possession created on death at any time, or by lifetime transfer before 22 March 2006 (see **Chapter 5**).

If it is a trust with a qualifying interest in possession, the life tenant is the 'transferor' and 'owner' of the agricultural property for the purposes of the relief. The life tenant must therefore satisfy the conditions of two years' occupation of the property or seven years' ownership of it. For other trusts, the trustees will instead be the 'transferors' and 'owners' of the agricultural property. The occasions of charge to IHT on discretionary trusts are discussed in **Chapter 10**.

Agricultural property relief is given in priority to any available business property relief.

4.3.6.2   Business property relief (IHTA 1984, ss 103–114)

Business property relief operates to reduce the value transferred by a transfer of value of relevant business property by a certain percentage.

A reduction of 100% of the value transferred is allowed for transfers of certain assets. They are:

(a)   a business or interest in a business (eg, a partnership share);

(b)   shares which are not quoted on the Stock Exchange (companies on the Unlisted Securities Market and the Alternative Investment Market (AIM) count as unquoted for this purpose).

A reduction of 50% of the value transferred is allowed for transfers of any other assets which qualify for business property relief. They are:

(a)   shares which are quoted on the Stock Exchange and where the transferor had control; control exists broadly where the transferor's entire holding yields over 50% of the votes on all resolutions;

(b)   land, buildings, machinery or plant owned by the transferor personally but used by a partnership of which he is a member or by a company of which he has control.

The relevant business property must have been owned by the transferor for at least two years immediately prior to the transfer. An exception to this rule applies where a spouse inherits business property under the will or intestacy of the deceased spouse. In that circumstance only, the surviving spouse is deemed to have owned the property from the time it was originally acquired by the deceased spouse.

> **Example 1**
> In 2004, James acquired 75% of the shares in X Ltd, a private company. James died in June 2010 leaving those shares to his wife Kim. In May 2011, Kim dies leaving all her estate, including the shares, to her son. The 100% relief will be available on Kim's death.

The exception does not apply where the relevant business property is transferred to the spouse *inter vivos*.

> **Example 2**
> In Year 1, Judy sets up her own business, Y Ltd, and holds 100% of the shares.
> In Year 5, she transfers 20% of those shares to her civil partner, Kelly.
> In Year 6, Kelly dies leaving the 20% shareholding to her son.
> No relief is available against the value of the 20% holding as Kelly has owned the shares only for one year.

These inter-spouse transfer rules also apply to agricultural property relief.

Lifetime transfers – availability of relief

Where the charge to IHT arises as a result of a PET or chargeable lifetime transfer (eg, a transfer to discretionary trustees) which is followed by the death of the transferor within seven years, any IHT (or additional IHT) will be calculated with the benefit of business property relief *provided*:

(a)   the transferee still owns the assets (or replacement assets which qualify as business property) at the death of the transferor (or, if earlier, the transferee's own death); and

(b)   the asset qualified as business property immediately before the transferor's death but (for this purpose) ignoring the two-year ownership requirement.

There is, therefore, the danger that at the time of the death relief will not be available.

Business property in settlements

As with agricultural property relief, relief can be available where business property is held by trustees.

If it is a trust with a 'qualifying' interest in possession (see **4.3.6.1** above), the availability of this relief is gauged by reference to the position of the life tenant. If the *life tenant* satisfies the two-year ownership test, 100% relief is available where the assets in the trust are either a business or unquoted shares; 50% relief is available for controlling holdings in quoted companies and for land, buildings, machinery or plant in the trust used in the life tenant's own business or a company which he controls.

For other trusts, relief will be available if the *trustees* satisfy the conditions. The occasions of charge to IHT on trusts are discussed in **Chapter 10**.

4.4   Capital gains tax

4.4.1   Rates

Since 23 June 2010, CGT is charged on disposals made by an individual at 18% and/or 28%, depending on whether the tax payer is a higher rate tax payer for income tax purposes. The gains are added to the tax payer's income for the year, and to the extent that these exceed the threshold for higher rate tax they are taxed at 28%. The gains below the threshold are taxed at 18%. Personal representatives and trustees are charged to CGT at 28%.

In the period 6 April 2008 to 23 June 2010 CGT was charged at a flat rate of 18% for individuals, personal representatives and trustees.

As the change in rate was unusually introduced part way through a tax year (in the budget of 22 June 2010) there are special rules to deal with the disposals occurring before 23 June 2010. Broadly these rules allow a tax payer who makes disposals in both periods of the 2010/11 tax year to deduct losses and apply the annual exemption in a way that is most advantageous to him.

For disposals made before 6 April 2008, individuals were taxed by treating the gains as the top slice of their income, and trustees were taxed at 40%.

4.4.2   Calculation

The gain is calculated as the difference between the disposal consideration (less the costs of selling) and:

(a)   the acquisition cost (less the cost of buying); and

(b)   any cost of improvements/enhancing expenditure.

Capital losses are normally set against capital gains of the same year. To the extent that losses exceed gains for the year, they can be carried forward to the following year.

For disposals made before 6 April 2008, it was possible to deduct an indexation allowance, removing inflationary gains from CGT, when calculating gains (but not losses) on any asset owned between 31 March 1982 and 5 April 1998. This allowance has been abolished for disposals made on or after 6 April 2008 (although it remains relevant in certain circumstances, for example where a held-over gain included an allowance for indexation).

Taper relief, which was introduced in April 1998, has been abolished for disposals on or after 6 April 2008.

4.4.3 Exemptions

These include the following:

(a)   The first £10,100 (£5,050 for trustees) of chargeable gains each year. (Note that a husband and wife is each entitled to the annual exemption.)

(b)   Any gain arising on the disposal by gift or sale of the tax payer's main or only residence. Where a tax payer owns more than one residence, he may elect for one to be treated as his main residence. A husband and wife living together have only one principal private residence exemption.

(c)   Any gain on the disposal of a property owned by trustees where the property is the residence of a beneficiary entitled to occupation under the terms of the trust or at the discretion of the trustees.

For a further discussion of the points mentioned in paragraphs (b) and (c) above and other matters relating to the main residence, see **4.7.3** and **4.7.4**.

4.4.4 Death (Taxation of Chargeable Gains Act 1992 (TCGA 1992), s 62)

Death provides an automatic CGT-free revaluation of assets. The probate value becomes the acquisition cost for subsequent disposals by PRs, beneficiaries and trustees if a trust arises under the will or intestacy. This is because there is no disposal on death but there is an acquisition by the PRs, etc. One consequence is that inbuilt gains accruing during the lifetime of the deceased person are not charged to CGT. This point needs careful consideration as part of general estate planning. Disposal of the same asset during lifetime could well result in immediate liability to tax if the gain exceeds the annual exemption and where hold-over relief is not available.

No liability arises when assets are vested in legatees by the PRs; the PRs' acquisition (on death) is taken to be the legatees' acquisition for their future CGT purposes. A 'legatee' includes any person inheriting under a will or intestacy whether beneficially or as a trustee if a trust arises following the death.

Example

Shares worth £50,000 at death were acquired by the testator 10 years earlier for £5,000. The gain of £45,000 over the period of ownership does not attract CGT. Gains on all subsequent disposals will be based on an acquisition cost of £50,000. If instead the shares were given away by lifetime gift, the gain on the disposal would attract CGT unless relief was available.

A similar CGT-free revaluation of trust assets occurs when the life tenant of a qualifying interest in possession trust dies (TCGA 1992, s 72) (see **4.3.6.1** above for the meaning of 'qualifying').

Example

Since the trust was created in 2000, trustees have been holding £100,000 of quoted shares 'for Susan for life, remainder to George'. Susan has just died and the shares are worth £250,000.

(a)   The gain of £150,000 during the trust period does not attract CGT.

(b)   The trustees are 'deemed' to dispose of the investments at market value at Susan's death.

> (c)   The investments transferred to George are 'deemed' acquired by him for his future CGT purposes at their market value at Susan's death. Not all the investment will be transferred to George because some will have been sold by the trustees to pay IHT due as a result of Susan's death.

The position of the trustees where a 'deemed disposal' occurs is considered further in **10.1.4.2**.

4.4.5 Reliefs

4.4.5.1 Inter-spouse transfers

Inter-spouse transfers are deemed to occur at no gain no loss. Effectively, tax on any gain since the acquisition by the donor spouse is deferred until there is a disposal by the donee spouse (TCGA 1992, s 58).

> **Example**
>
> In 1999, Archie bought a painting for £10,000. He gave his painting to his civil partner, Brian, in 2010 when its value had increased to £18,000.
>
> | | £ |
> |---|---:|
> | Archie's deemed disposal consideration | 10,000 |
> | *less:* Acquisition cost | 10,000 |
> | | nil |
>
> Brian's acquisition cost is Archie's disposal consideration, ie, £10,000. If Brian sells the painting two years later for £22,000, he will make a gain of £12,000.

4.4.5.2 Hold-over relief

Hold-over relief is provided in relatively limited circumstances by TCGA 1992, ss 165 and 260. These two provisions operate in the same way, by permitting gains which accrue to the donor to be held over. Tax is effectively deferred by permitting the donee to acquire the gifted property at the donor's acquisition cost. Tax remains deferred until the donee disposes of the property when he either cannot or chooses not to make a further hold-over election. Entrepreneurs' Relief (if available) is not applied if hold-over relief is claimed (see **4.4.5.3**).

To obtain hold-over relief, an election is required by both the transferor and the transferee, although where the transferee is a trustee only the election of the transferor is required. Once made, the result of the election is that:

(a)   the amount of any chargeable gain which the transferor would otherwise have made on the disposal; and

(b)   the value at which the transferee would otherwise be regarded as having acquired the asset,

shall be reduced by an amount equal to the held-over gain on the disposal.

> **Example**
>
> John gives his shares in his personal company, which he acquired in 1999, to his daughter Julia. Their market value is £100,000.
>
> A joint election for hold-over relief under s 165 is made.
>
> | | | £ |
> |---|---|---:|
> | (a) | Disposal consideration (market value) | 100,000 |
> | | *less:* Cost price (say) | 30,000 |
> | | held-over gain | 70,000 |
>
> 1.   John's gain on disposal is reduced to nil.
>
> 2.   Julia's acquisition cost is reduced to £30,000 (£100,000 – £70,000).

> (b)   Julia sells her shares for £150,000. Her gain is calculated as follows:
>
> | | £ |
> |---|---|
> | Disposal consideration (sale proceeds) | 150,000 |
> | *less:* Cost price (see above) | 30,000 |
> | gain | 120,000 |
>
> Julia's chargeable gain is made up of the gain during her period of ownership of £50,000 (£150,000 – £100,000) and £70,000 (the gain held over).

Disposal of business assets within s 165

Under s 165, hold-over relief applies where a person makes a gift (either outright or into a trust) of business assets.

Section 165 defines business assets as:

(a)   An asset, or an interest in an asset, used for the purposes of a trade, profession or vocation carried on by:

    (i)   the donor; or

    (ii)   his personal company; or

    (iii)   a company which is a member of a trading group of companies of which the holding company is the donor's personal company.

(b)   Shares or securities of a trading company or of the holding company of a trading group where:

    (i)   the shares or securities are not quoted on a recognised stock exchange; or

    (ii)   the trading company or holding company is the transferor's personal company.

(c)   Agricultural property, or an interest in agricultural property, which is not used for the purposes of a trade carried on as mentioned in (a) above.

A 'personal' company is one in which the individual owns not less than 5% of the voting rights.

Disposal of business assets held in settlements

Section 165 relief in a modified form is extended to deemed disposals of business assets owned by trustees by TCGA 1992, Sch 7. The asset must be used in a business carried on by the trustees, ie, the trustees of a discretionary settlement, or by a beneficiary of a settlement with an interest in possession in the settled property, ie, the life tenant. In the case of disposals of shares in a trading company by trustees, the company must be unquoted, or at least 25% of the voting rights must be exercisable by the trustees.

Disposals within s 260

Private client practitioners are likely to meet three types of disposal which attract hold-over relief under s 260:

(a)   *Chargeable transfers within the meaning of IHTA 1984 (and transfers which would be chargeable transfers but for IHTA 1984, s 19 (the annual exemption)) and which are not potentially exempt transfers (s 260(2)(a)).*

The effect of this relief is that a gift which is immediately chargeable to IHT (even at 0%) is not also charged to CGT at the time. A double charge to tax is thus avoided. PETs do not attract IHT (at least immediately) and so CGT will normally arise on the disposal (unless s 165 relief applies).

If the donor dies within seven years of making a PET and as a result the PET becomes chargeable, relief is still not available since it was not immediately chargeable when made. The lifetime creation of all types of trusts, except trusts for the disabled, on or after 22 March 2006 is an immediately chargeable transfer, and so relief will be available under s 260. There are other circumstances involving the termination of certain types of trust where there will be an immediate charge to IHT and also relief under s 260 (see **Chapter 10**).

Example

Kathy transfers assets valued at £325,000 to the trustees of her newly created discretionary settlement. She has made no other transfers. Even though no IHT is actually payable there is an occasion of immediate charge (at 0%). Hold-over relief is available at Kathy's election. The trustees do not need to join in the election.

(b) *Exempt transfers within IHTA 1984, s 24 (transfers to political parties), s 26 (transfers for public benefit), s 27 (transfers to maintenance funds for historic buildings) and s 30 (transfers of designated property) (s 260(2)(b)).*

(c) *Termination of accumulation and maintenance trusts, trusts for bereaved minors and 'age 18–25 trusts', where a beneficiary becomes absolutely entitled to the settled property (s 260(2)(d)).* (See **Chapters 8** and **12**.)

The termination of these types of settlement is specifically within the provisions even though IHT is not chargeable (see **Chapter 10**).

The creation and termination of trusts is dealt with in **Chapters 5** and **10**.

Hold-over relief and settlor interested trusts

Since 10 December 2003, hold-over relief has not been available under s 260 or s 165 for any disposal to a trust which is 'settlor interested' immediately after the disposal. If the settlement later becomes a settlor interested trust the relief is clawed back.

When this anti-avoidance measure was introduced a 'settlor interested' trust meant one where any property may be payable to the settlor or the settlor's spouse in any circumstances. From 6 April 2006 it also includes a trust which may benefit the settlor's unmarried minor children (see **6.2.11**). This restriction severely limits the occasions on which hold-over relief can be claimed (see **Chapter 5**).

Hold-over relief and the foreign element

Neither s 165 nor s 260 applies where the transferee is neither resident nor ordinarily resident in the UK. Thus, disposals of chargeable assets to non-resident individuals or settlements are, for this reason, not particularly attractive.

A clawback of CGT can arise where the donee emigrates within six years following a hold-over election. If the donee ceases to be resident and ordinarily resident in the UK, CGT liability on the held-over gains is immediately triggered. The CGT is primarily payable by the donee (now overseas). If he fails to pay the tax within 12 months it can be recovered from the donor who has a (probably worthless) right of recovery from the donee.

Because of the risk of a clawback charge, the donor should be advised to consider insurance cover, retention of part of the gifted property for six years and indemnities from the donee (see **Chapter 15**).

Gifts attracting IHT and CGT

If chargeable gains on a disposal are held over, the transferee may add any IHT paid on the transfer to him to his CGT acquisition cost. In this way, some relief against the overlap between IHT and CGT is available.

Example

Jason transferred assets worth £200,000 to the trustees of his recently established discretionary settlement. They elected to hold over the gain of £80,000. Assume £20,000 IHT was paid. The trustees now sell the assets for £250,000 and re-invest the proceeds. The calculation of the trustees' CGT liability is:

	£	£
Disposal consideration		250,000
less: acquisition cost		
(200,000 – 80,000)	120,000	
IHT paid	20,000	140,000
gain		110,000

Note: the principle illustrated in the example also applies if the lifetime gift was a PET which later becomes chargeable. Provided a CGT hold-over election was made by the donor and donee, the IHT payable on the donor's death can be added to the transferee's acquisition cost, as in the example.

Some planning considerations in relation to hold-over relief

The fact that hold-over relief is not generally available on lifetime gifts may make them less attractive for tax planning purposes.

A gift which attracts CGT at 18% or 28% now made to save IHT at 40% in the future may not be particularly attractive in cash-flow terms. The same gift made by will would avoid CGT and give the donee the benefit of an uplift in his acquisition price (to market value at the date of death) for future CGT purposes.

However, CGT is charged on gains whereas IHT is charged on full values (subject to reliefs).

Gifts of assets expected to appreciate in value may attract an immediate CGT charge on the gain to date but IHT will be limited to the value of the asset at the time of the gift, ie, 'asset freezing' applies should the PET become chargeable. If the value of the assets is within the transferor's nil rate band, there may be an advantage to transferring the assets to a discretionary settlement (a lifetime chargeable transfer, but chargeable at 0%) and then claiming hold-over relief.

Section 165 of IHTA 1984 provides that CGT paid by the donee reduces the value transferred by the chargeable transfer for IHT. Normally CGT is payable by the donor but, in circumstances where hold-over relief is not available, consideration should be given to the donee paying the tax to take advantage of s 165. For this to happen, agreement must be reached between the donor and donee.

A disposal (such as a PET) giving rise to a chargeable gain which cannot be held over, followed by the death of the donor within seven years, could cause IHT to become payable by the donee. In such a case any CGT paid by the donor will not be treated as part of the loss to the estate (IHTA 1984, s 5(4)). As discussed in the previous paragraph, if the donee pays the CGT, the value transferred is treated as reduced by the CGT paid (IHTA 1984, s 165(1)) and therefore the IHT bill for the donee will be reduced.

Example

A gift (PET) of quoted shares worth £500,000 results in a CGT liability of £50,000.

(a)   If the donor pays the CGT, the value transferred for IHT is £500,000. It is not £550,000, ie, the loss to the estate of the donor is not increased by the CGT paid.

> (b)   If the donee pays the CGT, the value transferred for IHT is £450,000, ie, it is reduced by the CGT paid.
>
> Obviously the donee will need to be in a position to fund both tax liabilities. Insurance against the potential IHT may be possible but not the CGT because this is an immediately quantifiable amount.

4.4.5.3   Entrepreneurs' Relief

This relief was introduced by the Finance Act 2008 and is contained in ss 169H–169R of the TCGA 1992. The relief applies only in relation to disposals (by sale or gift) made on or after 6 April 2008.

The relief applies where there is a 'qualifying business disposal'. This occurs where there is a disposal of certain types of business asset, which meet certain further criteria.

(1) The disposal of the whole or part of a business

This includes a business run by a sole trader or a partnership, and the disposal may be of:

(a)   the business (or part of it) as a going concern; or

(b)   the assets used in the business following the cessation of that business.

However, in either case only those assets used for the purposes of the business carried on by the sole trader or partner are eligible for relief. Shares and other assets held for investment purposes are not eligible.

Where the disposal is of the business (or an interest in it), the transferor must have owned his interest in the business for the period of one year ending with the date of disposal.

Where the disposal is of assets following the cessation of a business then the transferor must have owned the business for one year ending on the date of cessation of the business, provided that the disposal occurs within three years after the cessation of the business.

(2) The disposal of company shares

To qualify for the relief:

(a)   the company must be a trading company;

(b)   the transferor must have a shareholding that gives at least 5% of the voting rights (the transferor's 'personal company'); and

(c)   the transferor must be an officer or employee of the company.

and all these conditions must be satisfied:

(a)   either during a one-year period ending with the date of disposal; or

(b)   during a one-year period ending with the date when the company ceases to be a trading company, provided that the disposal occurs within three years after the company ceases to be a trading company.

(3) The disposal of assets owned by an individual but used by a partnership or company

To qualify for the relief:

(a)   the assets disposed of must have been used for the purposes of a business run by:

(i)   a partnership in which the transferor was a partner; or

(ii)   a trading company which was the transferor's personal company and of which the transferor was an officer or employee; and

(b)   the disposal of the assets must be associated with a qualifying disposal of the transferor's interest in the partnership or company arising from the withdrawal of the transferor from the business; and

(c)   the assets were in use for the purposes of the business during the period of one year ending with the earlier of:

(i)   the date of disposal of the partnership interest or company shares with which the asset disposal is associated; and

(ii)   the cessation of the business of the partnership or company using the asset.

Effect of the relief

The relief is not automatic. Where there has been a qualifying business disposal, the transferor may choose to claim the relief. If he does so, the effect is that any losses arising from the qualifying disposal are first offset against the gains from that disposal. For disposals made before 23 June 2010 the overall net gain was reduced by four-ninths, and the reduced gain formed part of the transferor's total gains for the relevant tax year.

For disposals on or after 23 June 2010 the net gain is not reduced by four-ninths, but is instead taxed at 10% (rather than 18% or 28%). As the tax payer may deduct the annual exemption in the way that is most beneficial to him, he can deduct this from gains that do not qualify for the relief before applying it to those that do.

For the tax year 2010/11 there are special rules to allow a person who makes disposals qualifying for the relief in both parts of the tax year to apply the annual exemption in the way that is most advantageous to him.

The use of the relief is subject to a lifetime cap. This cap was set at £1 million qualifying net gains for disposals made during the period 6 April 2008 to 5 April 2010, but rose to £2 million for the period 6 April 2010 to 22 June 2010, and to £5 million for disposals made on or after 23 June 2010. Each time a person claims the relief, the value of the net gains for which he claims is added to his lifetime total, and once the person exceeds the limit he will not be able to claim the relief in relation to any further qualifying gains.

Example

For the last five years Nicky has been a director of two companies, A Ltd and B Ltd and has held a 10% holding in each company. In August 2010 Nicky sells his holding in A Ltd, realising a gain of £2 million.

If Nicky elects to take the relief, his net gain of £2 million is taxed at 10%. Nicky now has only £3 million remaining of his £5 million lifetime limit.

If he sells his shares in B Ltd in the next tax year, realising a gain of £4 million, he can claim the relief only in relation to £3 million of this gain, and the remaining £1 million is taxed at Nicky's top rate.

There is an important planning point here. Someone who is a director and shareholder may wish to cease active involvement with the company but retain the shares. If the individual is likely to later sell the shares, it may be worth continuing as a director until the date of the sale to retain the benefit of the relief.

The total of qualifying disposals for any person will include not only those made by that person as an individual but also those made by a trust where the person is a 'qualifying beneficiary' (see below).

It is not possible to claim this relief to reduce a gain and claim hold-over relief.

Entrepreneurs' Relief and settlements

The relief also operates in limited circumstances in relation to business assets held within a settlement.

For the relief to apply, there must be a disposal of trust business assets. This occurs where:

(a)   the trustees of a settlement make a disposal of 'settlement business assets';

(b)   there is an individual who is a 'qualifying beneficiary'; and

(c)   s 169J(4) and (5) of the TCGA 1992 is satisfied.

Settlement business assets are:

(a)   company shares; and

(b)   assets used for the purposes of a business (as indicated above, these will not include shares or other investment assets);

which are part of the settled property.

A person is a qualifying beneficiary if he has an interest in possession in the settlement in the whole of the settled property or the part of it which includes the settlement business assets being disposed of. If the interest in possession is for a fixed term, for example for a period five years, the beneficiary is not able to be a qualifying beneficiary.

The further requirements contained in s 169J(4) and (5) of the TCGA 1992 are that:

Where the disposal is of shares:

For a one year period ending not later than three years before the disposal:

(a)   the company was:

    (i)   a trading company; and

    (ii)   the qualifying beneficiary's personal company; and

(b)   the qualifying beneficiary was an officer or employee of the company.

Where the disposal is of assets used within a business:

(a)   the assets must be used for the purposes of the business carried on by the qualifying beneficiary (including a business carried on by a partnership of which he is a partner) for the period of one year ending not earlier than three years before the disposal; and

(b)   the qualifying beneficiary must have ceased to carry on the business on the date of the disposal or within the three-year period before the disposal.

Both the trustees and the qualifying beneficiary must claim the relief.

Where it is claimed, the effect will be similar to the position for an individual claiming the relief. The lifetime cap also applies, and will include not only gains made by the trustees involving this qualifying beneficiary but also any qualifying gains made by the qualifying beneficiary as an individual.

4.5 Transfers between spouses and civil partners

4.5.1 Financial and estate planning

Although since 9 October 2007 there is the opportunity to transfer unused nil rate band from the first to die to the estate of the survivor on the latter's death, it is still advisable for the wealth of a married couple to be split between them. Whilst the division need not be equal, it is inadvisable for one spouse to own the majority of the assets. 'Equalisation' will provide greater financial security for the 'poorer' spouse, and the greatest scope for tax planning.

4.5.1.1   Life insurance

Insurance on the tax payer's own life

Most clients who have partners or young children should consider personal life insurance (see **Appendix 2**). If nothing further is done when the life cover is purchased, the insured sum will be paid to the PRs on the death of the insured and will form part of his estate.

A grant of representation will be required before the proceeds are available, and the amount will be taxable if left to a beneficiary other than the deceased's spouse (or charity). Both problems can be avoided if the life insurance policy is written in trust.

Where a new policy is being purchased as part of financial advice, it can be written in trust from the outset. Life insurance companies have standard trust documents which the insured can complete with the names of the trustees and the chosen beneficiary or beneficiaries.

Existing policies can also be written in trust but whenever possible it is better to create the trust at the time of purchase. This is because existing policies may have a surrender value, meaning that if the insured cancels the policy before his death he will receive a lump sum based on the amount of premiums he has paid. When an existing policy is written in trust, the insured gives up this surrender value to his beneficiary and this is a transfer of value for IHT purposes. Usually the policy will be valued for IHT at the higher of the market value or cost of providing the policy, ie, the premiums already paid (IHTA 1984, s 167). In practice this is rarely a problem as the value in the first few years is relatively small compared with the maturity value and is likely to be covered by the insured's £3,000 annual IHT exemption. To the extent this is exceeded the transfer of the surrender value will be a PET. It does mean, however, that in the year the policy is put into trust, the annual IHT exemption may not be available to set against other non-exempt gifts.

Once a policy has been written in trust, the annual premiums paid by the insured to the insurance company are paid by the insured for the benefit of the beneficiary. These premiums are transfers of value for IHT but, unless disproportionately large when compared with the annual income of the insured, they should be exempt as normal expenditure out of income, or if not then covered by the £3,000 annual exemption. They are not PETs (IHTA 1984, s 3A).

Insurance on the life of another

Where a couple have young children it is quite possible that one parent, usually the mother, does not have paid employment. The couple should calculate how much it would cost to employ a housekeeper and nanny or purchase child care if the mother were to die. Where the father's income is unlikely to be sufficient to cover the cost, he might consider insuring the mother's life, ie, he pays premiums and receives a lump sum if the mother dies. As the insurance cover is likely to be required only whilst the children are of school age, term assurance (see **Appendix 2**) could be considered.

Example

Adam and Betty have two children aged 6 and 4 respectively. Betty does not work and Adam's income is £32,000 per annum. He calculates the family's expenditure to be £22,000 per annum, and believes home help and child care would cost an extra £12,000 per annum if Betty died. This could not be supported by his income. If he insured Betty's life he would receive a lump sum on her death from which to pay the £12,000 per annum.

4.5.1.2   The matrimonial home

Sole ownership versus co-ownership

The matrimonial home is often the major asset owned by an individual or married couple. Unless there are personal reasons for not doing so, spouses should consider property being owned as co-owners rather than in the sole names of either.

Co-ownership can reflect the contributions each has made to the purchase price, or may provide a non-contributing spouse with the security of legal ownership. The couple may make the initial purchase as co-owners, or a sole purchaser may subsequently transfer an interest in the property to the other. Most lenders insist that a property which is to be used as a matrimonial home is held as co-ownership. This may be either a joint tenancy or a tenancy in common.

Joint tenancy

Holding a property as joint tenants means that on the death of one spouse his or her interest in the property immediately and automatically passes to the surviving spouse, ie accrues by survivorship. This cannot be prevented by anything said about the property in the will. All that the surviving joint owner needs to prove absolute ownership of the property is the death certificate of his or her spouse. Joint tenancy therefore avoids the costs and delays involved in obtaining a grant of representation on the death of the first joint tenant to die and, because the survivor is the spouse, the interest in the property is IHT exempt on that first death.

> **Example**
> Carla and David own a house worth £600,000 as joint tenants. David dies and the house vests in Carla absolutely. There is no IHT payable as the transfer is spouse exempt. Assuming that David did not use his nil rate band, he therefore had 100% unused nil rate band. Carla dies six weeks later, in November 2010, leaving her estate (the house) to Emma. There is no IHT as Carla's nil rate band of £325,000 is increased by 100% to £650,000.

Tenancy in common

Property held under a tenancy in common passes by will or intestacy, not automatically to the surviving co-owner. A tenancy in common provides greater flexibility as it allows the first spouse to die to leave his share to someone other than the survivor, for example his child. However, as the effect would be shared ownership between the surviving spouse and child, there is a danger that the child may want the house sold to realise his inheritance.

Mortgage

Where the matrimonial home, however owned, is subject to a mortgage, that mortgage debt should be covered by suitable insurance (see **Appendix 2**). This will enable the mortgage to be paid off in full on the death of the borrower without the need for the house or other assets to be sold to meet the debt. Where two people are jointly responsible for the mortgage, they can choose whether the insurance should pay out on the first or second death.

4.5.2   Transferring assets (other than the matrimonial home) into joint ownership

4.5.2.1   Practical reasons

The reasons for making such a transfer are likely to be practical. The transfer allows each spouse access to particular assets and means that, on the death of the first spouse to die, the survivor automatically becomes sole owner of those assets. There is no need to obtain a grant of representation (so the administration is quicker and cheaper) and the survivor has immediate access to finances.

4.5.2.2   Effect for IHT

Joint ownership offers no IHT saving. Although on the first death the transfer is spouse exempt, the combined estates are taxed on the second death. If the second spouse dies on or after 9 October 2007 he or she will have the benefit of any nil rate band unused on the death of the first spouse. However, this is no different from the owning spouse dying and leaving the assets to his or her spouse. The same unused proportion of nil rate band can be transferred to the surviving spouse.

4.5.2.3   Effect for income tax

The basic rule is that any income arising from a jointly held asset will be treated as belonging equally to the husband and wife (ITA 2007, s 836). This is so irrespective of how they contributed to the account or purchase of the asset or account (eg, with a bank or building society).

> **Example**
>
> Harry has a building society account into which he periodically pays additional savings. He transfers this account into the joint names of himself and his wife Isobel. Isobel makes no contributions to the account. For income tax purposes she is nevertheless treated as owning one half of the annual income.

Spouses can override this general 50:50 rule by making a declaration to HM Revenue & Customs of how they in fact beneficially enjoy the income. The declaration relates to the income and to the underlying property. The income cannot be shared in proportions different from the property which produces it. The maximum split is 1:99. The declaration has effect from its date; notice must be given to the Inspector of Taxes within 60 days of a declaration which must be made on Form 17.

Where one spouse has insufficient income from his or her own resources to be paying income tax, or is paying income tax at the basic (20%) rate whilst the other spouse is a higher (40%) or additional (50%) rate income tax payer, it may be sensible to transfer some part of the beneficial ownership in the jointly owned property to the spouse with the lower tax rate, followed by a declaration that that spouse is entitled to an equivalent proportion of the income. The transfer of the beneficial ownership will generally be by declaration of trust made by the spouses.

> **Example**
>
> John and Kate are the joint holders of a building society account. The annual interest is £100 gross. John pays income tax at 40%. Kate pays income tax at 20%.
>
> (a) Without a declaration
>
> | | | | |
> |---|---|---|---|
> | John will pay 40% tax on his one half | £50 × 40% | = | £20 |
> | Kate will pay 20% tax on her one half | £50 × 20% | = | £10 |
> | Total income tax | | | £30 |
>
> (b) Transfer of beneficial ownership and declaration that Kate is entitled to 90% of the interest
>
> | | | | |
> |---|---|---|---|
> | John will pay 40% tax on his 10% share | £10 × 40% | = | £ 4 |
> | Kate will pay 20% tax on her 90% share | £90 × 20% | = | £18 |
> | Total income tax | | | £22 |

4.5.2.4   Effect for CGT

The transfer of an asset from a sole name into the joint names of the husband and wife is at 'no gain no loss' (see **4.4.5.1**).

On a subsequent disposal, whether a sale or by gift, each spouse will be regarded as owning a half share of the asset and charged to CGT accordingly. This allows each spouse to use his or her annual exemption and to make the best use of the lower rate of CGT.

Example

Len transfers a shareholding which he bought for £2,000 into the joint names of himself and his wife Mary. Len is a higher rate tax payer and Mary pays at basic rate.

The shares are sold for £24,200 (assume that they make no other disposals in the tax year).

	Len will pay	*Mary will pay*
	£	£
Disposal consideration	12,100	12,100
less: Acquisition cost	1,000	1,000
	11,100	11,100
less: Annual exemption	10,100	10,100
	1,000	1,000
Chargeable gain	£1,000 @ 28%	£1,000 @ 18%
	= £280	= £180

If Len had sold the shares without sharing ownership with Mary, he would have realised a gain of £22,200 (£24,200 – £2,000). Setting only his annual exemption against this would result in a tax liability of £3,388 (£12,100 @ 28%).

Where a declaration as to the beneficial enjoyment of the income from a jointly owned asset has been made, it will have a corresponding effect for CGT purposes.

Example

Rafael and Maya declare that the income from a shareholding is enjoyed 25:75. They will have a corresponding beneficial ownership of the shareholding. The shares were bought for £400 and have just been sold for £16,000. Assume that they make no other disposals in the tax year.

	Rafael's chargeable gain		*Maya's chargeable gain*	
	£	£	£	£
Disposal		4,000		12,000
less: Acquisition cost	100		300	
less: Annual exemption	10,100		10,100	
		10,200		10,400
Chargeable gain		nil		1,600

4.5.2.5 Conclusion

Transferring assets into joint names may provide beneficial effects. It allows both spouses access to the assets. It is a means of making provision for the recipient spouse without the donor spouse losing control of the property. Since 9 October 2007 there is no IHT disadvantage in joint ownership as any unused nil rate band from the first spouse to die can be transferred to the second spouse.

Some clients value the independence and control of having assets in their sole name over and above any tax saving which may result from holding assets jointly.

4.5.3 Transferring assets outright from one spouse to another

Another way to achieve the 'equalisation' of a couple's estates is for the wealthier spouse to make an outright transfer of assets to the poorer spouse.

4.5.3.1   Income tax reasons

As seen in 4.5.2, wherever possible, a husband and wife should ensure that they each utilise their own personal allowance as well as their own basic rate bands before either of them starts paying income tax at the higher rate. If one spouse is an additional rate tax payer it is even more worthwhile, and even if the other spouse is a higher rate tax payer there is still a 10% saving in the taxation of the income.

4.5.3.2   CGT reasons

A transfer from one spouse to another is at 'no gain no loss'. A husband and wife are both entitled to an annual exemption of £10,100, but any unused annual exemption cannot be transferred to the other spouse nor can it be carried forward for use in future years. All clients (whether married or not) should be advised to use the exemption each year if possible.

It is also sensible to take advantage of one spouse paying CGT at only 18%, rather than 28%.

4.5.3.3   IHT reasons

Inheritance tax savings are often the main purpose in making inter-spouse transfers. Whilst no tax saving is achieved from the transfer itself, because such transfers are IHT exempt, having assets in the individual ownership of each spouse does allow maximum use of exemptions and reliefs for passing on family wealth during lifetime to children and other relatives.

Example

Henry has assets of £500,000, but his wife, Sarah, has assets of only £9,000. The couple would like to make some immediate gifts to their family. They decide to each give away £3,000 each year to their children, to utilise the annual exemption for IHT. Unless Henry transfers some of his wealth to Sarah she can only make gifts using the annual exemption on three occasions.

Using lifetime exemptions

There are several lifetime exemptions. For example, each parent can give £5,000 to a child on the occasion of the child's marriage; each parent can make annual gifts of £3,000; each parent can make gifts using the normal expenditure out of income exemption. Before these exemptions can be claimed, each parent must have sufficient assets to make the gifts. Unused exemptions cannot be transferred from one spouse to the other.

Anti-avoidance rules

The anti-avoidance legislation and cases (see **4.10**) should not be a problem in the context of straightforward family estate planning, provided that at the time of the inter-spouse transfer the recipient spouse is not under a binding obligation to use the property as directed by the donor spouse.

Transfer of nil rate band on death

Before 9 October 2007 it was also important to transfer assets between spouses to ensure that each member of the couple could make maximum use of his or her nil rate band when making gifts by will. This reason is less important since 9 October 2007 because of the possibility of the transfer of unused nil rate band between spouses.

> **Example**
>
> Assume Sarah in the Example above dies before Henry has a chance to transfer any of his wealth to her, leaving her £9,000 estate to Henry. There is no tax on Sarah's death and she has a 100% unused nil rate band. It does not matter that she could not have used more than £9,000 of her nil rate band because of the size of her estate. Henry then dies in the tax year 2010/11, leaving his £509,000 estate to his children. The nil rate band available for Henry's estate is increased by 100% to £650,000, so there is no IHT payable.

Loss of business or agricultural property relief

It may not be sensible to make a transfer of property qualifying for business or agricultural property relief because of the risk of losing the relief if the donee spouse dies within two years of the transfer.

> **Example**
>
> Peter and Rose wish to minimise the amount of IHT that their daughter Susan will pay on their deaths. Peter transfers his 40% shareholding in their private company Z Ltd worth £800,000 to Rose as part of the 'equalisation' process. He has owned the shares for four years. Rose dies six months later leaving everything to Susan.
>
> The shareholding is taxable on its full value as Rose has not owned the shares for two years (see **4.3.6**).
>
> Had Peter retained the shares and given them by lifetime gift or by will to Susan, 100% business property relief would have been available.

4.6 Transfers from parents to children and remoter issue

Most parents wish to provide for their children, and those who can actually afford to do so wish to ensure that such provision is made in the most tax-effective way.

It is not always possible to achieve the client's intentions and avoid a tax bill. The skill is to put forward ideas that will satisfy the practical objectives at the minimum tax cost.

Again, the solicitor must be aware of the interaction of the capital taxes; for example, is the CGT cost of a course of action less than the IHT bill which will arise if the action is not taken?

The choice for parents is a lifetime gift either outright or through the creation of a trust (see **4.6.4**), or by will which is either an outright gift or gift into trust. The use of will trusts is discussed in **Chapter 11** and will not be considered in detail here.

4.6.1 Outright gifts

A gift is an immediate outright transfer of property from one person to another. There can be no conditions attached.

When making gifts of small sums of money or family possessions, or wishing to benefit an adult child, an outright gift may be the most sensible and appropriate course of action. However, where the intended recipient is a minor or is irresponsible with money, the donor may feel that it is inappropriate to hand over valuable assets or large amounts of cash. In such circumstances, consideration might be given to the provision of the intended benefit via a trust (but see **4.6.4.1**). A minor is unable to hold the legal estate in land so it is impossible to make an outright gift of land to a person under 18 years of age. Where such a gift is attempted, statute imposes a trust.

4.6.2   The taxation of outright gifts

4.6.2.1   Inheritance tax

The current IHT legislation encourages lifetime giving, whether by a parent, grandparent or others, and, wherever possible, clients should take full advantage of the exceptions and reliefs offered (see **4.3.4**).

PETs (IHTA 1984, s 3A) – 'asset freezing'

All gifts between individuals are PETs when they are made, but the lifetime creation of all trusts, except trusts for the disabled, on or after 22 March 2006, will be an immediately chargeable transfer (charged at half the death rate). The effect of the PET is that no IHT is payable at the time of the transfer. The transfer becomes exempt from IHT if the transferor lives for seven years. Should the transferor die within the seven-year period, the PET becomes chargeable. The value which is taxed is the value of the property at the date of the transfer, unless the value has fallen when it is the lower value which is taxed – see below. It is therefore sensible for clients to consider giving away assets which are likely to increase in value. Rates at the date of the death are used unless they have increased since the gift. If so, the rates at the date of the gift are used instead.

Example

Keith owns a painting by an elderly living artist. He paid £20,000 for it and believes that its value will quadruple after the artist's death. Keith utilises his annual exemptions on other transfers.

Year 1: Keith gives the painting (value £20,000) to Laura (PET).

Year 4: Keith dies and the painting is valued at £115,000. IHT rates have not increased subsequently. The gift of the painting becomes a chargeable transfer and tax is charged on £20,000, which, assuming Keith had made no previous transfers, will be covered by his nil rate band.

Where a PET is of an amount which exceeds the transferor's nil rate band, IHT will be payable by the donee if the transferor dies within seven years. Whilst this tax cannot be avoided, the transferee or transferor can mitigate its effect by insuring the transferor's life for seven years (for an explanation of such term assurance, see **Appendix 2(16)**) for a sum equal to the potential tax bill. If the transferor insures his own life the insurance policy should be written in trust for the transferee.

Example

Mike, a divorcee, who has made no gifts other than of £3,000 per annum, gives his daughter Nina £345,000 to buy a house.

If Mike dies within seven years, Nina could face a tax bill of up to £8,000.

Unless she insures her father's life (which she may not be able to afford to do) Nina therefore has the choice of only spending £337,000 and putting the rest aside to meet the anticipated tax bill, or having to sell or mortgage the house on Mike's death to raise the tax.

Alternatively, Mike could insure his life for £8,000 for seven years and give the benefit of the insurance policy to Nina. The annual premiums should be covered by his normal expenditure out of income exemption. If Mike dies within seven years, Nina receives cash of £8,000 with which to pay the tax and so can safely spend the full £345,000 on buying her house.

PETs – loss in value

If property other than cash is given away and the property falls in value between the date of the PET and the death, relief is provided by IHTA 1984, s 131. Inheritance tax is calculated on the reduced value instead of the original value (the relief applies similarly following a lifetime chargeable transfer). This relief reduces the value which is taxed; it does not affect the value of the original PET. This means that the original value remains in the transferor's cumulative total when calculating any IHT on later lifetime transfers and on the estate on the death. Any taper relief is based on the IHT actually payable, ie, the IHT payable on the reduced value.

Inheritance tax is charged at the rate(s) in force at death unless the rates have increased, in which case the rates in force at the date of the PET are used.

Example

In January 2006 Harold gave his grandson his shares in Z plc, which were then worth £400,000. Harold died in May 2010 when the shares were worth £341,000. Apart from using his annual exemptions, Harold has made no other transfers.

(a)   On Harold's death within seven years, the PET becomes chargeable on the reduced value of £341,000.

(b)   IHT, at rates in force when Harold died:

		£
nil rate band	£325,000	nil
balance	£16,000 @ 40%	6,400
		6,400

(c)   Taper relief – Harold died more than four but less than five years later.

£6,400 @ 60% = £3,840 (payable by Harold's grandson).

(d)   The original value of £400,000 remains in Harold's cumulative total when calculating the IHT due on his estate at death.

Note: if Harold's grandson had sold the shares for £341,000, IHT on Harold's death would be calculated in the same way as above. If he had given them away, no relief is given and IHT would, instead, be calculated on the full value in 2006, ie, £400,000 (IHTA 1984, s 131(1)).

Order of gifts – some considerations

Clients planning a number of gifts, some PETs and some lifetime chargeable transfers such as transfers into a settlement, should be advised that the possible IHT consequences may differ depending upon the order of the gifts.

Transfers made on the same day (IHTA 1984, s 266)

If a number of PETs are intended and all are made on the same day, there is, of course, no IHT payable at the date of the gifts. If the donor should die within seven years so that IHT becomes payable, it is charged on each PET on a pro rata basis. Each gift benefits from a proportion of any available nil rate band. Had the gifts been made on separate days, the earlier gifts would benefit from the donor's available nil rate band whereas the donees of later gifts would suffer IHT once the nil rate band was exceeded.

PETs and relevant property trusts (lifetime chargeable transfers – LCTs)

Discretionary settlements and all lifetime settlements created after 22 March 2006 (except trusts for the disabled) can be referred to as 'relevant property trusts'. Such trusts have their own IHT rate, which is calculated partly on the value of transfers from the settlement and partly on the settlor's cumulative total immediately before he created the settlement (see **Chapters 5** and **10**). This makes the order of gifts important.

There is an advantage to the later taxation of relevant property settlements if the settlement is made before (or at the latest on the same day as) the PETs. If the PETs come first and later become chargeable, they will be taken into account when calculating IHT payable by the trustees during the life of the relevant property settlement. This liability of the trustees is considered in **Chapter 10**. If the client intends creating more than one settlement, the gifts to the trustees should be made on different days so as to avoid the settlements being treated as 'related settlements' (IHTA 1984, s 62). The effect of related settlements on the calculation of the trustees' IHT liability is considered at **10.2.4**.

Effect on PETs and relevant property settlements (LCTs) of death between three to seven years

Although it is beneficial to the subsequent taxation of relevant property settlements to make the LCT before the PET, there are circumstances where this can result in the payment of more tax on the transfers themselves. This occurs where the donor dies more than three years, but less than seven years after his gifts, as illustrated in the examples which follow. Assume that no annual exemptions are available.

Example 1: PET precedes LCT by one day

			IHT £
(a)	PET	£330,000	nil
(b)	LCT	£466,000	
	first	£325,000 – nil	
	balance	£141,000 @ 20%	28,200
(c)	Donor dies after six years.		
	PET	£330,000 – £325,000 = £5,000	
		£5,000 @ 40% × 20% (taper relief)	400
	LCT	£466,000 @ 40% × 20% (taper relief)	37,280
		credit (tax already paid)	(28,200)
	IHT due on LCT		£9,080
	Total IHT – £37,680		

Example 2: LCT precedes PET by one day

			IHT £
(a)	LCT	£466,000	
	first	£325,000 – nil	
	balance	£141,000 @ 20%	28,200
(b)	PET	£330,000	nil
(c)	Donor dies after six years.		
	LCT	£466,000	
	first	£325,000 – nil	
	balance	£141,000 @ 40% × 20% (taper relief)	11,280
		credit (tax already paid – no refund)	(28,200)
			no IHT due
(d)	PET	£330,000 @ 40% × 20% (taper relief)	£26,400
Total IHT – £54,600			

Lifetime transfers – transfers on death

Clients who are estate planning through a combination of lifetime giving and gifts by will should be aware of the effect of PETs on their death estates. Lifetime gifts which become chargeable on death have first call on the deceased's nil rate band and this may result in more IHT being payable on property passing under the will.

Example

Oswald has always used his annual exemption but otherwise has made no previous lifetime transfers.

Year 1: Oswald makes a will leaving a legacy of £325,000 to his children and the residue to his wife.

Year 2: He makes a PET of £100,000 to his eldest son.

Year 3: Oswald dies.

Step 1: The PET becomes chargeable, but as Oswald had made no previous lifetime transfers the £100,000 is covered by his nil rate band.

Step 2: The £100,000 is cumulated with his death estate and means that only the remaining £225,000 of the nil rate band is available to set against the legacy to his children. The balance of the legacy (£100,000) is taxable at 40% (subject to grossing up); the residue is exempt.

Use of a 'formula clause' limiting the legacy to the amount available of the nil rate band at death (here £100,000) when drafting the will can anticipate and avoid this situation (see **12.5.1**).

Using the reliefs

Property which attracts business property relief or agricultural property relief (especially at 100%) should, where possible, be given to non-exempt beneficiaries rather than exempt ones, as otherwise the benefit may be wasted. There is also the danger of losing the relief completely where the conditions for business property relief are not fulfilled at the date of death (see **4.3.6.2** for an example).

It may be preferable to make the gift of such property by will because there is a risk that the donee will no longer own the property on the death of the donor within seven years of the transfer, thus losing the relief.

Excluded property – inheritance tax

Section 5 of IHTA 1984 defines a person's estate as including everything 'to which he is beneficially entitled ... but does not include excluded property'. By IHTA 1984, s 48 a reversionary interest (with three anti-avoidance exceptions – see below) is excluded property. Section 47 defines any future interest under a settlement as a reversionary interest, whether the interest is vested or contingent, and includes the interest expectant on the termination of an interest in possession, ie, the interest which falls into possession on the death of a life tenant. The interest of a beneficiary under a discretionary settlement is not, therefore, within the definition.

Because a reversionary interest is not included in an individual's estate, it can be given away as part of estate planning without liability to IHT (and without CGT liability, see below).

Perhaps the most common example of excluded property is 'an interest in remainder' following a qualifying life interest.

Example

In 2000 S settles property on Angela for life, remainder to Bernard absolutely.

S ────────▶ Angela for life
                │
                ▼
        remainder to Bernard

While Angela is alive Bernard has an 'interest in remainder'. Assume Bernard is wealthy and has a house, shares and cash totalling £400,000. He is divorced and intends to leave everything to his daughter Davina.

(a)   If Bernard does nothing:

On Angela's death the trust fund, then valued at £355,000, is taxable as part of Angela's estate. (Assume that she is unmarried, her residuary estate is exempt and her cumulative total is zero.)

IHT of £12,000 is payable on the trust fund.

Bernard receives £343,000.

When Bernard dies his estate is £343,000 + £400,000 and Davina will pay IHT of £167,200.

(b)   If Bernard gives his interest in remainder to Davina while Angela is still alive.

There will be no IHT (IHTA 1984, s 5) and no CGT on the gift (see below; TCGA 1992, s 76)

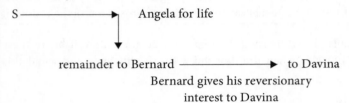

On Angela's, death, Davina will receive £343,000 (as Bernard did in (a)).

When Bernard dies his estate is £400,000 as the trust fund no longer forms part of his taxable estate. Davina will now pay IHT of £30,000 on her father's estate. This represents a tax saving of £137,200, ie, IHT at 40% on the £343,000 trust fund.

The three anti-avoidance exceptions within s 48 where the reversionary interest is not excluded property are:

(a)   where the interest was purchased for money or money's worth;

(b)   where the interest is one to which the settlor or his spouse is beneficially entitled;

(c)   where it is the lessor's interest expectant on the ending of a lease granted for life; where such a lease for life is granted, a settlement exists for IHT.

Excluded property – capital gains tax

No gain arises for CGT where a beneficiary disposes of his beneficial interest under a settlement, provided that it had never previously been acquired for a consideration in money or money's worth (other than consideration consisting of another interest under the settlement, for example, on a 'swap' of interests by beneficiaries). Once any consideration in money or money's worth has been given, all future disposals of the interest will attract CGT (TCGA 1992, s 76).

If, in the previous example, Bernard had sold his interest to Davina, no CGT would be payable by him (assuming no prior consideration had been given for the interest) because s 76 would apply. On Davina's later disposal (by sale or by gift) she would be liable to CGT on any gain she realises.

If instead Bernard had given his interest to Davina, neither he nor Davina would pay CGT. Whether she sold or gave away the interest subsequently, she would not pay CGT.

4.6.2.2   Capital gains tax

Although a gift may not result in an IHT charge, it may attract an immediate charge to CGT. A gift is a disposal by the donor and, if it is of a chargeable asset, CGT will be calculated in the usual way (subject to appropriate reliefs and exemptions).

Example

Susan gives quoted shares worth £60,000 to her daughter Tina and cash of £50,000 to her son Vernon.

Both gifts are PETs for IHT purposes and the cash is not a chargeable asset for CGT.

Susan will pay CGT on the difference between the purchase price of the quoted shares and their open market value at the date of the gift to Tina, after taking into account the annual exemption.

Where the gift is of a business asset hold-over relief will be available (for the definitions and conditions, see **4.4.5.2**), but if the donor's annual exemption is available or he has unused losses, it may be better not to claim the relief.

Example

William gives his 10% shareholding in O Ltd to his daughter Yasmin. William acquired the shares for £300 and they are currently worth £10,500. Yasmin expects to sell the shares within the next two years. Last year, William made capital losses of £2,000. (Assume that the annual exemption and tax rate remain unchanged in future years.)

(a)   If hold-over relief claimed:

William pays no CGT and retains losses of £2,000.

Yasmin acquires the shares at £300.

In two years' time she sells the shares for £11,400. Assume Yasmin makes no other disposals in the tax year.

CGT is payable on any chargeable gain.

	£
Disposal consideration	11,400
less: Acquisition cost	300
	11,100
less: Annual exemption	10,100
Chargeable gain	1,000

(b)   If hold-over relief not claimed and assuming neither makes other disposals in the relevant tax year:

William's gift is a disposal of a chargeable asset.

	£	£
Disposal consideration	10,500	
less: Acquisition cost	300	
		10,200
Part of unused losses	100	
Annual exemption	10,100	
		10,200
William's chargeable gain		nil

When Yasmin sells:

	£	£
Disposal consideration		11,400
less: Acquisition cost	10,500	
less: Annual exemption (part)	900	11,400
Yasmin's chargeable gain		nil

Note: Brought forward losses need only be used to reduce gains to the level of the annual exemption, unlike current year losses which must be used to reduce gains to zero before any portion of the loss can be carried forward.

Payment of CGT by instalments (TCGA 1992, ss 280, 281)

31 January following the end of the tax year of the disposal is the normal date for payment of a CGT liability. In limited circumstances, the tax may be paid by equal yearly instalments starting on 31 January. Interest is payable on the outstanding tax.

CGT may be paid by instalments if the following apply.

(a)   Sales (s 280) – if the consideration is payable over a period exceeding 18 months and the Revenue is satisfied payment of the tax in a lump sum would cause hardship. The instalment period is eight years (or the payment period if the consideration is payable over a shorter period).

(b)   Gifts or deemed disposals by trustees (s 281 – see **10.2.7**) – where the property is land, a controlling shareholding in either a quoted or an unquoted company, or a minority holding in a company whose shares are unquoted, provided that hold-over relief was not available under either TCGA 1992, s 165 or s 260, ie, neither the asset (s 165) nor the occasion (s 260) was appropriate to enable hold-over relief to be claimed. Failure to make the appropriate election for hold-over relief, in cases where it is available, does not mean that the tax can then be paid by instalments. When available, the CGT may be paid by 10 equal annual instalments.

4.6.2.3   Income tax

An outright gift of an income-producing asset to an adult child by his parent will give the child an increase in his taxable income (taxable at his own rates) and a corresponding decrease in the level of the parent's taxable income (and a saving of tax at his own rates). The potential saving of tax, possibly at 40% or 50%, by the parent makes such gifts attractive, particularly when the child's rate of tax may be at basic rate or less.

Parental gifts for minor children (ITTOIA 2005, s 629)

Despite the obvious practical advantage of an outright gift, there is a potential income tax problem if the child is unmarried and under 18 years when the gift is made. Income tax rules state that any income (of more than £100) paid to or for the benefit of the unmarried minor child from a 'settlement' created by his parent will be taxed as though it is still the income of the parent (s 629). This is deliberate policy to prevent a parent who pays income tax at 40% or 50% from benefiting the child who pays income tax at lower rates or possibly is not a tax payer at all. If income is accumulated and not paid to or for the benefit of the minor child, it will not be taxed as income of the settlor.

'Settlement' is defined in very wide terms by ITTOIA 2005, s 620, as including 'any disposition, trust, covenant, agreement, arrangement or transfer of assets'. An outright gift by a parent to a minor child is clearly within the provision, so that any income of the property given away is taxed as if it still belongs to the parent. The actual 'ownership' of the income does not belong to the parent even though it is deemed his for income tax purposes. The parent has a right of reimbursement from the child for the extra tax suffered where the income is deemed to be his for income tax purposes (s 646). Once the child attains 18 or marries, s 629 ceases to apply. The income is then taxed as the child's, not his parent's.

4.6.3   Post-death disclaimers and variations

Where a parent leaves assets by will to a wealthy adult child, that child may in turn decide to give that property to his own children. A post-death alteration of the will may be the most tax-effective way of passing inherited property to the next generation (see **Chapter 13**).

4.6.4 Gifts into trust

The practical advantage of a gift into trust over an outright gift is flexibility. By using a settlement, the settlor (the person making the gift into the trust) can determine who will benefit, when and how. Conditions can be imposed, for example, 'To Ben if he attains 21 years of age', so that Ben will receive the trust fund (gift) only if he reaches his 21st birthday; or to limit the amount of the gift received, for example 'the income to Carol during her life and on her death the income and capital to Doreen'. This is not possible with an outright gift.

There are various types of trust, and each trust has its own particular uses and conditions. The most commonly used types are considered in more detail in **Chapter 5**. Trusts with trustees resident outside the UK also play a considerable role in tax and estate planning. These are considered in **Chapter 15**.

4.6.4.1 Parental settlements (ITTOIA 2005, s 629)

The income deeming provisions discussed at **4.6.2** apply to 'settlements' as defined by s 620. If, therefore, a parent creates a trust of any of the types just mentioned of which his minor unmarried child is a beneficiary, s 629 will apply to income paid out to the child for so long as the child remains under 18 years and unmarried. The provision does not apply if income is accumulated. The income produced by the property in the settlement will be taxed as though it is still the income of the parent/settlor. The income remains the income of the trustees who will use it under the terms of the trust for the benefit of the beneficiaries. The parent/settlor has a right to recover from the trustees the extra income tax he pays because of these provisions.

4.6.5 Gifts with a reserved benefit (Finance Act 1986, s 102 and Sch 20)

No estate planning involving gifts can take place without at least a brief consideration of the rules governing 'reservation of benefit'. Anybody, whether parent, grandparent, uncle, etc, making a gift must ensure that the donor does not continue to have any interest (with minor exceptions) in the subject matter of the gift or the gift will be ineffective for IHT purposes. This principle applies to outright gifts and gifts into trust, and is illustrated by the following examples.

Example 1

Gina says to Henry 'I give you the Matisse which hangs in my drawing room'. Henry lets Gina keep it on her wall.

Example 2

For many years, Ian has owned a country cottage in which he spends his holidays. Ian transfers the ownership of the cottage to his son John but spends his holidays there as before.

In both examples there has been a valid gift for succession and CGT purposes and a PET for IHT purposes. However, the Revenue will not fully recognise the gift for IHT purposes because there has been a reservation of benefit – the continued enjoyment of the Matisse and the occupation of the cottage.

The death of the donor within seven years will attract IHT in the usual way on the PET. However, because the gift is caught by the 'reservation of benefit' provisions, the property will also be taxable as part of the donor's IHT estate at death. This prima facie double liability is, to an extent, alleviated by the Inheritance Tax Double Charges (Relief) Regulations 1987 (SI 1987/1130).

If the reservation ends before the donor's death, he is treated as making a PET at that time. Again, the 1987 Regulations provide relief should each PET (the original gift and the ending of the reservation) be within seven years of the donor's death.

The reservation of benefit provisions apply where an individual disposes of any property by way of gift and either:

(a)   full possession and enjoyment of the property is not bona fide assumed by the donee at or before the beginning of the relevant period (s 102(1)(a)); or

(b)   at any time in the relevant period the property is not enjoyed to the entire exclusion, or virtually to the entire exclusion, of the donor by contract or otherwise (s 102(1)(b)).

The relevant period means the period ending on the date of the donor's death and beginning seven years before that date, or if it is later, on the date of the gift.

Example 1

David gives away (ie, transfers the legal title to) his house to his only child Ella.

(a)   If Ella moves in and David dies two years later – full possession and enjoyment at the beginning of the relevant period (of two years) – no reservation.

(b)   If Ella moves in and David dies eight years later – as before, no reservation.

(c)   If after one year David resumes occupation for six months to write his autobiography, the property is no longer enjoyed to the entire exclusion of David – gift with reservation.

Example 2

Fiona settles a property on discretionary trusts naming herself as one of the discretionary beneficiaries. Even though she has no more than an expectation of benefiting as a beneficiary of a discretionary settlement, all the trust property will remain taxable as part of her estate on death.

Section 102(1)(b) (above) requires that 'the property' is 'enjoyed to the exclusion ...' etc. Identifying the property given is not normally difficult but is obviously essential before the rules can be applied appropriately. It also requires 'virtually entire exclusion' from the gifted property. Some continued enjoyment of the property is therefore possible. There is no statutory definition but the Revenue interprets the phrase as meaning (and therefore including) 'cases in which benefit to the donor is insignificant in relation to the gifted property' (Inland Revenue Tax Bulletin Issue 9, November 1993). Flexibility is applied by the Revenue when applying the interpretation so that a donor can have limited access to the property given away.

The following are some of the situations which, according to the Revenue, will not bring the rules into play:

(a)   A house which becomes the donee's residence but where the donor subsequently:

(i)   stays, in the absence of the donee, for not more than two weeks each year, or

(ii)   stays with the donee for less than one month each year.

(b)   Social visits, excluding overnight stays, made by a donor as a guest of the donee, to a house which he had given away. The extent of the social visits should be no greater than the visits which the donor might be expected to make to the donee's house in the absence of any gift by the donor.

(c)   A temporary stay for some short-term purpose in a house the donor had previously given away, for example:

(i)   while the donor convalesces after medical treatment;

(ii)   while the donor looks after a donee convalescing after medical treatment.

(d)   A house together with a library of books which the donor visits less than five times in any year to consult or borrow a book.

(e)   A motor car which the donee uses to give occasional (ie, less than three times a month) lifts to the donor.

(f)   Land which the donor uses to walk his dogs or for horse riding, provided this does not restrict the donee's use of the land.

Conversely, the following are instances (in the Revenue view) where the rules may apply:

(a)   A house in which the donor then stays most weekends, or for a month or more each year.

(b)   A second home or holiday home which the donor and the donee both then use on an occasional basis.

(c)   A house with a library in which the donor continues to keep his own books, or which the donor uses on a regular basis, for example because it is necessary for his work.

(d)   A motor car which the donee uses every day to take the donor to work.

Inland Revenue Tax Bulletin Issue 9 also provides some guidance on the meaning of the exclusion provided by FA 1986, Sch 20, para 6(1)(a). By this provision, if land or chattels are given away and the donor provides full consideration for his future enjoyment of the property, the reservation provisions do not apply. What constitutes full consideration for the use has caused estate planners problems. Would anything less than full consideration be fatal? In the context of rent payable for the future use of property the Revenue view is:

> While we take the view that such full consideration is required throughout the relevant period – and therefore consider that the rent paid should be reviewed at appropriate intervals to reflect market changes – we do recognise that there is no single value at which consideration can be fixed as 'full'. Rather, we accept that what constitutes full consideration in any case lies within a range of values reflecting normal valuation tolerances, and that any amount within that range can be accepted as satisfying the para 6(1)(a) test.

Further aspects of the reservation rules and the family home are discussed at **4.7.4**.

The reservation of benefit provisions do not apply (inter alia) to transfers qualifying for the four following IHT exemptions:

(a)   the spouse exemption;

(b)   the small gift exemption;

(c)   the gift in consideration of marriage exemption; and

(d)   the gifts to charity exemption.

Income tax charge on pre-owned assets

The FA 2004 introduced income tax provisions (s 84 and Sch 15) with the aim of catching situations not covered by the IHT reservation of benefit regime. The effect is that where a person owns certain assets (land, chattels or intangible property) and disposes of them, other than by sale at arm's length, but still derives some benefit from them, that person will suffer an income tax charge on the annual value of this benefit. The charge also applies if a person has contributed towards the purchase of such property by another, and derives some benefit from

the property. These provisions came into effect on 6 April 2005, but the charge affects anyone who has owned and disposed of assets since 17 March 1986, or contributed to the purchase of an asset since that date.

This charge will not apply in various situations, including:

(a)   where under the reservation of benefit rules the asset is treated as part of the IHT estate of the donor;

(b)   where the annual value of the benefit is below £5,000; or

(c)   where the asset is owned by the donor's spouse.

4.7   The family home

The principal tax-saving opportunity available to the home owner is the CGT private residence exemption. As a substantial asset in its own right, home owners will frequently raise questions about gifts of the home, or at least an interest in it, as part of estate planning with a view to saving, principally, IHT on its value at death. There are many problems associated with gifts of this type, some of which are discussed later.

4.7.1   Insurance cover

It is sensible to provide insurance cover designed to repay the mortgage secured on the family home. In the case of property owned jointly by a husband and wife the policy will normally mature on the death of the first spouse to die leaving a mortgage-free property for the survivor. Various types of policy are available and are discussed in **Appendix 2(16)**.

4.7.2   Joint tenancy and tenancy in common

Joint tenancy and tenancy in common have already been discussed (see **4.5.1.2**) as the two common ways property is held by spouses. For IHT purposes, there is no distinction made between joint tenancy and tenancy in common; it is the beneficial interest behind the trust of the legal estate that is important when considering the 'estate' of each spouse. The differences between joint tenancy and tenancy in common from a succession point of view have also been considered earlier.

4.7.3   Capital gains tax private residence exemption (TCGA 1992, ss 222–226)

Gains made on the disposal by sale or by gift of an individual's dwelling house used as his only or main residence, including grounds of up to 0.5 hectares (or such larger area as is reasonably required for its enjoyment), are exempt. It is a question of fact in each case as to what constitutes a dwelling house. A caravan was held to be a dwelling house in *Makins v Elson (Inspector of Taxes)* [1977] 1 All ER 572 but not in *Moore v Thompson* [1986] STC 170 (the caravan not having its own water or electricity supply).

Problems can also arise in deciding whether separate buildings can constitute the tax payer's residence. For example, a separate bungalow occupied by a caretaker and situated in the grounds of the tax payer's house was within the exemption when sold, ie, physical separation of the buildings did not deny the tax payer the exemption (*Batey (Inspector of Taxes) v Wakefield* [1982] 1 All ER 61). Later cases (where CGT was payable) show that the separate building must be physically close to the main building so as to enhance the tax payer's enjoyment of it (*Markey (Inspector of Taxes) v Sanders* [1987] 1 WLR 864 – bungalow 130 metres away), or within the 'curtilage' of the main building (*Lewis (Inspector of Taxes) v Lady Rook* [1992] 1 WLR 662 – cottage 200 yards away).

4.7.3.1   Land and residence disposed of separately

The order of disposals can be important where the tax payer plans to sell or give away land used with the main residence and the main residence itself. Land of up to 0.5 hectares (or a permitted larger area) is within the exemption if used in connection with the residence. Thus disposal of the residence with its grounds will be exempt, but gains on the later disposal of the retained land will be chargeable (*Varty (Inspector of Taxes) v Lynes* [1976] 3 All ER 447).

4.7.3.2 Part business user

Use of part of the house exclusively for business purposes will mean that part of the gain on the disposal is chargeable. Exclusive use can easily be avoided, for example, by having a television set in a room otherwise used as an office for a business run from home.

4.7.3.3 More than one residence

A tax payer with more than one residence can elect for one to be treated as his main residence (TCGA 1992, s 222(5)). This avoids difficult questions as to which of two or more residences is the only or main residence for the purposes of the relief. The election should be made within two years of acquiring the second residence. Failure by the tax payer to elect will mean that the Inspector of Taxes will do so. The relative CGT liability on each property will generally influence the election of a particular property, for treatment as the tax payer's main residence.

A husband and wife can have only one main residence between them, and the same is true of civil partners. When a couple marry, each owning a residence, the election for treatment as their main residence must be made within two years of the marriage or civil partnership.

4.7.3.4 Periods of absence

Exemption is available if a tax payer occupies a property as his only or main residence throughout the period of ownership. Periods of absence will therefore cut back the exemption so that a proportion of the gain on disposal is chargeable.

Certain periods of absence can be ignored (so not prejudicing the exemption). These include:

(a) the first 12 months' ownership due to delay in building or alteration (Statement of Practice D4);

(b) periods not exceeding three years in total provided there was no other available residence and the property was occupied before and after the periods of absence;

(c) the last three years of ownership, for example, where the owner moves into new property and has delay in selling the former.

4.7.3.5 Private residences occupied under the terms of a trust (s 225)

If the trustees sell a dwelling house occupied by a beneficiary as his main residence under the terms of the trust, their capital gain is exempt. The exemption will apply where the beneficiary has an interest in possession, ie, he is entitled to occupy under the terms of the settlement.

The exemption will also apply if he occupies as a result of the exercise of a discretion, for example, where he is a beneficiary of a discretionary trust and the trustees exercise a power in the settlement to permit him to occupy (*Sansom and Another v Peay (Inspector of Taxes)* [1976] 3 All ER 375).

Chapter 5 discusses the essential differences between interest in possession and discretionary trusts.

Since 10 December 2003, the TCGA 1992, s 226A provides that where hold-over relief is claimed under TCGA 1992, s 260 on a transfer of a house to a discretionary settlement, the principal private residence exemption will not be available if the trustees allow a beneficiary to occupy that house and the trustees then dispose of it. If hold-over relief is not claimed when the house is transferred to the settlement, the principal private residence exemption will be available on a later disposal by the trustees (assuming that they have first allowed a beneficiary to occupy the house).

4.7.4 Estate planning and the family home

The dilemma here is, on the one hand, the wish to give away part or all of the value of the home to save IHT; and on the other hand, the necessity to maintain a roof over the donor's head. Saving tax in relation to the home (bearing in mind its value in the client's estate) is an obvious consideration but the best advice is often 'don't let the tax tail wag the dog', ie, it is frequently better not to enter into arrangements just to save IHT. Joint tenancy between a husband and wife may often be the most practical approach for spouses.

Normally, IHT planning considerations will revolve around a gift of the house, or of an interest in it, to another individual who will usually be the donor's child.

There is a danger in giving the family home to a child. The child may become bankrupt or be divorced. The donor's house would then be taken by the child's trustee in bankruptcy, or be at risk in the divorce settlement.

The gift with reservation of benefit provisions (FA 1986, s 102) and the pre-owned assets regime discussed at **4.6.5** present the main obstacle to estate planning where the family home is involved. There are some exceptions to the reservation rules, the more important of which are discussed below.

4.7.4.1   'Occupation virtually to the entire exclusion of the donor' (FA 1986, s 102(1)(b))

A gift of the home to a child followed by occasional visits (as interpreted by the Revenue in Tax Bulletin Issue 9, November 1993) should have no adverse IHT consequences.

4.7.4.2   'Occupation resulting from change of circumstances of the donor' (FA 1986, Sch 20, para 6(1)(b))

A gift of land which is subsequently reoccupied by the donor following unforeseen and unintentional change in his circumstances is excluded by para 6 provided:

(a)   the donor is through age or infirmity unable to maintain himself;

(b)   the reoccupation is reasonable provision by the donee for the care of the donor; and

(c)   the donee is a relative of the donor or his or her spouse.

The scope of this exemption is clearly limited as shown in the following example.

> **Example**
> A father on his retirement gives to his daughter the family bungalow. He later returns to live there following serious ill health. No IHT consequences should follow from the reoccupation.

4.7.4.3   'Occupation of land and possession of a chattel for full consideration in money or money's worth' (FA 1986, Sch 6, para (1)(a))

A gift of the home and the arrangement of a right of continued occupation through a lease or licence should have no adverse IHT consequence. Full consideration is required throughout the period of occupation so that a full rent, reviewed regularly, will be essential (see the Revenue's view as to this published in Tax Bulletin Issue 9, referred to at **4.6.5**). A scheme using this paragraph will reduce the donor's estate for IHT but requires the donor to have sufficient income to pay the rent in full and regularly.

4.7.4.4   'Co-ownership' between the parents (donors) and the children (donees)

The parents could give the child(ren) an interest in the house as tenant(s) in common. A gift of the beneficial interest as tenant in common is a PET and carries with it the right to occupy the entire property with the other co-owner(s). The donor's continued occupation is not treated as a reservation of benefit provided the donor does not receive any benefit (such as payment) from the transfer (FA 1986, s 102B). Even if schemes of this sort work, the practical result is ownership and occupation shared with other (younger) members of the family. Often this will make such schemes unattractive. In view of the legal and practical uncertainty, the best advice is probably not to 'tax plan' with the matrimonial home.

4.8   Gifts to charity

In addition to, or perhaps instead of, gifts to family and friends, a tax payer may wish to make gifts to his favourite charity or charities.

Although not always considered part of estate planning, such gifts can be achieved in a number of tax-efficient ways and the method chosen will normally be determined by the timing and anticipated amount of the gift.

4.8.1   Inheritance tax

All gifts to a charity, whether made by lifetime gift or by will, and regardless of the amount, are exempt from IHT (IHTA 1984, s 23). A wealthy client may well make sizeable lifetime gifts to charity. These will be exempt and never enter his cumulative total.

Many clients will not be able to afford or wish to make such lifetime donations but will make provision for a charity in their will. This may take the form of a legacy or a gift of residue. The amount given must be deducted as an exemption in the calculation to find the deceased's total chargeable estate.

The will or intestacy of a deceased person may also be varied (see **Chapter 12**) to provide an exempt gift to charity.

4.8.2   Capital gains tax (TCGA 1992, s 257)

The most common form of charitable gift is of cash and therefore CGT is not relevant.

Where, however, a tax payer is transferring chargeable assets to a charity, the gift will be at no gain no loss (the rule works in a similar way to inter-spouse transfers, see **4.4.5.1**).

For property left to charity by will, the organisation will receive the property at probate value at the testator's death. As with inter vivos gifts, when the charity disposes of the property any gains should be exempt from CGT.

4.8.3   Income tax

There are various schemes for lifetime payments to charity which are income tax effective for the donor and which should, therefore, be especially attractive to higher rate tax payers. These include payroll giving (ITEPA 2003, s 713), gift aid (ITA 2007, ss 414–416) and charitable gift relief (ITA 2007, ss 431, 434).

4.9   Stamp duty and stamp duty land tax

Stamp duty is a tax on documents, not transactions. It applies in relation to transactions involving shares, interests in partnerships, loan capital and bearer instruments. Therefore where a document effects the transfer of these types of property, that document is subject to stamp duty. Where the transfer is a voluntary disposition there is no *ad valorem* stamp duty, but there is fixed duty (currently £5) and a requirement that the document be sent to the stamp office for a formal 'adjudication' stamp. However, for documents executed on or after 1 May 1987 which fall within any of the categories in the Schedule to the Stamp Duty (Exempt Instruments) Regulations 1987 (SI 1987/516) these requirements are removed.

Category

A   The vesting of property subject to a trust in the trustees of the trust on the appointment of a new trustee, or in the continuing trustees on the retirement of a trustee.

B   The conveyance or transfer of property the subject of a specific devise or legacy to the beneficiary named in the will.

C   The conveyance or transfer of property which forms part of an intestate's estate to the person entitled on intestacy.

D   The appropriation of property in satisfaction of a general legacy of money or of any interest of surviving spouse in an intestate's estate.

E   The conveyance or transfer of property which forms part of the residuary estate of a testator to a beneficiary entitled under the will.

F   The conveyance or transfer of property out of a settlement in or towards satisfaction of a beneficiary's interest, not being an interest acquired for money or money's worth, in accordance with the provisions of the settlement.

G   The conveyance or transfer of property on and in consideration only of marriage to a party to the marriage or to trustees to be held on a marriage settlement.

H   The conveyance or transfer of property in connection with divorce, etc.

I to K (not relevant to estate planning)

L   The conveyance or transfer of property as a voluntary disposition inter vivos.

M   The conveyance or transfer of property by a post-death variation. (Note: as a post-death variation is a voluntary disposition, it could be certified as falling within Category L.)

N   The declaration of any use or trust of or concerning a life policy, or property representing, or benefits arising under, a life policy.

To be exempt the document making the transfer must be certified as coming within one or more of the categories. The certificate can be included in or endorsed on the document. Most commonly for private client work this will arise on a voluntary transfer of shares where the stock transfer form will be the document effecting the transfer. Usually the certificate is found printed on the reverse of the form. A solicitor can sign the certificate in the name of his firm on behalf of the transferor (if, as is usual, it is not signed by the transferor personally).

Form of certificate

> I/we hereby certify that this instrument falls within Category ... in the Schedule to the Stamp Duty (Exempt Instruments) Regulations 1987.

From 1 December 2003 stamp duty was abolished in relation to land transactions. Instead, transactions in land are subject to stamp duty land tax.

A transaction in land is subject to the charge if, according to FA 2003, it is:

(a)   a land transaction;

(b)   effected for consideration;

(c)   which is not exempt.

Voluntary transactions are, thus, not liable to the tax. It is necessary for the transferee to complete a Revenue certificate to the effect that a stamp duty land tax return is not required, and this is then sent to Land Registry when the application is made to register the transfer of the land. The transferee must sign the certificate and his solicitor cannot do so on his behalf.

4.10 Conclusion

Financial planning is concerned with maximising the wealth (capital and income) of the individual. Estate planning is concerned with the passing on of that wealth within the family. This can be achieved by lifetime transfers or by will or a combination of the two. Each client is unique and requires a personal plan. The task of the solicitor is to identify the possibilities for estate planning. However much the solicitor believes in a course of action, the decision whether or not to take it is the client's alone.

Tax avoidance through the use of available reliefs and exemptions as in the previous paragraphs is a legitimate activity. However, some schemes designed for tax payers by their advisers have been so contrived, and the potential savings so great, that legislation has been enacted to combat their effectiveness. The Revenue has successfully challenged some schemes in the courts (see, for example, *Ingram and Another (Executors of the estate of Lady Ingram, deceased) v Inland Revenue Commissioners* [2000] 1 AC 293). Where the tax saving is achieved through a series of artificial steps carried out as a tax-saving measure only, the Revenue may be able to ignore the intervening steps and therefore negate the effect of the scheme. All practitioners need to be aware of the anti-avoidance legislation and cases (eg, ICTA 1988, s 674A; ITA 2007, Pt 13; IHTA 1984, s 268; and a series of cases beginning with *WT Ramsay Ltd v Inland Revenue Commissioners; Eilbeck (Inspector of Taxes) v Rawling* [1982] AC 300 and *Furniss (Inspector of Taxes) v Dawson* [1984] 1 AC 474) in putting forward tax-saving schemes.

In the FA 2004 a new regime was created requiring promoters of certain tax-avoidance schemes and, in some cases, tax payers using such schemes to disclose details of the scheme to the Revenue.

The Revenue registers each scheme reported to it by promoters and provides a reference number for it. This reference number is provided by the promoter to each tax payer using the scheme, and the tax payer has to disclose this in his tax return.

Summary – Lifetime Estate Planning

Topic	Summary	Reference
Financial planning	The object is to maximise a person's wealth with appropriate financial and investment planning to achieve the short, medium and long-term aims of the client. This includes considering what balance of income and capital growth the client needs, what level of risk the client can take and the tax position of the client.	Chapter 2
	Solicitors working in this area must comply with the relevant statutory provisions governing regulation.	Chapter 2 and Appendix 2
Enduring and lasting powers of attorney	Enduring and lasting powers of attorney, unlike ordinary powers of attorney, do not cease to be effective if the donor loses mental capacity.	Chapter 3
Enduring powers of attorney (EPAs)	EPAs cannot be created after 1 October 2007, but any created before then will continue to be valid and operate as normal. EPAs had to be created in a specific format. Unless restricted, an EPA is effective upon execution. The attorney has a duty to apply to register the EPA if the attorney has reason to believe that the donor is or is becoming mentally incapable. Once registered, the EPA can then continue to be used despite the donor's loss of capacity. The attorney can only deal with the donor's property and affairs, and, unless restricted, may make certain gifts of the donor's property.	3.2
Lasting powers of attorney (LPAs)	LPAs can only be created on or after 1 October 2007. The power must be made in a specific format, and contain a certificate by a prescribed person confirming that the donor understands the purpose of the LPA and that there is no fraud or undue pressure. The power is only valid once it is registered with the Public Guardian, which can be done at any time after the power has been executed. There are two types of LPA: the property and affairs LPA, allowing attorneys to deal with decisions on property and affairs, and the personal welfare LPA, allowing attorneys to deal with decisions on personal welfare. A person can choose to create both types of power or just one and can appoint the same person or different people to act as an attorney under each power.	3.4

Topic	Summary	Reference
Making lifetime outright gifts	A client may wish to reduce his estate for IHT purposes by giving away assets during his lifetime, usually to family members. Clients should consider the impact of all taxes, and the practical consequences of giving particular types of asset, and should not give away more than they can spare.	Chapter 4
	Clients should make the most of the various lifetime exemptions and reliefs for IHT and CGT. If clients are married or in a civil partnership they should consider equalisation of estates to ensure they can both use their nil rate bands to make lifetime gifts. Where a person dies on or after 9 October 2007, having survived a spouse or civil partner, the proportion of nil rate band unused on that earlier death can be transferred to the estate of the surviving spouse/civil partner on his or her death. However, the first spouse to die may prefer to use his or her nil rate band to make immediate provision for other family members.	4.3, 4.4, 4.5 and 4.7
	When making lifetime gifts there are a number of possible tax pitfalls to consider, including the rules on reservation of benefit, the possible loss of BPR if the donee does not retain the business property and the income tax consequences of making gifts to minor children.	4.6.5 and 4.6.2.3

Chapter 5
Introduction to Settlements

5.1 Settlements

The term 'settlement' has a variety of meanings depending upon the context in which it is used. In the private client department, the term is commonly used to include any arrangement whereby an individual 'settles' property of any kind upon trust for a beneficiary or group of beneficiaries. The term 'settlement' refers to the whole arrangement; the 'trusts' are the terms upon which the property is held.

Contrast the following statutory uses of the term:

(a) Under the SLA 1925, a 'settlement' or 'strict settlement' is a trust of land where no trust for sale is imposed. Under the SLA 1925 a beneficiary who has the right to enjoy the land (the tenant for life) has many of the powers over the property which would normally be vested in the trustees (eg, the power to sell the land). The TLATA 1996 prevents the creation of any new strict settlements. (The TA 2000, Sch 2 provides that SLA 1925 investments will be made at the discretion of the trustees and no longer at the direction of the tenant for life.)

(b) In tax statutes, the term 'settlement' is frequently used and is defined in a variety of different ways. For example, a parental 'settlement' for income tax purposes includes not only a settlement upon trust, but also an outright gift (see **4.6.4.1**).

5.1.1 Trusts background – some reminders

5.1.1.1 Fixed interest trusts

When an individual ('the settlor') settles property upon trust, he may wish to determine the precise extent to which his chosen beneficiaries are to enjoy the settled property in the future. He may, for example, divide their enjoyment of the property by creating successive interests, or he may prevent beneficiaries from obtaining access to the capital before a certain age by giving them contingent interests.

Where capital or income is to be divided between a group of individuals, the settlor may determine the extent of each beneficiary's share. It is possible to define beneficiaries by reference to a description rather than by naming them (eg, my grandchildren), provided that the description is sufficiently clear to enable the beneficiaries to be identified with certainty.

The settlor who creates such a trust gives fixed equitable interests to the beneficiaries. Each beneficiary has a bundle of rights resembling an interest in property which he may sell or give away (provided that any such assignment complies with s 53(1)(c) of the LPA 1925).

If the beneficiaries are between them entitled to the whole equitable interest and are all of full age and capacity, they may by agreement put an end to the trust, calling for the trustees to distribute the capital between them in such shares as they may agree (the rule in *Saunders v Vautier* (1841) 4 Beav 115 – see **10.1.3**).

Under TLATA 1996, s 19, such beneficiaries can require the existing trustees to retire and appoint specified new trustees to replace them. This procedure is often preferable to bringing the trust to an end as it avoids the potential CGT liability which arises when a trust ends.

Neither option is available if any beneficiary is a minor, or if there are potential beneficiaries who may be born in the future, although the court has power to consent on behalf of such beneficiaries under the VTA 1958 (see **13.2.3.1**).

The period during which the settlor may dictate how the property is to be held is limited by the rule against remoteness of vesting; interests which do not vest within the perpetuity period will fail (see **6.2.7**). If the trusts in the settlement should fail for this or any other reason, the property will revert to the settlor (or his estate if he is dead).

5.1.1.2 Discretionary trusts

A settlor may not wish to determine in advance the precise extent of each beneficiary's entitlement. In such a case, he may nominate a category of beneficiaries and give his trustees the power to determine how much (if anything) each potential beneficiary should receive.

The trustees' discretion may simply concern the distribution of income. If the trustees are obliged to distribute the income, the trusts are said to be 'exhaustive'. Alternatively, the settlor may widen the trustees' discretion to allow them to retain or accumulate the income as they think fit ('non-exhaustive' trusts). The period during which a power to accumulate income may continue is limited by the rule against accumulations in the case of settlements not governed by the Perpetuities and Accumulations Act 2009 (PAA 2009). In the case of settlements governed by the PAA 2009, trustees can accumulate throughout the lifetime of the settlement unless the settlor has provided otherwise (see **6.10**).

A discretion over the distribution of income may be combined with fixed interests in capital. A common example is to leave capital 'to such of my children as reach the age of 25 equally if more than one', with a direction that the trustees can apply income arising before the capital vests as they see fit.

Alternatively, the trustees' discretion may extend to capital as well as income, giving the trustees the power to distribute capital to one or more of the designated class of beneficiaries at any time (and thus, if they think fit, bring an end to the trust).

A beneficiary under a discretionary trust cannot claim any property as of right. He has only a hope that the trustees will exercise their discretion in his favour. Although in principle the rule in *Saunders v Vautier* would allow all the potential beneficiaries to end the trust by agreement, this is unlikely to be possible in practice as the class will be too widely drawn.

Any discretion over income or capital must be limited to the perpetuity period in order to comply with the rule against remoteness of vesting. A fixed period is usually specified in the trust instrument and the trustees will normally distribute the whole fund within that period. See **6.9** below.

If, however, all members of the class of beneficiaries should die before the trustees have distributed the capital, the trusts will fail. The property will pass to the beneficiary entitled in default if the settlement has been drafted to include one. If no default beneficiary is named, the property will revert to the settlor (or his estate, if he is dead) on a resulting trust. For tax reasons, it is important to avoid any possibility of 'reverter to settlor' (see **6.15**) and so an 'ultimate default' provision is usually included (see **6.15.4**) to ensure that the property cannot revert.

There is a difficult distinction between a power of appointment and a discretionary trust or 'trust power'. A trust power arises where the settlor's overriding intention is to benefit a particular class of beneficiaries, giving a power of selection to his trustees. A power of appointment involves no such overriding intention: if the power is not exercised, the property will pass in default of appointment. The distinction was once important because there was a different test for certainty of objects. However, the tests are now the same (*McPhail and Others v Doulton and Others* [1971] AC 424) and the distinction is largely academic. In practice, the trustees' power of selection is commonly expressed as a widely drawn power of appointment enabling them not only to give capital outright to a beneficiary, but also to resettle it on new trusts for the benefit of particular members of the class (see **Chapter 9** and **Appendix 3**, clause 6.2).

5.1.2   Settlements in practice

There are many rules of equity and statutory provisions which have a practical effect on the creation and use of settlements. The most important of these are the tax provisions which govern the treatment of the settlement for tax purposes on its creation, during its life and when it comes to an end. The FA 2006 introduced substantial changes to the way in which settlements are treated for IHT purposes. Unfortunately this has complicated matters, as it means that there are pre- and post-2006 rules to get to grips with.

This chapter is mainly concerned with the lifetime creation of settlements. **Chapter 12** considers how to create settlements in wills and their tax effects.

The purpose of this chapter is to look at the main types of lifetime settlement and to explore:

(a)   what can be achieved by using a settlement; and

(b)   the taxation cost to the settlor;

with the aim of enabling the selection of the appropriate type of settlement for a particular client.

5.2   Inheritance tax and settlements

5.2.1   The significance of 22 March 2006

22 March 2006 was Budget Day. Without any warning or consultation, the Chancellor introduced huge changes to the way in which trusts are treated for IHT purposes. It seems that the Treasury formed the view that settlements were being used primarily to escape IHT and was determined to make them less attractive. The intention was to encourage people to make outright gifts rather than to use trusts. There was concerted opposition from professional advisers and the press, who pointed out that trusts are used for all kinds of tax-neutral reasons. The Treasury backed down to some extent in relation to settlements created on death, but made very few concessions in relation to lifetime settlements. The date, therefore, remains a significant watershed in the tax treatment of settlements.

In the case of trusts created before 22 March 2006, the crucial question is whether or not the settlement has an interest in possession (see **5.2.2** below). This is because the IHT treatment of the two types of settlement is entirely different. It makes no difference whether the settlement is created by lifetime transfer or on death.

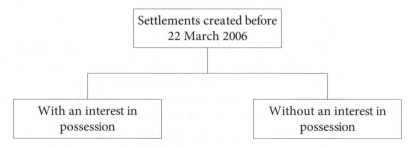

In the case of settlements created on or after 22 March 2006, the main question is whether the settlement is created by a lifetime transfer or on death. With one exception for disabled beneficiaries, all lifetime settlements are treated in the same way irrespective of whether or not a beneficiary has an interest in possession. Settlements created on death on or after 22 March 2006 have some special rules, which we will look at in **Chapter 12**.

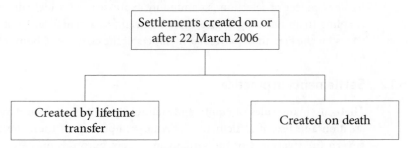

This chapter deals with the tax implications of creating *lifetime* settlements. However, for completeness, there is a brief summary of the rules applying to settlements created on death at **5.2.5**.

5.2.2   What is an interest in possession?

An 'interest in possession' was defined in *Pearson and Others v IRC* [1980] 2 All ER 479 as 'a present right to the present enjoyment' of income or assets. Put more simply, it means that the trustees have to pay the annual trust income to a beneficiary, or allow the beneficiary to have the use of assets.

The simplest example of an interest in possession is a life interest.

> **Example**
> Adam gives £100,000 to trustees to hold on trust for Brenda for life with the remainder to Colin. Brenda has an interest in possession. She is entitled to all the income generated by the trust fund of £100,000. The trustees must pay that income to her.

The purpose of this type of settlement is to provide successive interests. There are various ways to achieve this:

(a)   The settlor may want to benefit several people, one after the other.

> **Example**
> Diana wants to benefit her son and daughter-in-law by giving them extra income. She also wants to benefit her grandson. She might set up a trust giving:
> (i)   the income to her son for life; and on his death
> (ii)   the income to her daughter-in-law (if still living) for life; and on the death of the survivor of her son and daughter-in-law
> (iii)   the capital to the grandson absolutely.

(b)   The settlor may wish to give one person the right to income for a given time and then the capital to somebody else.

> **Example**
> Ernest wants to provide finance for his granddaughter while she studies to be an architect. He thinks she will need his support for about eight years, but ultimately he wants all his money to go to his favourite charity. He might set up a trust giving:
> (i)   the income to his granddaughter for eight years or until she qualifies as an architect, whichever is the shorter period; and then
> (ii)   the capital to the charity absolutely.

(c)   The settlor may want to stagger a beneficiary's entitlement to property.

Example

Fred wants to give a substantial sum of money to his grandson George, who is 19. George is in urgent need of some money, but Fred does not want him to receive everything immediately. Fred might set up a trust giving:

(i)   the income to George until he is 25 years of age; and then

(ii)   the capital to George absolutely.

Note: If the trustees have the power to decide whether or not to pay income to a beneficiary, it is not an interest in possession trust.

5.2.3   Settlements created before 22 March 2006

As we have already seen in the flowchart at **5.2.1,** it is essential from an IHT point of view to determine whether or not a settlement created before 22 March has an interest in possession. Settlements that do have such an interest are subject to a different IHT regime from those that do not.

A beneficiary with an interest in possession in settled property created before 22 March 2006 is treated as beneficially entitled to the property in which the interest subsists (IHTA 1984, s 49(1)). This means that the beneficiary is treated as the owner of the underlying trust property, with important IHT consequences:

(a)   on creation; and

(b)   on termination of the beneficiary's interest in possession.

Interests in possession in existence on 22 March 2006 are often referred to as 'qualifying' interests in possession. It makes no difference whether the settlement is created by lifetime transfer or on death.

Where no beneficiary has a qualifying interest in possession the trust itself is taxed. Again, it makes no difference whether the settlement is created by lifetime transfer or on death.

Settlements created for the benefit of disabled beneficiaries are often created without an interest in possession. These settlements receive special IHT treatment which continues after 22 March 2006.

5.2.3.1   Settlements with an interest in possession created before 22 March 2006

Inheritance tax on creation

The settlor's transfer to the settlement is a PET in so far as not exempt (IHTA 1984, s 3A). It might be exempt because an annual exemption is available, or because the beneficiary is a spouse or civil partner.

Where a settlor dies within seven years of creating the settlement, the PET becomes chargeable. The trustees will pay the tax from the settlement funds.

Example

On 1 March 2006 Harriet transfers £340,000 in cash and shares to a settlement for her brother for life, remainder to her nephew. She has already made chargeable transfers which exhausted her nil rate band and has no annual exemptions available.

Harriet dies on 8 February 2010 with assets of £130,000, which she leaves to her sister.

The lifetime transfer to the settlement is a PET under IHTA 1984, s 3A, so no IHT is paid at the time of the transfer. However, on Harriet's death the PET becomes chargeable. Taper relief applies as Harriet died more than three years but less than four years after the PET.

	£
Value transferred	340,000
IHT on £340,000 @ 40%	136,000

80% of £136,000 is payable because of taper relief, ie £108,800.

The tax is due six months from the end of the month in which Harriet died and must be paid by the trustees from the trust fund, so reducing the present value of the trust fund by £108,800. The whole of her death estate will be taxed at 40% as the transfer to the trust has exhausted her nil rate band.

Harriet could avoid the fund being reduced by the tax chargeable on her death by insuring her life for seven years and writing the policy in trust for the trustees of the settlement. The trustees would receive the proceeds of the policy as additional trust property after her death.

Inheritance tax on termination of the beneficiary's interest

A beneficiary with a qualifying interest in possession is treated as the owner of the trust property so:

(a)   if the beneficiary dies, the trust property is aggregated with his death estate; and

(b)   if the interest terminates in any other way (eg by surrender or assignment), the beneficiary is treated as making a transfer of value.

Note: All interests in possession in existence on 22 March 2006 will continue to be taxed in this way.

Transitional serial interests

The FA 2006 contains provisions relating to 'transitional serial interests'. In certain circumstances an interest in possession which arises after 22 March 2006 but which follows a qualifying interest in possession in existence on that date is treated for IHT purposes as if it had been created before 22 March 2006.

One example is a surviving spouse taking an interest following the death of his/her spouse.

Example

Sam creates a settlement in February 2000 for 'my daughter for life, remainder to her husband for life, remainder to her children absolutely'. The daughter dies in 2028; the husband is treated as if he had a pre-22 March 2006 interest in possession.

Another example of a transitional serial interest occurs where an interest in existence on 22 March 2006 ended in the period between 22 March 2006 and 1 October 2008 and was replaced by a further interest in possession.

We will not consider transitional serial interests further in this book. The relevant legislation is IHTA 1984, ss 49B–E.

5.2.3.2   Settlements without an interest in possession created before 22 March 2006

No beneficiary is treated as owning the underlying trust property so there are no charges to IHT when a beneficiary dies, or when one beneficiary's interest terminates and is replaced by another. Instead the property held in the settlement is subject to an entirely different IHT regime. This regime is sometimes referred to as the 'relevant property' regime, because IHTA 1984, s 58 calls property in which there is no qualifying interest in possession and which does not qualify for privileged IHT treatment 'relevant property'. See **Chapter 10** for a fuller discussion of the relevant property regime.

Inheritance tax on creation

The settlor's transfer to the settlement is a lifetime chargeable transfer in so far as not exempt. Annual exemptions may be available, but there can be no spouse exemption even if one of the beneficiaries is the settlor's spouse.

At the time of the transfer IHT is charged at half the death rates. If the settlor dies within seven years of creating the settlement, the transfer becomes chargeable at the full death rates, although credit is given for any IHT already paid.

Let us consider the Harriet example from **5.2.3.1** on the basis that the trust created is a discretionary settlement for the benefit of her brother and his children rather than a life interest settlement.

Example

On 1 March 2006, Harriet transfers £340,000 in cash and shares to a discretionary settlement for her brother and his children. She had already made chargeable transfers which had exhausted her nil rate band and had no annual exemptions available.

Harriet dies on 8 February 2010 with assets of £130,000, which she leaves to her sister.

The initial transfer is charged at half the death rates.

Assume that the IHT is paid from the funds transferred to the trustees, so there is no need to gross up the transfer. (If Harriet agreed to pay the IHT, it would be necessary to gross up the transfer.)

	£
Value transferred	340,000
IHT on £340,000 @ 20%	68,000

On Harriet's death within seven years, the lifetime transfer will become chargeable at the full death rates, although credit will be given for the IHT already paid. Taper relief will be available as she has died more than three years but less than four years after the transfer.

	£
Value transferred	340,000
IHT on £340,000 @ 40%	136,000
80% after taper relief	108,800
Less the IHT already paid	(68,000)
IHT to pay	40,800

As at **5.2.3.1** above, the tax is due six months from the end of the month in which Harriet died and must be paid by the trustees from the trust fund. The whole of her death estate will be taxed at 40% as the transfer to the trust has exhausted her nil rate band.

Charges to IHT after creation

No beneficiary is treated as owning the underlying trust property and so there are no charges to tax when a beneficiary dies, or when one beneficiary's interest terminates and is replaced by another. Instead, the settlement itself pays a charge to tax every 10 years (often called an anniversary charge) and there is also an exit charge when property leaves the settlement. The calculation of these charges is dealt with at **10.2** below.

5.2.4 Lifetime settlements created on or after 22 March 2006

All lifetime settlements created on or after 22 March 2006 (with the exception of those for disabled beneficiaries) are treated in the same way. They are all subject to the relevant property regime mentioned at **5.2.3.2** above. It is irrelevant for IHT purposes whether or not there is an interest in possession.

5.2.4.1 Lifetime settlements for the disabled

The transfer into the settlement will be a PET in so far as not exempt, if, and only if, it fulfils the qualifying conditions and is created for:

(a)   the benefit of a beneficiary who is 'disabled' within the meaning of IHTA 1984, s 89; or

(b)   the settlor's own benefit at a time when the settlor is suffering from a condition that it is reasonable to expect will lead to the settlor becoming 'disabled' within the meaning of IHTA 1984, s 89.

Trusts for the disabled are beyond the scope of this book and are not considered further.

5.2.4.2 All other lifetime settlements

Inheritance tax on creation

The creation of a lifetime settlement will be a lifetime chargeable transfer. It is irrelevant whether the settlement created is discretionary, has contingent interests or has an interest in possession. All lifetime trusts (except those qualifying as disabled trusts) are subject to the relevant property regime mentioned at **5.2.3.2**.

Let us consider the way in which the Harriet example from **5.2.3.1** will be treated if the transfer takes place on or after 22 March 2006. The settlement is subject to the relevant property regime.

Example

On 31 March 2008, Harriet transfers £340,000 in cash and shares to a settlement for her brother for life with the remainder to her nephew. She had already made chargeable transfers which had exhausted her nil rate band and had no annual exemptions available.

Harriet dies on 8 February 2010 with assets of £130,000, which she leaves to her sister.

The initial transfer is charged at half the death rates.

Assume that the IHT is paid from the funds transferred to the trustees, so there is no need to gross up the transfer. (If Harriet agreed to pay the IHT, it would be necessary to gross up the transfer.)

	£
Value transferred	340,000
IHT on £340,000 @ 20%	68,000

On Harriet's death within seven years, the lifetime transfer will become chargeable at the full death rates, although credit will be given for the IHT already paid. There will be no taper relief as she has died within three years of the transfer.

	£
Value transferred	340,000
IHT on £340,000 @ 40%	136,000
Less the IHT already paid	(68,000)
IHT to pay	68,000

As above, the tax is due six months from the end of the month in which Harriet died and must be paid by the trustees from the trust fund. The whole of her death estate will be taxed at 40% as the transfer to the trust has exhausted her nil rate band.

If the settlor has annual exemptions available, the value transferred by the lifetime chargeable transfer will be reduced appropriately. If the trust property is held for the settlor's spouse for life, no spouse exemption is available because the spouse is not treated as beneficially entitled to the settled property.

Inheritance tax treatment during the lifetime of the trust

No beneficiary is treated as owning the underlying trust property so there are no charges to tax when a beneficiary dies, or when one beneficiary's interest terminates and is replaced by another. Instead the trust itself pays a charge to tax every 10 years and there is an exit charge when property leaves the settlement. The calculation of these charges is dealt with at **10.2.3** below.

5.2.5 Settlements created on death on or after 22 March 2006

We will look at settlements created on death in **Chapter 12**. However, for completeness it is useful to know that there are three types of settlement which qualify for special IHT treatment:

(a) *Trusts for the disabled*

There are no anniversary or exit charges. Instead the beneficiary will be treated as beneficially entitled to the underlying trust assets. The settled property will be aggregated with the disabled beneficiary's own property when the beneficiary dies.

(b) *Immediate post-death interests*

These are settlements where a beneficiary has an interest in possession, eg 'to Fred for life'. The beneficiary will be treated as beneficially entitled to the underlying trust assets. The settled property will be aggregated with the beneficiary's own property when the beneficiary dies or when the interest terminates (eg by surrender or assignment). In other words, the beneficiary has a 'qualifying' interest in possession.

(c) *Trusts for bereaved minors and young people*

Settlements for the benefit of a parent's own child contingent on reaching an age not greater than 25 will not be subject to anniversary charges provided the requirements of IHTA 1984, s 71A or s 71D are satisfied.

If settlement property is paid to the child at or before 18, there will be no exit charge (s 71A and s 71D).

If settlement property is paid to the child after 18 and before 25, there will be an exit charge calculated on the length of time the property has remained in the settlement since the child's 18th birthday(s 71D).

5.2.6 Special IHT treatment for settlements without an interest in possession created for young people before 22 March 2006

Before 22 March 2006, certain settlements without an interest in possession were singled out for privileged IHT treatment. These settlements were called 'accumulation and maintenance' settlements. It did not matter whether the settlement was created by lifetime transfer or on death.

To qualify the settlement had to meet the conditions set out in IHTA 1984, s 71. Broadly, the beneficiaries had to become entitled to income or capital at or before age 25. For example, a settlement 'for my daughter contingent on her reaching 18' would qualify. Lifetime transfers to accumulation and maintenance settlements were PETs and not lifetime chargeable transfers, and there were no anniversary or exit charges.

No new accumulation and maintenance settlements can be created on or after 22 March 2006, and existing settlements lost their privileged status on 6 April 2008 unless they complied with stringent conditions. (This is true for all accumulation and maintenance settlements, whether initially created by lifetime settlement or on death.) See **Chapter 8**.

5.2.7 Settlements and inheritance tax planning

There is now a tax disincentive for tax payers to create lifetime settlements. The creation of any lifetime settlement will be a lifetime chargeable transfer and will give rise to an immediate charge to IHT unless:

(a)   the amount transferred is within the settlor's nil rate band or annual exemption; or

(b)   the assets transferred attract business or agricultural property relief.

Moreover, there will be a continuing cost as, after creation, there will be anniversary and exit charges to pay to the extent that the trust assets exceed the level of the nil rate band.

Some tax payers may prefer to make outright gifts to beneficiaries, which will be treated as PETs and give rise to no further IHT liability provided the transferor survives for seven years after making the gift.

5.2.8   Further inheritance tax points on settlements

5.2.8.1   Inheritance tax and grossing up

Where a settlor transfers funds to a lifetime settlement and IHT is payable on that transfer, he can either:

(a)   allow the tax to be paid from the sum transferred, in which case the settlement will receive less; or

(b)   provide additional funds to meet the tax, in which case the settlement will receive more.

Inheritance tax is calculated on the loss to the transferor, so if the settlor provides additional funds to cover the charge to IHT, there is a greater loss and more IHT will be payable. When calculating the IHT liability it will be necessary to gross up.

In the Harriet example at **5.2.4.2**, we assumed that the trustees paid the IHT due from the funds transferred by Harriet, and we said that there was no need to gross up. However, if Harriet felt more generous and was willing to transfer £340,000 to the settlement *and pay the IHT due as well*, grossing up would be required. She will lose not just the £340,000, but also the amount required to pay the tax.

> **Example**
>
> Harriet had already made chargeable transfers which had exhausted her nil rate band and had no annual exemptions available.
>
> She wants the full £340,000 to go into the discretionary trust. The £340,000 is net of 20% IHT. Inheritance tax on the gross gift will be calculated as follows:
>
> Gross up the value transferred at the appropriate tax rates:
>
> | Net | Gross equivalent |
> |---|---|
> | £ | £ |
> | $340,000 \times \dfrac{100}{80}$ | 425,000 |
>
> The settlement receives £340,000.
>
> The Revenue will receive IHT of £85,000 from Harriet (£425,000 – £340,000 = £85,000).
>
> Any charge which arises as a result of Harriet's death within seven years will be based on a value transferred of £425,000.

5.2.8.2   Cumulation

Because of the way cumulation works, a tax payer who makes a lifetime chargeable transfer (eg settles property on discretionary trusts before 22 March 2006, or on any trusts on or after that date) has to survive for 14 years before it ceases to have any impact.

> **Example**
>
> | May 2005: | Jake, who is divorced, settles £200,000 on discretionary trusts. |
> | May 2009: | Jake makes a gift of £125,000 to his sister Susan. |
> | May 2011: | Jake makes a gift of £200,000 to his granddaughter. |

January 2014:   Jake dies.

Ignore annual exemptions and assume rates and bands continue to be the same as in 2010/11.

Step 1

The transfer to the discretionary settlement was a lifetime chargeable transfer (LCT) made more than seven years before death and so no further tax is due on it. However, as we shall see, it remains relevant to the calculation of IHT on the transfers in 2009 and 2011.

Step 2

The gift in 2009 was made less than seven years before death and so the PET becomes chargeable. Look back seven years from that transfer to see if there are any chargeable transfers. If so, they must be cumulated. The existence of the 2005 LCT reduces the nil rate band available when calculating IHT on the 2009 transfer.

	£	£
Transfer – PET now chargeable		125,000
Cumulative total – LCT	200,000	
Nil rate band (part)	200,000	
Nil rate band (balance)		125,000
		nil

IHT on failed PET – nil

Step 3

The 2011 gift was a PET when made but has also become chargeable. It must be cumulated with all chargeable transfers made in the preceding seven years. In this case, the cumulative total of chargeable transfers is £325,000 (the 2005 LCT and the 2009 PET which is now treated as chargeable) and so exhausts the nil rate band.

	£	£
2011 PET now chargeable		200,000
Cumulative total – the failed PET and the LCT	325,000	
Nil rate band	325,000	
Nil rate band (balance)		nil
		200,000

IHT on £200,000 @ 40% payable by the trustees. Taper relief is not available as three years have not elapsed since the gift.

Step 4

Jake's estate on death is cumulated with chargeable transfers made in the previous seven years, ie the gifts in 2009 and 2011 which are now treated as chargeable.

As these together give a cumulative total of chargeable transfers of £325,000, Jake's estate is prima facie taxable at 40%. The LCT to the discretionary settlement was made more than seven years ago and drops out of cumulation for the death estate.

5.2.8.3 Order of gifts and same day transfers (IHTA 1984, ss 62, 66 and 68)

As we saw at **4.6.2**, where a client is proposing to create a lifetime settlement (for example, a discretionary settlement) and to make a PET, there is an advantage to the later taxation of the settlement in making the discretionary settlement before the PET. If the PET comes first and later becomes chargeable, it will be taken into account when calculating IHT payable by the trustees during the lifetime of the discretionary settlement. See **Chapter 10**.

5.3   Capital gains tax and lifetime settlements

5.3.1   Capital gains tax on creation

The basic CGT treatment of disposals to settlements is not affected by the type of settlement involved. However, on certain disposals a settlor may claim hold-over relief under TCGA 1992, s 165 or s 260 (see para **5.3.2** below).

The transfer of property by a settlor to trustees is a disposal (TCGA 1992, s 70). If chargeable assets are settled, a chargeable gain (or allowable loss) may result. The gain (if any) will be the settlor's, and he will bear the tax unless there is an agreement to the contrary.

Example

In December 2010, Ilyana (a higher rate tax payer) settles her quoted shares worth £37,000 (acquired for £6,900) and cash of £30,000. She has made no other disposals in that tax year. The beneficiaries are her daughter for life, with remainder to her grandchildren. No Entrepreneurs' Relief is available and she has no available losses.

Calculate the CGT on the disposal.

Cash is exempt.

Shares:	£
Market value at disposal	37,000
less: acquisition cost	(6,900)
	30,100
less: annual exemption	(10,100)
Chargeable gain	20,000

CGT @ 28% on £20,000 = £5,600

Calculate the cost of the settlement to Ilyana.

	£
Value of shares	37,000
Cash	30,000
CGT	5,600
	72,600

The acquisition cost of the shares to the trustees for the purpose of any future capital gains on a disposal by them is £37,000.

The creation of this settlement is also a lifetime chargeable transfer for IHT purposes of £61,000 (ie, £30,000 plus £37,000 minus 2 × £3,000 annual exemptions). As a result of IHTA 1984, ss 5(4) and 164, the reduction in Illyana's estate caused by the payment of CGT (and any disposal costs involved in the transfer) is ignored for IHT purposes, ie this reduction in value of the estate is not included when calculating the amount of IHT payable.

Capital gains tax on subsequent disposals by the trustees

Once the settlement has been created, any sale of trust assets by the trustees (see **14.5.1**) or a transfer of the trust fund, or part of it, to a beneficiary (see **10.1.4.2**) will be a disposal by the trustees giving rise to a CGT charge.

From 23 June 2010, CGT on any gains made on disposals by trustees is paid at 28%. (Between 6 April 2008 and 22 June 2010 the rate was 18%, between 6 April 2004 and 5 April 2008 the rate was 40%, between 6 April 1998 and 5 April 2004 it was 34%, and for earlier years the rate depended on the type of settlement.)

Trustees have an annual exemption of half that available to an individual, ie £5,050 per annum in the tax year 2010/11. Where a settlor has created more than one settlement, the annual exemption is divided between them.

> **Example**
>
> Albert creates two separate settlements. Each settlement will have an annual exemption of £2,525 (£5,050 ÷ 2).

There is, however, a minimum exemption per settlement of £1,010.

5.3.2 Capital gains tax and hold-over relief on creation of lifetime settlements (TCGA 1992, s 165 and s 260)

Where a settlor disposes of business assets (see **4.4.4**) to a settlement, he can claim hold-over relief under s 165 (unless the anti-avoidance provisions apply – see **5.5** below). Only the settlor need elect for s 165 hold-over relief.

Hold-over relief is available on transfers chargeable to IHT under TCGA 1992, s 260:

(a)   irrespective of the nature of the asset being settled, therefore including land and quoted shares; and

(b)   even if the transfer is chargeable at 0% or exempt (see Example 2 below).

The lifetime disposal of property by a settlor into a settlement post 22 March 2006 is a chargeable event for CGT (unless the asset being settled is cash).

Only the settlor need elect for s 260 hold-over relief.

> **Example 1**
>
> In January 2011 Lesley settles her country cottage, which she bought for £50,000 and which is now worth £280,000, on her children. She has made no previous transfers.
>
> The transfer is chargeable to IHT, but at 0% because the £280,000 falls within Lesley's nil rate band.
>
> Lesley has made a gain of £230,000 but can claim CGT hold-over relief. If she claims the relief, the trustees will acquire the cottage at £280,000 less Lesley's chargeable gain, ie an acquisition value of £50,000. If Lesley had incurred allowable expenditure of £5,000, her gain would be £225,000 and the trustees would be treated as acquiring the property for £280,000 less £225,000 = £55,000.

> **Example 2**
>
> In January 2011 Morris settles quoted shares purchased for £1,000 and now worth £6,000. He has made no other transfers but has made chargeable gains this year of £10,100 on disposal of other assets.
>
> The transfer to the discretionary settlement is a chargeable transfer. However, for IHT purposes the value transferred is nil because of Morris's unused annual exemptions.
>
> CGT hold-over relief is available.

Since 10 December 2003, hold-over relief is not available if the settlor or his spouse, or his minor children who have neither married nor entered into a civil partnership have an interest in the settlement (see **4.4.5.2** and **5.5.2**).

Sales by the trustees after the settlement has been created will be subject to CGT, depending on the availability of the trustees' exemptions and reliefs. Transfers of capital from the trust fund to a beneficiary may also attract CGT, although hold-over relief may then be available (see

10.1.4.2). Trustees pay a flat rate of 28% on gains irrespective of the level of income of the settlement.

5.4   Income tax and settlements

The creation of a settlement should have no income tax consequences for the settlor (other than saving of income tax on any actual loss of income, unless the settlor or spouse has retained an interest, when the settlor will continue to be assessed to income tax on the income).

Once the trust is established the trustees will have an income tax liability in relation to the trust income. The income tax rules which apply depend on whether the beneficiaries have a right to income, or whether the trustees have a discretion. This is so no matter when or how the settlement is created.

5.4.1   Trusts where the beneficiaries have a right to income

The trustees pay income tax at basic rate (20%) and dividend ordinary rate, depending on the type of income. In many cases, they will receive only dividends, which carry a tax credit of 10%, and interest, where 20% tax is deducted at source. As a result, no further income tax will be payable by the trustees (see further **14.5.2**).

5.4.2   Trusts where the beneficiaries have no right to income

The usual rate of income tax on all trust income over £1,000 is a single flat rate of 50% (or 42.5% on dividends). The trustees pay income tax at basic rate on the first £1,000. In the case of small trusts where the income does not exceed £1,000, the trustees will have no further tax liability as the dividend tax credit and lower rate deduction on savings income will satisfy their basic rate tax liability. See **Chapter 14**.

Note that for the tax year 2009/10 the usual rate of income tax on trust income was 40% (and 32.5% on dividends).

5.5   Anti-avoidance provisions

There are anti-avoidance provisions in all three taxes, designed to prevent tax payers purporting to give away property while continuing to derive a benefit from it.

5.5.1   Inheritance tax

Property will continue to be treated as part of a settlor's estate if he is not excluded or virtually excluded from benefit.

5.5.2   Capital gains tax

If the settlor, or his spouse or civil partner, or the settlor's minor unmarried child has an 'interest in the settlement', it is not possible to claim hold-over relief on creating the settlement (see **5.3.2**).

5.5.3   Income tax

Trust income applied for the settlor's minor unmarried children will be taxed as the settlor's, as will income which could be applied for the benefit of the settlor, his spouse, or civil partner.

5.6   Choice of settlement

Any settlor who is thinking of creating a settlement should consider the tax implications before taking any final step.

Prior to 22 March 2006, a settlor who wanted to create a lifetime settlement would have had his choice of settlement influenced by the fact that different types of settlement were treated in different ways for IHT.

On or after 22 March 2006, the type of settlement is neutral from an IHT point of view. The decision for the settlor will be whether or not he wants a settlement at all in the light of the tax consequences.

A settlor is likely to consider three options:

(a)   making an outright gift;

(b)   transferring assets to a lifetime settlement;

(c)   retaining assets and leaving them by will.

If the tax payer concludes that a lifetime settlement is desirable, the decision as to what type of settlement to choose will not be influenced by IHT considerations as all lifetime settlements are treated in the same way (apart from settlements for the disabled). Instead, the decision will depend on what the tax payer wants to achieve.

The following points will be relevant:

(a)   Discretionary trusts are useful for making long-term provision for a class of beneficiaries, where the settlor is unsure which beneficiaries will turn out to have the greatest needs.

The settlor identifies the beneficiaries whom he wishes to benefit, but leaves it to the trustees to select which of these beneficiaries is to benefit and how and when. Discretionary trusts are the most flexible type of settlement because the decision as to beneficial entitlement can be deferred and does not have to be determined at the time the trusts are created. The trustees will normally have a discretion over both the capital and income of the trust fund.

Example

Barry wishes to benefit his grandchildren, Cora, Doris and Edward. All three are under 5 years of age, and he does not know how they will develop and whether their needs will be the same. He settles £150,000 on discretionary trusts.

Twenty years later Cora has just qualified as a lawyer; Doris is a hairdresser and single parent; Edward is a bank clerk and physically disabled as a result of an accident several years ago. The trustees decide to distribute the money unevenly between the three beneficiaries.

(b)   A settlement with successive interests is useful where a settlor wants to make income provision for one beneficiary while preserving the capital for others. The trustees will hold the income for one beneficiary and the capital for another.

Example

Hari's first wife died five years ago and he has just married again. He wants to make sure that his second wife has income from a gift of property, while preserving the capital for the children of his first marriage. He will give the property to trustees to hold for his wife for life, remainder to his children.

Often a settlor creating successive interests will also give the trustees a discretion to allow them to appoint capital in case of need either to the life tenant or to the remaindermen. The additional flexibility is useful, but means that the settlor will be less certain of what will happen after establishing the settlement.

(c)   Where a settlor wishes to make fixed provision for young children, a settlement with contingent interests is likely to be appropriate. The children will not be entitled to the capital unless and until they reach the specified age. The trustees will normally have a discretion as to how they deal with income, although the terms of the settlement may provide that the beneficiary becomes entitled to income at a specified age. The trustees may also be given a discretion to advance capital at an earlier age in case of need.

Example

Saleena transfers £200,000 to trustees to hold for such of her four children as reach 21, equally if more than one. The trust provides that the trustees have a discretion as to whether to use income from each child's presumptive share for maintenance or to accumulate it until each beneficiary reaches 18; thereafter the child has a right to receive the income from the share.

5.7 Summary – tax on creation of settlements

Lifetime settlements created before 22 March 2006

	IHT	CGT
Interest in possession	PET	Disposal – hold-over relief TCGA 1992, s 165 only
Discretionary	LCT: 0% and/or 20%	Disposal – hold-over relief available (TCGA 1992, s 260 and s 65)

Lifetime settlements created on or after 22 March 2006

	IHT	CGT
Settlement for a disabled beneficiary	PET	Disposal – hold-over relief TCGA 1992, s 165 only
Any other settlement	LCT: 0% and/or 20%	Disposal – hold-over relief available (TCGA 1992, s 260 and s 165)

Summary – Creation of Lifetime Settlements

Topic	Summary	Reference
Types of settlement	Settlements may have fixed interests or be held on discretionary trusts. They may have vested interests or contingent interests. Settlors need to consider which type of settlement is most suitable for the needs of the beneficiaries and also the tax regimes which will apply to different types of settlements.	5.1
IHT and settlements created before 22 March 2006	The IHT treatment of settlements created before 22 March 2006 depends on whether or not the settlement has an interest in possession. An interest in possession is a present right to present enjoyment of income or assets. A beneficiary with an interest in possession is treated as the owner of the underlying trust capital. The creation of the settlement is a PET by the settlor (unless the beneficiary is a spouse in which case it is exempt). There is a charge to IHT when the interest comes to an end. The beneficiary is treated as making a transfer of value of the trust capital.	5.2.3
	Settlements where the beneficiary does not have an interest in possession are called relevant property settlements (unless the settlement is for a disabled beneficiary or fulfils the requirements of IHTA 1984, s 71 – rare after 6 April 2008 – in which case the settlement qualifies for special treatment). The creation of a relevant property settlement is a lifetime chargeable transfer by the settlor. There are charges to IHT on the tenth anniversary of creation of the settlement and exit charges when property leaves the settlement.	5.2.3
IHT and settlements created on or after 22 March 2006	All settlements created on or after 22 March 2006 are now relevant property settlements unless they are created: (a) for a disabled beneficiary, or (b) on death for: (i) a beneficiary with an immediate interest in possession, in which case the beneficiary will be treated as entitled to the underlying trust capital, or	5.2.4 5.2.5

Topic	Summary	Reference
	(ii) a child of the deceased who will become entitled to capital no later than 18, in which case there will be no anniversary or exit charges, or (iii) a child of the deceased who will become entitled to capital no later than 25, in which case there will be no anniversary charges and exit charges will only be payable if the property continues to be held in trust once the beneficiary reaches 18.	
CGT and the creation of settlements	The transfer of assets to a settlement is a disposal by the settlor. CGT may be payable if the assets have increased in value since acquisition. However, hold-over relief can be claimed under: (a) TCGA 1992, s 165 if the assets are business assets, or (b) TCGA 1992, s 260 if the transfer to the settlement is chargeable to IHT; transfers to relevant property settlements are chargeable. Hold-over relief is not available if the settlement includes the settlor or spouse or minor unmarried children of the settlor.	5.3

Chapter 6

Drafting Lifetime Settlements: Some Common Points

6.1 Introduction

We saw in **Chapter 5** that settlements differ depending on what the settlor is trying to achieve. They may have fixed interests, for example 'To X for life and then absolutely' or 'to such of my children as reach 25', or the capital and income may be held at the discretion of the trustees to apply as they see fit amongst a class of beneficiaries. Some settlements are a mixture, giving beneficiaries fixed interests but allowing the trustees overriding discretions to alter those fixed interests by terminating interests and/or advancing capital to beneficiaries early.

However, all settlements follow the same general structure, and in this chapter we will look at that general structure and some particular drafting points.

As each client is unique, the available 'standard' precedents may not be appropriate for that client's requirements. In modifying an existing deed or drafting from scratch, those drafting settlements must be aware of the effect of every clause included and the effect of excluding a particular clause. In addition, they should aim for a consistency of style and not use both 'modern' and 'traditional' styles in the same trust instrument.

The basic structure of a settlement is set out in the following table. It is not a definitive list of what should always be included in a settlement. Some clauses are not required if the settlement is a simple life interest settlement. Where a clause may not be necessary for a particular type of settlement, we have included a note explaining this in the comment column.

To keep the content of this chapter relatively brief, the drafting of the trusts of beneficial interests is dealt with mainly in **Chapter 7**. Additional powers required by trustees and their use are examined in **Chapters 9** and **10**. The administrative provisions are discussed in **Chapter 14** but are broadly similar to those in will drafting (see **Chapter 11**).

Structure of settlement

Clause	Comment
Date	
Parties	
Recitals	
Definitions	
Beneficiaries	A separate clause defining beneficiaries is not always required. Beneficiaries may be defined within the definitions clause or, if there are only two or three, they may be named in the clause setting out the beneficial interests.
Perpetuity period	Not required where all interests are already vested, eg in a life interest trust. Required for settlements with interests which are not vested, such as discretionary settlements or those with contingent interests. In the case of settlements not governed by the Perpetuities and Accumulations Act 2009 (PAA 2009), it was important to state the perpetuity period expressly as the settlement would otherwise be subject to the less satisfactory common law rules. In the case of settlements governed by the PAA 2009, the period will be 125 years irrespective of what, if anything, the settlement says (see **6.9**).
Accumulation period	Only required where trustees have power to accumulate income rather than being able to pay it out each year. In the case of settlements not governed by the PAA 2009, the accumulation period is limited to various statutory periods. In the case of settlements governed by the PAA 2009, there are no statutory limitations and income can be accumulated throughout the life of the settlement with the result that, unless the settlor provides otherwise, there will be no restriction on the power to accumulate (see **6.9**).
Trust (for sale)	
Trusts of the beneficial interests	This is the most important part of the settlement as it explains the terms on which the trustees hold the trust property and who is entitled to what.
Trustee discretions in relation to the beneficial interests	In a very simple trust, the interests may be fixed and the trustees may have no discretions. However, this is increasingly rare. Even in a simple life interest trust, it is common to give trustees an unfettered power to give capital to the life tenant or remainderman in case of need.
Administrative provisions	
Appointment of new trustees	
Exclusion of TLATA 1996, ss 11, 12 and 19	
Exclusion of settlor and spouse from any benefit	

Clause	Comment
Schedules	Schedules are optional. They can make complex documents more comprehensible by keeping detail away from the main body of the document. Some practitioners consign everything except the clauses directly related to the beneficial interests to a series of Schedules. For example: (1) Definitions; (2) The Trust Property; (3) Administrative Provisions.
Signatures	

6.2 The date and opening words

It is usual for the date on which the settlement was made to be set out at the beginning of the trust instrument. In modern style settlements, this may be preceded by a table of contents. The date may be important for subsequent time-limits and the chronology of events where a settlor has made more than one settlement. Some settlements are known by titles which include their dates, for example, 'Mrs Brown's Grandchildren Settlement of 4 April 1990'.

Sample clause

This Settlement is made the   day of   Two thousand and

6.3 Parties

The settlor and the initial trustees must be clearly identified. How this and the opening words are set out will also determine the style for the rest of the document, ie is it to be modern (Clauses 1 and 2) or traditional (Clause 3)?

Sample clause 1

BETWEEN
(1)   DAVID SMITH of [address] ('the Settlor')
(2)   TONY TUBBS of [address] and TOM THOMAS of [address] ('the Trustees') which expression shall where the context admits include the trustee or trustees for the time being of this Settlement

Sample clause 2

PARTIES:
(1)   [   ] (the 'Settlor'); and
(2)   [   ] (the 'Trustees').

Sample clause 3

Between DAVID SMITH of [address] (hereinafter called 'the Settlor') of the one part and TONY TUBBS of [address] and TOM THOMAS of [address] (hereinafter called 'the Trustees' which expression shall where the context so admits include the trustee or trustees for the time being of the Settlement) of the other part

The definition of the trustees may instead come later in a clause which collects together all definitions used in the settlement.

6.4 Recitals

Recitals appear immediately after the parties, and in traditional style settlements are introduced by the word 'Whereas'. The numbers or letters to the recital clauses are normally placed in brackets, which distinguishes them from 'operative' clauses, ie the clauses declaring the beneficial interests.

Recitals explain the background to the settlement: why it has been created and the settlor's intentions.

A declaration that the settlement is to be irrevocable means that the settlor cannot subsequently change his mind about having created the settlement and demand his money or property back from the trustees. Whilst revocable settlements are possible, in the UK they are uncommon because of their unfavourable tax treatment. Where there is a power to revoke the trusts, the result is that the fund may revert to the settlor or his spouse.

Sample clause

Whereas

(1)   The Settlor wishes to make this Settlement and has transferred or delivered to the Trustees the property specified in the Schedule

(2)   It is intended that this Settlement shall be irrevocable.

6.5   Table of contents, clause headings, definitions and Schedules

6.5.1   Table of contents

Because settlements are often long and complex, modern precedents generally start by setting out in a table of contents the constituent parts of the settlement, showing the operative parts separately from the administrative provisions. Whilst a table simplifies the use of the settlement, it is important that a further clause ensures that the use of the table does not affect the meaning of the settlement (see **6.5.2**).

6.5.2   Clause headings

Some draftsmen like to give each clause a heading, as this enables a person who is reading the trust instrument to see quickly and clearly what each clause concerns. This can be particularly useful once the settlement is in use. For example, a trustee may want to know what powers of investment the trustees have. Rather than having to read every clause until he finds the investment clause, he need only look at the clause headings to identify the one he needs to study. It is a matter of personal preference as to whether or not clause headings are used, but they should either be used for every clause, or not at all. Where headings are used, it should be made clear by an additional clause that they are only for administrative convenience, ie, they do not affect the construction of the trust instrument.

Sample clause

Clause headings

The clause headings are included for reference only and do not affect the interpretation of this Settlement

6.5.3   Definitions

Many descriptions and phrases will need to be repeated, often several times, in drafting a settlement. It is, therefore, convenient to give these descriptions and phrases a 'name' by which they can be identified throughout the trust deed.

Example

Adam is settling a house, some cash and several holdings of quoted shares on discretionary trusts.

Reference needs to be made to these assets being held on trust, being available for distribution, being invested and so forth.

Unless a 'name' is used, each time reference is made to them the trust deed will have to read: 'The Trustees shall hold the freehold house known as [address], £x cash, 500 shares in A plc etc upon trust …'.

> It is much neater and simpler to call the combined assets 'the Trust Fund' so that the clause would read: 'The Trustees shall hold the Trust Fund upon trust ...'.

It is good practice to give the first letter of the 'names' a capital letter to indicate to the reader that they are definitions.

There is a choice of where to record the definitions of the 'names':

(a) Definitions can be dealt with as and when they arise in the body of the deed, for example:

> The Trustees shall hold the Trust Fund upon trust for such of them, David, Sue and Charles (hereinafter together called 'the Beneficiaries') as shall attain 18 years of age and if more than one in equal shares

The problem with this approach is finding the definition when subsequently using the trust instrument. For example, Brenda is a trustee of a settlement set up for the settlor's young relatives contingent on their reaching 21. She wants to know if the trustees have a power to apply income for the maintenance of a particular beneficiary. A glance through the clause headings shows her that she needs to study clause 18. In reading this clause, she comes across the expression 'the Accumulation Period'. She has no idea what it means and will have to read all the preceding clauses until she finds where the expression was used for the first time.

(b) Definitions can be contained in a Schedule to the deed. A person reading the trust instrument who comes across a 'name' such as 'the Beneficiary', will know to turn to the Schedule whenever he meets a 'name'.

(c) All the definitions can be set out in clause 1 of the trust instrument. This is common practice in modern style settlements.

Sample clause

> (1)   Definitions
> In this deed where the context so admits
> (a)   'the Trust Fund' shall mean ...
> (b)   'the Beneficiaries' shall mean ...

6.6 Identifying the beneficiaries

6.6.1 Need for clarity

Every settlement needs to identify the beneficiaries. In the case of a simple life interest trust, there will be only a small number of beneficiaries and this will not be difficult. They may simply be named in the clause setting out the beneficial interests:

Sample clause

> The Trustees shall pay the income of the Trust Fund to [Arshad] during [his] life and after his death shall pay the capital to [Jemima]

or defined in the Definitions clause and then referred to by reference to that definition:

Sample clause

> The Trustees shall pay the income of the Trust Fund to the Life Tenant during [his] life and after [his] death shall pay the capital to the Remainderman

6.6.2 Identification by description

It is not possible to name beneficiaries where there is a class which includes unborn or unascertained individuals. This is commonly the case for discretionary settlements or settlements with contingent interests. Here the beneficiaries must be identified by description, and it is vital that the class is described with sufficient clarity to enable the trustees to say with certainty whether or not a particular individual is within the class of beneficiaries, eg 'the children of my niece, Sally'.

Sample clause

'The Beneficiaries' shall mean the following persons (whether now in existence or who come into existence during the Trust Period)

(a)   the Settlor's children and remoter issue and the spouses' widows and widowers (but not such widows or widowers as have remarried) of such children and remoter issue

---

Example

Twenty years ago, Aisha created a settlement, which is still continuing, and she used the above clause. When she set up the trusts, she had three adult children, Ben, Cora and Deirdre, and one grandson, Edwin. The trustees wish to know who are the current beneficiaries.

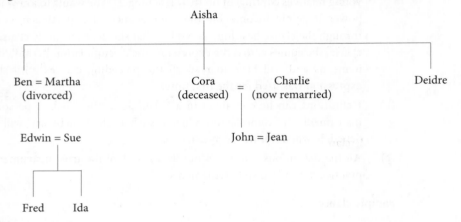

The beneficiaries are:

(a)   Ben, Deirdre, Edwin, John, Fred and Ida because they are the issue of the settlor; and

(b)   Sue and Jean because they are the spouses of the settlor's issue.

Martha and Charlie have been within the class of beneficiaries, but are now excluded. Martha's divorce from Ben means she is no longer his spouse; although Charlie was the spouse and then widower of the settlor's child, he has remarried.

If a person who was within the class of beneficiaries is subsequently excluded because of a change in status, he does not have to pay back to the settlement any previous benefit he may have received from it.

Example

The facts are the same as in the previous example. After Cora's death the trustees gave Charlie £5,000. Charlie remarried two years later. He does not have to repay the £5,000 but cannot receive anything more from the settlement.

6.6.3   Particular points on contingent interests

6.6.3.1   Include age of living beneficiaries

Where gifts are contingent on reaching a specified age, it is normal practice to include each living beneficiary's date of birth, since this enables the trustees to calculate the beneficiary's age and to know the date when his interest will vest.

Sample clause for a trust with contingent interests

The 'Primary Beneficiaries' shall mean:

(1)   The existing [grand]children of the Settlor namely [   ] who was born on
[   ]; [   ] who was born on [   ]; [   ]
who was born on [   ]; and [   ] who was born on
[   ]; and

(2)   every other [grand]child of the Settlor born after the date of this Deed and before
the Closing Date.

6.6.3.2   Include a closing date for a class which is open at the time the settlement is created

A settlor may wish to add later born beneficiaries to the class, for example where a settlor settles property for 'my grandchildren' and at the time of creation has only got one or two grandchildren but anticipates further grandchildren. This is perfectly acceptable, but the clause must specify that the class is to close on the date when the first beneficiary attains a vested interest in the capital of the trust fund, ie when the contingency is first satisfied, or at the end of the trust if this is earlier.

This is because the trustees will have to distribute a share of the trust property to the beneficiary who has become entitled; for example, if there are four beneficiaries, they will distribute one-quarter. However, if the class remains open, additional beneficiaries may be added to the class after the distribution date. The trustees will have paid the first beneficiary too much, and this will amount to a breach of trust.

Sample clause

The 'Closing Date' shall mean whichever shall be the earlier of:

(1)   the date on which the first Primary Beneficiary to do so attains the age of 25; and

(2)   the date on which the Trust Period shall determine.

6.6.3.3   The meaning of 'child' and 'spouse'

The expression 'child or grandchild', etc will normally include adopted and legitimated (grand) children, and those whose parents are not married to each other. If the settlor wants to exclude any such person, a clause to that effect (eg, as in the sample clause) should be included.

Sample clause

References to the children, grandchildren and issue of any person shall include his children, grandchildren and remoter issue, whether legitimate, legitimated [, illegitimate] or adopted [, but shall exclude any illegitimate person and his descendants].

The expression 'spouse' does not include civil partner unless the trust instrument makes express provision. If the settlor wishes to include civil partners and former civil partners, they must either be added to the class, which is rather clumsy, or a separate clause can be inserted, extending the meaning of spouse.

Sample clause

In this will, 'marriage' includes civil partnership as defined in the Civil Partnership Act 2004 and 'spouse', 'husband', 'wife', 'widower', 'widow', are to be construed accordingly

The Human Fertilisation and Embryology Act 2008 (HFEA 2008) contains provisions about parenthood where a child is born as a result of certain types of fertility treatment (artificial insemination or placing an embryo or sperm and eggs in a woman). These provisions came into force on 6 April 2009 and affect the meaning of 'children' in wills and trusts, whenever made, where the children are born as a result of fertility treatment received after that date.

The Act does not state that the provisions are subject to contrary intention but settlors are free to include and exclude individuals from the class of beneficiaries as they see fit.

The HFEA 2008 provides as follows:

(a)   The woman who carried the child is treated as the child's mother (s 33).

(b)   If the woman is married at the time of the treatment, her husband is treated as the child's father, unless he did not consent to the treatment (s 35).

(c)   If the woman has a civil partner, the couple will be treated in the same way as married couples. The woman who carries the child will be treated as the child's mother, and her civil partner will be treated as the child's second parent unless she did not consent to the treatment (s 42).

(d)   If the woman is not married or in a civil partnership but has a male partner at the time of the treatment, he is treated as the child's father if the 'agreed fatherhood' conditions are satisfied at that time provided no other man is treated as the child's father under s 35 and no woman is treated as a parent under s 42. The 'agreed fatherhood' conditions are set out in s 37. Broadly, both parties must have consented in writing to the man being treated as the father and the partners must not be within the prohibited degrees of relationship, which exclude close relatives.

(e)   Similarly if the woman has a female partner at the time of the treatment, that partner is treated as the child's female parent if the 'agreed female parenthood' conditions are satisfied at that time provided no man is treated as the child's father under s 35 and no other woman is treated as a parent under s 42. The 'agreed female parenthood' conditions are set out in s 44. Broadly, both parties must have consented in writing to the woman being treated as the parent and the partners must not be within the prohibited degrees of relationship, which exclude close relatives. No man will be treated as the child's father.

The HFEA 2008 does not affect the position of male civil partners and same-sex couples. The man who is not the child's genetic father will be treated as a second parent only if he adopts the child. Where there is a surrogacy arrangement, the woman carrying the child remains the mother unless and until a parental order (similar to an adoption order) is obtained.

6.7 The trust fund

The settlement needs some property to be the subject-matter of the trusts from the outset. The settlor may add to the original trust property from time to time and other people may also transfer property to the settlement. The original trust property will be described in detail in the Schedule. The definition of the 'Trust Fund' will refer to the property set out in the Schedule plus any additions.

When property is transferred from the settlor to the trustees, the correct mode of transfer must be used or the transfer will be ineffective. For example, unquoted shares must be transferred by signed stock transfer form and land by deed.

6.8 Trust or trust for sale?

Before TLATA 1996, it was usual practice for the trustees of lifetime settlements to hold property on an express trust for sale. This ensured that a strict settlement under SLA 1925 could not arise where land was settled property. The TLATA 1996 prevents any new strict settlements being created after 31 December 1996 but does not prevent settlements being drafted with an express trust for sale. An express trust will probably be included only where the settlor wishes the trustees to be under a duty to sell. If, instead, a power of sale is considered sufficient, the trustees will be directed to hold the settled property 'on trust' and will be given power of sale in the administrative provisions of the settlement.

If a trust for sale is used, it has five constituent parts, as shown in the sample clause.

Extracts from sample clause – trust for sale

(1)   The Trustees shall hold the Trust Fund upon trust as to investments or property other than money in their absolute discretion to sell, call in or convert into money all or any of such investments or property

(2)   But with power to postpone such sale, calling in or conversion

(3)   To permit the same to remain as invested

(4)   Upon trust as to money with the like discretion to invest the same in their names or under their control in any of the investments authorised by this Settlement or by law

(5)   With power at the like discretion from time to time to vary or transpose any such investments for others so authorised

6.9 Perpetuity period

6.9.1 No perpetual trusts

English law does not allow a private trust (as opposed to a charitable trust) to be perpetual. It must come to an end and the capital vest in a beneficiary within a limited period of time. The time from the creation of the settlement to the moment when the capital must vest is called 'the perpetuity period'. Although not necessary, many settlements also have a defined trust period which is the period within which the trustees can exercise their powers. This is usually defined as the same period as the perpetuity period but could be a shorter period.

6.9.2 What is the perpetuity period?

6.9.2.1 Trusts not governed by the PAA 2009

At common law, the perpetuity period is that of a life or lives in being plus 21 years. The life or lives in being could be expressly selected, eg '21 years from the death of my son, John' or, more creatively, '21 years from the death of the last grandchild of Queen Elizabeth II living at my death'. If no life is expressly selected, the relevant life or lives will be identified from the particular disposition. For example, in the case of a gift to 'the first child of X to reach 21', X is the life in being.

The Perpetuities and Accumulations Act 1964 (PAA 1964) allowed settlors to select a fixed period of anything up to 80 years. The trust instrument must state expressly that it selects a particular number of years as the perpetuity period. Where a period is selected, it is defined in the trust instrument as 'the perpetuity period'. If no mention of a perpetuity period is made in the trust instrument, the common law rules apply.

Sample clause – the trust and perpetuity period

The trust period shall mean the period ending on the last day of the period of 80 years from the date of this Settlement which period shall be the applicable perpetuity period.

6.9.2.2 Trusts governed by the PAA 2009

The PAA 2009 provides a new perpetuity period of 125 years which will apply to lifetime trusts taking effect and will trusts created in wills executed on or after 6 April 2010 irrespective of the terms of the trust instrument. Trusts already in existence at that date or will trusts coming into effect under wills executed before that date are not affected. The new 125-year period will take precedence over whatever the trust instrument may say, and if the trust instrument is silent the perpetuity period will still be 125 years. It is helpful to include an express statement as to the length of the perpetuity period, as in 20 years time lawyers may not necessarily remember the date on which the PAA 2009 came into force.

Sample clause – the trust and perpetuity period

> The trust period shall mean the period ending on the last day of the period of 125 years from the date of the creation of this settlement which period (and no other) shall be the applicable perpetuity period.

The PAA 2009, s 6(2) provides that the perpetuity period for an instrument created in the exercise of a special power of appointment will begin on the date on which the instrument creating the power took effect.

Example

A trust created on 1 July 1980 with an 80-year perpetuity period from that date includes a special power of appointment which is exercised after 6 April 2010 to resettle the property on new trusts. The perpetuity period for the new trusts created by the power will be 80 years starting on 1 July 1980.

The PAA 2009, s 12 allows trustees of pre-Act trusts to opt for a fixed period of 100 years from the date the trust commenced in one limited case. This is where the perpetuity period is defined by reference to a life or lives in being and it is difficult, or not reasonably practicable, to ascertain whether the lives have ended. The trustees must execute a deed stating that they believe there is such a difficulty and that the instrument is to be treated as if it specified a period of 100 years (no other period is possible).

6.9.3   What does 'vest' mean?

Property does not have to vest *in possession* provided it has vested *in interest* by the end of the perpetuity period.

Example 1

Property is settled on Agnes for life with the remainder to Bert. Agnes has an immediate interest in possession (ie, the right to the income) and Bert is guaranteed the capital, although the actual receipt of the capital will be delayed until Agnes dies.

Agnes's interest is vested in possession. Bert's interest is vested in interest.

You will not need to consider the perpetuity rules as the interests are already vested.

Example 2

Property is settled on Connie for life with the remainder to the first child of David to attain 25 years of age.

At the time the settlement is created, David has no children, but shortly afterwards he has one child, Edward. Edward will become entitled to the settled property only if he reaches 25. Until then his interest is contingent. Connie's interest is vested in possession. Here it is necessary to consider the perpetuity rules.

6.9.4   Which settlements need a perpetuity period?

As we saw, no perpetuity period is required when all the interests have already vested, as in Example 1. A perpetuity period is required for settlements where the gifts are contingent upon the beneficiaries reaching a specified age, as in Example 2.

A perpetuity period is also required for discretionary settlements. Trustees select the beneficiary from within a class of beneficiaries and decide how much of the trust property to give that beneficiary. They must exhaust the trust fund, ie give a vested interest in the trust property, within the perpetuity period. A failure to do so will render void the trusts over any remaining property.

> **Example**
>
> In 2008 £10,000 is settled on discretionary trusts for the children of X.
>
> There are three children: Rose, Arthur and Kate. The stated perpetuity period is 10 years.
>
> If the trustees make the following appointments which exhaust the fund in the sixth year, there will be no perpetuity problems.
>
>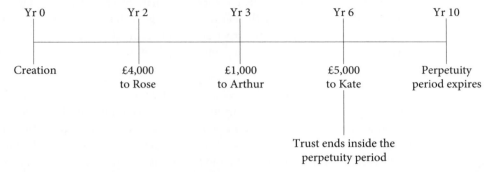
>
> If, at the end of year 10, funds still remained, the trust would become void and the surplus funds would revert to the settlor (unless there was a gift over in default).

When drafting a settlement where there is any possibility that an interest might vest outside the perpetuity period, it is important to include provisions making this impossible rather than simply relying on the trustees to make sure that funds are appointed out before the end of the perpetuity period. As we will see later, the mere possibility of funds reverting to the settlor (however unlikely it is to happen) is enough to produce adverse tax consequences.

To ensure that 'reverter to settlor' can never happen, the settlement should contain an ultimate default trust, ie, a clause directing who should receive any surplus left in the trust at the end of the trust (perpetuity) period.

This ultimate beneficiary must be living or in existence (eg, a charity) and be given a vested interest in the trust fund at the date of the settlement. A settlor will often choose a charity as the ultimate default beneficiary.

Sample clause

> Subject as above and if and so far as not wholly disposed of for any reason whatever by the above provisions, the capital and income of the Trust Fund shall be held in trust for [name] absolutely

> **Example**
>
> Many years ago, property was settled on discretionary trusts for the settlor's children and remoter issue with a charity as ultimate default beneficiary. The perpetuity period is 80 years. The settlor had one child (Tracy) when the trust was set up. Tracy had two sons, Wayne and Calvin.
>
> Since the settlement was created the trustees have distributed £170,000 of the trust fund, but Wayne died when he was 6 years old, Tracy died three years ago and Calvin has just died having never had any children.
>
> There are no other issue of the settlor and a surplus of £30,000 remains within the trust. The trustees must transfer this to the charity and bring the trust to an end.

6.10 Accumulations

6.10.1 Meaning of accumulations

In the case of discretionary settlements and those where the interests of the beneficiaries are contingent on reaching a certain age, the beneficiaries will not normally have a right to receive income as it arises. However, the trust property is likely to be earning income all the time. If the trustees choose not to pay it out to a beneficiary, they will retain it within the trust. Such retained income is said to be 'accumulated'.

Historically, there was a fear that allowing income to be accumulated for long periods within settlements would result in such a concentration of wealth in private hands that it might compromise the economic independence of the nation. There have, therefore, been successive statutory provisions limiting the period for which trustees can accumulate income. Once the relevant period has expired, the trustees cannot accumulate income and must pay it out. The most recent rule against excessive accumulations of income is set out in s 13 of the LPA 1925 and s 13 of the PAA 1964.

In recent years, there has been a relaxation in fears of excessive accumulations, and the PAA 2009 abolishes the statutory rule against excessive accumulations in the case of lifetime trusts created after the date the Act comes into force and will trusts created in wills executed after that date. It will, therefore, be possible to accumulate throughout the lifetime of a settlement. Pre-PAA 2009 trusts will remain bound by the terms of the original instrument.

The PAA 2009 does not override provisions in trust documents, so the unrestricted power to accumulate will be subject to any express provisions in the trust instrument.

6.10.2   Accumulation periods

For trusts not governed by the PAA 2009, there is a limit to the number of years during which income can be accumulated. The PAA 1964 sets out a choice of maximum periods for which income can be accumulated. Most trust draftsmen specify that income can be accumulated for a fixed period of 21 years from the date of the settlement. Although this period is possibly shorter than PAA 1964 would allow, a fixed period provides for certainty. The specified accumulation period must not exceed the perpetuity period applicable to the settlement. At the end of the accumulation period, all income arising in each future year must be paid out to the beneficiaries, unless the beneficiary is a minor (see **6.10.3**).

Example

Property is settled on discretionary trusts for the benefit of Susan, John and Harry. The accumulation period is 21 years. The trust income is £300 per annum.

		Susan	John	Harry	Accumulated
Accumulation period	Yr 1	100	–	–	200
	Yr 7	–	300	–	–
	Yr 8	100	100	100	–
	Yr 15	–	–	–	300
After accumulation period ends	Yr 22	100	200	–	–
	Yr 23	100	100	100	–
	Yr 24	150	–	150	–

Sample clause

The Accumulation Period shall mean the period of twenty-one years from the date of this Settlement or the Trust Period if shorter

6.10.3   Extension of accumulation period under Trustee Act 1925, s 31

Where a beneficiary is a minor at the end of the PAA 1964 accumulation period and s 31 of TA 1925 applies to the trust, the trustees can continue to accumulate the income of the minor's share of the trust fund until he is 18 years of age.

Example

Three brothers were the beneficiaries of a discretionary settlement. The two older boys both died, leaving Adam (aged 16) the only beneficiary. The settlement's accumulation period has just ended. The trustees may accumulate income for a further two years.

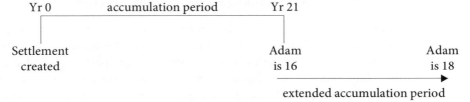

Where s 31 of TA 1925 is substantially modified by the terms of the trust instrument, it is usual to limit the alteration to the accumulation period. This is to prevent any suggestion that the statutory provision has been replaced by the express provision.

6.10.4   Perpetuities and Accumulations Act 2009

As explained at **6.10.1** above, the PAA 2009 abolishes the rule against excessive accumulations for trusts governed by the PA 2009. The abolition is achieved by repealing ss 164–166 of the Law of Property Act 1925 and s 13 of the 1964 Act. The result is that trustees would be able to accumulate income throughout the lifetime of a trust (which will normally be 125 years – the new perpetuity period).

The PA 2009 does not override provisions in trust documents, so the unrestricted power to accumulate will be subject to any express provisions in the trust instrument.

Most settlors will want to give their trustees maximum flexibility in relation to accumulating income and so will not want to limit their freedom. The settlement can either be silent as to accumulations, in which case the trustees will be able to accumulate throughout the lifetime of the settlement, or the settlement can define the accumulation period expressly.

Sample clause – the accumulation period

> The accumulation period shall mean the period ending on the last day of the period of 125 years from the date of my death

In the case of settlements not governed by the PA 2009, if trustees use their special powers of appointment to resettle property on new trusts, the old accumulation period will continue to apply to the new trusts (in the same way that such resettlements retain the original perpetuity period).

6.11   Trusts of the beneficial interests

In many ways, this is the most important section of the trust as it sets out the terms on which the trustees are to hold the trust property.

It is important that the whole of the beneficial interest is dealt with. If any of the trust property could revert to the settlor because the trusts were not exhaustive, adverse tax consequences follow.

A simple life interest trust

This will deal first with the payment of income and then with entitlement to capital. It may name the beneficiaries within the clause or may use defined terms.

> The Trustees shall pay the income of the Trust Fund to the Life Tenant during [her] life
>
> Subject to the above the Trustees shall hold the capital of the Trust Fund upon trust for the Remainderman absolutely

Because all the interests are vested, there is no possibility of the Trust Fund reverting to the settlor. If the remainderman dies before the life tenant, the trust capital will be paid to the remainderman's personal representatives and will pass as part of his estate.

Drafting the beneficial trusts where there are discretionary or contingent interests is slightly more complicated. To avoid overcomplicating this chapter, points relevant to drafting these beneficial interests are dealt with in **Chapter 7**. One important point that we will look at there is the importance of including a default beneficiary to take if the main beneficial interests fail. This will prevent the adverse tax consequences that arise if property can possibly revert to the settlor.

6.12 Trustees' discretions in relation to beneficial interests

It is becoming increasingly common to give settlements added flexibility by giving trustees additional discretions. A settlor may think that he wants to leave a life interest to his spouse and the capital to his children absolutely, but it is impossible to know what may happen in the future. A spouse may have unexpected need of capital; one child may become very much more wealthy than another.

This could be dealt with by making the settlement fully discretionary, but many people prefer to create a settlement with fixed interests and then to give the trustees overriding powers to alter those interests in case of need.

Typical overriding powers would be:

(a)   to appoint trust capital to the life tenant;
(b)   to terminate a life tenant's interest early;
(c)   to advance capital to one or more of the remainder beneficiaries early;
(d)   to distribute the capital to the remainder beneficiaries unequally.

6.13 Appointment of new trustees

If a new trustee needs to be appointed because, for example, one of the original trustees has died or wishes to retire, in the absence of anything to the contrary in the trust instrument, the choice and appointment rests with the continuing trustee(s) under TA 1925, s 36.

A settlor who wishes to continue to exercise sole control over the selection of trustees during his lifetime can do so only if the trust instrument gives him the appropriate power (see **14.4.2**).

Sample clause

> During the lifetime of the Settlor the power of appointing new trustees shall be vested in the Settlor

As it is relatively common for settlors to wish to retain control over the appointment of trustees or to nominate close family members to exercise such control, it is important that those advising trustees do not simply assume that the continuing trustees have the power to make new appointments but check the trust instrument. Errors over appointments are amongst the most common of mistakes made in relation to the administration of trusts. They are very serious, as any acts carried out by a person invalidly appointed will be invalid.

Some settlements appoint a third party as a 'Protector'. The Protector can perform a variety of roles, but it is common to give the Protector power to appoint and remove trustees.

6.14 Excluding the effect of TLATA 1996, ss 11, 12 and 19

6.14.1 Consultation

Under TLATA 1996, s 11(1), the trustees of a trust of land who are exercising any function relating to the land subject to the trust must consult any beneficiary who is of full age and beneficially entitled to an interest in possession (eg, a co-owner) and, so far as consistent with 'the general interest of the trust', give effect to the wishes of the beneficiary or (in the case of dispute) the majority (according to the value of their combined assets).

Section 11 will not apply if there is a provision to that effect in the trust instrument (s 11(2)). If appropriate, a declaration excluding the s 11 requirement for consultation can be included in the settlement. It is common to include such a declaration.

Sample clause

> The provisions of section 11 of the Trusts of Land and Appointment of Trustees Act 1996 shall not apply so that it shall not be necessary for my Trustees to consult any Beneficiaries before carrying out any function relating to land or for the avoidance of doubt any other property.

6.14.2 Occupation of land by beneficiaries

Section 12 gives a beneficiary who is entitled to an interest in possession (eg, a co-owner) in land, even if not of full age, a right to occupy the land in certain circumstances.

In order to have this right of occupation, a beneficiary must establish either that the purposes of the trust include making the land available for his occupation or that the land is held by trustees so as to be so available.

The trustees have the right to impose conditions on an occupying beneficiary (eg, the payment of outgoings or expenses in respect of the land (s 13)). These conditions may include making payments by way of compensation to a beneficiary whose entitlement has been restricted.

A settlor cannot exclude ss 12 and 13. However, where a settlor does not wish beneficiaries to have a right to occupy, he can include a declaration that the purposes of the trust do not include making land available for occupation.

Sample clause

> The purposes of the trust in clause [   ] do not include making land available for occupation of any Beneficiary.

6.14.3 Right to direct retirement and appointment of replacement trustees

The TLATA 1996, s 19 (unless expressly excluded by the trust instrument) gives beneficiaries who are *sui juris* and entitled to the whole beneficial interest the right to direct trustees to retire and appoint specified replacement trustees (see **14.4.2**).

Settlors can exclude the s 19 right, but beneficiaries who are *sui juris* and entitled to the whole beneficial interest would still be able to remove the trustees by bringing the trust to an end and then resettling the trust property with different trustees. Ending the trust would be likely to involve a charge to CGT as it will be a disposal. It is likely to be preferable in most cases, therefore, to allow beneficiaries to retain the s 19 right. However, there may be settlors who wish to exclude it.

Sample clause

> Section 19(2)(a) of the Trusts of Land and Appointment of Trustees Act 1996 shall not apply to this trust.

6.15 Exclusion of settlor (and spouse/civil partner)

To prevent settlors using settlements to obtain an unfair tax advantage for themselves, there are a number of anti-avoidance provisions in the tax legislation. Broadly, these apply where settlors, spouses, civil partners and minor children can benefit from settled property. The most important provisions relating to income tax, CGT and IHT are set out at **6.15.1** to **6.15.3** below.

6.15.1 The general income tax avoidance rules (ITTOIA 2005)

These complex, wide-ranging provisions are intended to prevent a higher rate tax payer from avoiding income tax on income by transferring the property which produces it to another person, who either pays no income tax or pays at a rate lower than the transferor.

The rules apply to 'settlements'. 'Settlement' is defined very widely (ITTOIA 2005, s 620) to include 'any disposition, trust, covenant, agreement, arrangement or transfer of assets'. They apply to settlements where the settlor retains an interest in the settled property (s 624) and they apply specifically to settlements by parents for the benefit of their minor unmarried children (s 629; see **4.6.2.3** and **4.6.4.1**).

Under s 624 the income of settled property 'is treated . . . as the income of the settlor and of the settlor alone if it arises . . . from property in which the settlor has an interest'. Section 625 states that a settlor is treated as having an interest in settled property if there are any circumstances in which the settled property is or may become payable to or applicable for the benefit of the settlor or the settlor's spouse.

Typically (but not exclusively), s 624 will apply where:

(a)   the settled property will revert to the settlor, for example where the property is settled on A for life with the remainder to the settlor. Such a settlement might be considered if a settlor wished to provide an elderly relative with an income but at the same time wanted to ensure return of the settled property when the relative died;

(b)   the settled property could revert to the settlor because the beneficial interests are not exhaustive;

(c)   the settlement contains a power of revocation whereupon the settled property would revert to the settlor or his spouse;

(d)   the settlement contains a discretionary power to benefit the settlor or his spouse or civil partner, ie they are among the objects of the trustees' discretion.

Example

Thomas creates a discretionary settlement during his lifetime under which he and his wife Agatha may benefit because they are included in the class of beneficiaries, ie they are among the objects of the trust. Even if neither Thomas nor Agatha actually benefits, for example because the trustees of the settlement accumulate the income or apply all of it for other beneficiaries, all of the income of the settled property will be taxed as though it belonged to Thomas.

Where the rules apply, the income of the property in the settlement is treated as belonging to the settlor for all income tax purposes, although generally he can recover from the trustees any tax he has to pay on the income. Now that many trusts pay income tax at 50% (see **Chapter 14**) there is the possibility that the settlor will pay income tax at a lower rate than that of the trust. Legislation is proposed to prevent any advantage being derived from such a situation.

Although the rules treat the income as belonging to the settlor for income tax purposes, they do not affect the entitlement of the settlement trustees to receive the income and to use it for the beneficiaries.

6.15.2 CGT where the settlor has an interest in the settlement

For tax years before 2008/09, CGT was payable at different rates depending on the circumstances of the individual tax payer. There was, therefore, the possibility of paying a lower rate of tax by manipulating assets to make sure that gains were realised by a person liable to CGT at a lower rate. Hence, anti-avoidance provisions (TCGA 1992, ss 77 and 78) applied which were similar to the income tax provisions.

These anti-avoidance provisions were repealed with the introduction of the flat rate of CGT for tax years 2008/09 onwards and have not been reinstated.

Anti-avoidance provisions of a different kind continue in relation to hold-over relief.

Since 10 December 2003, the settlor cannot claim hold-over relief under TCGA 1992, ss 165 or 260 on a transfer into a settlement in which he, his spouse or his unmarried minor child is interested (see **4.4.5.2**). Hold-over relief already claimed will be clawed back if the settlement becomes settlor interested within six years of the tax year of creation.

6.15.3 Reservation of benefit and IHT

Although the phrase 'an interest in the settlement' is not found in FA 1986, s 102, none the less the concept lies behind the reservation of benefit provisions. These have been discussed at **4.6.5**. If settled property is subject to reservation of benefit for the settlor, s 102 will apply, with the result that the property is still within the settlor's estate for IHT. Note that the rules apply only where the *settlor* derives a benefit. They do not apply if the settlor's spouse or unmarried minor child benefits.

6.15.4 Drafting the settlement

Because of the adverse tax consequences that will follow if the settlor, spouse or minor unmarried child of the settlor can benefit from the trust, it is important to include provisions to ensure that this does not happen. Civil partners are subject to the same anti-avoidance provisions as spouses and so must also be excluded from benefit.

It is important that beneficial interests are drafted to ensure that there is no possibility of property reverting to the settlor. In discretionary and contingent settlements, where the interests are not immediately vested, an ultimate default clause will always be included.

In addition to the default clause, a settlement with discretionary powers will normally contain two references to the exclusion of the settlor, spouse and minor unmarried children; the first, in relation to the power to add new beneficiaries and the second in relation to the exercise of the administrative powers (see **Appendix 3**, clauses 3(3) and 14).

(1)   The trust instrument may give the trustees very wide powers and discretions over the trust fund (see **Chapter 9**). For example, if the trustees can use their powers to benefit the settlor, his spouse or minor unmarried children, even though the power is never used, the settlor is deemed to have an interest in the trust property.

(2)   A clause should be included in the settlement deed to the effect that the settlor, his spouse or minor unmarried child cannot and must not benefit from the trust. This clause serves as a prohibition against trustees ever exercising a trust power in favour of the settlor or his spouse.

Sample clause

> No discretion or power conferred on the Trustees by this Settlement or by law shall be exercised and no provision in the Settlement shall operate, directly or indirectly so as to cause or permit any part of the capital or income of the Trust Fund to become in any way payable to or applicable for the benefit of the Settlor or the spouse [or civil partner] or minor unmarried children of the Settlor

6.16 Stamp duty and stamp duty land tax

It is not uncommon for a settlor to transfer shares into a settlement. Where shares are transferred for no consideration the document transferring them is exempt from stamp duty if the transaction falls within the schedule to the Stamp Duty (Exempt Instruments) Regulations 1987 (SI 1987/516) (see **4.9**). If, very unusually, the settlement deed is the document making the transfer of shares to the trustees it should contain a certificate that the transaction does come within these regulations.

Sample clause

> It is hereby certified that this instrument falls within Category L in the Schedule to the Stamp Duty (Exempt Instrument) Regulations 1987

However, it is much more likely that the transfer to the trustees will be by separate stock transfer form, and it is this document that should contain this certificate.

If land is transferred to the trustees, the transferor must provide a separate certificate to the effect that a stamp duty land tax return is not required.

6.17 Signatures

A trust instrument is a deed and must be signed as such by the settlor, and by the trustees as well to show their acceptance of the trusts. One witness is required to each signature.

Sample clause

> Signed as a deed and delivered
> by [name of Settlor]
> in the presence of

Chapter 7
Drafting Beneficial Interests

7.1 Introduction

We looked in **Chapter 6** at points which are generally relevant when drafting settlements. In this chapter we will look at points which are relevant when drafting the beneficial interests in discretionary settlements and settlements with contingent interests.

Both these forms of settlement commonly give trustees extensive discretions and it is, therefore, desirable that the settlor prepare a letter of wishes indicating the factors which the settlor would like the trustees to take into account. Such a letter is not binding on the trustees but it will be helpful for them to know what the settlor regarded as important. It will normally set out the settlor's views on matters such as the appropriate age for receiving capital, what sort of things capital should be provided for, and the extent to which the trustees should strive for equality between the various beneficiaries.

7.2 Settlements creating discretionary trusts

The discretionary trusts apply to both income and capital of the trust fund. There are separate clauses for each. The component parts of these clauses are discussed at **7.2.1** and **7.2.2**. A full precedent of the clauses is found in **Appendix 3**.

7.2.1 Discretionary trusts of income

7.2.1.1 The primary trust

The primary trust enables the trustees to decide how to distribute the income of the trust fund amongst the beneficiaries.

Sample clause

> The Trustees shall pay or apply the income of the Trust Fund to or for the benefit of such of the Beneficiaries as shall for the time being be in existence, in such shares and in such manner generally as the Trustees shall in their discretion from time to time think fit

The clause gives trustees the choice not only of which beneficiaries to benefit, but also how to provide that benefit.

Example

Property is settled on discretionary trusts for the settlor's two grandchildren, Adam and Debbie. The annual income is £1,000 net. Adam is at university, reading medicine; Debbie is 16, at school and wants to be an actress.

For the last two years the trustees have made an outright payment of £1,000 per annum to Adam as he is finding it difficult to manage financially on the amount available from other sources.

This year the trustees decide to buy one year's membership to the local theatre club for Debbie at a cost of £80 and pay the insurance premium (£20) on the bicycle she has bought herself to save bus fares. They give the balance to Adam.

7.2.1.2 Power to accumulate income

We saw at **6.10** that, in the case of settlements not governed by the PAA 2009, the trustees cannot accumulate income indefinitely. The PAA 1964 limits the length of time that income can be accumulated. The accumulation period selected must be stated in the settlement but there is no need to grant an express power to accumulate. Once the accumulation period is selected, the trustees have power to retain income during the selected period.

At the end of the accumulation period, the trustees lose the power to retain income (apart from the power conferred by s 31 of the Trustee Act 1925 to accumulate during the minority of a beneficiary) and must pay out the trust income every year.

In the case of settlements governed by the PAA 2009, trustees can accumulate throughout the life of the settlement (unless the settlor has imposed limitations) so the issue of the accumulation period expiring before the end of the trust period will not arise.

7.2.1.3 Power to use accumulated income

As a general rule, income received during the accumulation period and accumulated becomes part of the capital of the trust fund and so unavailable as income of future years. However, the settlor may wish to give the trustees more flexibility.

Sample clause

> The Trustees may under sub-clause [   ] apply the whole or any part of the income accumulated as if it were income arising in the then current year.

The effect of this clause is that any income retained from previous years can be made available to increase the income available in the current year.

Example				
Property is settled on discretionary trusts for Gail and Martin. The accumulation period is 21 years and the annual income £100 net.				
	Gail	Martin	Accumulate	Total of income available for distributions
Year 1	75	25	–	nil
Year 2	–	–	100	100
Year 3	90	–	10	110
Year 4 etc	60	60	–	90

7.2.1.4 Accumulated income at the end of the accumulation period

Where the accumulation period is shorter than the trust period, the settlement will direct what is to happen to any undistributed income at the end of the accumulation period.

Extract from clause

> ... and subject to sub-clause [ ] shall hold such accumulations as an accretion to capital

Any accumulated income which has not been spent by the end of the accumulation period is added to the capital of the trust fund.

Example

In 2008 £5,000 is settled on discretionary trusts for Penny and Nick. The accumulation period is 21 years and the annual income £100 net.

	Penny	Nick	Total of accumulated income	Capital
Year 20	90	–	320	5,000
Year 21	100	100	<u>220</u>	5,000
Year 22	60	40		5,220
Year 23	50	50		5,220
etc				

7.2.2 Discretionary trusts of capital

The trusts over capital enable the trustees to decide how, when and to which beneficiaries to distribute the capital of the trust fund. The trustees will give effect to their decision by the exercise of a power of appointment. Powers of appointment are dealt with in **Chapters 9** and **10**.

7.2.2.1 The primary trust

Sample clause

> The Trustees may pay or apply the whole or any part of the capital of the Trust Fund to or for the benefit of all or such of the Beneficiaries, eg, in such shares and in such manner generally as the Trustees shall in their discretion think fit

Example

£10,000 is settled on discretionary trusts for Alice and Bertram. Each year, the trustees pay all available income to the beneficiaries. So far as capital is concerned:

Year 1:   Trustees decide not to pay out any capital.

Year 2:   Bertram is buying a car and the trustees decide to give him £2,000.

Year 15:   For 13 years the trustees exercised their power by not distributing any capital but this year gave £1,000 to Alice to help towards the cost of looking after her new baby and £5,000 to Bertram for alterations to his house.

Year 16:   The trustees decide that the costs of running the settlement outweigh its benefits and so bring it to an end by giving what is left equally to Alice and Bertram.

7.2.2.2 Transfers on to other trusts

Sample clause

> The Trustees may, subject to the application (if any) of the rule against perpetuities pay or transfer any income or capital of the Trust Fund to the trustees of any other trust, wherever established or existing, under which any Beneficiary is interested (whether or not such Beneficiary is the only object or person interested or capable of benefiting under such other trust) if the Trustees in their discretion consider such payment or transfer to be for the benefit of such Beneficiary

The trustees may feel it appropriate to benefit a particular beneficiary by 'resettling' property on new trusts of which he is a beneficiary. Without such a clause, trustees could only use trust funds for the purposes set out in the trust instrument; they would have no power to resettle on different trusts. This clause enables them to do so. The exercise of such a power is considered in **Chapter 10**.

7.2.2.3 Ultimate default trusts

As we saw in **Chapter 6** it is important that there is no danger of property reverting to the settlor at the end of the perpetuity period.

All the capital and income of the trust fund must be fully distributed or be subject to vested interests by the end of the trust (perpetuity) period so that the trusts are not void for perpetuity. If for any reason the trustees have not distributed everything, the property remaining in the trust fund will revert back to the settlor. Even though in practice this never happens because the trustees do distribute fully, the fact that it could happen means that the settlor has an interest in the settlement and suffers adverse tax consequences (see **6.9.3**).

7.3   Settlements with contingent interests

The principal trusts

This clause will state the primary intention of the settlor, namely that the trustees will hold the capital of the trust fund for the beneficiaries until they attain the specified age.

Sample clause

> The Trust Fund shall be held upon trust for such of the Primary Beneficiaries as:
> (a)   attain the age of 25 before the end of the Trust Period; or
> (b)   are living and under that age at the end of the Trust Period
> and, if more than one, in equal shares absolutely.

Commentary on the clause: capital provision

Perpetuity rules

To comply with the perpetuity rules, the contingent interests must vest within the perpetuity period applying to the trust; currently this will normally be a period of 80 years or 125 years depending on whether the settlement is governed by the PAA 1964 or the PAA 2009.

This trust provides contingent gifts which are to vest in beneficiaries at the age of 25 years. Any beneficiary attaining that age within the trust period, ie the perpetuity period of the trust, will have a vested entitlement. Any beneficiary who is still under the age of 25 years when the trust period ends will immediately acquire a vested entitlement to a share of the trust fund.

It is of course possible that by the end of the perpetuity period no beneficiaries have or can take a vested interest.

Example

Fred creates a lifetime settlement for such of his grandchildren as reach 25. At the time the settlement is created he has one grandchild aged two. This grandchild is killed in a climbing accident, aged 24. No further grandchildren are born. At the end of the perpetuity period there are no beneficiaries who can take a vested interest. The property will revert to the settlor unless the settlement includes an ultimate default clause.

As we saw in **Chapter 6** adverse tax consequences follow if there is any possibility of property reverting to the settlor, so settlements creating contingent interests should, like discretionary trusts, always include an ultimate default clause. This will give someone (typically, a charity) a vested interest subject to the preceding contingent interests.

Right to capital to vest at 25 years

The sample clause above provides that a beneficiary's entitlement to capital will vest at or before the age of 25. However, as we have seen, it is equally possible to give a beneficiary a right to income contingent on reaching a certain age and leave the entitlement to capital to the trustees' discretion (subject to vesting within the perpetuity period).

Trustee Act 1925, s 32

Section 32 of TA 1925 gives the trustees power to apply capital for the advancement or benefit of a beneficiary who has an interest in the capital of the settlement. The power may be exercised where the beneficiary has a contingent interest even though the beneficiary may never satisfy the contingency, for example, because he dies before the age stipulated for the vesting of the capital. In the absence of contrary provision, s 32 will automatically apply to a settlement with contingent interests to enable the trustees to advance up to one half of a beneficiary's presumptive, ie contingent, entitlement to capital irrespective of the age to which the right to the capital has been delayed by the terms of the settlement.

The implied power may be modified when drafting the settlement to enable the trustees to advance up to the whole of a beneficiary's presumptive entitlement in the same way as the power is often extended when drafting a will.

Commentary on the clause: income provision

Income entitlement at 18 years

This clause contains no express reference to income. In particular, the clause does not vary the implied provisions of s 31 of TA 1925 by substituting a later age of up to 25 years for the statutory age of 18 years. Income entitlement of the primary beneficiaries and the trustees' duty to accumulate surplus income is, therefore, determined in accordance with s 31 of TA 1925.

Trustee Act 1925, s 31

Unless expressly excluded, s 31 of TA 1925 will automatically apply to the settlement.

The implied power is often modified when drafting settlements with contingent interests to defer the entitlement to income to an age exceeding 18. The trustees' discretion then continues until the specified age. However, when deferring entitlement to income, it is important to check the length of the accumulation period. Trusts created before the Perpetuities and Accumulations Act 2009 came into force will always have a limited accumulation period. Those created afterwards may have limitations imposed by the settlor (although this would be unusual) (see **6.10**).

7.4 Summary of Chapters 6 and 7

(a) There are many different types of settlements, for example settlements with fixed vested interests, discretionary settlements and settlements with contingent interests.

(b) However, all lifetime settlements have many elements in common.

(c) They all need to appoint trustees, define the trust property, declare the beneficial interests and exclude the settlor, spouse, civil partner and minor unmarried children from benefit to avoid adverse tax consequences.

(d) Unless the settlement is a simple one where all interests are vested and the trustees have no discretions, they will need in addition:

(i) an ultimate default clause to make sure that there cannot be funds left over at the end of the perpetuity period which would revert to the settlor; and

(ii) in the case of settlements not governed by the PAA 2009, a clause selecting the perpetuity period and a clause selecting the accumulation period.

(e) If the trustees have any discretions, the settlor should prepare a letter of wishes to help the trustees exercise their discretions.

Chapter 8
Accumulation and Maintenance Settlements

8.1 Introduction

Individuals often want to provide funds for the benefit of young people but do not necessarily want the young people to have free access to those funds until they are sufficiently mature. Creating a settlement is useful as it allows the trustees to control the availability of funds.

Before 22 March 2006 a particular form of settlement created for young people, called an accumulation and maintenance (A & M) settlement, attracted privileged tax treatment. No new settlements of this type can be created on or after 22 March 2006, but settlements in existence on that date continue to attract privileged treatment provided they comply with certain conditions.

You will continue to meet such settlements for some time to come, although they will become less and less common.

8.2 What are A & M settlements?

Accumulation and maintenance settlements were originally settlements created before 22 March 2006 which fulfilled the requirements of IHTA 1984, s 71. They received IHT privileges (see **8.3**).

On 6 April 2008 existing A & M settlements lost their privileged status unless they fulfilled the requirements of s 71 as amended by FA 2006.

8.2.1 The requirements

The original s 71 laid down three requirements, all of which had to be satisfied:

(a) One or more beneficiaries will, on or before attaining a specified age not exceeding 25, become beneficially entitled to the settled property or to an income from it.

(b) No interest in possession subsists in the settled property and the income from it is to be accumulated so far as it is not applied for the maintenance, education or benefit of such a beneficiary.

(c) Either:

    (i) not more than 25 years have elapsed since the day on which the settlement was made; or

    (ii) all the beneficiaries are grandchildren of a common grandparent, or are children, widows or widowers, or surviving civil partners of such grandchildren who were themselves beneficiaries but died before becoming entitled as in (a) above.

8.2.2 The requirements of amended s 71

Accumulation and maintenance settlements in existence on 22 March 2006 continued to qualify for privileged IHT treatment until 6 April 2008. On 6 April 2008 an amended s 71 came into effect, and existing A & M settlements continue to qualify for IHT privileged treatment only if they satisfy the requirements of the amended s 71.

The second and third requirements (see **8.2.1**) are unchanged, but the first requirement is substantially amended as from 6 April 2008 as follows:

> One or more beneficiaries will, on or before attaining a specified age not exceeding 18, become beneficially entitled to the settled property.

The reduction of the age of entitlement to 18 and the requirement that beneficiaries must become entitled to capital and not merely income at 18, means that many settlements ceased to qualify as A & M settlements on 6 April 2008.

Section 71D of IHTA 1984, introduced by FA 2006, provides for limited IHT privileges for certain types of settlements for young people created on death. It also provides that any A & M settlement in existence on 22 March 2006 may qualify for the same limited privileges from 6 April 2008. To qualify, the settlement must provide that the beneficiaries will become entitled to capital at or before 25, and satisfy certain other requirements set out in s 71D. See **Chapter 12** for details of the IHT treatment of s 71D settlements. Broadly, there will be no anniversary charges but there will be an exit charge when a beneficiary becomes entitled to capital, calculated on the length of time property remains settled after the beneficiary's 18th birthday. (Settlements that fulfil the even more restrictive requirements of s 71A will qualify as s 71A settlements, but this will be unusual.)

Settlements which meet neither the amended first requirement of s 71 nor the requirements of s 71D are converted into relevant property settlements on 6 April 2008 without any charge to IHT.

During the period 22 March 2006 to 6 April 2008, trustees had to review the terms of their settlements to decide what would happen in 2008. Some trustees allowed their settlements to be converted into relevant property settlements. Some used powers of appointment or advancement to distribute all the capital to the beneficiaries before 6 April 2008, thus bringing the settlement to an end, or to resettle the property on different trusts. Others applied to court to vary the terms of the settlement to allow them to retain their status as A & M settlements.

Because some settlements will still qualify as A & M settlements under the amended s 71, we will look briefly at each of the three requirements.

8.2.3   The three elements of the amended s 71

8.2.3.1   At least one beneficiary will become entitled to the trust property on or before his 18th birthday

The requirement is that a beneficiary will become entitled to the capital of the trust fund or a portion of it at or before age 18.

Example

Sam settles £10,000 in 2001 on trust for Adam if he attains 18 years of age.

If Adam reaches 18 years (ie, satisfies the contingency) the trustees must give him the £10,000.

If Adam dies, say, aged 15 years, the trust will fail. The £10,000 will not form part of Adam's estate.

The requirement that a beneficiary 'will' become entitled does not require absolute certainty. It should be read as meaning 'will become entitled, if at all, at or before the age of 18'. Death can always prevent entitlement but the possibility does not mean that this requirement is unsatisfied.

Section 71(4)(b) provides that tax will not be charged on the death of a beneficiary below the specified age. Therefore, the death of all the intended beneficiaries before the specified age does not prevent the settlement being an A & M settlement (see further *Inglewood (Lord) and Another v IRC* [1983] STC 133).

The existence of powers which, if exercised, could result in property vesting beyond the specified age or being appointed to a non-beneficiary will, however, prevent a settlement having A & M status.

Example

Shazia settles property on Bhopal in 2005 contingent on his reaching 18, but the settlement gives the trustees power to appoint the trust property to Shazia's husband if they see fit. This settlement is not an A & M settlement, as it is not possible to say that Bhopal *will* become entitled.

8.2.3.2   No beneficiary may have an interest in possession and any income not applied must be accumulated

There are two elements to this requirement:

(a)   no interest in possession; and

(b)   income must be accumulated to the extent that it is not applied for beneficiaries.

Both are normally satisfied while the beneficiary is a minor as a result of the effect of s 31 of TA 1925.

8.2.3.3   The trust must not have lasted for more than 25 years unless all the beneficiaries have a common grandparent, etc

Where the beneficiaries do not share a common grandparent, the settlement can have A & M status for only 25 years. If it continues as a settlement after the expiry of 25 years, a charge to IHT may then arise.

The grandparent must be common to all the beneficiaries, but need not have any blood tie to the settlor.

This requirement is designed to prevent more than one generation from benefiting from A & M status. Even so, a second generation can benefit in some cases, as the provisions permit substitution where an original beneficiary has died.

8.3   Taxation of existing A & M settlements from 6 April 2008

8.3.1   Inheritance tax

Be aware of the following points:

(a)   The lifetime creation of an A & M settlement before 6 April 2006 was a PET (IHTA 1984, s 3A). Hence if the settlor dies within seven years of the transfer, IHT will become payable. Tapering relief is available after three years.

(b)   There are no anniversary or exit charges (unless a settlement created for beneficiaries without a common grandparent lasts for more than 25 years, when there is an exit charge). This means that these settlements defer the beneficiaries' entitlement to capital without incurring any IHT charges for the settlement.

8.3.2   Capital gains tax

There is only one special CGT advantage for A & M settlements. Hold-over relief is available when a beneficiary of an A & M settlement becomes absolutely entitled to capital assets. See **4.1.2**.

8.3.3   Income tax

There are no special income tax provisions relating to A & M settlements. The normal income tax rules applying to settlements apply. See **Chapter 14**.

8.4 Summary

(a)   A & M settlements had important IHT benefits. They were not subject to anniversary or exit charges.

(b)   These benefits continued until 6 April 2008 for all A & M settlements in existence on 22 March 2006.

(c)   At that date an A & M settlement lost its privileged status and the property within it became subject to the relevant property regime *unless* the settlement satisfied certain conditions, in particular that the beneficiaries are entitled to capital at:

   (i)   age 18; or
   (ii)   age 25.

(d)   Settlements which fulfilled the conditions on 6 April 2008 retained their privileged IHT status. They are not subject to the relevant property regime, which means that there are no anniversary or exit charges payable.

(e)   Clients wishing to create lifetime settlements for young people on or after 22 March 2006 will have to create relevant property settlements (unless the beneficiary is disabled). The form of the settlement is immaterial.

(f)   A transfer to a relevant property settlement will be immediately chargeable to IHT, but there will be tax to pay only to the extent that the transfer exceeds the settlor's nil rate band.

Chapter 9

Trust Advances and Appointments

9.1 What are advances and appointments?

Whether the trustees exercise a power of advancement or a power of appointment, the result is generally the same. The trust property, or some part of it, will become subject to different beneficial interests. The property will either become the absolute property of a beneficiary, ie it ceases to be subject to the trusts of the settlement, or it will remain settled property subject to the trusts of the original settlement or of a new settlement. The trustees' powers may be sufficiently wide for them to 'declare new trusts' over some part of the trust property. The manner of the exercise of these powers is discussed further in **Chapter 10**.

A power of advancement may be available to the trustees as a statutory power (ie, the power to advance trust capital under TA 1925, s 32) or as an express power through provision in the trust instrument. Powers of appointment can exist only as express powers. Modifying the statutory power of advancement by express provision and the drafting of express powers are considered at **9.4.3** and **9.5**.

9.2 Legal similarities and differences

9.2.1 Similarities

Both types of power are fiduciary and are dispositive in nature. Either can be exercised to create new beneficial interests for the beneficiaries of the trust. Generally, the powers are exercisable by the trustees for the benefit of beneficiaries who have been selected by the settlor of the settlement.

9.2.2 Differences

There are differences which relate to the existence of the powers and the manner of their exercise.

9.2.2.1 Existence of the powers

Only the power of advancement is statutory. Section 32 of TA 1925 will be implied into every settlement, but its effect may be extended or restricted by express provision in the settlement depending on the instructions given by the settlor at the time the settlement was created. Section 32 of TA 1925, and its possible modification, are considered at **9.4.3**.

A power of appointment can exist only if there is an express provision in the trust instrument creating it. A power which is widely drafted may permit advancements of the type permitted by s 32 and so render that provision superfluous. Drafting powers of appointment is considered further at **9.5**.

9.2.2.2 Exercise of the powers

Power of advancement

When trustees exercise a power of advancement, they apply capital for the benefit of a beneficiary. For example, they may hold the trust property for a beneficiary contingently on his attaining 25 years. If the trustees exercise the power in TA 1925, s 32 (or an equivalent express power) and give capital to the beneficiary when he is aged 21 to buy a flat, this is an advancement.

Power of appointment

A power of appointment in a settlement allows trustees to grant a beneficiary income or capital from the settlement, or change the terms on which property is held. Such powers are typically (but not exclusively) found in discretionary settlements. For an example of this in a will creating interest in possession trusts, see **12.7.2**.

The exercise of a power of appointment may have an effect similar to the exercise of a power of advancement. Alternatively, the exercise of the power of appointment may change the beneficial entitlement to the trust property while leaving the property subject to trusts. Those trusts may be the trusts established in the original trust instrument, or they may be new trusts specifically created by the instrument which exercises the power.

Example

Trustees are holding property on trust for the settlor's grandchildren. There is a wide power of appointment over the settled property and its income, enabling the trustees to appoint the property among the beneficiaries at such times and in such proportions and for such purposes as they think fit. In default of appointment, the trust property will pass equally to such of the settlor's grandchildren living at the date of the settlement who attain 18.

The trustees may exercise a power of this nature:

(a) To provide capital for the absolute benefit of any single beneficiary, or group of beneficiaries, even before the age of 18 years. They must exercise their powers in proper manner having regard to their fiduciary nature.

(b) To provide capital for one or more of the beneficiaries on their attaining 21 years, ie, the power of appointment is executed to create new trusts in favour of beneficiaries selected from the class beneficiaries. If the power is exercised in this way, care must be taken to observe the perpetuity period applicable to the original settlement (see **6.2.7**).

9.2.3 General and special powers of appointment

Powers of appointment are generally characterised as either special or general powers of appointment.

9.2.3.1 General powers

These powers permit the trustees to appoint to any person they may choose and are, therefore, uncommon. The settlor will generally wish to select the class of beneficiaries among whom the trustees may exercise the power. For this reason most settlements contain special powers of appointment.

9.2.3.2 Special powers

These permit the trustees to appoint to beneficiaries within a class chosen by the settlor. Two areas in particular require prior consideration before the trustees exercise a special power of appointment.

The objects of the power

No power may be exercised in a manner which exceeds any limitations laid down by the settlor in the settlement. The exercise of the power of appointment must, therefore, be for the benefit of a member or members of a class of beneficiaries selected by the settlor. Although the settlor and his spouse can be included within the class of beneficiaries, generally they will be excluded for tax reasons. Minor unmarried children will normally be excluded for the same reasons. See **6.2.11**.

The perpetuity period

The property must vest in interest in the beneficiary in whose favour the power is to be exercised before the perpetuity period relevant to the settlement expires. In the case of special powers, this period is the period established by the settlement and which starts to run from the date of creation of the settlement (see **6.2.7**).

Example

The facts are the same as in the example at 9.2.2.2. The perpetuity period is 80 years. Fifteen years after the settlement is created, the trustees appoint one quarter of the trust funds on trusts for the settlor's grandchild, Millie (aged 1) if she attains 21 years. There is an ultimate gift over to charity.

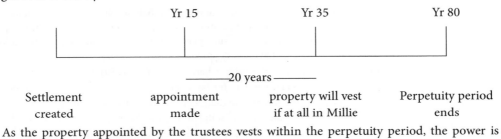

| Settlement created | appointment made | property will vest if at all in Millie | Perpetuity period ends |

As the property appointed by the trustees vests within the perpetuity period, the power is properly exercised.

9.3 Practical similarities

The exercise of either power will require the execution by the trustees of a deed of advancement or a deed of appointment depending on the method selected by the trustees.

The initiative for the exercise of the power will generally come from one or more of the beneficiaries, normally because they need money. The trustees must, on each occasion, consider whether they have adequate powers to satisfy the beneficiary's request and, if so, whether they wish to exercise those powers.

Any exercise of a power pursuant to such a request will have taxation implications. These should be fully considered before any power is exercised. Taxation aspects of the exercise of powers are considered in **Chapter 10**.

Sometimes, the trustees rather than the beneficiaries will take the initiative as to the need to exercise a power and begin discussion with the beneficiaries on the manner and method of exercise of the power. This often happens where the trustees foresee a tax problem which they can avoid by using their powers. These aspects of the use of the trustees' powers are considered further in **Chapter 10**.

The exercise of either power may cause settled property to cease to be subject to trusts. In such cases the trustees will need to transfer the trust property to the beneficiary. Similarly, if property becomes subject to new trusts, the trustees of the original settlement may need to transfer the property to the trustees of the new settlement. The manner of vesting trust property in beneficiaries or new trustees is considered at **14.4.3**.

9.4 The statutory power of advancement

9.4.1 The power of advancement

Section 32 of TA 1925 states:

(1) Trustees may at any time or times pay or apply any capital money subject to a trust, for the advancement or benefit, in such manner as they may, in their absolute discretion, think fit, of any person entitled to the capital of the trust property or of any share thereof, whether absolutely or contingently on his attaining any specified age or on the occurrence of any other event, or subject to a gift over on his death under any specified age or on the occurrence of any other event, and whether in possession or in remainder or reversion, and such payment or application may be made notwithstanding that the interest of such person is liable to be defeated by the exercise of a power of appointment or revocation, or to be diminished by the increase of the class to which he belongs:

Provided that—

(a) the money so paid or applied for the advancement or benefit of any person shall not exceed altogether in amount one half of the presumptive or vested share or interest of that person in the trust property; and

(b) if that person is or becomes absolutely and indefeasibly entitled to a share in the trust property the money so paid or applied shall be brought into account as part of such share; and

(c) no such payment or application shall be made so as to prejudice any person entitled to any prior life or other interest, whether vested or contingent, in the money paid or applied unless such person is in existence and of full age and consents in writing to such payment or application.

(2) This section applies only where the trust property consists of money or securities or of property held upon trust for sale calling in and conversion, and such money or securities, or the proceeds of such sale calling in and conversion are not by statute or in equity considered as land, or applicable as capital money for the purposes of the Settled Land Act 1925.

(3) This section does not apply to trusts constituted or created before the commencement of this Act.

9.4.2 Commentary on the statutory power

9.4.2.1 The power is discretionary: the trustees 'may'

Beneficiaries cannot compel trustees to exercise the power. Before exercising this power, the trustees must ensure their intended use of the power is for a legitimate purpose. If not, it will be an improper exercise of the power which will be invalid, and which may cause the trustees personal liability for loss suffered by the trust fund.

9.4.2.2 Interest in capital of the trust fund (or part)

Only beneficiaries with an interest in the capital may benefit from exercise of the power. However, the interest may be any of the following:

(a) absolute or contingent (on attaining any age or on any other event occurring);

(b) in possession, remainder or reversion.

It does not matter that a beneficiary's interest is liable to be defeated or diminished by the occurrence of a future event, for example because the beneficiary may die at a young age and never reach the age at which the interest vests.

> **Example**
> Trustees are holding £30,000 on trust for Saul contingent upon his attaining the age of 25 years (if he dies under the age of 25 the money is to go to charity). On his 18th birthday, the trustees advance £12,000 to enable Saul to go to university. This is a proper exercise of the power even though Saul may die before his 25th birthday.

Beneficiaries of a discretionary trust do not have an interest in the capital of the settlement. They have a mere hope of benefiting if the trustees exercise their discretion in their favour. While their interest is discretionary, they cannot benefit from s 32.

9.4.2.3 Limitations on the exercise of the power

The trustees may exercise their power only where it is for 'the advancement or benefit' of the beneficiary. 'Advancement' is normally considered to cover capital payments designed to 'set the beneficiary up in life (often in a business)' or payments made on the occasion of marriage. 'Benefit' has a particularly wide meaning. It has been held *Pilkington and Another v Inland Revenue Commissioners and Others* [1964] AC 612 to have a meaning wide enough to permit the trustees to exercise their power of advancement by creating new trusts in relation to settled property if such is for the benefit of the beneficiary (a *'Pilkington* advance').

Example

Trustees are holding £100,000 on trust for Martha contingent on her reaching 25 years. She is now aged 24, is wealthy and has two children aged 1 and 3 years. She would prefer the funds to be transferred to trustees for her children so that IHT may be avoided if she should die soon after her 25th birthday. The trustees may exercise their power and advance some of the settled funds into a settlement for Martha's children.

Courts have held the following to be for the 'benefit' of beneficiaries:

(a) a settlement on the beneficiary's children relieving him of the 'considerable obligation in respect of making provision for their future' which he would otherwise have owed (*Re Hampden's Settlement Trusts* [1977] TR 177);

(b) a transfer from a substantial trust fund to a family charitable foundation discharging the moral and social obligations felt by the beneficiary (*Re Clore's Settlement Trusts* [1966] 1 WLR 955).

The statutory power limits the trustees to paying or applying 'not more than one half' of a beneficiary's presumptive or vested share. If the power is exercised, the amount paid or applied must be 'brought into account' if the beneficiary later becomes entitled to a share in the trust property.

9.4.2.4 Prior life or other interests

The statutory power can be exercised only if consent is obtained from a beneficiary with a prior interest. For example, if property is held on trust for a beneficiary for life and then for other beneficiaries in remainder, the trustees could not exercise their power in favour of the remaindermen without the consent of the life tenant.

9.4.3 Modifying the statutory power

Normally, only minor amendments, as discussed below, need to be made to the statutory form of the power. They are similar to those made when drafting a will for a testator. As mentioned at **9.2.2**, it is often the case that a settlement contains a wide power of appointment. If so, the trustees may prefer to exercise this power rather than the statutory power, even in modified form.

The alterations made by express provision to the statutory power of advancement are normally:

(a) to permit the trustees to pay or apply up to the whole (not merely one half) of a beneficiary's presumptive or vested share;

(b) to remove the requirement that the distribution has to be brought into account;

(c) to remove the requirement for a person with a prior interest to consent to the advance.

It is unnecessary to consider extending the circumstances in which the statutory power can be exercised by the trustees. The phrase 'advancement or benefit' is generally considered sufficiently wide, especially in view of the particularly wide meaning of the word 'benefit'.

9.5 Drafting powers of appointment

As there is no statutory power of appointment, all powers must be drafted as express powers in a trust instrument. The precise form which the power takes will depend upon the particular settlement which is to be drafted.

9.6 Taxation aspects of the exercise of powers of advancement and appointment

As each power is exercisable in relation to the trust capital, ie, the property in the settlement, it follows that the IHT and CGT aspects of the exercise of the power need be considered by the trustees before the power is actually exercised. These are discussed in **Chapter 10**.

Chapter 10

The Exercise of Powers of Advancement and Appointment

10.1 Interest in possession settlements created before 22 March 2006 or on death

In this section we will look at the taxation of interests in possession created by lifetime transfer before 22 March 2006 or on death. In both of these cases the person with the interest in possession is treated as beneficially entitled to the underlying trust capital. Such interests are often referred to as 'qualifying' interests in possession.

Interests in possession can be created by lifetime transfer after 22 March 2006, but the person with the interest in possession will not be treated as beneficially entitled to the underlying trust capital for IHT purposes.

10.1.1 The nature of the trusts and the powers

Settlements with an interest in possession are usually created because the settlor or the testator is seeking to provide one person (often a spouse) with an income for life while controlling the ultimate devolution of the capital. They are normally created by will.

After the trust comes into effect, the trustees may be asked by beneficiaries to exercise their powers to apply capital.

Since the introduction of TLATA 1996, it is usual for trustees of interest in possession settlements to hold the settled property 'on trust' and have an appropriate power of sale among the administrative provisions of the settlement. The beneficial trusts provide the life tenant with an income for life and the remainderman with an interest which vests in possession on the life tenant's death. Until then, it is vested in interest only.

> **Example**
> Trustees hold settled property currently worth £200,000 on trust to pay the income to Aida for life, thereafter for Carmen in remainder. Aida has an interest in possession, ie the right to income produced by the trust property. Carmen has the right to receive the trust property when Aida dies.

Carmen's interest, in the example, is an interest in remainder but is often called (albeit incorrectly) 'a reversionary interest'. It is an asset which can be professionally valued, ie a value can be placed on Carmen's right to receive the trust property when Aida dies. Since Carmen has the right to receive the trust property only when Aida dies, the value of the interest in remainder may be significantly less than the current value of the settled property. The value will be influenced (inter alia) by the prospective life expectancy of Aida. Carmen's interest in remainder is an asset which she may consider selling or possibly giving away as part of her estate planning arrangements (see **4.6.2**).

Example

If Carmen waits until Aida dies, she will receive the full trust fund (currently valued at £200,000). Carmen, however, is in need of some money immediately and decides to sell her interest in remainder to David.

(a)   Assuming Aida is 84 years old, David might pay Carmen £175,000 for the right to receive the trust fund when Aida dies.

(b)   Assuming Aida is 35 years old, David might pay Carmen £40,000 for that right.

If Carmen's sale is for full market value, no IHT or CGT would be payable by her. If, instead, she gave her interest in remainder to David, no tax would be payable (see 4.6.2) because:

(a)   her interest in remainder is 'excluded property' for IHT purposes, ie, it is not in Carmen's 'estate' and so may be given away free of IHT; and

(b)   as a beneficial interest in settled property acquired without any payment by Carmen, it is exempt from CGT on a disposal whether by sale or gift.

The trustees' power to advance capital to the remainderman in s 32 of TA 1925 applies to an interest in possession settlement, although it may have been modified by express provision in the trust instrument. Any exercise of the statutory power to pay or apply trust property would, unless also suitably modified, require the prior consent of the life tenant.

10.1.2   Provision of capital for the beneficiaries of an interest in possession settlement

Apart from capitalisation of a life interest on an intestacy, there are three methods of providing the beneficiaries with capital from the trust:

(a)   By the exercise of an express power of advancement or appointment.

Only if the trust instrument contains express provision can the trustees apply capital to or for the benefit of the life tenant.

(b)   By the exercise of the statutory power in s 32 of TA 1925 in favour of the remainderman (with consent of the life tenant, unless modified).

The decision to exercise either of these powers is a matter for the trustees. Their decision will generally follow an approach by the beneficiary with a request for the advance of some money. The trustees' decision should be formally recorded either:

(i)   by a minute in the trustees' minute book for the trust (if any); or

(ii)   by signing a separate notice to the effect that, in exercise of a power contained in the settlement or in s 32 of TA 1925 certain property is advanced from the settlement to a named beneficiary. This notice should be retained with the trust instrument and records.

(c)   By partitioning the trust fund by agreement between the life tenant and the remainderman (see **10.1.3**).

10.1.3   Partitioning the trust fund

In the absence of an express power to advance capital to a life tenant, capital may be provided by 'breaking the trust' under the rule in *Saunders v Vautier* (1841) 4 Beav 115. 'Trust busting' under this rule allows beneficiaries who are of full age and capacity and together entitled to the whole beneficial interest in the trust fund to bring the settlement to an end and to direct the trustees to transfer the property as they wish.

If the beneficiaries decide to end the trust in this way, they will need to reach agreement as to the value of their respective beneficial interests, ie, a value needs to be placed on the life tenant's right to receive income for life and on the remainderman's right to receive the capital of the trust on the life tenant's death. Agreement may be reached informally between the beneficiaries or by formal valuation by an actuary instructed to act on their behalf.

> **Example**
>
> Trustees hold £10,000 on trust for Mary for life, remainder to William. Mary and William agree that their respective interests are worth 40% and 60% of the settled property. They may direct the trustees to sell the trust property and to divide the sale proceeds between them in the agreed proportions.

Instead of directing the trustees to sell the trust property as in the example, the beneficiaries may prefer to direct the trustees to divide the assets between them so that each beneficiary receives the appropriate proportion of the trust fund. This method of division will require each asset to be valued separately. It may be necessary for the trustees to use cash to achieve exactly the correct proportions of the funds for each beneficiary.

> **Example**
>
> The facts are the same as in the previous example. The £10,000 trust fund is made up of shares in A plc valued at £5,000, shares in B plc valued at £4,000, and £1,000 cash.
>
> William will receive:
>
> £3,000 A plc shares;
>
> £2,400 B plc shares;
>
> £600 cash.
>
> Mary will receive:
>
> £2,000 A plc shares;
>
> £1,600 B plc shares;
>
> £400 cash.

Before the settled property is actually distributed among the beneficiaries, the trustees must first consider the taxation implications.

10.1.4 Taxation implications of provision of capital for the beneficiaries

The exercise of the statutory or express power of advancement has capital tax implications which the trustees must consider before releasing the formerly settled property from their control. The trustees will often become personally liable for tax as a result of the exercise of a power. They should retain some of the trust property in their own names until all liabilities have been discharged.

10.1.4.1 Inheritance tax

A person with a qualifying interest in possession (created by lifetime transfer before 22 March 2006 or on death) is treated as beneficially entitled to the property in which he has an interest (IHTA 1984, s 49).

> **Example**
>
> Trustees of a will trust hold a fund of £50,000 for Leonard for life, remainder for his daughter, Rachel. Leonard has assets of his own which amount to £100,000. His estate for IHT purposes will be valued at £150,000.

The lifetime termination of a qualifying interest in possession in a will trust or pre-22 March 2006 lifetime trust is a transfer by the life tenant. If the property is then held for one or more of the beneficiaries absolutely, ie, the settlement comes to an end, the transfer will normally be a PET. If, however, the property is held by the trustees for a spouse or civil partner of the life tenant absolutely, the transfer will be exempt. Tax (calculated in the normal manner where there is a 'failed' PET) will be payable only if the former life tenant dies within seven years of termination of the settlement (IHTA 1984, ss 52(1) and 3A). Inheritance tax may, therefore, become payable where a power is exercised to provide capital to beneficiaries in the three ways mentioned below. If IHT is payable, it is the trustees of the settlement who must pay it to the Revenue and who should therefore reserve funds for the purpose.

If such an interest in possession is terminated to create a further trust, there will be a lifetime chargeable transfer by the life tenant.

Method 1: Express power to appoint capital to life tenant

If the trustees of a qualifying interest in possession trust exercise a power to advance all of the capital to the life tenant, his interest in possession in the capital advanced will end. However, no IHT will be payable. This is because there is no fall in the value of his estate, since for IHT purposes he is deemed already to own that property which is actually being advanced (IHTA 1984, s 53(2)).

Example

Assume that in the previous example the trustees advance the whole fund to Leonard.

Before the advance:

Leonard's estate	£100,000
Trust fund	£ 50,000
	£150,000

After the advance:

Leonard's estate £100,000 + £50,000 advanced = £150,000.

Method 2: Statutory power of advancement to remainderman

If the trustees of a qualifying interest in possession trust exercise their power to advance the capital to the remainderman, the life tenant's interest in possession ends in that part of the settled property. The life tenant makes a PET which becomes chargeable only if he dies within seven years of the advance (IHTA 1984, ss 3A and 52(1)).

Example

Assume that the trustees holding the trust property for Leonard for life, remainder to Rachel, had advanced £10,000 to Rachel. Leonard is treated as making a PET. If it becomes chargeable, any IHT payable on the £10,000 (ie, the value of the property in which Leonard's interest in possession has ended) is payable by the trustees from the trust fund.

Note: The statutory power requires the life tenant's consent, although the need for consent can be removed in the trust instrument.

Method 3: Partition of the trust fund

If, by agreement, the fund is partitioned, the life tenant's interest in possession ends in the trust property which passes to the remainderman. This too is a PET made by the life tenant. Inheritance tax is payable by the trustees on that portion of the trust fund if the life tenant dies within seven years of the partition (IHTA 1984, s 52(2)).

Example

Assume that Leonard and Rachel in the previous example agreed to partition the £50,000 fund between them in proportions of 30:70. Leonard makes a PET of £35,000 (£50,000 – £15,000 = £35,000). If Leonard dies within seven years of the PET, IHT is payable by the trustees from the partitioned trust fund (which they should remember).

10.1.4.2 Capital gains tax

Liability to CGT occurs only if there is a disposal of chargeable assets. Disposals may be actual or deemed. No actual disposal occurs on the exercise by the trustees of their power of advancement. However, in each case there is a deemed disposal. (Actual disposals by trustees are considered in **Chapter 14**.)

Deemed disposals (TCGA 1992, s 71, as amended by FA 1999, s 75)

A deemed disposal occurs when an individual becomes 'absolutely entitled' to settled property against the trustees, for example, on any of the occasions mentioned in **10.1.2**. The trustees are deemed to dispose of each item of settled property at its market value and to re-acquire it immediately at the same value as nominees for the beneficiary, ie they continue to hold the property in their names as bare trustees for the beneficiary. The property is no longer settled property but belongs to the beneficiary whose acquisition cost of the property is the market value when the re-acquisition occurred.

Example

Trustees appoint 1,000 ABC plc shares worth £20,000 to Leonard, the life tenant of an interest in possession settlement. The shares were worth £2,000 when the settlement was created. Entrepreneurs' Relief is not available. A deemed disposal occurs at the date of the appointment.

Value at deemed disposal	£20,000
Less: acquisition cost	£2,000
Chargeable gain	£18,000

Leonard's acquisition cost of the shares is £20,000.

Reliefs, exemptions and rate of tax

If any tax is due, it is calculated at 28% of the gain (for disposals on or after 23 June 2010) and is payable by the settlement trustees. As their deemed disposal gave rise to the gain, any tax is their liability. They pay the tax from the settled funds. If a loss occurs, the trustees can claim relief for it by setting the loss against their gains on other disposals of trust assets in the same or future tax years.

Before calculating their liability to tax, the trustees may deduct an annual exemption (£5,050 in 2010/11), ie, one half of the exemption available to individuals.

On the joint election of the trustees and beneficiaries, hold-over relief will be available when assets leave a settlement if:

(a)   the settled property comprises business property (see **4.4.5.2**); or

(b)   the occasion is chargeable to IHT, ie, it is not a PET.

If they claim hold-over relief, the annual exemption will not be available.

In very limited circumstances Entrepreneurs' Relief may be available (see **4.4.5.3**). If claimed, hold-over relief is not available.

Beneficiaries' and trustees' losses

If a loss arises on the deemed disposal, the trustees may claim relief for it by deducting it from:

(a)   gains which accrued to the trustees on disposals in the same tax year as the deemed disposal; or

(b)   gains accruing on the deemed disposal, ie, gains on the assets to which the beneficiary is entitled.

If relief is not available to the trustees (because they have insufficient gains), the loss may be transferred to the beneficiary. He may use the loss to offset future gains made on the disposal of assets received from the settlement only. In other words, the loss is not generally available to offset gains on disposals of his other assets.

10.1.5 Drafting a deed of partition

Heading and date

Sample clause

> DEED OF PARTITION
> DATE: [   ]

Parties

Normally, there will be three parties:

(a)   the life tenant (who gives up the right to income in part of the trust fund); and

(b)   the reversioner (who gives up the right to part of the capital of the trust fund); and

(c)   the trustees.

Sample clause

> (1)   [name and address] ('the Life Tenant');
>
> (2)   [name and address] ('the Reversioners'); and
>
> (3)   [name and address] ('the Trustees')

Recitals

The recitals will explain the background circumstances giving rise to the partition.

Sample clause

> RECITALS
>
> (A) This Deed is supplemental to the settlement ('the Settlement')
> [and to the other documents and events] specified in the First Schedule.
>
> (B) The Trustees are the present trustees of the Settlement.
>
> (C) Under and by virtue of the Settlement and in the events which have happened, the Life Tenant is entitled to the income of the Trust Fund for life and, subject thereto, the capital and income of the Trust Fund is held upon trust for the Reversioners [in equal shares] absolutely.
>
> (D) The Trust Fund presently consists of the property described in Parts 1 and 2 of the Second Schedule.
>
> (E) It has been agreed between the Life Tenant and the Reversioners that the Trust Fund shall be partitioned so that [   ] per centum as described in Part 1 of the Second Schedule ('the Life Tenant's Share') shall be held for the Life Tenant absolutely and the balance remaining being [   ] per centum as described in Part 2 of the Second Schedule ('the Reversioners' Share'), shall be held for the Reversioners in equal shares absolutely.
>
> (F) The Trustees have agreed, following the joint request of the Life Tenant and the Reversioners, to release the Trust Fund to the parties respectively entitled under the above agreement.
>
> [(G) This partition is carried out following and in accordance with actuarial advice.]

The clauses assume that there is more than one reversioner and that the reversioners agree to divide their share equally between them. They will need amendment if there is only one reversioner. If the parties did not obtain actuarial advice, delete clause G.

The operative part

Normally, there will be two clauses, one each for the life tenant and the reversioner, whereby they respectively assign and surrender to the other their interest in the income or capital of the trust fund. The consequence is that the trust property is freed from the trust and may be transferred by the trustees in accordance with the arrangement mentioned in the recitals.

Sample clause

> OPERATIVE PROVISIONS
>
> 1. Definitions and construction
>
> In this Deed, where the context admits, the definitions and rules of construction contained in the Settlement shall apply.
>
> 2. Assignment by Life Tenant
>
> The Life Tenant hereby assigns [his/her] interest in the Reversioners' Share to the Reversioners in equal shares absolutely, to the intent that such interest shall merge and be extinguished in the reversion and that the Reversioners shall become entitled to the Reversioners' Share [in equal shares] absolutely.
>
> 3. Assignment by Reversioners
>
> The Reversioners hereby assign their respective interests in the Life Tenant's Share to the Life Tenant absolutely, to the intent that the life interest and the reversion shall merge, the life interest shall be enlarged and the Life Tenant shall become entitled to the Life Tenant's Share absolutely.
>
> 4. Payment of tax
>
> Without prejudice to the provisions contained in clause 5, it is hereby agreed and declared that any inheritance tax occasioned by the partition in respect of the Reversioners' Share shall be borne by that share and any capital gains tax occasioned by the partition shall be borne by the Life Tenant and the Reversioners in the same proportions as they become absolutely entitled to the Trust Fund.
>
> 5. Trustees' lien
>
> Nothing in this Deed shall prejudice or impair in any way any lien to which the Trustees are entitled in respect of any claim for costs, charges or expenses or in order to protect themselves against any tax liabilities.

Clauses 4 and 5 above deal with liability to IHT and CGT which may arise following the partition and the position of the trustees who are liable for that tax. This was considered at **10.1.4**.

Schedules

The First Schedule will give details of the settlement which is to be ended, ie the date and parties to it. A Second Schedule will detail the division of the trust property between the life tenant and the reversioner in accordance with the agreement stated in the recitals.

10.2   Relevant property settlements

Relevant property settlements are those without a qualifying interest in possession. They may be discretionary settlements, settlements with a contingent interest or settlements with an interest in possession created by lifetime transfer on or after 22 March 2006.

10.2.1   The nature of the trusts and the powers

In the case of discretionary settlements and settlements where the beneficiaries have merely contingent interests, it is not normally possible for the beneficiaries to divide up capital by consent under the rule in *Saunders v Vautier* for the following reasons:

(a)   some of the beneficiaries may not be of full age;

(b)   there may be an enormous number of beneficiaries potentially within the class so that it is impossible to identify them all;

(c)   it will be difficult for a large number of beneficiaries to agree on the correct basis of distribution.

Drafting the dispositive provisions of a discretionary settlement is considered in detail in **Chapter 7**. Generally, the trusts are drafted in as wide a form as possible. Such wording permits maximum possible flexibility for the trustees. They can pick and choose between beneficiaries. They have power to appoint absolute interests or to make trust appointments, ie, to create new trusts in favour of the beneficiaries. Unless and until this power is exercised, the trust fund and its income will be subject to default provisions.

In the case of settlements where the beneficiaries have contingent interests, it is normal to give the trustees wide powers to advance capital to the beneficiaries. Even if the trustees have no express powers, they will normally have the statutory power to advance capital implied under the TA 1925, s 32, although this will be limited to half the beneficiary's vested or presumptive entitlement.

In the case of settlements created by lifetime transfer on or after 22 March 2006 where a beneficiary has a right to income, the same powers to appoint capital, advance it or partition the trust that we looked at in relation to settlements with a qualifying interest in possession at **10.1.4.1** exist. However, the IHT implications are different, as we will see at **10.2.3** below.

10.2.2   Taxation implications of exercising the power of appointment

The exercise of the power will affect the capital of the settlement. Before exercising it, the trustees must consider the IHT and CGT implications. Having done so, additional clauses may be inserted in the deed of appointment dealing with the payment of the tax (see **10.2.8**).

10.2.3   Inheritance tax

All relevant property settlements are subject to the same IHT regime, no matter what the nature of the beneficiaries' interests. The settlement is a taxable entity in its own right.

A beneficiary may have a right to receive income, but this does not mean that the beneficiary is treated as beneficially entitled to the underlying trust assets. Trustees can give beneficiaries rights to income and remove those rights without any IHT implications. The only occasion when the trustees' action will give rise to a charge to IHT is where the trustees appoint capital out of the settlement.

The regime charges IHT on the value 'relevant property', ie settled property in a settlement in which there is no qualifying interest in possession. Rates of tax are limited to half the rates applicable on death, ie a maximum rate of 20% applies, although tax is often charged at rates considerably less than 20% (see **10.2.4**).

There are a two types of charge to IHT on relevant property settlements (in addition to the charge which may have arisen when the settlement was created, see **Chapter 5**). These are a periodic charge and a distribution (exit) charge.

10.2.3.1   The periodic charge

This is an anniversary charge at 10-yearly intervals on relevant property in the settlement immediately before the 10th anniversary. The anniversary is calculated from the date of the settlement (or the date of death if the relevant property settlement was created by will).

Example

A discretionary settlement is created on 1 July 2000; the first 10-year anniversary charge falls on 1 July 2010 and the second on 1 July 2020, etc.

10.2.3.2 The distribution (exit) charge

A charge also arises when certain events occur, ie, when property ceases to be 'relevant property' by leaving the settlement, for example, on the exercise of a power of appointment by the trustees.

This charge is a proportion of the rate charged on the previous 10-year anniversary. The proportion is calculated by reference to the number of complete quarters (periods of three months) the property has been in the settlement since its creation or the previous periodic charge. There are 40 quarters in a 10-year period. If property has been in the settlement for five years, 20 quarters will be used to calculate the charge. The proportionate rate is applied to the value of the property leaving the fund.

There are special rules for calculating exits in the first 10 years of a settlement's life because there is no previous anniversary charge on which to base the calculation (see **10.2.4** below).

There is no distribution charge, however, if the date when the property ceases to be relevant property is within three months after the creation of the settlement, or within three months after any 10-year anniversary of the creation of the settlement (IHTA 1984, s 65(4)).

10.2.4 Calculating the distribution (exit) charge before the first 10-year anniversary

In the case of distributions of capital made before the first 10-year anniversary, there has to be a special rule for calculating the rate of tax. This is because there has been no previous anniversary and therefore no previous anniversary rate to take a proportion of.

To calculate the liability to IHT, it is necessary to calculate a rate of tax for the settlement (the settlement rate) and then to apply that rate to the value of the trust fund property leaving the settlement. To calculate the exit charge, it is necessary to follow five steps.

Step 1: Ascertain the value of a hypothetical chargeable transfer

This is done by adding together:

(a)   the value of the trust property on creation; and

(b)   the value of property added to the settlement after its creation, if any (using the value when added); and

(c)   the value of property in any related settlement at the date of creation (ie, any other settlement created by the settlor on the same day).

Step 2: Ascertain the tax on this hypothetical transfer

The rate of tax is ascertained from the current table of rates. Tax is calculated at 0% or 20%, ie, half the death rate, even if the discretionary settlement was created by will. Any chargeable transfers made by the settlor in the seven years before the settlement was created will reduce the nil rate band available. However, no account is taken of any transfers made on the same day as the settlement. Thus, if the discretionary settlement is created by a will, no account is taken of the rest of the deceased's estate (although his cumulative total of chargeable transfers will be relevant).

Step 3: Ascertain the settlement *rate* of tax

The tax calculated in Step 2 is converted to an estate or average rate. The rate at which tax is then charged, 'the settlement rate', is 30% of this rate. Thus the maximum rate is 30% × 20% (Step 2) = 6%.

Step 4: The charge to IHT

Inheritance tax is charged on the fall in value of the trust property, as a result of the exercise of the power of appointment, at the rate of one-fortieth of the settlement rate for each complete quarter (three months) between the setting up of the settlement and the event giving rise to the liability. If an appointment occurs within the first quarter, there is no liability.

Step 5: Paying the IHT

If the tax is paid from the amount to be distributed there is no grossing up and the amount calculated at Step 4 is paid. If the tax is paid from the balance of the trust fund, it is necessary to gross up the distribution to calculate the tax payable.

Example 1

A settlor settles £100,000 on discretionary trusts on 1 July 2010. On 1 February 2013 the trustees appoint £50,000 to a beneficiary.

Assume that at the time the settlement was created the settlor had made no previous transfers, ie, he had no cumulative total, no property has been added and there were no related settlements.

Step 1:	Find value of hypothetical chargeable transfer	
	No property added or related settlements, therefore just the original valued settled	£100,000
Step 2:	Ascertain tax on hypothetical chargeable transfer	
	The settlor made no chargeable transfers in the 7-year period before 1 July 2010 and so there is a full nil rate band available	
	Portion of nil rate band available	£100,000
	IHT	nil
Steps 3–5	Need not be made	
	The charge to IHT is nil on the £50,000 appointed	

Example 2

As above, but assume that the settlor's cumulative total of chargeable transfers was £235,000.

Step 1:	Find value of hypothetical chargeable transfer	
	No property added or related settlements, therefore just the original valued settled	£100,000
Step 2:	Ascertain tax on hypothetical chargeable transfer	
	The settlor has made chargeable transfers totalling £235,000 in the 7-year period before 1 July 2010	
	Balance of nil rate band remaining	£90,000
	Portion of hypothetical chargeable transfer taxed at 20%	£10,000
	IHT @ 20% × £10,000 = £2,000	
Step 3:	Ascertain settlement rate	
	First find the Average Rate of tax by dividing the tax by the value of the hypothetical chargeable transfer:	

$$\frac{£2,000}{£100,000} \times 100 = 2\%$$

Then convert to the Settlement Rate which is 30% of the Average Rate:

$$30\% \times 2\% = 0.6\%$$

Step 4: Ascertain the charge to IHT

Apply the Settlement Rate to the number of complete quarters which have occurred in the period between the date the settlement was created and the date of the appointment, divided by 40

(1 July 2010–1 February 2013 = 10 complete quarters)

and apply this to the value by which the trust property has fallen as a result of the appointment

IHT on the appointment of £50,000 is

$$0.6\% \times \frac{10}{40} \times £50,000 = £75$$

Step 5: Paying the IHT

If the beneficiary pays, the IHT will be £75

If the trustees pay, grossing up applies.

Example 3

As above but the settlor had a cumulative total of £325,000, ie, his nil rate band was already exhausted when the settlement was created.

Step 1: Find value of hypothetical chargeable transfer

No property added or related settlements, therefore just the original valued settled £100,000

Step 2: Ascertain tax on hypothetical chargeable transfer

The settlor has made chargeable transfers totalling £325,000 in the 7-year period before 1 July 2010

As there is no available nil rate band the whole of the hypothetical chargeable transfer is taxed at 20%

IHT @ 20% × £100,000 = £20,000

Step 3: Ascertain settlement rate

First find the Average Rate of tax by dividing the tax by the value of the hypothetical chargeable transfer:

$$\frac{£20,000}{£100,000} \times 100 = 20\%$$

Then convert to the Settlement Rate which is 30% of the Average Rate:

30% × 20% = 6%

Step 4: Ascertain the charge to IHT

Apply the Settlement Rate to the number of complete quarters which have occurred in the period between the date the settlement was created and the date of the appointment, divided by 40

(1 July 2010–1 February 2013 = 10 complete quarters)

and apply this to the value by which the trust property has fallen as a result of the appointment

IHT on the appointment of £50,000 is

$$6\% \times \frac{10}{40} \times £50,000 = £750$$

Step 5: Paying the IHT

If the beneficiary pays, the IHT will be £750

If the trustees pay, grossing up applies

The effect of the settlor's cumulative total of chargeable transfers

If the settlor has made no chargeable transfers before making the settlement – as in Example 1 (and had created no related settlement nor added any property to the discretionary settlement) – then a full nil rate band is available to the trustees. Thus, if the hypothetical chargeable transfer in Step 1 (the value of the property at the start of the settlement) does not exceed £325,000, the rate of tax on *all* exit charges before the first 10-year anniversary will be a nil rate as established in Step 3.

Increases in the value of the trust fund after creation and before the first 10-year anniversary do not increase the rate of tax charged. Earlier transfers from the settlement in the first ten years are also irrelevant. The rate in this period is calculated only by reference to the settlor's cumulative total and the value of the trust property at creation.

Trustees of a discretionary settlement not yet 10 years old can take advantage of this nil rate to distribute all the settled property without liability to IHT. This is an important planning point for the trustees.

10.2.5 The first 10-year anniversary charge

This charge is on the value of the property in the settlement (including any accumulated income) immediately before the anniversary of the creation of the settlement.

Step 1: Ascertain the value of a hypothetical chargeable transfer

This is done by adding together:

(a)   the current value of the relevant property in the settlement; and

(b)   the value at creation of any property in a related settlement (if any); and

(c)   the value at creation of other property in the settlement (if any).

Items (b) and (c) are anti-avoidance provisions which rarely apply. Thus, any charge will usually relate only to the current value of the settled property. For this purpose income will be included as relevant property once it has been accumulated. Income is accumulated for this purpose when the trustees take an irrevocable decision to accumulate (or perhaps after the lapse of a reasonable period of time in which to distribute). Although this is not clear from the legislation, it is the view adopted by the Revenue (see Inland Revenue Statement of Practice (SP 8/86)).

Step 2: Ascertain the tax on this hypothetical transfer

The tax is ascertained from the table of rates. Two cumulative totals are relevant to this:

(a)   the settlor's cumulative total of chargeable transfers in the seven years before the settlement was created, and

(b)   the settlement's own cumulative total of chargeable transfers made in the first 10 years.

Tax is calculated at 0% or 20%, ie, half the death rate (even if the settlement is created by will).

Step 3: Ascertain the settlement rate of tax

The tax calculated in Step 2 is converted into an estate or average rate. The settlement rate is 30% of this rate.

Step 4: The charge to IHT

Inheritance tax is charged at the settlement rate applied to the property in the settlement at the anniversary date.

Step 5: Paying the IHT

The trustees will pay the tax from the trust fund.

Example 1

On 1 July 2010 a settlor settled £100,000 on discretionary trusts. The first 10-year anniversary charge falls on 1 July 2020 when the trust fund is worth £140,000 as a result of sound investment by the trustees. No income has been accumulated.

Assume that the settlor had no cumulative total when he created the settlement and no appointments have been made.

Step 1:	Find value of hypothetical chargeable transfer	
	No related settlements or non-relevant property in this settlement, therefore just the value of relevant property at the date of the first 10-year anniversary	£140,000
Step 2:	Ascertain tax on hypothetical chargeable transfer	
	The settlor made no chargeable transfers in the 7-year period before 1 July 2010 and there have been no chargeable transfers out of the settlement in the 10 years since creation, so there is a full nil rate band available	
	Portion of nil rate band available	£140,000
	IHT	nil

Steps 3–5: Need not be made

Example 2

As above, but assume that in 2010 the settlor had a cumulative total of £235,000 from an earlier transfer of value.

Step 1:	Find value of hypothetical chargeable transfer	
	No related settlements or non-relevant property in this settlement, therefore just the value of relevant property at the date of the first 10-year anniversary	£140,000
Step 2:	Ascertain tax on hypothetical chargeable transfer	
	The settlor has made chargeable transfers totalling £235,000 in the 7-year period before 1 July 2010	
	There have been no chargeable transfers out of the settlement in the 10 years since creation	
	Balance of nil rate band remaining	£90,000
	Portion of hypothetical chargeable transfer taxed at 20%	£50,000
	IHT @ 20% × £50,000 = £10,000	
Step 3:	Ascertain settlement rate	
	First find the Average Rate of tax by dividing the tax by the value of the hypothetical chargeable transfer:	
	$\frac{£10,000}{£140,000} \times 100 = 7.14\%$	
	Then convert to the Settlement Rate which is 30% of the Average Rate:	
	30% × 7.14% = 2.14%	

Step 4:	Ascertain the charge to IHT
	Apply the Settlement Rate to the value of relevant property at the date of the first 10-year anniversary
	IHT on the first 10-year anniversary is
	2.14% × £140,000 = £2,996
Step 5:	Paying the IHT
	The trustees pay the IHT from the trust fund.

Example 3

As above, assume that the settlor had a cumulative total of £235,000 in 2010, but that during the first 10 years of the settlement the trustees made an appointment of £50,000 to a beneficiary.

Step 1:	Find value of hypothetical chargeable transfer	
	No related settlements or non-relevant property in this settlement, therefore just the value of relevant property at the date of the first 10-year anniversary	£140,000
Step 2:	Ascertain tax on hypothetical chargeable transfer	
	The settlor has made chargeable transfers totalling £235,000 in the 7-year period before 1 July 2010	
	There has been a chargeable transfer of £50,000 out of the settlement in the 10 years since creation	
	The cumulative totals of the settlor and the settlement are together £235,000 + £50,000 = £285,000	
	Balance of nil rate band remaining	£40,000
	Portion of hypothetical chargeable transfer taxed at 20%	£100,000
	IHT @ 20% × £100,000 = £20,000	
Step 3:	Ascertain settlement rate	
	First find the Average Rate of tax by dividing the tax by the value of the hypothetical chargeable transfer:	
	$\frac{£20,000}{£140,000} \times 100 = 14.29\%$	
	Then convert to the Settlement Rate which is 30% of the Average Rate:	
	30% × 14.29% = 4.29%	
Step 4:	Ascertain the charge to IHT	
	Apply the Settlement Rate to the value of relevant property at the date of the first 10-year anniversary	
	IHT on the first 10-year anniversary is 4.29% × £140,000 = £6,006	
Step 5:	Paying the IHT	
	The trustees pay the IHT from the trust fund.	

The effect of cumulative totals of chargeable transfers of the settlor and the settlement

Transfers by the settlor and by the trustees reduce or extinguish the nil rate band available to the settlement on the occasion of the anniversary charge. Uniquely, the settlor's own cumulative total at the time he made the settlement remains relevant to IHT calculations for as long as the settlement continues. It does not 'drop out' in the way it does for an individual after seven years.

The settlement's own cumulative total ceases to be relevant once an anniversary has passed, although subsequent exit charges will cause the settlement to acquire another cumulative total which will remain relevant until the next 10-year anniversary charge and so on. These factors are particularly relevant to the trustees when considering whether to make distributions, ie, appointments of settled property or to 'break' the settlement.

10.2.6 Subsequent distribution and anniversary charges

Later distribution (exit) charges are brought about by the same events as discussed previously (see **10.2.3**). Inheritance tax is charged on the fall in the value of the settled property at a rate based on the rate at the previous 10-year anniversary charge. The number of quarters (periods of three months since then) will be relevant.

Example 3 (continued) – Exit charge

A discretionary settlement created on 1 July 2010 had a settlement rate of 4.29% on its first 10-year anniversary (1 July 2020). On 1 January 2023 (10 quarters later) the trustees appoint £40,000 to a beneficiary. The rate will be one-fortieth of the settlement rate for each complete quarter since the first 10-year anniversary.

The rate of IHT will be $4.29\% \times \dfrac{10}{40} = 1.07\%$

IHT payable will be £40,000 × 1.07% = £428

Later anniversary charges are calculated in the same way as the first anniversary charge. Any cumulative total of chargeable transfers of the settlor before he created the discretionary settlement are taken into account but only exits since the last anniversary charge will be relevant.

Example 3 (continued) – Anniversary charge

The facts are the same as in the previous example. To calculate the anniversary charge in 2030 when the value of the trust fund has increased to £190,000 and no further distributions have been made:

Step 1:   Find value of hypothetical chargeable transfer

No related settlements or non-relevant property in this settlement, therefore just the value of relevant property at the date of the second 10-year anniversary   £190,000

Step 2:   Ascertain tax on hypothetical chargeable transfer

The settlor has made chargeable transfers totalling £235,000 in the 7-year period before 1 July 2010

There has been a chargeable transfer of £40,000 out of the settlement in the 10 years since the previous 10-year anniversary

The cumulative totals of the settlor and the settlement are together £235,000 + £40,000 = £275,000

Balance of nil rate band remaining   £50,000

Portion of hypothetical chargeable transfer taxed at 20%   £140,000

IHT @ 20% × £140,000 = £28,000

> Step 3:   Ascertain settlement rate
>
> First find the Average Rate of tax by dividing the tax by the value of the hypothetical chargeable transfer:
>
> $$\frac{£28,000}{£190,000} \times 100 = 14.74\%$$
>
> Then convert to the Settlement Rate which is 30% of the Average Rate:
>
> $$30\% \times 14.74\% = 4.42\%$$
>
> Step 4:   Ascertain the charge to IHT
>
> Apply the Settlement Rate to the value of relevant property at the date of the second 10-year anniversary
>
> IHT on the second 10-year anniversary is
> $$4.42\% \times £190,000 = £8,398$$
>
> Step 5:   Paying the IHT
>
> The trustees pay the IHT from the trust fund.

10.2.7   Capital gains tax

As in the case of interest in possession settlements, a deemed disposal by the trustees will occur on their exercise of a power of appointment whereby someone becomes 'absolutely entitled' to the settled property against the trustees.

10.2.7.1   Deemed disposals

Deemed disposals have been considered at **10.1.4.2** in relation to interest in possession settlements. The principles discussed apply equally to appointments by trustees from discretionary trusts in favour of individuals.

If the appointment by the trustees creates new trusts of which there are new trustees, these new trustees may become absolutely entitled to the settled property as against the 'old' trustees. If so, the old trustees will make a deemed disposal to the new trustees. However, if the property appointed remains subject to some of the original trusts and trust instrument, there will be no deemed disposal.

There is often a fine line between the two situations. This is considered further at **10.4**.

10.2.7.2   Reliefs, exemptions and rates

The rate of CGT for all trustees for disposals on or after 23 June 2010 is 28% of the net chargeable gains. An annual exemption of £5,050 is available to the trustees. Disposals in the earlier part of the tax year are taxed at 18%.

Hold-over relief will generally be available when assets leave a discretionary settlement (see **10.1.4**). The relief can be claimed, inter alia, if the occasion which gives rise to the disposal is also an occasion of immediate liability to IHT. The relief will be available even if the rate at which IHT is charged is at 0% – for example, because the transfer is within the nil rate band.

However, because s 65(4) of IHTA 1984 provides that there is no charge to IHT if assets leave the discretionary trust within three months after the date of creation, or three months after the date of any 10-year anniversary, hold-over relief is not available if the exit occurs during this time (unless the assets qualified as business assets under s 165 of TCGA 1992).

If the trustees and the beneficiaries agree to claim hold-over relief, it is convenient to add an appropriate clause to the deed of appointment containing their hold-over election. As a joint election of the beneficiaries and the trustees is required, they should all be made parties to the deed of appointment. If preferred, the election can be contained in a separate document.

> **Example**
>
> Trustees of a discretionary settlement appoint 5,000 DEF plc shares worth £20,000 to Johan in August 2010. The shares were worth £4,950 when they were acquired two years ago. There are no other disposals in the tax year.
>
> Disposal consideration£20,000
>
> *Less:* Acquisition cost £4,950
>
> Chargeable gain£15,050
>
> (a)   No hold-over relief election:
>
> Trustees pay tax on £15,050 – £5,050 (annual exemption) = £10,000 @ 28% = £2,800. Johan acquires the shares at a cost of £20,000.
>
> (b)   Hold-over relief election:
>
> There are two consequences:
>
> (i)   the trustees pay no CGT
>
> (ii)   Johan's acquisition cost is reduced
>
> | | |
> |---|---:|
> | Market value of shares at appointment | £20,000 |
> | *Less:* held-over gain | £15,050 |
> | Johan's acquisition cost | £4,950 |
>
> Johan does not benefit from the trustees' annual exemption.

Note that on the facts of the above example the trustees could make two separate disposals of shares. They can then have the benefit of the annual exemption on one disposal and claim holdover relief on the other.

10.2.8   Drafting a deed of appointment

It is good practice for trustees to make all appointments by deed even though an absolute appointment may be made less formally by the trustees making a memorandum note in their records. However, making the appointment by deed has the advantage of providing all the relevant details in a clear form which can be referred to easily in subsequent documents.

Heading and date

Sample clause

> DEED OF APPOINTMENT
> DATE: [   ]

Parties

There will be two parties to a deed if an absolute appointment is intended:

(a)   the appointors, sometimes defined as 'the trustees'; and

(b)   the beneficiary.

If an appointment on further trusts with the same trustees is to be made, the deed will normally be made by the appointors alone.

Sample clause

> BETWEEN
> (1)   [name and address] ('the Appointors')
> (2)   [name and address] ('the Beneficiary')

Recitals

The recitals should explain the circumstances surrounding the exercise of the power. They will be confined to a brief statement that the trustees intend to exercise their power of appointment under the settlement in the manner indicated in the operative part of the deed.

Sample clause

RECITALS

(A) This Deed is supplemental to the settlement ('the Settlement')

[and to the other documents and events] specified in the [First] Schedule.

(B) The Appointors are the present Trustees of the Settlement.

(C) [   ] is a member of the class of Beneficiaries.

(D) The Appointors wish to exercise their power of appointment under clause [   ] of the Settlement in the following manner.

The operative part

Sample clause

OPERATIVE PROVISIONS

1.   Definitions and construction

In this Deed:

1.1   'the Appointed Fund' shall mean [that part of] the Trust Fund [specified in the Second Schedule]; and subject thereto,

1.2   where the context admits, the definitions and rules of construction contained in the Settlement shall apply.

2. Appointment

The Appointors, in exercise of the power of appointment conferred by clause [ ] of the Settlement and of all other relevant powers, hereby [ir]revocably appoint and declare that the Appointed Fund shall henceforth be held upon trust for [   ] absolutely.

[3. Application of Settlement provisions

The trusts, powers and provisions contained in the Settlement shall continue to be applicable to the Appointed Fund so far as consistent with the provisions of this Deed.]

[4. Payment of tax and expenses

Any inheritance tax or capital gains tax and all other costs, expenses and other liabilities occasioned by the appointment contained in this Deed shall be borne by [the Appointed Fund] [the balance of the Trust Fund.]

5. Trustees' lien

Nothing in this Deed shall prejudice or impair in any way any lien or charge to which the Trustees are entitled in respect of any tax and other liabilities whatever for which they are or may become accountable.

[6. Capital gains tax hold-over relief

The parties claim relief under the provisions of s [165] [260] of the Taxation of Chargeable Gains Act 1992 in respect of the appointment contained in this Deed.]

[7. Power of revocation

The Trustees shall have power, at any time during the Trust Period, by deed or deeds wholly or partly to revoke the appointment contained in this Deed.]

Clause 3 will not be required if the appointment is both irrevocable and gives the beneficiary an absolute interest. If the appointment is onto trusts, clause 3 can be used to indicate that the powers under the original settlement are to apply to the Appointed Fund (where those powers are considered suitable). Clause 3 will also be required where the appointment is revocable. Clause 4 deals with the division of capital tax liability where part only of the trust fund is appointed. If the whole fund is appointed, it can be omitted.

Clause 6 is a claim by the parties for hold-over relief on the basis that the appointment is an occasion of charge to IHT (s 260). An equivalent claim could be made under TCGA 1992, s 165 if the assets appointed from the settlement were business assets. Hold-over relief is considered at **4.4.5.2** and see **10.1.4**. Clause 7 will not be required if, as is usual, the appointment is irrevocable.

Schedules

Schedules will give details of the settlement under which the appointment is made and of the trust fund (or part) which is being appointed.

10.3 Trusts for bereaved minors and bereaved young people

10.3.1 The nature of the trusts and the powers

These are settlements created on death for the deceased's own children. To qualify as a settlement for bereaved minors, children must become entitled to capital at or before 18; and to qualify as a settlement for bereaved young people, they must become entitled at or before 25. These settlements are considered in detail in **Chapter 12**.

As we will see, trustees are allowed only limited powers of appointment. They can have the statutory power of advancement under s 32 of TA 1925, or an express power in the same terms widened to allow trustees to advance up to the whole of a beneficiary's capital entitlement. There must be no possibility of using the power to appoint capital away from the deceased's children to others, eg the deceased's spouse, or the settlement will not qualify. However, the power of advancement can be used to settle property on further trusts provided it is for the benefit of the same beneficiary.

10.3.1.1 Inheritance tax

These settlements have IHT advantages when it comes to capital entitlement. An appointment from a relevant property settlement would give rise to an exit charge. If the trustees use the power of appointment to give a beneficiary capital at or before 18, there will be no exit charge. If the power is used to give a right to capital after 18, there will be a charge to IHT but only for the period from the beneficiary's 18th birthday.

Example

Trustees of a trust created on death by Sunita's will hold £100,000 for her two children, contingent on their reaching 25. The children are aged 6 and 4.

The trustees appoint £50,000 to one child on her 18th birthday. There is no charge to IHT. They appoint the remaining £50,000 to the other on her 21st birthday. There will be a charge to IHT for the three years that have elapsed since her 18th birthday.

10.3.1.2 Capital gains tax

A deemed disposal will occur when a beneficiary of either settlement becomes absolutely entitled to the trust property as against the trustees.

Deemed disposals

The principles discussed at **10.2.7.1** in relation to discretionary settlements apply equally to appointments by trustees from settlements for bereaved minors or bereaved young people.

Reliefs, exemptions and rate

The rate of tax is 28% of any net chargeable gain for disposals on or after 23 June 2010 and 18% for disposals in the first part of the tax year. An annual exemption of £5,050 is available to the trustees. Holdover relief is available under TCGA 1992, s 260 when beneficiaries of either type of trust become absolutely entitled as against the trustees. Relief is available under TCGA 1992, s 165 if the assets qualify as business assets (see **4.4.5.2**).

Example 1

Trustees of a trust for bereaved minors hold property for Rajid contingent on reaching 18. He does so in June 2010. The settlement ends and Rajid becomes absolutely entitled to the settled property. Any gain made by the trustees on the deemed disposal may be held over on an election being made by the trustees and Rajid.

Example 2

Trustees of a trust for bereaved young persons hold property for Amy contingent on reaching 25. In June 2010 the trustees appoint all the assets to Amy on her 21st birthday. The settlement ends and Amy becomes absolutely entitled to the settled property. Any gain made by the trustees on the deemed disposal may be held over on an election being made by the trustees and Amy.

10.4 Accumulation and maintenance settlements

10.4.1 The nature of the trusts and the powers

As we saw in **Chapter 8**, A & M settlements are a particular type of settlement without an interest in possession, created before 22 March 2006 and complying with the requirements of the amended s 71(1) of IHTA 1984. Beneficiaries must become entitled to capital at or before 18.

A power of appointment may be inserted in an A & M settlement. There must be no possibility of using the power to prevent beneficiaries becoming entitled to income or capital at age 18 or the settlement will not qualify as an A & M settlement.

10.4.1.1 Inheritance tax

An appointment from an A & M settlement to a beneficiary will not give rise to an exit charge. There are no anniversary charges.

10.4.1.2 Capital gains tax

A 'deemed' disposal will occur when a beneficiary of an A & M settlement becomes 'absolutely entitled' to the trust property against the trustees.

Deemed disposals

The principles discussed in **10.2.7.1** in relation to discretionary settlements apply equally to appointments by trustees from A & M settlements.

Reliefs, exemptions and rates

The rate of tax for A & M trustees is 28% or 18% of any net chargeable gain depending on whether the disposal is made before or on or after 23 June 2010. An annual exemption of £5,050 is available to the trustees.

Hold-over relief is available under TCGA 1992, s 260, or if the assets disposed of are business assets (TCGA 1992, s 165) – see **4.4.5.2**.

10.5 Resettlements

10.5.1 Absolute entitlement for CGT?

So far, this chapter has concentrated upon deemed disposals where an individual has become absolutely entitled to settled property against the trustees. Modern settlements are drafted in flexible form and usually include fiduciary powers for the trustees to 'declare new trusts' in relation to some or all of the settled property. The possibility of exercising a power either of advancement or appointment in this way is mentioned in **Chapter 9** (see **9.1**). Although the statutory power of advancement (TA 1925, s 32) is generally used to give an individual absolute entitlement to property freed from any continuing trusts, it has been held that the section may also be used to create trust advances, ie, to advance property in such a way that it is to be held in trust for a beneficiary, see *Pilkington and Another v Inland Revenue Commissioners and Others* [1964] AC 612 where a settled advance was for a beneficiary's 'benefit' within s 32 (see **9.4.2.3**).

The phrase 'absolutely entitled against the trustees' does not mean 'absolutely and beneficially entitled'. It is therefore possible that one set of trustees (whether they are the same people or not) may, following the exercise of a fiduciary power, become absolutely entitled against another set of trustees. However, this does not necessarily mean that there will be a separate settlement. If there is not, then the usual rule in TCGA 1992, s 69 that the trustees are a single and continuing body of persons will apply, ie, there will be no deemed disposal and so there can be no question of liability to CGT arising.

If trustees propose exercising their power to declare new trusts, they need to consider whether or not the exercise of the power will amount to a deemed disposal. This is an area of some uncertainty, although clarification was provided through the Inland Revenue Statement of Practice (SP 7/84) following the decision in *Bond (Inspector of Taxes) v Pickford* [1983] STC 517 (see **10.5.2** and **10.5.3**).

10.5.2 A separate settlement or not?

In *Roome and Another v Edwards (Inspector of Taxes)* [1982] AC 279, the leading case in this area, Lord Wilberforce suggested that the existence of separate trustees, trusts and trust property was not necessarily conclusive as to the existence of a separate settlement. In the following extracts from the judgment, he draws a distinction between a special power of appointment (its exercise being unlikely to create a separate settlement) and the exercise of a wider form power which is more likely to create a separate settlement because property may be removed from the original settlement and subjected to other trusts:

> ... trusts declared by a ... special power of appointment are to be read into the original settlement ... If such a power is exercised, whether or not separate trustees are appointed, I do not think that it would be natural ... to say that a separate settlement had been created, still less so if it were found that provisions of the original settlement continued to apply to the appointed fund, or that the appointed fund were liable, in certain events, to fall back into the rest of the settled property.

> If such a [wider form] power is exercised, the natural conclusion might be that a separate settlement was created, all the more so if a complete new set of trusts were declared as to the appropriated property, and if it would be said that the trusts of the original settlement ceased to apply to it. There can be many variations on these cases each of which will have to be judged on its facts.

In *Bond (Inspector of Taxes) v Pickford*, there were three relevant powers in the settlement whereby the trustees could:

(a)   pay or apply funds to or for the benefit of the beneficiaries;

(b)   allocate funds to beneficiaries either absolutely or contingently on attaining a specified age;

(c)   resettle funds for the benefit of the beneficiaries.

What was the effect of an allocation of funds for named beneficiaries on attaining 22 years of age under (b) above: did it create a separate settlement? The Court of Appeal held that a new settlement had not been created and in doing so distinguished between powers in the 'narrower form' and powers in the 'wider form'. The former do not permit property to be freed from the original settlement; the latter do permit this. It is not so much the description given to the power in the trust instrument which is significant, it is what it permits the trustees to do. The Court of Appeal held that the power in (b) above was a narrower form power in that it permitted a reorganisation internally within the original settlement and not the removal of funds from the settlement.

The manner of exercise of any given power is crucial. The mere fact that a wider form power may be exercised to free property from the original settlement does not necessarily mean it has been exercised in this way. It will be a matter of intention; the trustees may decide to exercise it in a narrower form way. If they wish to avoid a separate settlement, and the associated deemed disposal for CGT, they will exercise the power in a narrower way; the property will remain subject to the original trusts. See *Swires v Renton* [1991] STC 490.

10.5.3   Inland Revenue Statement of Practice (SP 7/84)

This Statement of Practice followed the Court of Appeal decision in *Bond (Inspector of Taxes) v Pickford* and contains the following:

> … the Board considers that a deemed disposal will not arise when … [powers in the wider form, which may be powers of advancement or certain powers of appointment, are] … exercised and trusts are declared in circumstances where:
>
> (a)   the appointment is revocable, or
>
> (b)   the trusts declared of the advanced or appointed funds are not exhaustive so that there exists a possibility at the time when the advancement or appointment is made that the funds covered by it will on the occasion of some event cease to be held upon such trusts and once again come to be held upon the original trusts of the settlement.
>
> Further, when such a power is exercised the Board considers it unlikely that a deemed disposal will arise when trusts are declared if duties in regard to the appointed assets still fall to the trustees of the original settlement in their capacity as trustees of that settlement … Finally, the Board accepts that a power of appointment or advancement can be exercised over only part of the settled property and that the above consequences would apply to that part.

By this Statement of Practice, the Revenue accepts that a new settlement can be created only if a wider form power is exercised. There are, however, limitations when a new settlement would not be created, ie, where the exercise is revocable, the trusts are not exhaustive in the sense that some of the property could again become subject to the original trusts and where the trustees of the original settlement have continuing duties in relation to the settled property.

10.5.4   Drafting the trustees' power of appointment

Powers of appointment given to trustees should be drafted as separate clauses in such a way as to make it abundantly clear whether they are wider form or narrower form powers. Trustees, having considered the effect of the exercise of their powers fully (including the CGT consequences) can then specifically exercise by deed a narrower or a wider form power. By so doing, difficulty of construction and effect for CGT of the deed of appointment should be avoided.

10.5.5   The CGT consequences of a separate settlement

If a separate settlement is created by the exercise of the power of appointment, the new trustees become absolutely entitled against the old (whether they are the same people or not) so that there is a deemed disposal for CGT. The calculation of the gain (or loss) follows normal principles (including the deduction for the trustees' annual exemption of £4,800). The trustees pay any tax due from the settled property.

If cash is appointed, no liability to CGT will arise. Otherwise, hold-over relief may be available to the trustees under TCGA 1992, s 165 or s 260 depending on the circumstances, but in this case, the annual exemption will not be available.

10.5.6   The documentation if a separate settlement

In addition to a deed of appointment drafted in the manner discussed earlier, the trustees of the old settlement will need to sign stock transfer forms to transfer the settled stocks and shares to the new trustees. If they are the same people, stock transfer forms will still be required but it may be sensible specifically to designate the transferees as trustees of the newly created settlement so as to avoid confusing the share certificates in their own names for the investments in the new settlement with those belonging to them as trustees of the original settlement.

10.5.7   Summary

Tax on exercise of powers of appointment and advancement.

Settlement	IHT	CGT
Qualifying interest in possession	PET (except to the extent the life tenant benefits)	Deemed disposal No hold-over relief (unless business assets)
Discretionary	Exit or periodic charge	Deemed disposal (if absolute entitlement) Hold-over relief available
Bereaved minors or young people	No exit or periodic charge	Deemed disposal (if absolute entitlement) Hold-over relief available
Accumulation and maintenance	No exit or periodic charge	Deemed disposal (if absolute entitlement) Hold-over relief available

Summary – Trust Advances and Appointments

Topic	Summary	Reference
Trust advances and appointments	Once a trust has been created, whether by lifetime transfer or on death, trustees may wish to allow beneficiaries to receive trust capital before they are entitled to it. This may be because of beneficiaries' needs, the wishes of the settlor, or to save tax. Trustees may have a statutory power (advancement) or an express power (appointment).	Chapter 9
Power of advancement	This statutory power (Trustee Act 1925, s 32) applies to all trusts, unless excluded. It allows trustees to pay or apply capital to or for a beneficiary who has a vested or contingent interest in the trust capital. It does not apply to beneficiaries who only have an interest in income, or to those who have only a hope of benefiting from a discretionary trust. The power permits outright advances of capital or advances on further trust. Any advance must be for the 'advancement or benefit' of the beneficiary and comply with other restrictions in s 32(1)(a)–(c). It is common for trusts to modify these restrictions.	
Power of appointment	Express powers allowing beneficiaries to have early access to trust capital are known as powers of appointment. Commonly, they are drafted very widely allowing trustees to appoint capital outright or on further trusts.	
The exercise of powers of advancement and appointment	It is usual for trustees to exercise their powers by deed. Before exercising their powers trustees should consider the tax consequences of appointing or advancing capital.	Chapter 10 10.2.8
Trusts with a qualifying interest in possession (IIP) [IIP trusts created before 22 March 2006, and IPDI trusts created on or after this date]	**IHT** *Capital appointed to the beneficiary with the qualifying IIP* – this person is treated as owning the underlying capital so there is no transfer of value on the appointment. *Capital appointed to other beneficiaries* – the beneficiary with the qualifying IIP makes a PET. **CGT** *Capital appointed to any beneficiary* – the appointment is a deemed disposal by the trustees. Holdover relief is only available if business assets are appointed (TCGA 1992, s 165).	

Topic	Summary	Reference
Relevant property trusts [discretionary trusts created on or before 22 March 2006 and lifetime trusts created on or after this date, other than trusts for disabled persons]	**IHT** There is a periodic or anniversary charge every 10 years from the date of creation of the trust. In addition, when capital is appointed to any beneficiary there is an exit charge. **CGT** When capital is appointed to any beneficiary there is a deemed disposal by the trustees. Holdover relief is available under TCGA 1992, s 260 because the transfer is immediately chargeable to IHT (and under s 165 if business assets are appointed).	See 10.2.4–10.2.6 for calculating these charges
Trusts with privileged treatment [trusts for bereaved minors, bereaved young people]	**IHT** There are no periodic charges. There are no exit charges if an appointment is made on or before the beneficiary reaches 18, but a modified exit charge if the appointment is made after this. **CGT** When capital is appointed to any beneficiary there is a deemed disposal by the trustees. Holdover relief is available under TCGA 1992, s 260 because of the nature of the trust (and under s 165 if business assets are appointed).	
Beneficiaries ending a trust	Any trust may also be brought to an end and the capital distributed at the request of the beneficiaries under the rule in *Saunders v Vautier*. The rule requires that the beneficiaries must be adult, of full capacity, and together entitled to the whole beneficial interest. The tax consequences of the trust ending in this way are similar to those where capital is appointed or advanced under the trustees' powers.	

Chapter 11
Basic Will Drafting

This chapter deals with the basic content of a will, and the typical provisions likely to appear in all types of will. The next chapter deals with the special provisions required for the creation of different types of trust within a will. For further exploration of the subject, refer to practitioners' books such as Withers, *Practical Will Precedents* (Sweet & Maxwell), *Williams on Wills, Wills Probate and Administration* (Butterworths).

It is important to be aware that, since the House of Lords' decision in *White v Jones* [1995] 1 All ER 691, will drafting is the fastest growing area for negligence claims against solicitors. Many firms prohibit anyone who is not a specialist from attempting it.

11.1 Preliminary matters

A solicitor taking instructions for a will should be aware of the need for the testator to have the requisite capacity and intention. This is considered in LPC Guide, *Legal Foundations*.

The solicitor should also be aware of the tax consequences of the testator's instructions, and be able to advise on tax savings where possible. Inheritance tax on death is considered in LPC Guide, *Legal Foundations*, para 4.3, and general tax planning is considered in **Chapter 4** above.

The solicitor should also be aware of relevant issues of professional conduct. For example, instructions must be taken from the client and not from an intermediary. The solicitor must not draft a will giving a significant amount to him/herself, a partner or member of the solicitor's family unless the client has obtained independent advice.

The Civil Partnership Act (CPA) 2004 came into effect on 5 December 2005. It has important implications for will drafting. The CPA 2004 allows same sex couples who are not closely related to each other to register a civil partnership.

Persons who have registered a civil partnership are, in effect, treated as spouses for the purposes of succession to property. Basically the provisions of the Married Women's Property Act 1882, s 11 and enactments relating to wills and administration of estates, and the Inheritance (Provision for Family and Dependants) Act 1975 are amended to apply in relation to civil partnerships as they do to marriages.

The main provisions relating to wills and administration that are amended are:

(a) revocation by marriage/civil partnership unless a will is made in expectation of marriage or civil partnership;

(b) gift in will to former spouse/civil partner treated as lapsed where divorce/dissolution of civil partnership occurs;

(c) gifts attested by spouse/civil partner are void;

(d) entitlement on intestacy including rights to take 'matrimonial home' in or toward satisfaction of absolute entitlement on intestacy; and

(e)   civil partners have same rights as spouses to make applications under the Inheritance (Provision for Family and Dependants) Act 1975.

11.2   Basic content of a will

All wills should contain the following:

(a)   opening words or commencement;

(b)   revocation clause;

(c)   date;

(d)   appointment of executors;

(e)   legacies and/or gift of residue;

(f)   attestation clause.

Although these provisions may be sufficient for a very simple will, most wills require additional provisions. For example, if any of the legacies is to a charity, it is desirable to make provision for the possibility that the charity may amalgamate or cease to exist. If any of the legacies give rise to a continuing trust, it may be necessary to supply express trust administration powers for the trustees.

11.2.1   Opening words or commencement

The main purpose of this clause is to identify the testator and the nature of the document.

The full name and address of the testator should be stated. If the testator holds property in any other name, it will be helpful when the application for the grant of representation is later made if the will also states this other name and indicates that the testator is also known by it. Details of the testator's occupation may also be included as further identification.

A statement that the document is the 'last will' or 'last will and testament' (there is no legal difference between these phrases) should be included. This helps demonstrate that the testator had an intention to make a will, which is a legal requirement.

The date may appear within the commencement or at the end of the will. A space should be left as the will is dated on execution.

If the testator intends to marry in the near future, he should state that the will is made in expectation of that marriage and that he does not wish the marriage to revoke the will. In the absence of such a statement the will is automatically revoked by subsequent marriage. Formation of a civil partnership has the same effect.

11.2.2   Revocation clause

The purpose of this clause is to indicate that all earlier wills and codicils are expressly revoked. Any later will impliedly revokes earlier wills and codicils, but only to the extent that the later will is inconsistent with the earlier provisions. An express revocation avoids the risk of an earlier will or codicil not being wholly revoked by the implied revocation.

The revocation clause may appear by itself, but it is also commonly incorporated into the commencement. It should appear near the beginning of the will.

11.2.3   Appointment of executors (and trustees)

The purpose of this clause is to appoint the persons that the testator has chosen to administer his estate (the executor(s)). If the testator does not take the opportunity to name his own choice, the Non-contentious Probate Rules 1987 (SI 1987/2024) will govern who may act as administrator (see LPC Guide, *Legal Foundations*).

It is sometimes sensible to create an express trust of the estate (see below for where this is the case). Where this happens, the testator should appoint persons to be trustees. It is often convenient to name the same people as both executors and trustees, although it is not essential. Such people will act as executors while they collect in the estate, pay debts and distribute the estate. When they have completed that stage, they will transfer the property that is to be held on trust to themselves to hold in the new capacity of trustee.

11.2.3.1 How many executors?

In principle there is no maximum number of executors that can be named in the will. However, as only a maximum of four can apply for the grant of probate to the same assets, there is little point in naming more than four.

It is possible to limit the appointment of executors to particular parts of the estate. For example, a testator may appoint specialists to deal with his business assets or literary effects and members of his family to deal with his general assets. In such a case each appointment can be of up to four people.

The minimum number is one, and this will often be sufficient for a small, simple estate where the executor is the sole or main beneficiary. (A sole executor can give a good receipt for the proceeds of sale of land held in the estate.) However, there is a risk that the sole executor may pre-decease the testator or be unable to act for some other reason. For example, the effect of a divorce on a will is that the spouse is deemed to have died at the date of the divorce, so that any appointment of the spouse as executor will not take effect (Wills Act 1837, s 18A). The dissolution of a civil partnership has the same effect. It is therefore prudent to appoint at least two persons, or name a substitute for a sole executor.

If the executors will also be trustees, it is sensible to appoint at least two so that they can give a good receipt for the proceeds of sale of any land held in the trust.

11.2.3.2 Whom to choose?

The testator may appoint any combination of:

(a)   individuals who are not professionals (eg, family or friends);

(b)   solicitors or other professionals (as individuals or as a firm);

(c)   banks or other trust corporations.

A testator may ask for advice on the type of person he should appoint and the solicitor should therefore be able to discuss the relevant considerations allowing the testator to make an informed choice.

11.2.3.3 Non-professional individuals

Choosing family members or close friends whom the testator can trust will have the advantage of ensuring that persons familiar with the testator and his affairs will deal with the estate. A further advantage is that such persons are unlikely to want to charge the estate for their time spent in dealing with it. However, this advantage may be more apparent than real. If the estate is other than straightforward, it is likely that the individuals will lack the expertise necessary to complete the administration and will have to employ a solicitor. The costs of this will be paid from the estate.

Naturally the testator should only choose those responsible enough to deal with the estate, and should not appoint anyone barred from taking out a grant of probate (such as a minor or a convicted criminal).

11.2.3.4   Solicitors or other professionals

Choosing a solicitor or other professional will mean that the executor will have the necessary expertise to administer the estate. Family and friends will be spared the burden at a time when they may be grieving. However, the professional executor will expect to be paid not just for expenses incurred but also for the time spent doing the work.

An individual solicitor may be appointed, but there is a risk that this person may die or retire. To avoid this possibility the firm of solicitors can be appointed.

If the testator decides to appoint a firm of solicitors there are some drafting considerations:

(a)   The firm, being a partnership, has no legal identity and so cannot be appointed. Instead the appointment is of the partners in the named firm. As these will change from time to time it is important to specify that it is the partners in the firm at the date of death who are appointed. Otherwise the appointment will be of those at the date of the will. It is usual to express the wish that only two partners will take the grant and act in the administration.

(b)   The firm may change its name, amalgamate or become a limited liability partnership (LLP) between the date of the will and the date of death, and it is sensible to provide for this. Usually the testator will indicate that the appointment is of the partners in the new or amalgamated firm. To allow for a firm becoming a LLP there should be a reference to the solicitors who are the directors or members of, or beneficial owners of shares in, a firm that has become a LLP.

Many wills were drafted before it became possible for a firm to become a LLP, and so the clause appointing the partners in a firm merely refers to the substitution of *partners* in any new or amalgamated *firm*. For a while Probate Registrars took the view that such clauses did not provide for the appointment of solicitors in a LLP, which was a different legal entity. This approach was tested in the case of *Re Rogers (Deceased)* [2006] EWHC 753, where it was held that Probate Registrars should recognise members of an LLP as successors to the original firm, thus saving the need for existing wills to be re-drafted when a firm became a LLP. The judge emphasised that in any firm it is only the profit-sharing partners (as opposed to the salaried partners) who are true partners, although a testator is free to choose a salaried partner to act as an executor if he wishes. Firms where salaried partners are in the habit of taking grants of probate may widen the meaning of 'partner' by including a statement that 'in this will "partner" includes a salaried partner'.

Banks or other trust corporations

A testator may consider appointing a bank as executor. Most high street banks have a trustee department, and it is able to act via the mechanism of a trust corporation. Appointing this type of executor has some similar advantages to appointing a firm of solicitors: the corporation will not die or retire, and there should be financial and some legal expertise. Disadvantages include the fact that the corporation may seem large and impersonal to the family. The charging methods of banks may also be disadvantageous, as they usually charge a percentage of the value of the estate, which can be a significant expense.

11.2.3.5   Charging provisions

Whether an individual professional or a firm is appointed, there will be a need to consider the charging arrangements. An executor or trustee is a fiduciary and unable to profit from his position, unless authorised. The Trustee Act (TA) 2000, s 29 allows the payment of reasonable remuneration to a trustee for time spent and work done (even if such work could have been done by a lay person), but only if the trustee is either:

(a)   a trust corporation; or

(b)   a trustee 'acting in a professional capacity', but who is not a sole trustee and who has got the written consent of all his co-trustees.

'Acting in a professional capacity' means acting in the course of a profession or business which involves providing relevant services to trusts.

Trustees may only charge for services carried out after 1 February 2001, although the provision applies to all trusts unless excluded.

An express charging provision will always be required to allow any trustee who does not fall within s 29 to charge for time spent and work done. It may also be desirable to include express provisions allowing:

(a)   a trust corporation to be paid in accordance with its standard terms and conditions; and/or

(b)   a trustee to retain remuneration he has received for services given as a director of a company in which the trust holds shares.

It is usual in any express charging clause to state that the solicitor or other professional may charge for work done, even though it could have been done by a non-professional. Again, although the TA 2000 now provides for this, it is better to have clear express drafting within the will.

Where an express charging provision is included it may appear early on together with the clause appointing the executors, or later among the administrative provisions. It does not matter which approach is used.

Until the TA 2000 came into force, a charging clause was treated as a legacy in the will. Under s 15 of the Wills Act 1837, a beneficiary loses his benefit if he or his spouse (or civil partner) witnesses the will. Therefore, in the past if a will had a charging clause, it could not be witnessed by the individual solicitor appointed or any of the partners in the firm appointed, or any spouses or civil partners. The TA 2000 now provides that a charging clause does not qualify as a legacy for these purposes. (However, the TA 2000 only operates for this purpose on wills where death occurred after 1 February 2001.)

11.2.4   Non-residuary gifts

A testator may wish to make gifts of specific assets or of money. Traditionally a legacy is a gift of personalty and a devise is a gift of land. The term 'gift' applies to either. There are various types of gift.

11.2.4.1   Specific gifts

This is a gift of a specific item or items or specific piece of land which the testator owns, for example, 'I give my diamond engagement ring to my daughter'. If the testator does not own the specific item or property at death, the gift fails ('adeems'). The beneficiary gets nothing in place of the gifted item unless the will expressly provides for substitution.

11.2.4.2   General gifts

This is a gift of an item corresponding to a description. If the testator does not own this item at death, it must be obtained using funds from the estate, for example, 'I give 100 shares in Z plc to my son'. If the testator does not own 100 such shares then they must be purchased.

11.2.4.3   Demonstrative gift

This is a gift that is general in nature but is directed to be paid from a specific fund, for example, 'I give £500 to X to be paid from my Nationwide savings account'. If the account exists at the date of the death and contains £500 or more, the legacy is paid from the account and is classified as specific. If there is no account (or if it contains less than £500), the legacy is paid, in whole (or in part), from the rest of the estate and to that extent is classified as general.

11.2.4.4   Pecuniary gift

This is a gift of money. This gift will usually be general, but could be demonstrative, or possibly even specific, for example, 'I give the £100 held in the safe in the study'.

Note: Where there are insufficient assets in an estate to pay all debts and expenses and pay the legacies in full, legacies will be reduced ('abate') proportionally. General legacies will be reduced first, and only if they are insufficient will specific legacies be taken.

Where a testator wishes to include non-residuary gifts, there are a number of matters to consider and upon which instructions should be obtained.

11.2.4.5   The beneficiary

Identification

This person must be clearly identified in the will, otherwise the gift will fail for uncertainty. Accurately stating the name and address is important, and including the relationship to the testator will also help. Where the gift is to a person, rather than a group, it is unwise only to describe that person by relationship, for example, to 'my nephew', because there may be more than one person answering that description. A gift to 'my nephews', though, will not suffer this problem.

Where the identity of the person who fits the description changes, it is the person who fits that description at the date of the will who is construed as the beneficiary. For example, a gift to 'my son's wife' will mean his wife at the date of the will, even if by the date of death he is married to someone else.

For the meaning of 'children' and 'grandchildren', see **6.6.3.3**.

The Gender Recognition Act 2004

The Gender Recognition Act 2004 came into force on 4 April 2005. It provides transsexuals who have obtained a full gender recognition certificate with legal recognition in their acquired gender.

The effect of legal recognition is that, for example, a male-to-female transsexual person will be legally recognised as a woman in English law for all purposes (s 9(1)). However, s 15 provides that a change of gender does not affect the distribution of property under a will or other instrument made before the day on which the Act came into force. For wills or other instruments made after that day, the general principle stated in s 9(1) will apply.

For example, if a will made after the Act came into force refers to the 'eldest daughter', and a person who was previously a son becomes the 'eldest daughter' following recognition in the acquired gender, that person (subject to s 18) will inherit as the 'eldest daughter'.

Neither the Act nor the explanatory notes which accompany it give any guidance on how to construe a gift 'to my son, John' where John becomes Joanna after the will is made. It may be advisable to direct that the will is to be construed without reference to any certificates issued under the Act and as referring to persons who fulfilled a particular description at the date the will was made.

Under s 18 the court has power to make orders to deal with the situation where the devolution of property under a will or other instrument is different from what it would be but for the change of gender.

If, for example, a will left property to 'eldest daughter' of X, and there is an older brother whose gender becomes female under the Act, then the person who was previously the 'eldest daughter' may cease to enjoy that position. A person who is adversely affected by the different gender can apply to the court.

The court, if it is satisfied that it is just to do so, may make such order as it considers appropriate in relation to the person benefiting from the different disposition of the property.

Vested or contingent?

Where the testator wishes to benefit persons who may be minors, or relatively young, he should consider whether he wishes to make outright or contingent gifts.

A vested gift imposes no conditions, and the beneficiary will be immediately entitled to it merely by outliving the testator. For example, 'I give £10,000 to my grandson, Oliver'. If the beneficiary is under 18 then he will be unable to give a good receipt to the executors (unless the will permits it) and there will be a trust of the gift until he is 18. Here, therefore, if Oliver were over 18 at his grandfather's death he would receive his gift straight away. If he were under 18, he would receive his gift as soon as he became 18. If he were to die under age 18, the money would form part of his estate.

A contingent gift imposes conditions to be satisfied before the gift can vest. The most common contingency is to require the beneficiary to reach a certain age, for example, 'I give £10,000 to my grandson, Oliver, provided he reaches the age of 25'. Only if Oliver reaches 25 will he be entitled to the £10,000. If he is under 25 when his grandfather dies, the money will be held on trust until he reaches 25. If he were to die under age 25 his estate will not be entitled to the cash, which will instead pass to the person(s) expressed to be entitled in default or, if none, with the residue of his grandfather's estate.

The testator must decide how he will make the gift and, if contingent, the nature of the contingency. For further discussion of this topic see **12.6**.

Lapse

A beneficiary who predeceases the testator is not able to take a legacy. The legacy will normally fail or 'lapse' and will pass with residue unless the will provides for a substitute beneficiary.

The Wills Act 1837, s 33 provides a limited exception to the doctrine of lapse. It provides that where a gift to the testator's child or remoter descendent fails because that person predeceases the testator, but he or she leaves issue living at the testator's death, then those issue will take the gift.

Examples of effect of Wills Act 1837, s 33

Fred leaves his estate to 'such of my children who survive me'.

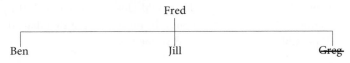

Ben and Jill survive Fred. Greg predeceases him. If Greg has no issue alive at Fred's death, the estate will be split equally between Ben and Jill. However, if Greg has issue who survive Fred, the one-third share which he would have taken will be divided among his issue.

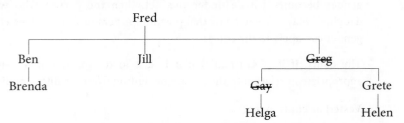

Nobody can take an interest under s 33 if he has a parent alive.

Brenda takes nothing because her father is alive. Greg's one-third share is divided into two. Helga takes the one-sixth her mother, Gay, would have taken. Grete takes the other one-sixth. Helen takes nothing as her mother, Grete, is still alive.

The section can be excluded by contrary intention expressed in the will. It is usual to include an express substitution provision rather than to rely on the implied provisions.

Burden of tax and debts charged on assets

It is important to consider where the burden of any tax or other costs associated with the gift may fall. Where the will is silent the statutory order contained in the Administration of Estates Act 1925 (AEA 1925) applies. Usually this means that tax is paid from the residue, and any debts charged on specific assets will be paid from that asset. It is important to vary this expressly if the testator does not want this to happen, and even where he does it is usual to state matters expressly.

The most common concern is usually whether the IHT attributable to the gift should be borne by the residue (in which case the gift should be stated to be 'free of tax') or by the beneficiary of the gift (in which case the gift should be stated to be 'subject to tax'). The testator should be made aware of the consequences of the different wording. In particular, in certain circumstances, it can make a difference to the overall amount of tax payable on the estate. This is the case where a partially exempt transfer occurs (see **11.3**).

11.2.5   Drafting considerations for certain types of beneficiary

11.2.5.1   Gifts to a class of beneficiary

Where the testator does not name his beneficiary but makes a gift to a class which could continue to grow after his death, it is sensible to impose a closing date for entry to the class. For example, a gift of '£20,000 to my nephews and nieces' would include those alive at the death of the testator and those later born, which would make the gift very inconvenient to administer. A sensible closing date would be the death of the testator, for example, 'to my nephews and nieces alive at my death'. However, if the will is silent there are a number of class closing rules which may apply to close the class at an artificially early date. In the example just given, the class closing rules would close the class at death provided there was at least one member; if there was no nephew or niece living at that date, the class would remain open until all possible members were ascertained.

11.2.5.2   Gifts to charitable bodies

It is important to identify accurately the charitable body. To avoid argument later the solicitor should include the address and registered charity number of the body for identification.

A further issue to consider is how the executors will obtain a receipt from the charity for the gift. Without express provision stating otherwise, all members of an unincorporated association would have to sign a receipt. To avoid this, it is normal to authorise the executors to accept the receipt of an authorised officer of the charity. The clause should provide that the receipt of the person who appears to be the treasurer or other proper officer of the organisation will be sufficient. This avoids the need for the executors to check the constitution of the body to establish the identity of the proper officers.

A further problem to consider is that the charitable body may dissolve, amalgamate or change its objects before the date of death. It is useful to state that the gift is to the body 'for its general charitable purposes'. This may help establish that the gift has not failed, because those purposes can continue to be performed by another organisation, or help establish that the testator had general charitable intention and so allow the gift to be applied cy-près to a similar charity. A further option is to provide in the will that the executors may choose a similar charity to pay to, if the original recipient charity has ceased to exist.

11.2.5.3 Will for spouse and children

We saw at **4.5.3.3** that, until the introduction of the transferable nil rate band between spouses and civil partners, it was efficient from an IHT perspective for the first spouse to die to leave assets up to the limit of the available nil rate band to his children and the balance to the spouse.

Many spouses will now choose to leave everything to the other either absolutely or on a terminable life interest (see **12.7** for discussion of terminable life interests). However, some may be uncertain about the wisdom of passing everything to the spouse and may prefer the flexibility of a nil rate band legacy.

The difficulty is how best to draft such a legacy. It is not possible to word the legacy as a gift of a fixed amount for two reasons: first, the testator will not know what the level of the nil rate band will be at death; and, secondly, the testator may not have a full nil rate band available at death, for example because he made transfers after the date of the will which have become chargeable.

It is therefore necessary to word the legacy as a gift of 'the maximum amount that can pass on the testator's death without attracting inheritance tax'.

Some clauses set out expressly all the things that will have to be taken into account when calculating the amount payable. These are:

(a)   lifetime chargeable transfers;

(b)   property passing on death to non-exempt beneficiaries under the will, the intestacy rules or by survivorship;

(c)   settled property passing to a non-exempt beneficiary where the deceased was treated as beneficially entitled to the underlying trust assets;

(d)   property given to a non-exempt beneficiary during the deceased's life but included in the deceased's estate under the reservation of benefit rules.

However, it is not necessary to list these things expressly. It is sufficient to state that the amount payable is equal to what is left of the testator's nil rate band at the date of death.

> **Example**
>
> Freda makes a will giving her goddaughter jewellery worth £10,000, her sons a legacy equal to the greatest amount that can pass without attracting IHT, and the residue to her husband. She dies in 2010/11 when the nil rate band is £325,000. Her estate is £1m.
>
> Freda always gave £1,500 to each of her two sons on 6 April to make use of her annual exemption, but two years before her death she also gave her grandson £45,000. She owned a holiday cottage as beneficial joint tenant with her sons. Her share is valued at £80,000.
>
> The legacy to her sons will be calculated as follows:

	£
Nil rate band at date of death	325,000
Less	
Lifetime chargeable transfer	(45,000)
Property passing by will to goddaughter	(10,000)
Property passing by survivorship	(80,000)
	190,000

The maximum amount that can pass to the sons without attracting IHT is £190,000, so that is the amount they will take under the legacy.

Testators whose main concern is to provide adequately for their spouse (or civil partner) need to think carefully before leaving assets away from the spouse. A reduction in the size of residue is particularly significant at present due to the low interest rates available. A surviving spouse may find it difficult to manage on what is left after the deduction of a nil rate band legacy.

Another matter that may concern testators is that the nil rate band may increase to such an extent that too little of the estate will be left to make adequate provision for the surviving spouse. It is possible to include a maximum limit on the amount payable to the non-exempt beneficiaries under the legacy.

Clients should always consider whether they would be happy with the distribution of their property in the event of a substantial increase in the size of the nil rate band. One of the policies proposed by the Conservative Party at its Conference in October 2007 was the introduction of a nil rate band of £1m for everyone. The introduction of the transferable nil rate band in October 2007 has increased the amount passing under nil rate band legacies and, therefore, caused decreases in the amount received by spouses, civil partners and charities.

Example

Edith made a will in June 2007 leaving the largest amount she could pass without payment of IHT to her godson and the balance of her estate to her favourite charity. At that time the nil rate band was £300,000. She died in November 2010 with the benefit of a nil rate band transferred from her husband who had died some years earlier leaving everything to Edith. Her estate was £1m. The godson receives £650,000 and the charity £350,000. This may or may not be what Edith would have wanted.

Rather than giving an outright legacy to the children, it is common for testators to leave the nil rate sum on discretionary trusts for issue and spouse. See **12.6.1.1**.

11.2.6   The subject matter of the gift

It is essential that the property which is the subject matter of the gift is clearly identified. This is particularly important for non-pecuniary gifts. There are several important drafting considerations for specific gifts.

11.2.6.1   Ademption

A general problem is ademption. This is the failure of the gift because the specific item described no longer exists within the testator's estate at death. A testator should be alerted to the fact that this could happen. For example, a gift of 'my gold and ruby necklace' could fail because during the testator's lifetime the testator gives it to someone else, sells it or loses it in a fire or burglary. This is the case even if the testator has bought another similar necklace to replace it. This is because the 'my' indicates that the testator is referring to the specific item in his possession at the date of the will and not to whatever item matching that description he happens to own at death. If the testator wants the beneficiary to have a substitute benefit if the original gift adeems, the will should provide for a replacement or substitute.

11.2.6.2   Burden of costs

There may be costs associated with the packing or transport of the specific gift. Unless the will provides otherwise the beneficiary will bear these costs. The testator should consider if these costs will be too great for the beneficiary and if so provide that the gift is free of these costs. As a result they will be paid from the residue of the estate.

11.2.6.3   Gift involving selection

The testator may leave a gift to several people inviting them to select an item from the estate. To prevent argument, the testator should indicate the order of choosing or provide for a means of resolving any dispute. It is normal to provide that the decision of the executors will be final. It is also wise to require the selection to be done within a time-limit to avoid delays in the administration.

11.2.6.4   Gifts of specific company shares

These are especially susceptible to ademption, not just because the owner may buy and sell shares on a regular basis, but also because the company may be renamed or taken over, and the will should provide for this. Shares may also be subject to a charge secured on them. The rule is that the beneficiary will take subject to this charge unless the will provides otherwise.

11.2.6.5   Gift of specific land

Again this type of gift is susceptible to ademption. A gift of the testator's main residence at death will avoid some problems but will not provide for situations where the testator owns no land at all, for example because the testator has gone into residential accommodation. A house or flat is also likely to be subject to a mortgage. As with gifts of shares it is necessary to expressly provide for a gift to be free of mortgage if the testator does not want the beneficiary to pay the mortgage, or to leave the benefit of any mortgage insurance policy to the beneficiary too.

11.2.7   Gift of the residue

It is important that the will contains a gift of the residue and that care is taken to ensure that it does not fail, as the result would be a partial intestacy.

11.2.7.1   Is a trust required?

Where the testator wishes to leave the residue on trust of some kind (for example, a life interest trust) then clearly there will be a trust expressly declared in the will. However, a trust may arise in less obvious circumstances. Where any of the beneficiaries is under 18 years at the death of the testator and the testator does not want the minor's parent or guardian to give a receipt on his behalf, there will need to be a trust of that person's entitlement until he reaches 18 and can give a good receipt. Where there is a possibility that this could occur (and even if all the primary beneficiaries are adults there may be a possibility of a substitution being made) it would be preferable to declare a trust expressly in the will and so control the terms and trustees.

It is also desirable to declare a trust where contingent gifts are made, so that property can be properly dealt with until the contingency is satisfied (or fails).

Where the residue is passing outright to adult (or charitable) beneficiaries, there is no need for an express trust. However, it is not unusual to create a trust of the residue in these circumstances as it does no harm.

Whether or not the residue is left on express trust, there should be an express direction for the payment of all debts, expenses and legacies to be made from the residue before it is distributed to the beneficiaries. In the absence of such a direction, the statutory order set out in the AEA 1925 will apply, and this can lead to problems.

11.2.7.2 Avoiding partial intestacy

If a gift of residue fails, the property will pass under the intestacy rules. The testator may be happy with this, but it is preferable to include substitutional gifts to cover the possibility of the primary gift failing. For example, where the residue is left to the testator's niece, there could be an express substitution of children of the niece. It is also worth considering a 'longstop' beneficiary to inherit if all the intended arrangements fail. Although this could be another person, it is also worth considering charitable bodies as there is little possibility of such a gift failing. The testator may prefer to benefit a favourite charity in preference to distant relatives or the Crown as *bona vacantia*.

A gift of the residue to more than one person also raises some drafting issues. For example, assume that the testator has three children, A, B and C and wishes to leave them an equal share. He could leave one-third to each named child. This carries risks. He may have more children before he dies who will be excluded. Also any or all of the children may predecease him. If this were to happen, Wills Act 1837, s 33 would provide for the failed one-third share to pass to any child of the dead child; but if there were none, the failed one-third share would pass on intestacy.

Therefore, it is wiser to omit names and specific shares in the residue, and refer only to any children the testator may have at the date of death. Using the phrase 'for such of my children as survive me and if more than one in equal shares' will ensure that there will be a partial intestacy only if all children predecease the testator. The testator will normally want to provide that the share of a child who predeceases should pass to his or her own children, if any.

The testator may desire to establish a trust rather than make an outright gift of the residue. Various types of trust that can be useful in a will are considered in **Chapter 12**.

11.2.8 Directions and declarations

It is common to include declarations of the testator's wishes. Examples of such declarations are set out below.

11.2.8.1 Survivorship

Unless a will states otherwise, a beneficiary only has to be alive at the death of the testator to acquire a vested interest. This may have an unfortunate effect where the beneficiary dies a very short time after the testator. This can happen where, for example, members of the same family are involved in a common accident.

The testator's property will pass in accordance with the will or intestacy provisions of the deceased beneficiary, which may mean passing to a person the testator would not want to inherit.

Example

Thelma leaves property to her married son. She dies and he dies a week after her. He leaves everything to his wife. Thelma might well have preferred her assets to pass to beneficiaries of her own choice rather than to her son's wife.

There will also be the burden and expense of the property being part of the administration of two different estates. Lastly, there may be adverse IHT consequences. For example, suppose Mildred leaves her estate of £300,000 to her divorced daughter, Diana, who has £300,000 of her own assets. Diana dies a week after Mildred, leaving everything to her son, Sam. Both Mildred and Diana have full nil rate bands available but do not have the benefit of any transferable nil rate band. Diana's estate now includes her mother's property and so IHT will be payable on the amount which exceeds Diana's nil rate band. Had Mildred left her estate directly to Sam, no IHT would have been payable as both estates would have been within the nil rate band.

To avoid unnecessary IHT and give the testator more control over the destination of his property, a survivorship clause may be used. This usually directs that the beneficiary must survive the testator by a minimum period of time. The time usually chosen is about a month, stated either as a calendar month, or as a period of 28 or 30 days. Using a longer period may lead to delays in the administration of the estate. The period should not exceed six months or the gift will be treated as creating a settlement without an interest in possession.

The testator may declare that a general survivorship period is to apply to all gifts in the will, or only to certain of the gifts.

There is one situation where including a survivorship clause can increase the amount of IHT payable. This is where spouses (or civil partners) die in quick succession and the assets of the first spouse or civil partner exceed the nil rate band while the survivor's do not.

Example

Harry and Wanda are married. Harry has assets worth £425,000. In tax year 2010/11 Harry dies with an estate of £425,000 and a full nil rate band. One week later his wife, Wanda, dies with assets of £200,000 and a full nil rate band.

(1)   *If Harry includes a survivorship clause*

Harry leaves his estate to Wanda but includes a survivorship clause giving the property to their children if Wanda fails to survive by 28 days. Harry's estate, therefore, passes directly to the children and IHT will be payable on £100,000. Wanda's estate passes to the children without any IHT as her estate falls within the nil rate band.

(2)   *If Harry does not include a survivorship clause*

Harry leaves his estate to Wanda absolutely. No IHT is payable on his death as the spouse exemption applies. Wanda has the benefit of the transferable nil rate band so the combined estates of £525,000 will fall within her enhanced nil rate band.

There is administrative inconvenience in passing assets from one estate to another and no way of knowing which spouse or civil partner will die first, so it may be more satisfactory to redistribute family assets so that each spouse or civil partner has sufficient to take advantage of a full nil rate band.

11.2.8.2   Directions concerning the body

Some testators wish to include directions concerning how their body is to be disposed of, for example cremation, woodland burial or donation for medical research. The testator should be aware that such directions have no legal effect. The testator must ensure that his close family and friends are aware of his wishes, and, where he wishes to donate organs, carry an organ donor card.

11.2.9   Administrative provisions

Personal representatives (PRs) and trustees have a number of statutory administration powers. The AEA 1925 gives certain powers to PRs, and the TA 1925 and TA 2000 give powers to both trustees and PRs. However, it is usual to extend or modify some of these statutory powers where they are not regarded as sufficient. Even where the statutory powers are adequate, it is common to put in an express provision on the basis that it makes the will easier to construe.

A will which might give rise to a trust (for example, because there is a substitutional gift to children of a primary beneficiary who predeceases the testator) will benefit from the inclusion of extensive express administrative provisions. However, even a simple will leaving everything to adults or to a charity will benefit from some express provisions.

We have divided the administrative provisions below into those that should be considered for inclusion in any will irrespective of whether or not it might give rise to a trust, and those which should be considered only if a trust might arise.

11.2.9.1 Administrative provisions to consider in relation to all wills

Power to charge

We have already dealt with this at **11.2.3.6**. If the testator wishes to give the executors (and trustees) power to charge, the power can either be included as part of the appointment clause or with the other administrative provisions. When drafting such a clause it is important to be clear whether a person engaged in *any* profession or business can charge for time spent on the administration (for example, a brain surgeon) or whether *only* a person whose profession involves administering estates and trusts can charge (for example, a solicitor or accountant).

Power for trust professional to charge

> Any Trustee who acts in a professional capacity may charge reasonable remuneration for any services provided to the trust.
>
> For this purpose a Trustee acts in a professional capacity if he acts in the course of a profession or business which consists of or includes the provision of services in connection with the administration or management of trusts.

Power for any business person to charge

> Any Trustee who is engaged in a profession or business may charge reasonable remuneration for any services provided to the trust.

Extended power to appropriate assets without consent of legatee

The AEA 1925, s 41 gives PRs the power to appropriate any part of the estate in or towards satisfaction of any legacy or any interest in residue provided that the appropriation does not prejudice any specific beneficiary. Thus, if the will gives a pecuniary legacy to a beneficiary, the PRs may allow that beneficiary to take chattels or other assets in the estate up to the value of his legacy, provided that these assets have not been specifically bequeathed by the will. The section provides that the legatee (or his parent or guardian if he is a minor) must consent to the appropriation.

It is common to remove the need for the legatee's consent.

Express amendment

Specimen clause

> Power to exercise the power of appropriation conferred by section 41 of the Administration of Estates Act 1925 without obtaining any of the consents required by that section.

This provision is commonly included in order to relieve the PRs of the duty to obtain formal consent. Nevertheless, the PRs would informally consult the beneficiaries concerned.

Power to insure assets

The statutory power to insure assets of the estate conferred by TA 1925, s 19 was inadequate and it used to be necessary to extend it. However, TA 2000 substituted a new s 19 which is much more satisfactory. It gives PRs and trustees power to insure assets against all risks, to the full value of the property, and to pay premiums out of income or capital.

It is no longer necessary to amend the statutory provision, which is now adequate. However, including an express provision makes life easier for lay PRs who will be able to see from the will itself exactly what they can do. The following is a typical provision.

Specimen clause

> Power to insure any asset of my estate on such terms as they think fit and to pay premiums at their discretion out of income or capital and to use any insurance money received either to restore assets or as if it were the proceeds of sale.

Power to accept receipts from or on behalf of minors

Under the general law, an unmarried minor cannot give a good receipt for capital or income. A married minor can give a good receipt for income only (LPA 1925, s 21). Parents and guardians used not to be able to give a good receipt on behalf of minors unless specifically authorised to do so in the will. This meant that without such authority the PRs would have to hold onto a legacy until the minor reached 18 and was able to give a good receipt. The AEA 1925, s 42 gives PRs the power to appoint trustees to hold a legacy for a minor who is absolutely entitled under the will. The receipt of the appointed trustees (who could be the child's parents or guardians) discharges the PRs from further liability. This power does not apply where the child has a contingent interest.

The Children Act 1989 provides that parents with parental responsibility have the same rights as guardians appointed under the Act. These rights are set out at s 3 and include the right to receive or recover money for the benefit of the child. Therefore, since the Children Act 1989, parents and guardians have been able to give a good receipt to PRs.

There are often tensions within families and a client may not be happy for a parent or guardian to give a good receipt for a legacy. In such a case, the will should be drafted to leave a legacy to trustees to hold for the benefit of the minor rather than to the child directly. Alternatively, the will may include a clause allowing the PRs to accept the receipt of the child himself if over 16 years old. The provision may be incorporated into the legacy itself or may be included in a list of powers in the will.

Power to continue a sole trader's business

Personal representatives have power only to carry on a business for the purpose of selling it as a going concern. When doing this, they have power to indemnify themselves from the assets of the estate for liabilities they incur.

It is helpful to authorise the PRs to postpone the sale of the business if they so wish and to carry on the business in the meantime. The clause should make clear which assets of the estate can be used in the business. The PRs will be able to indemnify themselves from those assets.

In practice few PRs are going to want to get involved in running a business. Professional trustees will normally refuse to take a grant in such cases. It is preferable to appoint the person(s) taking the business under the will as special executors limited to dealing with the business.

Note: A testator who is a member of a partnership should check that the partnership agreement deals adequately with arrangements for the death of a partner. The PRs of a deceased partner have no implied rights to take part in the running of the business.

A testator who runs a business through the medium of a limited company should also consider what will happen after death. The company will continue as a separate legal entity, but is there anyone in place who will be able to carry on the business?

Removing need to comply with the Apportionment Act 1870

Section 2 of the Apportionment Act 1870 provides that income such as rent and dividends is to be treated as accruing from day to day and apportioned accordingly. Thus, where assets in the estate produce income (such as bank or building society interest or dividends) which is received after death but which relates to a period partly before and partly after death, the income must be apportioned. The part accruing before death is a capital asset of the estate. The part accruing after death is income relating to the particular asset.

Unless the Act is excluded, s 2 will also have to be complied with where a will creates a trust which gives capital to one person and income to another. It also has to be complied with where there is no trust but a will gives an income-producing asset to one person and residue to another. If the apportionment applies, it is necessary to apportion the income between the two beneficiaries.

Example: Apportionment Act not excluded

The testator's will gives 'my ABC Co shares to Fred and my residue to Graham'.

ABC Co declares a dividend of £12,000 three months after the testator's death. The dividend is expressed to cover the previous 12 months.

Three quarters of the dividend relates to the pre-death period and is regarded as capital forming part of the residue of the estate. It will pass to Graham.

One quarter of the dividend relates to the post-death period and is regarded as income passing with the shares to Fred.

This calculation is time consuming and it is common to exclude the need to apportion so that all the income will pass with the income-producing asset.

Specimen clause

> Power to treat as income all the income from any part of my estate whatever the period in respect of which it may accrue and to disregard the Apportionment Act 1870.

Example

If the will in the previous example includes such a clause, the whole of the dividend is treated as relating to the post-death period and will pass with the shares to Fred.

Power to employ agents

The TA 2000, ss 11–15 replace in similar but clearer terms the provisions of TA 1925, s 23(1) by allowing non-charitable trustees to delegate to agents any or all of their 'delegable functions'. Functions personal to the trustees which cannot be delegated include:

(a)   decisions on distributing trust property to beneficiaries;

(b)   allocation of fees or payments to income or capital;

(c)   appointment of trustees;

(d)   appointment of nominees or custodians of trust assets.

Only in the case of delegation of their asset management function is agreement in writing required.

A trustee who satisfies the duty of care in TA 2000, s 1 in relation to the appointment and subsequent review of the appointment of an agent is not liable for the acts and defaults of the appointee. Typically, this power will be used by PRs to employ estate agents, stockbrokers or bankers to carry out executive functions in relation to the administration. For example, PRs may instruct estate agents to sell the deceased's house or stockbrokers to value shares for IHT purposes.

Delegation by power of attorney

The TA 1925, s 25, as substituted by Trustee Delegation Act 1999, s 5, allows trustees and PRs to delegate by power of attorney the exercise of any of the powers and discretions vested in them for a period not exceeding 12 months. However, in this case, the PRs remain liable for the acts of the delegate as if they were their own acts.

This provision is often used by PRs who, having obtained their grant, find that they are unable to be involved personally in the administration for some temporary reason, such as absence abroad on business or on holiday. If, before taking out the grant, a long absence is anticipated, the better course of action would be for the PR to renounce his right to a grant or for others to take a grant reserving power to any absentee executor. It is too late to renounce or reserve power if the grant has already been obtained or if an executor has accepted office by intermeddling in the estate.

11.2.9.2 Administrative provisions to consider in relation to wills which may give rise to a trust

Removing need to comply with the Apportionment Act 1870

We have already seen that a draftsman would consider excluding the Act where an income-producing asset goes to one person and residue to another.

It is normal to exclude the Act where a will creates a life interest trust.

Example: Apportionment Act not excluded

The testator's will gives 'my residue to Larry for life, remainder to Rob'.

ABC Co declares a dividend of £12,000 three months after the testator's death. The dividend is expressed to cover the previous 12 months.

Three quarters of the dividend relates to the pre-death period and is regarded as capital of the estate. It will be held for Larry for life and will eventually pass with the rest of the capital to Rob.

One quarter of the dividend relates to the post-death period and is regarded as income. It will be paid to Larry.

Example: Apportionment Act excluded

The whole of the dividend will be treated as income and paid to Larry.

It is also desirable to exclude the Act where there is a trust with contingent interests. Beneficiaries will fulfil the contingency at different times (or fail to fulfil it) and unless the Act is excluded there will have to be an apportionment of income each time there is a change in beneficial entitlement.

Example

A trust is created for three children contingent on reaching 18.

When the first child reaches 18 any income will have to be apportioned to the pre- and post-birthday period. The first child will be entitled to one third of the post-birthday income but all of the pre-birthday income will be a trust asset.

If the Act is excluded the first child will be entitled to one third of the whole receipt.

Removing need to comply with the equitable rules of apportionment

The equitable apportionment rules apply only where residuary personalty is left to one person for life, remainder to another.

The rules are designed to preserve a fair balance between the competing interests of the life tenant (who wants high income) and the remainderman (who wants capital growth).

Under the rule in *Howe v Dartmouth* (1820) 7 Ves 137, where property is left in this way, trustees are under a duty to sell assets which are either wasting (such as copyrights) or non-income producing (such as reversionary interests) and invest the proceeds in authorised investments.

Where there is a duty to sell and the trustees delay, the trustees must only pay 'a fair yield' to the life tenant and must treat the rest as capital. There is a complicated formula for calculating the fair yield.

Under the rule in *Re Earl of Chesterfield's Trusts* (1883) 23 Ch D 643, where trustees have delayed selling a non-income-producing asset, they must apportion the proceeds of sale and treat some as income and some as capital. Again there is a formula for the calculation.

Under the Rule in *Allhusen v Whittell* (1867) LR 4 Eq 295, debts of the estate must be treated as paid partly with capital and partly with the income that the capital produced. The burden is, therefore, apportioned between tenant for life and remainderman.

The principle behind these rules is admirable. However, the expense involved in making the calculations is rarely justified. It is usual to exclude them when drafting life interest trusts.

Specimen clause

> Power to disregard the rules of equity relating to apportionment including those known as the rules in *Howe v Dartmouth* and *Allhusen v Whittell* in all their branches.

Even where the equitable apportionment rules are excluded, trustees should still strive to achieve fairness between beneficiaries. For example, they must not invest for income at the expense of capital growth (see **14.3.2**).

Power to appropriate assets

Section 41 of AEA 1925 does not apply to trustees. It is necessary to include an express provision, equivalent to s 41, to permit the trustees to appropriate trust property towards beneficial interests arising under the trust.

Specimen clause

> Power to appropriate assets in or towards satisfaction of any beneficial interests arising under the trust without obtaining the consent of any beneficiary.

The power to invest

The TA 2000 contains a new 'general power of investment' giving trustees power to invest as if absolutely entitled to the trust assets (s 3). This general power does not permit investment in land other than by mortgage. However, s 8 allows trustees to acquire land in the UK for investment or occupation by beneficiary, or for other reasons, which means that all trustees will now have similar powers to a trustee of land with regard to acquiring land.

Trustees exercising any investment power, whether expressly given or under the TA 2000, must comply with various specific requirements, which include reviewing the investments chosen from time to time (s 4), taking proper advice before investing or reviewing the investments (s 5), and having regard to 'the standard investment criteria' which means considering the suitability to the trust of the investment type chosen and considering the need for diversification in so far as is appropriate to the circumstances of the trust (s 4).

Although an improvement on the previous provisions under the Trustee Investments Act 1961 (TIA 1961), it may still be desirable expressly to state the investment powers and make some modifications and additions to the effect of the TA 2000. For example, the trust instrument should contain express permission to:

(a) purchase foreign investments including land; and/or

(b) retain or purchase non income-producing investments, such as insurance policies; and/or

(c) retain investments originally settled, for example, shares in the settlor's family company; and/or

(d)   pursue an 'ethical' investment policy; and/or

(e)   borrow (and use trust property to be charged) for the purposes of investment; and/or

(f)   exclude the obligation to diversify the trust fund.

It is not possible to exclude s 4 (which requires the trustees to have regard to the need for diversification when investing). However, particularly where the trust contains primarily one type of asset and it is intended that the trustees should not sell this (for example, shares in a private company) it is advisable to state this expressly.

The TA 2000 provides that the management of trust assets can now be delegated (s 15) and that trustees may also appoint certain persons as nominees (s 16). Previously an express power was required for these actions. There are a number of special requirements to be observed if a trustee wishes to delegate asset management and investment decisions, for example, the trustee must create a written policy document to guide the delegates and review this from time to time. It is not clear whether this requirement applies to all trustees, or only to those exercising power under the TA 2000. In practice, though, it is usual for trustees to set out the investment aims of the trust when appointing managers to deal with the investment decisions.

See **14.3** for a further discussion of trustee investments.

Power to purchase land

The TA 2000, s 8 gives trustees power to acquire freehold or leasehold land in the UK for 'investment, for occupation by a beneficiary or for any other reason'. When exercising their power, the trustees are given 'all the powers of an absolute owner in relation to the land'.

Specimen clause

> My Trustees may apply trust money in the purchase or improvement of any freehold or leasehold dwelling-house and may permit any such dwelling-house to be used as a residence by any person with an interest in my residuary estate upon such terms and conditions as my Trustees may think fit.

This clause gives trustees an express power to use trust money to buy or improve land for use as a residence by the beneficiaries. It leaves the question of responsibility for the burden of repairs and other outgoings to the discretion of the trustees.

The statutory power does not authorise the purchase of land abroad, nor does it allow trustees to purchase an interest in land with someone else (eg, a beneficiary). An express power will be needed if the trustees are to have such powers.

Power to sell personalty

Trustees holding land in their trust have the power to sell it under their powers of an absolute owner under TA 2000 (see above). However, there is some doubt whether trustees who hold no land and where there is no express trust for sale have power to sell personalty. For this reason, some wills may continue to impose an express trust for sale over residue. The alternative solution is to include power in the will (among the administrative provisions) giving the trustees express power to sell personalty.

Specimen clause

> Power to sell mortgage or charge any asset of my estate as if they were an absolute beneficial owner.

Power to use income for maintenance of beneficiaries

Where trustees are holding a fund for a minor beneficiary, TA 1925, s 31 gives them power to use income they receive for the minor's maintenance, education or benefit.

Section 31 (as amended by TA 2000) states (inter alia):

(1)   Where any property is held by trustees in trust for any person for any interest whatsoever, whether vested or contingent, then, subject to any prior interests or charges affecting that property—

    (i)   during the infancy of any such person, if his interest so long continues, the trustees may, at their sole discretion, pay to his parent or guardian, if any, or otherwise apply for or towards his maintenance, education, or benefit, the whole or such part, if any, of the income of that property as may, in all the circumstances, be reasonable, whether or not there is—

        (a)   any other fund applicable to the same purpose; or

        (b)   any person bound by law to provide for his maintenance or education; and

    (ii)   if such person on attaining the age of eighteen years has not a vested interest in such income, the trustees shall thenceforth pay the income of that property and of any accretion thereto under subsection (2) of this section to him, until he either attains a vested interest therein or dies, or until failure of his interest:

Provided that, in deciding whether the whole or any part of the income of the property is during a minority to be paid or applied for the purposes aforesaid, the trustees shall have regard to the age of the infant and his requirements and generally to the circumstances of the case, and in particular to what other income, if any, is applicable for the same purposes; and where trustees have notice that the income of more than one fund is applicable for those purposes, then, so far as practicable, unless the entire income of the funds is paid or applied as aforesaid or the court otherwise directs, a proportionate part only of the income of each fund shall be so paid or applied.

(2)   During the infancy of any such person, if his interest so long continues, the trustees shall accumulate all the residue of that income by investing it, and any profits from so investing it, from time to time in authorised investments, and shall hold those accumulations … .

(3)   This section applies in the case of a contingent interest only if the limitation or trust carries the intermediate income of the property … .

Examples of the application of s 31

Example: Trust 1

The trustees are holding £100,000 for Mary (16) who has a vested interest in the capital. Under s 31(1), the trustees have the power to pay all or part of the income to Mary's parent or guardian or 'otherwise apply' it for Mary's maintenance, education or benefit. This could include paying bills (eg, school fees) directly.

The power is limited to so much of the income as is 'reasonable'. The proviso directs the trustees to take into account various further points such as Mary's age and requirements, and whether any other fund is available for her maintenance.

Section 31(2) directs the trustees to accumulate any income not used for maintenance and invest it.

Example: Trust 2

The trustees are holding £100,000 for Dora (14) who has an interest in capital contingent on reaching 21. They may pay or apply the income for Dora's maintenance, education or benefit in the same way as the trustees of Trust 1.

The trustees are also holding £100,000 for Charles (19) who has the same contingent interest in capital. Section 31(1)(ii) directs them to pay all the income from his share of the trust fund to Charles until his interest vests (ie, until he is 21), when he will receive the capital, or fails (ie, if he dies before he is 21).

The same will apply to the income from Dora's share from her 18th birthday onwards.

> ## Example: Trust 3
> The trustees are holding £200,000 for Henry for life with remainder to Stephen (10). They have no power to use the income for Stephen's benefit as Henry is entitled to it. If Henry dies while Stephen is still a minor, s 31 will apply to allow the trustees to apply income for Stephen's maintenance etc during the period from Henry's death until Stephen is 18 (when they will transfer the capital to Stephen).

Extending s 31: specimen clause

> Section 31 of the Trustee Act 1925 shall apply to the income of my estate as if the words 'as the Trustees shall in their absolute discretion think fit' were substituted for the words 'as in all the circumstances be reasonable' in paragraph (i) of subsection (1) thereof and the proviso to subsection (1) had been omitted and as if the age of 21 years were substituted for all references to the age of 18 wherever they occur in section 31 (references to 'infancy' being construed accordingly).

The clause begins by removing the 'reasonable' limitation in s 31. It gives the trustees complete discretion over whether to pay or apply income for minor beneficiaries and over how much income they pay or apply.

Secondly, it removes the right for a contingent beneficiary to receive all the income from the age of 18. The trustees' discretion under s 31 to pay or apply income for maintenance or to accumulate any surplus will continue until the beneficiary is 21. Thus in Trust 2 the trustees would have a discretion over the payment of income to Charles even though he is over 18.

Power to use capital for advancement of beneficiaries

The TA 1925, s 32 allows trustees in certain circumstances to permit a beneficiary with an interest in capital to have the benefit of part of his capital entitlement sooner than he would receive it under the basic provisions of the trust.

Section 32 states:

(1)   Trustees may at any time or times pay or apply any capital money subject to a trust, for the advancement or benefit, in such manner as they may, in their absolute discretion, think fit, of any person entitled to the capital of the trust property or of any share thereof, whether absolutely or contingently on his attaining any specified age ... and whether in possession or in remainder or reversion ...

Provided that—

(a)   the money so paid or applied for the advancement or benefit of any person shall not exceed altogether in amount one-half of the presumptive or vested share or interest of that person in the trust property; and

(b)   if that person is or becomes absolutely and indefeasibly entitled to a share in the trust property the money so paid or applied shall be brought into account as part of such share; and

(c)   no such payment or application shall be made so as to prejudice any person entitled to any prior life or other interest, whether vested or contingent, in the money paid or applied unless such person is in existence and of full age and consents in writing to such payment or application.

Examples of the application of s 32

> ## Example: Trust 1
> Mary has a vested interest in the £100,000 capital. Section 32 allows the trustees to release some of the capital for Mary's benefit. 'Benefit' is widely construed: money could be used to pay educational or living expenses. The amount the trustees may advance is limited to one half of Mary's entitlement, ie, £50,000.

Example: Trust 2

Charles and Dora have contingent interests in the capital, their presumptive shares being £100,000 each. Section 32 applies to allow the trustees to release up to £50,000 for the benefit of either beneficiary. The trustees could give money directly to Charles as he is old enough to give a valid receipt. The power applies even though the interests of Charles and Dora are contingent. If either beneficiary dies before the age of 21 there is no right to recover any advance even though that beneficiary's interest in capital has failed.

Section 32(1)(b) requires advances to be brought into account on final distribution. If the trustees give £50,000 to Charles now, he will receive £50,000 less than Dora when the fund is finally distributed to them.

Example: Trust 3

Henry has only an interest in income and s 32 does not permit the release of capital to him. The section does apply to Stephen's vested interest in remainder, and permits the trustees to apply up to £100,000 (half his interest) for Stephen's benefit.

Such an advance would prejudice Henry since his income would be substantially reduced. Section 32(1)(c) provides that no advance may be made without Henry's written consent.

Extending s 32: specimen clause 1

> Power to apply for the benefit of any Beneficiary as my Trustees think fit the whole or any part of the share of my residuary estate to which that Beneficiary is absolutely or presumptively entitled and I leave it within the discretion of my Trustees whether and to what extent the beneficiary shall bring into account any payments received under this clause.

This clause extends the limit in s 32(1)(a) to the full amount of the beneficiary's share. Up to £100,000 could be advanced for Mary (in Trust 1) or for Charles and Dora (in Trust 2). In Trust 3, the whole fund could be advanced for Stephen provided that Henry consents.

The second part of the clause supersedes s 32(1)(b) and means that if, in Trust 2 £50,000 was advanced to Charles, the trustees could on distribution still divide the remaining fund equally between Charles and Dora.

Extending s 32: specimen clause 2

> Power to pay or apply capital money from my residuary estate to any extent to or for the benefit of the Life Tenant.
>
> Power to advance capital money from my residuary estate to the Life Tenant by way of loan to any extent upon such terms and conditions as my Trustees may in their absolute discretion think fit.

These provisions would permit the trustees of a life interest trust like Trust 3 to give or lend capital from the fund to the life tenant even though he has an interest only in income, not capital. Such a clause may be included to give more flexibility in case the income proves insufficient for the life tenant's needs. The life tenant is dependent on the discretion of the trustees.

Note: Section 31 specifically allows trustees to pay income to the parents or guardian of a minor beneficiary, or 'otherwise apply it' for the minor's 'maintenance, education or benefit'. Similarly s 32 allows trustees to pay or 'apply' capital for the beneficiary's advancement or benefit. Thus, even without express authorisation, the trustees could take a good receipt from parents or guardians.

Control of trustees by beneficiaries

Section 19 of TLATA 1996 provides that, where beneficiaries are *sui juris* and together entitled to the whole fund, they may direct the trustees to retire and appoint new trustees of the beneficiaries' choice. This means that in a case where the beneficiaries could by agreement end the trust under the rule in *Saunders v Vautier* (1841) 4 Beav 115, they now have the option of allowing the trust to continue with trustees of their own choice. The provision may be expressly excluded by the testator. If, under the terms of the trust, the position could arise where all the beneficiaries are in existence and aged over 18 but the trust has not ended, the testator may wish to prevent the beneficiaries from choosing their own trustees.

Specimen clause

> The provisions of section 19 of the Trusts of Land and Appointment of Trustees Act 1996 shall not apply to any trust created by this will so that no Beneficiary shall have the right to require the appointment or retirement of any Trustee or Trustees.

Trusts of land

The TLATA 1996 gives special powers (see below) to a beneficiary under a trust of land who has an interest in possession. If, under the terms of the will, a trust with an interest in possession could arise, the will may amend those powers. The Act does not define 'interest in possession', so it presumably has its usual meaning; a beneficiary has an interest in possession if he is entitled to claim the income of the fund as it arises or enjoy an asset as of right (normally either because he has a life interest, or because he is over 18 and entitled to claim income or enjoyment under TA 1925, s 31).

Duty to consult beneficiaries

Trustees exercising any function relating to the land must consult any beneficiary who is of full age and beneficially entitled to an interest in possession in the land and, so far as consistent with the 'general interest of the trust', give effect to the wishes of any such beneficiary (TLATA 1996, s 11). The duty to consult may be excluded by the will.

Specimen clause

> The provisions of section 11 of the Trusts of Land and Appointment of Trustees Act 1996 shall not apply so that it shall not be necessary for my Trustees to consult any Beneficiaries before carrying out any function relating to land.

Beneficiary's rights of occupation

A beneficiary with a beneficial interest in possession, even if not of full age, has the right to occupy land subject to the trust if the purposes of the trust include making the land available for occupation by him or if the trustees acquired the land in order to make it so available (TLATA 1996, s 12). There is no power to exclude s 12, but a declaration that the purpose of the trust is not for the occupation of land may be included in the will.

Specimen clause

> The purposes of any trust created by this will do not include making land available for occupation of any Beneficiary [although my Trustees have power to do so if they wish].

11.3 Partially exempt transfers

Sometimes only a part of an estate on death is exempt for IHT purposes and the other part is not exempt. Difficulties may arise in determining how much tax is payable. Any tax relating to the non-exempt part of the estate can affect the calculation of the size of the exempt beneficiary's inheritance. Provisions designed to resolve these difficulties are contained in IHTA 1984, s 38. In general, these provisions apply relatively rarely and give rise to complicated calculations. It is, however, important to understand their effect where there are legacies on which tax is chargeable combined with a gift of residue to an exempt beneficiary. This could happen, for example, where the residue passes to a spouse and there are legacies to children.

Example

In her will, Polly gives £358,000 to her son Mark and the rest of her estate to her husband, Harry. Polly has made no lifetime gifts in the seven years preceding her death. Her estate is worth £800,000. The legacy to Mark exceeds Polly's nil rate band, and there will be tax to pay. Residue is exempt. The amount of tax payable depends on who is liable to pay the tax.

(a) If Polly's will gives the legacy to Mark 'subject to tax', simply calculate tax on the legacy in the usual way.

Calculate tax on £358,000		£
	£325,000 @ 0%	Nil
	£33,000 @ 40%	13,200
Distribution:	Tax bill	13,200
	Mark receives legacy (less tax)	344,800
	Harry receives residue	<u>442,000</u>
		<u>800,000</u>

(b) If Polly's will gives the legacy to Mark 'free of tax', the calculation is more complicated. Section 38(3) of the IHTA 1984 provides that the value transferred is the aggregate of the value of the gift and the 'tax which would be chargeable if the value transferred equalled that aggregate'.

The value transferred is, therefore, made up of the £358,000 which Mark takes (the net sum) PLUS the tax attributable to it.

In order to ascertain the value transferred, it is necessary to calculate what sum would, after deduction of tax at the appropriate rate, leave £358,000: ie, the legacy must be grossed up.

Gross up Mark's legacy:		£
	£325,000 (grossed up @ 0%)	325,000
	£33,000 (grossed up @ 40%) $33,000 \times \dfrac{100}{60}$	55,000
	Gross gift	380,000
Calculate tax on £380,000		
	£325,000 @ 0%	nil
	£55,000 @ 40%	22,000
Distribution:	Mark receives legacy	358,000
	Tax bill	22,000
	Residue to Harry (after payment of tax)	<u>420,000</u>
		<u>800,000</u>

It is particularly important to be aware of these provisions when drafting a will. If a legacy is given 'free of tax', the tax bill may be considerably higher than if the legacy were given 'subject to tax'. Compare the tax paid in the example above. The alternatives should be explained to the testator so that clear instructions can be taken and express provision included as to whether the legacy is to be free of tax or subject to tax.

A will may direct that residue is to be divided between an exempt and a non-exempt beneficiary. The share of the non-exempt beneficiary attracts tax whereas the share of the exempt beneficiary does not. The IHTA 1984, s 41 provides that an exempt share of residue shall not bear any part of the tax attributable to the non-exempt share of residue even if the will directs otherwise. The non-exempt share of residue must bear its own tax and the non-exempt beneficiary will receive less benefit from the gift than will the exempt beneficiary.

Example

Douglas (who has exhausted his nil rate band) leaves the residue of his estate after payment of debts, expenses and tax to be divided equally between his wife and his son, Henry.

After paying debts, expenses and tax attributable to non-residuary gifts, the residue is £600,000. His wife will receive £300,000. Henry will receive £300,000 less 40% tax ie, £180,000. Tax of £120,000 is paid on Henry's share of residue.

In this example, Douglas may object that he does not want his son to receive less than his wife. He may ask if the tax can be paid first and then what is left be divided into two equal shares. This is not possible because s 41 provides that a chargeable share of residue must bear its own tax and any provision to the contrary in a will is void.

However, he could direct that the residue be divided unequally between his wife and son in such proportions that after the payment of tax attributable to his son's share they each end up with the same amount. However, the calculation is difficult.

Summary – Basic Will Drafting

Topic	Summary	Reference
Basic content of a will	All wills should contain certain common elements: opening words to identify the document, revocation of previous wills, appointment of executors, legacies (if required) and gift of residue, attestation clause and date.	11.2
Additional provisions	It is often appropriate to include additional clauses to deal with particular problems, for example: a survivorship clause and substitutional gift in case a beneficiary predeceases or dies shortly after the testator; a default beneficiary in case contingent beneficiaries fail to attain a vested interest; directions as to whether the burden of debts charged on and IHT attributable to particular assets are to fall on the asset or on residue.	
	In all but the simplest will it is sensible to include administrative provisions to facilitate the administration of the estate, for example, a power for executors and trustees to charge, a power to appropriate assets without consent of the beneficiary, and extended powers to buy land. Where property is to be held for beneficiaries with contingent interests it is often desirable to vary the Trustee Act 1925, s 31 to give trustees an unfettered discretion and to remove the beneficiaries' right to income at 18, and to vary Trustee Act 1925, s 32 to remove the three limitations on the statutory power.	11.2
Nil rate band legacies	Married couples with children are often concerned about the impact of IHT. If the first spouse to die passes all the assets to the survivor, there is no immediate charge to IHT (because of the spouse exemption). Until 9 October 2007 there was a substantial charge when the survivor died because only one nil rate band was available. It was, therefore, IHT efficient for the first spouse to die to leave assets to his or her children up to the limit of his or her available nil rate band and the balance to their spouse. However, in the case of surviving spouses dying on or after 9 October 2007 the proportion of the nil rate band unused on the death of the first spouse can be passed to the survivor.	11.2.5.3

Topic	Summary	Reference
Provisions relating to partly exempt transfers	A testator may wish to divide assets between exempt and non-exempt beneficiaries in such a way that the non-exempt beneficiaries take more than the testator's available nil rate band. The calculation of IHT will be affected by the requirements of IHTA 1984, s 38 and s 41. IHT is paid from residue unless a testator directs otherwise. If the IHT on a legacy to non-exempt beneficiaries is paid from residue, the legacy must be grossed up to calculate the IHT due on it (s 38). If the residue is divided between the exempt and non-exempt beneficiaries, the non-exempt share of the residue must bear its own tax. Testators must consider whether the distribution of assets will be satisfactory once the effect of IHT is considered.	11.3

Chapter 12
Will Trusts

12.1 Introduction

The main contents of a will are the dispositive provisions, ie the clauses which actually leave property to the beneficiaries. The purpose of this chapter is to consider in more detail the different ways in which a testator may leave his property. Testators will frequently want to leave property on trust rather than making outright gifts.

The principles of drafting are identical whether a trust is created on death or by lifetime transfer. However, there are significant IHT differences between lifetime trusts and those created on death, which we will consider in this chapter. We will also look at ways of using trusts to provide flexible benefits by will.

12.2 Why include trusts in a will?

Testators are frequently uncertain about the precise nature of the gifts they want to make, because they do not know what the financial and personal position of the people thay want to benefit will be at the date of their death and in the years following. Instead of making fixed gifts in the will, testators may prefer to have a will which delays the decision as to who shall benefit on death until a later date. This can be achieved by including trusts in the will and authorising the trustees, or others, to determine the matter after death. These trusts may relate to non-residuary gifts and/or the gift of the residue.

There are a number of possibilities for the testator to consider when planning a will which delays the ultimate choice of beneficiary until after his death. A trust is usually involved, and in each case the succession and taxation implications must be balanced carefully. This chapter discusses each of these matters, as well as the drafting considerations which arise.

12.3 Special IHT treatment for certain settlements created on death

Most settlements created on death will be subject to the relevant property regime. However, there are the following exceptions:

(a)   settlements created for the disabled;

(b)   immmediate post-death interests;

(c)   trusts for bereaved minors;

(d)   trusts for bereaved young people.

12.3.1 Settlements created for the disabled

As in the case of lifetime trusts (see **5.2.4.1**), these are settlements fulfilling the qualifying conditions and created for the benefit of a beneficiary who is 'disabled' within the meaning of the IHTA 1984, s 89.

There are no anniversary or exit charges. Instead the beneficiary will be treated as having a qualifying interest in possession, ie, as beneficially entitled to the underlying trust assets. The settled property will be aggregated with the disabled beneficiary's own property when the beneficiary dies.

12.3.2 Immediate post-death interests

To qualify as an immediate post-death interest (IPDI), a person must have become beneficially entitled to an interest in possession in settled property on the death of the testator or intestate and must have continued to have such an interest at all times since the death (IHTA 1984, s 49A).

It is irrelevant that trustees may be able to terminate the interest. The settlement will be an IPDI settlement unless and until the interest is ended. If the interest does come to an end at any point, for example as a result of the trustees exercising a right to appoint the property elsewhere, the IPDI ceases. It cannot restart even if the original beneficiary reacquires the interest in possession.

A survivorship clause of not more than six months is ignored. The dispositions actually taking effect are treated as if they had had effect from the beginning of the period.

A person with an IPDI is treated as if beneficially entitled to the underlying trust property. There are no anniversary or exit charges. Instead the property is aggregated with the beneficiary's own estate on death. If the interest comes to an end before death, the beneficiary will be treated as making a lifetime transfer of value. The type of transfer depends on whether the property passes to someone absolutely, in which case there is a PET (to the extent that the transfer is not exempt), or whether the property passes on trust, in which case there is a lifetime chargeable transfer.

Example 1

Terri leaves property to Lucy for life, remainder to Rohan absolutely.

If Lucy surrenders her lifetime interest, the property will pass to Rohan absolutely. Lucy will make a PET. If, however, she was married to Rohan, the transfer would be exempt.

Example 2

Terri leaves property to Larry for life, remainder to Linda for life, remainder to Rocco.

If Larry surrenders his life interest, he will make a lifetime chargeable transfer, not a PET, because there is no absolute gift.

Linda will not have an IPDI because it is not taking effect immediately on the testator's death. The settlement will, therefore, continue as a relevant property settlement.

12.3.3 Trusts for bereaved minors

A trust for bereaved minors (BMT) is a trust which satisfies the conditions set out in IHTA 1984, s 71A. That is:

(a)   the trust must be created by will or on intestacy for the deceased's own child (the bereaved minor);

(b)   the bereaved minor must, on or before attaining 18, become entitled to the settled property, any income arising from it, and any income that has already arisen and been accumulated.

(c)   while the bereaved minor is living and under 18:

  (i)   any capital applied must be applied for the benefit of the bereaved minor,

  (ii)   the bereaved minor must be entitled to all the income from the settled property or no income may be applied for any other person.

The word 'must' in (b) above does not require absolute certainty. Death can prevent the beneficary taking an interest. The word should be read as meaning 'must, if at all'.

The power to advance capital under s 32 of TA 1925 allows trustees to advance capital for the 'benefit' of a beneficiary. 'Benefit' is a wide word and could include settling it for the beneficiary and close family members. This would seem to conflict with the requirement in (c) that capital must be applied for the bereaved minor. However, s 71A(4) makes specific provision for this problem. It provides that a settlement can still satisfy the capital condition if s 32 applies, or if the settlement widens the statutory power to allow up to the whole of the beneficiary's interest to be advanced.

A settlement which satisfies the s 71A requirements will not be subject to the relevant property regime. There will be no anniversary or exit charges.

Example

Mandy dies intestate on 5 June 2010, leaving three children aged 4, 3 and 2. The children will be entitled to the capital at age 18. No anniversary charge arises in June 2020, and no charges arise as each beneficiary reaches 18 and becomes entitled to a share of the capital.

Section 71B provides that no IHT is to be payable as a result of the death under age 18 of the bereaved minor.

Notice that these trusts are very restricted:

(a)   A grandparent cannot create a BMT for a grandchild.

(b)   Income and capital must be applied for the beneficiaries for whom the property is held. There must be no overriding powers to appoint elsewhere.

Note, however, that a settlement can be a BMT even if the beneficiary has a right to receive income.

A will may leave property to the testator's children contingent on their reaching 18, with a substitutional gift to a grandchild if a child predeceases the testator. The trust for the children will be a BMT, but if a grandchild is substituted for a child who has predeceased, that part of the settlement held for the grandchild will be subject to the relevant property regime.

Example

Trevor dies with an estate of £600,000 which he leaves on trust for his three children, Ann, Ben and Clare, contingent on reaching 18, with a substitutional gift to children of a child who predeceases also contingent on reaching 18.

On Trevor's death Ann is 24. Ben died, aged 22, but has left a child, Brady, who is aged 2; and Clare is 17.

Ann has a vested interest and is immediately entitled to her share; Clare's interest is a BMT; the portion held for Brady is subject to the relevant property regime.

Oddly, IHTA 1984, s 71A provides that where the trusts arise on intestacy, there will be a BMT for a substituted grandchild. Had Trevor died intestate in the above example, there would have been a BMT for Brady.

Section 71A is drafted by reference to a single beneficiary called the bereaved minor, suggesting that each bereaved minor must become entitled to his or her own 'share' of the trust capital and income. If this was the correct interpretation, it would be fatal to the status of the settlement for the trustees to have a power to alter the shares of individual beneficiaries to give more to one than the other. However, the Revenue issued guidance in July 2007 on the section, which said that this was not the correct interpretation. The Revenue considers that is possible to include a power for trustees to apply income unequally and/or to appoint capital in unequal shares, or even all to one at the expense of another.

Example

Extract from Trust Deed

> . . . to such of my children alive at my death as attain the age of 18 years and if more than one in such shares as the trustees shall from time to time by deed or deeds revocable or irrevocable appoint and in default of such appointment in equal shares absolutely at 18.

Fred died and left £400,000 to trustees to hold for his three children, contingent on reaching 18, and with a power to appoint capital in the above terms. The trustees decide to appoint £300,000 to the youngest child and the rest equally to the two older children. The trust fulfils the requirements of s 71A.

However, according to the Revenue guidance the power must not permit the trustees to vary the share of a child who has *already* reached 18. The Revenue also takes the view that once a child has been excluded from benefit, even revocably, the power cannot afterwards be used to benefit the excluded child. In the Revenue's view it is not possible under the s 71A regime for someone who is not currently benefiting to become entitled in the future. Trustees should therefore consider carefully before excluding a child from benefit or making a revocable appointment of all the trust funds to one child. The mere possibility of trustees exercising the power in this way in the future will not affect the status of the BMT.

To prevent problems the power of appointment should be limited in the following way:

> PROVIDED that no such appointment shall be made and no such appointment shall be revoked so as to either diminish or to increase the share (or the accumulations of income forming part of the share) of or give a new share (or new accumulations of income) to a child who at the date of such appointment or revocation has reached the age of 18 nor to benefit a child who has been excluded from benefit as a result of the exercise of the power.

Note that a BMT attracts no special treatment for CGT or income tax, except that when a beneficiary becomes absolutely entitled as against the trustees, hold-over relief is available under TCGA 1992, s 260.

12.3.4   Trusts for bereaved young people

As a result of public criticism of the very restricted trusts afforded privileged treatment for IHT, the Government amended the Finance Bill 2006 at a late stage and introduced s 71D into IHTA 1984. This allows entitlement to capital to be deferred beyond 18. However, the IHT privileges are restricted.

The following conditions set out in s 71D must be satisfied:

(a)   the trust must be created by will for the deceased's own child (B);

(b)   B must, at or before age 25, become entitled to the settled property, any income arising from it and any income that has already arisen and been accumulated;

(c)   while B is living and under 25:

    (i)   any capital applied must be applied for the benefit of B,

    (ii)   B must be entitled to all the income from the settled property or no income may be applied for any other person.

As was the case for a BMT (see **12.3.3**), the word 'must' does not require absolute certainty. Death can prevent the beneficiary taking an interest. The word should be read as meaning 'must, if at all'.

As was the case with a BMT, a settlement can still satisfy the capital condition if s 32 applies, or if the settlement widens the statutory power to allow up to the whole of the beneficiary's interest to be advanced. The power can be used to advance capital on relevant property trusts.

A settlement which satisfies the s 71D requirements will not be subject to the relevant property regime while the beneficiaries are under 18.

There will be an exit charge if a beneficiary becomes entitled to capital after the age of 18. The charge will be calculated on the amount of time the property has remained settled since the beneficiary's 18th birthday. There are no anniversary charges. The calculation of the exit charge is similar to the calculation of an exit charge in the first 10 years of a relevant property settlement (see **10.2**).

Section 71E provides that no IHT is to be payable as a result of the death under 18 of the beneficiary.

Settlements satisfying the s 71D requirements can be created only by parents for their own children.

A settlement can qualify as a s 71D trust a even if the beneficiary has a right to receive income. However, s 71D(5) of the IHTA 1984 provides that a settlement which gives a beneficiary a right to income arising immediately on death will be classified as an immediate post-death interest (IPDI), not a s 71D settlement. (This is not the case for s 71A settlements where a settlement fulfilling the s 71A requirements will be classified as a s 71A settlement even if it gives the beneficiary an immediate right to income.)

Section 71D is drafted by reference to a single beneficiary called 'B'. The Revenue guidance issued in July 2007 takes the same approach in relation to s 71D settlements as to s 71A settlements. Trustees can have a power to apply income and appoint capital unequally amongst the beneficiaries without affecting the status. As with s 71A settlements, the power must not be exercisable in favour of a child who has reached 25 and the trustees must not make an appointment to a beneficiary who has been excluded.

Most people making wills who want to benefit their children with as little IHT as possible will probably choose a s 71D settlement in preference to a s 71A one. The trustees of a s 71D settlement are free to advance the trust funds to the beneficiaries at age 18 if they choose, in which case there will be no charges to IHT. If, however, the beneficiary is too immature to deal with the funds at age 18, the trustees can allow the settlement to continue until age 25. There will be an exit charge at that point.

If the trustees are still doubtful as the maturity of the beneficiary as 25 approaches, they could use any power of advancement they may have to settle the trust funds on further trusts for the benefit of the beneficiary. The same exit charge will be payable as if the property went to the beneficiary absolutely. There will be subsequent anniversary charges and an exit charge, but this may be worthwhile if the beneficiary cannot be trusted to deal sensibly with the funds. (Trustees of a BMT can also make use of the power of advancement to settle the trust property on further trusts for the benefit of the beneficiary before his 18th birthday. There will be no exit charge at the time of the advance but, once the property is settled on the new relevant property trusts, there will be subsequent exit and anniversary charges on the property.)

Note that there is no special treatment for CGT or income tax, except that when a beneficiary becomes absolutely entitled as against the trustees, hold-over relief is available under s 260 of the TCGA 1992.

12.4   Precatory trusts

12.4.1   Misnomer

A so-called 'precatory trust' arises when a testator gives assets to a beneficiary and expresses a wish that the beneficiary will pass the assets on to others in accordance with an expression of wishes left by the deceased.

There is actually no trust at all. The beneficiary is free to ignore the testator's wishes.

To create a binding trust, there must be certainty of words, ie words of an imperative nature such as 'on trust', of subject matter and of objects, ie the beneficiaries. A testator who expresses a 'wish' or a 'hope' is not imposing any obligation. There is simply an expectation that the beneficiary will try to comply with the wish or hope.

12.4.2   Using the clause

Precatory trusts are normally used by testators when disposing of personal chattels, and in particular their jewellery. They are useful where the testator is undecided who should benefit from what on his death, especially in respect of property which may change in extent between the date of the will and the subsequent death. The clause introduces a degree of flexibility, giving the testator the opportunity to change his mind as to his wishes but without needing to change the will by codicil or, possibly, by executing a new will.

12.4.3   Drafting the clause

Sample clause

> I give and bequeath all my personal chattels as defined by section 55(1)(x) of the Administration of Estates Act 1925 to [my wife] for [her] own absolute use and benefit and I express the wish (but without imposing any legal obligation on [her]) that [she] should distribute such assets in accordance with any instructions I communicate to [her] whether orally or in writing at any time and from time to time.

12.4.3.1   Definition of personal chattels

Although it is convenient to adopt the definition used in the AEA 1925 for personal chattels, thought should be given as to whether it is appropriate. For example, if a testatrix wishes to make a gift of jewellery only, the clause should be modified by inserting an appropriate description of the gift in place of the words 'personal chattels as defined by section 55(1)(x) of the Administration of Estates Act 1925'.

12.4.3.2   The nature of the gifts

There is an absolute gift in the sample clause to the testator's wife. She could retain all the personal chattels, but the testator hopes that through the use of the precatory words she will retain only certain chattels and will distribute the rest. Flexibility is achieved since the instruction to the testator's wife can be changed as often as the testator pleases by giving further, non-testamentary instruction.

12.4.4   Taxation implications of the precatory trust

12.4.4.1   Inheritance tax (IHTA 1984, s 143)

The gift takes effect initially as an absolute gift to the beneficiary named in the clause. Inheritance tax is initially calculated on this basis. Thus, under the sample clause, no IHT will become payable because of the spouse exemption. If no exemption is available, IHT may be payable immediately on the testator's death.

Section 143 provides that where the named beneficiary transfers property in compliance with the testator's wish within two years after the death of the testator, 'this Act shall have effect as if the property transferred had been bequeathed by the will to the transferee'. Section 17(b) supports this by stating 'the transfer (by the named beneficiary) shall not be a transfer of value'. The benefit of s 143 is given automatically and does not need to be specifically claimed. Thus the distribution of the property by the named beneficiary in accordance with the 'precatory words' is not a PET by the beneficiary, and so will not attract IHT if the named beneficiary dies within seven years of the distribution.

Example

Martha by will leaves her jewellery to her daughter Emma, coupled with the wish that Emma shall distribute some of it to persons named in a letter handed to her before Martha's death. Emma distributes half of the jewellery to members of the family named in the letter and keeps the remainder.

No IHT exemption is available so, on Martha's death, tax is payable on the value of the jewellery. No adjustment of the position will be needed when Emma distributes one half of the jewellery (unless some is given to Martha's spouse or civil partner, in which case the spouse exemption will become available on those items given to the spouse or civil partner). Assuming no items are given to a spouse or civil partner, the IHT position will be unchanged, whether Emma keeps the items or distributes them. Emma makes no transfer of value provided she re-distributes the jewellery within two years of her mother's death.

12.4.4.2   Capital gains tax

There are no CGT provisions equivalent to s 143 of IHTA 1984. The named beneficiary will make a disposal of assets each time property is transferred in accordance with the precatory trust. However, CGT will be payable only if there is a gain on disposal which is beyond any available exemption or relief. In view of the timescale between the death and the later transfer of the property, it is unlikely that any taxable gain will arise.

Even if there are gains, they are likely to fall within the tangible moveable property exemption contained in s 262(1) of the TCGA 1992, which applies to disposals of non-wasting assets where the disposal consideration is £6,000 or less.

12.5   Wills containing discretionary trusts

12.5.1   Why have a discretionary will?

A testator cannot anticipate accurately the circumstances prevailing at his death, whether in relation to the extent of his property or his family, and so may decide his will should be drafted in 'flexible' form. This can be achieved by giving a legacy or the residue (or part of residue) to the executors and trustees on discretionary trusts together with wide powers of appointment over the capital and income. If the powers of appointment are not exercised by the trustees, the property will pass 'in default of appointment' to beneficiaries chosen by the testator and named in the will.

A will of this type enables the trustees to take into account the circumstances prevailing at the death of the testator and use the trust property as best suits those circumstances. For example, a testator's spouse may be financially well provided for and so not require any provision from the testator. If so, the trustees could exercise their powers over the income and capital in favour of the testator's children. If the circumstances were different and the spouse was in need of the testator's estate, the whole of it could be made available by exercise of the trustee's power of appointment in favour of the spouse.

12.5.2   Planning the discretionary will

Instructions will be required from the testator on various matters before the will can be drafted.

12.5.2.1   Legacy or residue on discretionary trusts?

A 'settled legacy', ie a legacy of property to be held on discretionary trusts, is often incorporated into a will which then leaves the residuary estate to other beneficiaries absolutely.

Sample clause – settled legacy

(1) I give to my Trustees free of all taxes the sum of [ ] thousand pounds (which said sum and all investments and property for the time being representing the same is hereinafter referred to as 'the Settled Legacy') upon the trusts and with and subject to the powers discretions and provisions contained in the succeeding paragraphs of this Clause

(2) For so long during the period of 125 years from my death (the perpetuity period applicable hereto) as any of the persons hereinafter mentioned is living my Trustees shall have power at any time and from time to time if and whenever they shall in their absolute discretion think fit to pay or apply the whole or any part or parts of the income or of the capital or of the income and the capital of the Settled Legacy to or for the benefit of all or any one or more exclusively of the others or other of the following persons that is to say my [spouse and issue] and with power to accumulate any income of the Settled Legacy not so paid or applied and to add any such accumulations to the capital thereof

(3) Subject to the foregoing provisions of this Clause and to any and every exercise of the powers and discretions hereinbefore conferred upon them my Trustees shall hold the Settled Legacy upon trust for such of my [children and grandchildren] ...

If there is no settled legacy, the will may provide absolute legacies, for example to the testator's children, and then leave the residuary estate on discretionary trusts for a class of beneficiaries possibly including the testator's spouse and issue.

If a will contains a settled legacy, it is generally inadvisable for the will to contain another settlement (eg, residue should not be given on discretionary trusts as well). This is because s 62 of the IHTA 1984 provides that if two settlements are made on the same day by the same person (the testator on the day he dies), they are 'related settlements'. The rate of IHT chargeable on each settlement will, therefore, be calculated on the basis of the value of the two settlements added together. That rate will be higher than it would have been had the will created a single settlement and made an absolute gift of the rest of the testator's property. However, s 80 of the IHTA 1984 provides that a life interest in favour of a surviving spouse will not be related to any other settlement created on death, so there is no harm if residue is left on IPDI trusts for the testator's spouse together with a settled legacy.

12.5.2.2   Duration of the discretionary trust

The discretionary trust, whether as a settled legacy or of residue, may be drafted so as to be capable of lasting for a full perpetuity period. Even if it is drafted in this way, it is unlikely that it will in fact last so long. Trustees will normally exercise their powers of appointment over capital far earlier.

Often, trustees will distribute all or a substantial portion of the assets within two years of death to take advantage of the IHT relief contained in IHTA 1984, s 144 (see **12.5.3.1**).

12.5.2.3   Extent of the property within the discretionary trust

Where the discretionary trust is a settled legacy, it may be limited to property to the value of the available nil rate band for IHT at the testator's death. Such 'nil rate band discretionary trusts' have the advantage that no IHT is payable when the trustees exercise their discretionary powers (see further **12.5.3.1**). However, there is nothing to prevent the testator leaving the entire estate on discretionary trusts.

12.5.3 IHT implications of discretionary trusts in wills

12.5.3.1 IHTA 1984, s 144

This section is specifically designed to permit distribution of property from a discretionary trust within two years of the testator's death, without liability to IHT.

The section applies where property is settled by a will if two conditions are satisfied:

(a)   no interest in possession subsists in the settled property; and

(b)   an event occurs in relation to the settled property within the period of two years after the death of the testator which would otherwise be chargeable to tax, for example the distribution of trust property by the trustees to a beneficiary.

If the conditions are met there are two consequences:

(a)   there is no exit charge to IHT when the property leaves the settlement; and

(b)   the will is treated as if it had left the property in the way the trustees have distributed it. A 'writing back' effect is, therefore, achieved in a manner similar to that which occurs with a post-death variation (see **13.2.1.1**).

Example

Mary by her will creates a discretionary trust of her residuary estate of £575,000. The beneficiaries are her husband Henry and their children and grandchildren. She dies in May 2010, having made no lifetime transfers.

Death of Mary: £100,000 IHT is payable (£575,000 – £325,000 = £250,000 @ 40%). The spouse exemption is not available.

Distribution by Mary's trustees in October 2010 (within two years of Mary's death) as follows:

£325,000 to trustees on discretionary trusts for the grandchildren: within nil rate band.

The rest to Henry absolutely: spouse exemption.

No IHT is now payable on Mary's death as the trustees' distributions are 'written back' into Mary's will.

This writing back effect is automatic; no election is required. The IHT paid by the PRs to obtain the grant of probate will be repaid (with interest) by the Revenue. Where (as is often the case) the PRs apply for the grant before making an appointment, they will have to pay IHT on the basis of there being no spouse exemption. When they make the appointment to the spouse, they will obtain a refund of IHT paid with interest.

The three-month trap

Section 144 works to provide the writing back effect only where a charge to IHT would otherwise have arisen on the distribution by the discretionary trustees. No exit charge arises if property leaves a settlement within the first three months of creation or of an anniversary; there must be at least one complete quarter (see **10.2.3**). Any appointment within three months of Mary's death would not be written back into her will. Spouse relief would not be available and, using the figures from the previous example, £100,000 IHT would remain payable (see further *Frankland v IRC* [1996] STC 735, where an enormous amount of IHT was irrecoverable by trustees).

The FA 2006 amended s 144 to make it clear that writing back will occur where property is appointed from a settlement without an interest in possession to create an IPDI, a bereaved minor's trust or a trust satisfying IHTA 1984, s 71D, even though such appointments would not give rise to a charge to IHT. In this case there will be reading back even if the appointment is made within three months.

Distributions after two years from death

Section 144 relief may only be claimed for distributions made within the two-year period. Later distributions will be taxable in accordance with normal principles which apply to relevant property trusts (see **10.2**). Will trusts often used to require trustees to distribute within two years of death, but this is now uncommon. It is often appropriate not to appoint all the property out within the first two years but to let the trust continue.

If the trust does continue, it will be treated for tax purposes as an ordinary discretionary trust created at the date of death of the testator.

Example

Tom, a widower, dies on 1 September 2010 leaving his entire estate on discretionary trusts for the benefit of his grandchildren. The estate is substantial and the grandchildren are all minors. The trustees decide that there is no need to make any immediate appointments and that they will allow the trust to continue.

The first 10-year anniversary will be 1 September 2020.

The rate of tax charged on distributions made after the first two years and within the first ten years will be calculated using the number of complete quarters that have elapsed since 1 September 2010.

12.5.3.2   Nil rate band discretionary trusts

Before the introduction of the transferable nil rate band, many testators who wanted to make use of their nil rate band chose to settle an amount equal to the unexhausted portion of their nil rate band on discretionary trusts and leave the residue to the surviving spouse.

This had a number of benefits:

(a)   no IHT was payable on the death estate;

(b)   the testator made use of his nil rate band;

Now that the nil rate band of the first spouse to die can be transferred to the survivor, these benefits can be obtained while leaving the whole estate to the surviving spouse either absolutely or as an IPDI. There are still some continuing benefits to using a nil rate band discretionary trust although these are much reduced. These benefits are:

(a)   There is the flexibility to make funds available to whichever beneficiaries are most in need. The surviving spouse, as well as the children and issue, can be included, so the testator will know that, if required, all the assets of the estate can be made available to the spouse. If the spouse does not need the assets, they can be made available to the children or issue. However, funds could also be made available to spouse and children by using a terminable life interest – see **12.7**. So a nil rate band discretionary trust is not the only way to get this particular advantage.

(b)   As the settlement is a nil rate band settlement, IHT will be charged at 0% during the first 10 years. However, the will must not contain any related settlement or the rate of IHT will be increased (see **12.5.2**).

Example

Raymond had made PETs of £125,000 which became chargeable on his death last year. By his will he creates a discretionary trust of the balance of his nil rate band of £200,000 and leaves the residue of his estate to his wife Wendy. The beneficiaries of the trust are Wendy, his children and grandchildren.

(1)   Calculate the IHT on Raymond's death.

No IHT is payable because:

> (a)   the funds in the nil rate band discretionary trust are taxed at 0% because the balance of Raymond's nil rate band is available (£325,000 − £125,000 = £200,000);
>
> (b)   the residuary estate has the benefit of the spouse exemption.
>
> (2)   Distribution by the trustees.
>
> Three years after Raymond's death, when the nil rate band has increased to £400,000, Wendy tells the trustees that she can manage without relying on the nil rate band discretionary trust fund and she asks if they will distribute it to the children. The trustees agree to do so. The value of the trust assets has risen to £450,000. No IHT is payable by the trustees from the discretionary trust. The settlement rate will be nil.
>
> Using the method illustrated in **10.2.4** (exit charge before the first 10-year anniversary), the calculation is:
>
> | Step 1: | Hypothetical chargeable transfer (value of funds settled by will) | | £200,000 |
> |---|---|---|---|
> | Step 2: | Ascertain tax payable | | |
> | | Raymond's cumulative total | £125,000 | |
> | | Nil rate band (balance) | | £200,000 |
> | Step 3: | Ascertain settlement rate | | nil |
>
> *Note:* the settlement rate will always be nil within the first 10 years so long as the funds entering the discretionary settlement at death are limited to the testator's available nil rate band:
>
> | Step 1: | Value of funds | £325,000 |
> |---|---|---|
> | Step 2: | Available nil rate band | £325,000 |
> | Step 3: | Ascertain settlement rate | nil |

The nil rate band discretionary settlement for the benefit of spouse and issue was one of the most common ways for married couples to leave their property. The settlor normally left a letter of wishes desiring the trustees to apply income for the benefit of the spouse unless not required.

However, there were always some practical problems with this course. Many couples own a valuable house as beneficial tenants in common but have little in the way of cash and investments. When the first spouse dies, the cash and investments in the estate may be far short of the current nil rate band. The PRs could transfer all or part of the deceased's interest in the matrimonial home to the trustees of the nil rate band settlement, but this is unlikely to be popular with the surviving spouse and may give rise to CGT problems when the property is sold.

12.5.3.3   Solution to problem of lack of liquid assets – use of a debt or charge

The availability of the transferable nil rate band between spouses provides an alternative approach to providing for spouse and issue in a tax efficient manner.

Before the transferable nil rate band was introduced, a solution which was commonly adopted was for the will creating the nil rate band settlement to give the PRs the right to require the trustees of the nil rate band settlement to accept a debt instead of assets.

The PRs normally secured the debt on the assets transferred to the spouse. The trustees of the nil rate band settlement have the right to enforce the charge against those assets during the spouse's lifetime but normally wait until death. If the spouse wants to sell the property, the charge has to be paid off, but the trustees can lend trust funds to the spouse for the purchase of a replacement property provided the trust instrument gives them suitable powers.

The will normally gives the trustees the right to claim interest on the debt or to index link it.

The benefits of this route are:

(a)   the surviving spouse has the use of all the assets of the couple;

(b)   on the death of the surviving spouse there is a debt which will reduce the IHT value of the estate.

Example

Fred and Georgia are married. They own the matrimonial home worth £800,000 as beneficial tenants in common. Fred dies first, and in addition to his half interest in the house he has £50,000 in cash and investments. His will leaves a nil rate band legacy on discretionary trusts for the benefit of Georgia and their children and grandchildren, and the residue to Georgia. It allows his executors to require the trustees of the nil rate band settlement to accept a debt.

The executors transfer all the assets of Fred's estate to Georgia, charged with a debt of £325,000 together with interest. Georgia dies four years later. The trustees will demand repayment of the debt with interest, which will reduce the IHT value of Georgia's estate. The trustees of the settlement can then distribute the settlement funds as they see fit.

Using a debt to fund the discretionary trust was enormously popular and many discretionary trusts have been set up in this way.

Because the use of the debt scheme has been so widespread, practitioners will be claiming the deduction for the debt on the death of the surviving spouse for many years to come. However, going forward, the introduction of the transferable nil rate band is likely to mean that far fewer nil rate band discretionary trusts will be created and so the number of debt arrangements will also fall.

12.5.4   CGT implications of discretionary trusts in wills

No special rules exist for CGT where distributions are made from discretionary trusts created by a will. In particular, there is no writing back effect for CGT corresponding to s 144 of the IHTA 1984. Thus, ordinary principles must be applied to calculate any liability (see further **10.2.7**). However, HMRC accepts that where the trustees exercise their powers of appointment during the administration period and before the PRs have vested assets in them, then the assets should be treated as passing direct to the appointee and never entering the trust at all.

The appointee then takes those asset(s) as legatee and therefore acquires the assets at probate value by reason of s 62(4) of the TCGA 1992. This means that there will be no liability to CGT resulting from the appointment.

This is clearly the best course for the trustees. If they wait until the PRs vest assets in them and then make the appointment, normal CGT principles apply and the position is as follows.

When a beneficiary becomes 'absolutely entitled' to trust property as against the trustees, the trustees are 'deemed to dispose' of the property at its market value and to re-acquire it at the same value as bare trustees, ie it remains in the names of the former trustees but is now the absolute property of the beneficiary.

Example 1: nil rate band discretionary trust – no IHT writing back

A testator's will creates a nil rate band discretionary trust. Three years after death the trustees appoint the trust property to the testator's spouse who thereby becomes absolutely entitled to it. Although the property will remain in the trustees' names (until it is actually transferred to the spouse), they now hold it as 'bare trustees' for the testator's spouse. Hold-over relief is usually available whenever property leaves the discretionary trust, so that no CGT liability will actually arise for the trustees provided the appropriate election is made by the trustees and beneficiary (TCGA 1992, s 260 – see **4.4.5.2**).

Example 2: nil rate band discretionary trust – with IHT writing back

A testator's will creates a nil rate band discretionary trust. The PRs have vested assets in the trustees. The trustees exercise the power of appointment within two years of death so that it is written back into the testator's will. As there is no chargeable transfer by the trustees, ie IHTA 1984, s 144 applies, hold-over relief will not be available under TCGA 1992, s 260. If the trust property is 'business assets', hold-over relief under TCGA 1992, s 165 may be available.

12.5.5 Income tax implications of discretionary trusts in wills

Once the discretionary trust is set up following the death, income over £1,000 from the settled property received by the trustees will attract tax at the trust rate or the dividend trust rate (Income Tax Act 2007, s 9). This, and the position of the beneficiaries, is considered in **Chapter 14**.

Distributions by trustees from discretionary trusts created by a will do not create settlements which fall within the income tax anti-avoidance provisions discussed at **4.6.2** and **4.6.4**.

Example

David appoints his wife, Sheena, as his executor and trustee. His will bequeaths her a substantial legacy and leaves his residuary estate on a two-year discretionary trust for Sheena and their children. David dies leaving two young children.

Within two years of David's death, Sheena distributes the residuary estate onto new s 71D trusts for their minor children. Even though the children's trust was created by appointment by their mother, the appointment onto the new trusts is not a 'settlement' by a parent on her child within the income tax anti-avoidance provisions. Sheena creates the new settlement in her capacity as trustee of David's will, not as a parent.

However, compare the position in relation to post-death variations (see **13.4.2**, where the anti-avoidance legislation can apply).

12.6 Drafting discretionary trusts of residue

The clauses which follow should be inserted into the will after the clauses directing the payment of the testator's debts, legacies, funeral and testamentary expenses and hence establishing the residuary fund to be 'the Trust Fund'. Many of the provisions used to create a discretionary trust by will are similar to those used to establish a discretionary trust by lifetime settlements. The comments on the clauses which follow are confined to those relevant only to will trusts.

12.6.1 Trust definitions

Sample clause

In my Will where the context so admits

(1) 'the Trust Fund' shall mean
   (a) my Estate after the payment of my debts funeral and testamentary expenses and legacies and
   (b) all money investments or other property accepted by the Trustees as additions and
   (c) all accumulations (if any) of income directed to be held as an accretion to capital and
   (d) the money investments and property from time to time representing the above

(2) 'the Trustees' shall mean my Executors or other of the trustees for the time being of the Trust Fund

(3) 'the Trust Period' shall mean the period ending on the earlier of

    (a)   the last day of the period of 125 years from the date of my death which period (and no other) shall be the applicable perpetuity period or

    (b)   such date as the Trustees shall by deed at any time or times specify (not being a date earlier than the date of execution of any such deed or later than a date previously specified)

(4)   'the Discretionary Beneficiaries' shall mean

    (a)   [my wife] [my husband]

    (b)   my children and remoter issue (whether living at my death or born thereafter)

    (c)   the husbands wives widowers and widows of my children and remoter issue

    (d)   any company trust or other body regarded as charitable under the law of England and Wales

(5)   'the Discretionary Period' shall mean [the period of two years (less one day) from the date of my death] [the Trust Period]

Clause (5) contains alternatives. If the period of 'two years (less one day) from the date of death' is selected, the trust necessarily will comply with the provisions of s 144 of IHTA 1984, ie a two-year discretionary trust will have been established. By limiting the trustees to a period of two years less one day, it is intended to remove uncertainty as to whether the distributions in fact occurred within two years of the testator's death. Difficulties can arise if an exact period of two years is used instead. Selecting the longer period means the settlement can continue as an ordinary discretionary trust.

12.6.1.1 Nil rate band discretionary trust

The clauses set out above may be used to establish a discretionary trust of the whole of the testator's estate after payment of debts, expenses and legacies. If a nil rate band discretionary trust is to be created, these clauses can be used but the definition of the trust fund must be altered to limit its extent.

Sample clause

'the Trust Fund' shall mean

(1)   the greatest value (if any) which such Trust Fund can have within the nil rate band of inheritance tax applicable at the date of my death which does not cause inheritance tax to be charged (other than at the said nil rate) in respect of my estate as a consequence of my death

(2)   (a)–(d) [as for (1) in the previous clause]

12.6.2 Residuary gift: discretionary trusts

Sample clause

(1)   The Trustees shall hold the capital and income of the Trust Fund upon such trusts in favour or for the benefit of all or such one or more of the Discretionary Beneficiaries exclusive of the other or others of them in such shares or proportions if more than one and with and subject to such powers and provisions for their respective maintenance education or other benefit or for the accumulation of income for any period (including administrative powers and provisions and discretionary trusts and powers to be executed or exercised by any person or persons whether or not being or including the Trustees or any of them) and so that the exercise of this power of appointment may be delegated to any extent and in such manner generally as the Trustees (subject to the application (if any) of the rule against perpetuities) by any deed or deeds revocable during the Discretionary Period or irrevocable and executed during the Discretionary Period shall appoint provided always that no exercise of this power shall invalidate any prior payment or application of all or any part or parts of the capital or income of the Trust Fund made under any other power or powers conferred by my Will or by law and provided further that this power may be exercised whether or not the

administration of my Estate has been completed and whether or not a transfer of the Trust Fund has been effected by my Executors under Clause [   ]

All powers and provisions established by the clause are exercisable by the trustees at any point in the administration period – even before the executors transfer the assets remaining in the estate to the trustees. This is almost certainly the position in any event, but the proviso removes any doubt by expressly authorising the trustees to exercise the powers in the way set out in the clause.

Sample clause (continued)

(2)   Until and subject to and in default of any appointment under sub-clause (1) the following provisions of this sub-clause shall apply to the Trust Fund during the Discretionary Period

   (a)   the Trustees shall pay or apply the income of the Trust Fund to or for the benefit of all or such one or more of the Discretionary Beneficiaries exclusive of the other or others of them as shall for the time being be in existence and in such shares if more than one and in such manner generally as the Trustees shall in their absolute discretion from time to time think fit

   (b)   notwithstanding the provisions of sub-clause (2)(a) the Trustees may in their absolute discretion instead of applying all or any part or parts of the income accumulate the same in the way of compound interest by investing or otherwise applying it and its resulting income from time to time in any applications or investments authorised by my Will or by law and subject to sub-clause (2)(c) below shall hold such accumulations as an accretion to capital

   (c)   the Trustees may apply the whole or any part or parts of the income accumulated under sub-clause (2)(b) as if it were income arising in the then current year

   (d)   notwithstanding the trusts powers and provisions declared and contained in this sub-clause the Trustees may

      (i)   at any time or times pay or apply the whole or any part or parts of the capital of the Trust Fund to or for the benefit of all or such one or more of the Discretionary Beneficiaries exclusive of the other or others of them in such shares if more than one and in such manner generally as the Trustees shall in their absolute discretion think fit

      (ii)   (subject to the application (if any) of the rules against perpetuities) pay or transfer any income or capital of the Trust Fund to the Trustees of any other trust wherever established or existing under which all or any one or more of the Discretionary Beneficiaries is or are interested (whether or not all or such one or more of the Discretionary Beneficiaries is or are the only objects or persons interested or capable of benefiting under such other trust) if the Trustees shall in their absolute discretion consider such payment or transfer to be for the benefit of all or such one or more of the Discretionary Beneficiaries

(3)   At the end of the Discretionary Period and subject to and in default of any appointment under sub-clause (1) the Trustees shall hold the Trust Fund upon trust for ...

If this clause is used to create a nil rate band settled legacy, the ultimate default trusts in clause (3) would generally provide that the property in the settled legacy should pass to the residuary beneficiary under the will of the testator.

12.7   Wills containing a terminable life interest

12.7.1   Form of the will

Many testators wish to provide adequately for their surviving spouse and yet wish to incorporate into their wills flexibility whereby other members of the family may benefit should the surviving spouse not require the provision when the testator dies.

Although a will containing discretionary trusts (see **12.5**) may be used to achieve the testator's wishes, the testator may prefer a will which gives his surviving spouse a direct benefit in the form of a life interest (coupled with powers of advancement in her favour over the capital), with 'an overriding power of appointment' allowing the trustees to appoint the property away from the spouse among a class of beneficiaries identified by the will.

There is an IHT advantage to drafting the will trust to leave a terminable life interest to the surviving spouse in that the property in which the spouse has an IPDI will attract the spouse exemption so no IHT will have to be paid on it. See **12.7.3.1** below. In the case of surviving spouses dying on or after 9 October 2007, any proportion of the nil rate band of the first spouse to die unused on his or her death can be transferred to the surviving spouse.

12.7.2 Drafting life interest trusts subject to an overriding power of appointment

After the usual provisions dealing with payment of debts, legacies, testamentary expenses etc, and after the residuary fund defined as 'my Trust Fund' has been established, the clauses creating the beneficial trusts should be set out. Extracts of the principal clauses are set out below in the order they usually appear, ie, the life interest for the surviving spouse follows the overriding power for the trustees.

Sample clause

> My Trustees shall hold the capital and income of the Trust Fund upon such trusts in favour or for the benefit of all or such one or more of the Beneficiaries exclusive of the other or others of them in such shares or proportions if more than one and with and subject to such powers and provisions for their respective maintenance education or other benefit or for the accumulation of income ... as my Trustees (subject to the application (if any) of the rule against perpetuities) by any deed or deeds ... shall appoint ...

This clause subjects the whole of the trust fund to a wide power of appointment. It may be exercised by the trustees to create absolute interests or interests under trusts in favour of the beneficiaries who will have been identified earlier in the will in a clause setting out various definitions (see **6.2.4**). Normally, the beneficiaries would include the testator's spouse, children and remoter issue and their respective spouses. The testator's intention would be that the trustees exercise this power only after consulting the surviving spouse (although there is no express provision requiring the consent of the spouse) and after they have taken into account all the circumstances existing at the testator's death. In such circumstances, it would not be unusual for the testator to appoint the surviving spouse as a trustee. The effect of exercising the power is to bring to an end the surviving spouse's life interest (see the following clause) in the whole or part of the trust fund, although if included in the class of beneficiaries, the trustees may appoint capital to the former life tenant.

Sample clause

> Until and subject to and in default of an appointment under clause [   ]
> (a)   My Trustees shall pay the income of the Trust Fund to the Life Tenant for life [or until remarriage] [if the Life Tenant shall survive me by [   ] days]
> (b)   (i)   My Trustees may at any time or times during the Trust Period as to the whole or any part of the Trust Fund in which the Life Tenant has for the time being an interest in possession transfer or raise and pay the same to or for the absolute use or benefit of the Life Tenant or raise and pay or apply the same for the advancement or otherwise for the benefit of the Life Tenant in such manner as my Trustees shall in their absolute discretion think fit
> (ii)   In this clause 'interest in possession' shall have the same meaning it has for the purpose of the Inheritance Tax Act 1984 and any statutory modification or re-enactment of such Act
> (c)   ...
> (d)   ...

This clause gives the spouse the right to receive the income from the fund until such time as the trustees choose to use the overriding power of appointment. It also gives the trustees express power to advance capital to the life tenant (who would also be identified in the definition clause in the will) should his circumstances so require. Sub-clauses (c) and (d) would set out the further trusts in the event of the trustees not exercising their overriding power of appointment.

12.7.3 Taxation implications of an overriding power

12.7.3.1 Inheritance tax

Death of the testator

No IHT is payable on the death of the testator since the spouse exemption is available as a result of the qualifying interest in possession given to the surviving spouse. Thus, a grant of probate can be obtained without the need to negotiate a loan to pay any IHT. This is an advantage which is not available where the property is left on discretionary trusts (see the 'Mary' example at **12.5.3.1**).

Exercise of the overriding power

The spouse has an IPDI. In so far as capital is appointed to the spouse, no IHT will arise.

If the power is exercised in favour of the other beneficiaries, the ending of the IPDI is a transfer of value which may be a PET (if an outright gift) by the life tenant so that IHT is payable only if death occurs within seven years (IHTA 1984, s 52), or may be a lifetime chargeable transfer (if the appointment is on continuing trusts). Thus, in both cases the IHT position is similar to that discussed at **10.1.4.1** in relation to partitioning trust funds.

12.7.3.2 Capital gains tax

If the exercise of the power results in someone becoming 'absolutely entitled' to the settled property against the trustees, there is a deemed disposal by the trustees. Absolute entitlement can occur where property leaves the trust following an outright appointment in favour of a beneficiary, or where the trustees appoint property to trustees to hold on new trusts (see further **10.4**). Either of these methods is possible under the power of appointment set out at **12.7.2**.

The calculation of the trustees' liability, the exemptions, reliefs and rates of tax is also similar to that for lifetime trusts (see **10.1.4.2**).

12.7.4 Drafting the deed of appointment

The drafting of the deed, and its contents, will follow closely the drafting of the deed of appointment discussed at **10.2.8**.

12.8 IHT treatment of settlements created on death on or after 22 March 2006

Trusts for testator's own children	Bereaved minor's trust (BMT) (18): • No exit or anniversary charges. • Beneficiary not treated as owning underlying capital. Section 71D (18–25): • As above except that there are exit charges once beneficiary reaches 18, calculated on the length of time elapsed since beneficiary reached 18.

Immediate life interest for anyone	Immediate post-death interests (IPDI): • Beneficiary treated as beneficially entitled to underlying trust capital for IHT.
All other trusts	Relevant property regime, ie exit and anniversary charges. (NB. Section 144 'writing back')

Summary – Will Trusts

Topic	Summary	Reference
Special IHT treatment of trusts created on death	Many wills create trusts. The Finance Act 2006 contains special IHT provisions relating to trusts created on death. A person who has an interest in possession arising on death (eg a life interest) has an 'immediate post-death interest' (IPDI). Such a person is treated as entitled to the underlying trust capital. It is irrelevant that the trustees have power to terminate the interest. Until they terminate the interest, the beneficiary has an IPDI.	12.3.2
	A settlement created on death for the deceased's own child where the child will become entitled to capital at or before 18 and which complies with the other requirements of IHTA 1984, s 71A will be a trust for bereaved minors (BMT). BMT settlements will not be subject to anniversary or exit charges.	12.3.3
	A settlement created on death for the testator's own child where the child will become entitled to capital at or before 25 and which complies with the other requirements of IHTA 1984, s 71D will be a trust for bereaved young persons (BYP). BYP settlements will not be subject to anniversary charges. They will only be subject to exit charges if property remains settled after the beneficiary reaches 18.	12.3.4
Flexible will drafting	Testators may not be certain who they want to benefit and may wish to incorporate flexibility. There are a number of ways of achieving flexibility.	
	(a) *Precatory trusts* – a beneficiary passes assets bequeathed by will to other people in accordance with a record of wishes left by the testator. Provided the beneficiary carries out the wishes within 2 years of death, IHT is charged as if the property had been left in accordance with the wishes of the deceased (IHTA 1984, s 143).	12.4
	(b) *Residue left on discretionary trusts* – this ensures maximum flexibility. The trustees will deal with the estate as they see fit although the testator will normally leave a letter of wishes. The settlement will be a relevant property settlement subject to anniversary and exit charges. However, if the trustees distribute more than 3 months after and within 2 years of death, IHT will be charged as if the property had been left in the way the trustees have distributed it (IHTA 1984, s 144).	12.5

Topic		Summary	Reference
	(c)	*Nil rate band discretionary trust for spouse and issue, residue to spouse* – this gives flexibility in relation to the property held in the nil rate band trust. As in (b) above there can be writing back under s 144 if distributions are made after 3 months and within 2 years of death. If assets are retained, there will be no exit charge on assets distributed in the first 10 years because of the way the tax charge is calculated in the first 10 years.	12.5.3.2
		Many couples have a valuable house and little else in the way of assets so that it is difficult to transfer assets to the nil rate band trustees. A popular solution is for the PRs to transfer all the deceased's assets to the spouse charged with a debt to the nil rate band trust. The debt will reduce the estate of the surviving spouse on death.	12.5.3.3
	(d)	*Terminable life interest for spouse, residue to issue* – this gives the surviving spouse a right to the income from the settled property and secures the spouse exemption. However, it gives flexibility as the trustees can terminate the life interest and appoint capital to the spouse or issue depending on their respective needs. If the appointment is to the spouse, there will be no IHT implications. If the appointment is to the issue, the spouse will be treated as making a PET.	12.7

Chapter 13

Post-death Arrangements

13.1 Types of arrangement

13.1.1 Introduction

Beneficiaries and trustees may wish to rearrange dispositions of property in an estate following a death. Reasons for rearrangements include:

(a)   a beneficiary's wish to redirect benefits to other members of the family who are less well provided for, either as a result of the death or generally; and

(b)   the saving of tax, usually IHT, particularly where the disposition of the estate does not fully utilise the deceased's nil rate band.

There are many ways of redirecting assets. Most methods take advantage of specific statutory provision while others use taxation exemptions and reliefs. The following are among the more usual.

13.1.1.1 A lifetime gift by the beneficiary of an inheritance under a will or under an intestacy

This may be an outright gift by the beneficiary. If so, it will constitute a PET for IHT and a disposal for CGT by the beneficiary. If instead the beneficiary transfers the property to trustees to hold on trust, it will be a PET or lifetime chargeable transfer depending upon which type of trust is selected. For CGT, a gift to trustees will be a disposal whichever type of trust is selected. Creation of trusts by lifetime gift is considered in **Chapter 5**.

13.1.1.2 'Precatory trusts' and wills creating two-year discretionary trusts

These are flexible dispositions created by the testator. The exact testamentary effect of the will is, effectively, determined after death by the act of the personal representatives (and in some cases, the beneficiaries), and not by the testator at the time of making the will. Wills containing this type of provision were considered in **Chapter 12**.

13.1.1.3 Orders made under the Inheritance (Provision for Family and Dependants) Act 1975 and the capitalisation of a life interest on an intestacy

Both of these amount to rearrangements of the disposition of an estate on death. In either case, the estate is treated as if left in accordance with the terms of the rearrangement. This 'writing back' effect will affect the extent of the liability to IHT on the estate on death. (See further LPC Guide, *Legal Foundations*.)

13.1.1.4 Post-death variations of the dispositions of the deceased's estate

If the variation is made in the appropriate form, the effect is to write the provisions of the variation back into the terms of the deceased's will or the intestacy law for tax purposes. The estate on death is then charged to IHT on the basis of the amended provisions but the beneficiary suffers no adverse tax consequences. If the writing back effect is not obtained, the beneficiary is left in the position of making lifetime gifts as discussed above. Variations are discussed further at **13.2**.

13.1.1.5   Disclaimer of benefit

A disclaimer may not achieve the objectives of the beneficiary wishing to make the post-death rearrangement. Disclaimers amount to a rejection of the benefit of the gift under the will or the intestacy law. They will be appropriate for use only if, following the rejection, the property passes to the person whom the original beneficiary intends to benefit. However, despite this limitation on their use, in some cases disclaimers offer advantages not available in the case of variations.

13.1.2   Variation or disclaimer?

These provisions permit the redirection of property after a death by a beneficiary whether the deceased died testate or intestate. They offer estate planning opportunities for the beneficiary who can afford 'not to receive' property for whatever reason.

It is very important to think through the effect of a disclaimer carefully, especially where the statutory trusts on intestacy are involved. *In re DWS (Deceased); In re EHS (Deceased); TWGS (A Minor) v G and Others* [2000] 3 WLR 1910 illustrates this. A child of the deceased was unable to take on intestacy (his interest was forfeited because he had killed his parents). The child's own children could not replace him because issue are entitled under the statutory trusts only where a child predeceases the intestate. Section 47(2) provides that unless issue take an 'absolute vested interest', the intestate is to be treated as having left no issue and those next entitled on intestacy will take. Thus, the deceased's grandchildren took nothing and the property went to the relatives next in line. The principle will apply just as much to disclaimer as to forfeiture.

Post-death variations and disclaimers are both used to redistribute property among members of the family following a death, but variations offer wider possibilities. A variation permits the beneficiary positively to redirect the devolution of the property whereas a disclaimer is merely 'negative' in its operation, ie, the beneficiary rejects the gift. As the variation permits redirection by the original beneficiary, it is possible to introduce 'new beneficiaries' into the terms of the deceased's will or the provisions of the intestacy law. If not used to redirect the property among the family, a variation will often be used to provide charitable payments by will attracting the IHT exemption.

A beneficiary can control the devolution of the property by using a variation but not by using a disclaimer. Thus, if the disclaimed property would pass to the 'wrong beneficiary', a variation will be required to redirect its devolution as appropriate. Although a variation will enable the desired rearrangement to be achieved, the lack of 'writing back' provisions for income tax can cause difficulties where the original beneficiary wants to vary in favour of his/her own minor children. These income tax difficulties are considered at **13.4.2**. The advantage of redirecting property by disclaimer is that there is no equivalent income tax disadvantage. Thus, where possible, a disclaimer by a parent is the favourable method of effecting a post-death rearrangement in favour of minor children.

13.2   Post-death variations

13.2.1   The conditions (IHTA 1984, s 142 (as amended by FA 2002, s 117); TCGA 1992, s 62 (as amended by FA 2002, s 51))

13.2.1.1   Inheritance tax

To achieve the desired writing back effect, the beneficiary must enter into the variation, in writing, within two years of the deceased's death. For variations made on or after 1 August 2002, there must be a statement in the instrument of variation, by the persons making it, that

IHTA 1984, s 142(1) is to apply to the variation. If the variation will result in additional IHT being payable on the estate of the deceased, the personal representatives must also join in this statement, and they can refuse to do so only if they do not hold sufficient assets to meet the additional tax liability.

A further requirement is that the variation must not be made for any consideration in money or money's worth (although there is not a problem if the consideration arises from other variations or disclaimers of the same estate). This is an anti-avoidance measure, illustrated by *Margaret Lau v Revenue and Customs Commissioners* [2009] STC (SCD) 352. In this case the deceased's will gave his children substantial gifts free of tax, and the residue to his wife. As this was a partly exempt estate, the IHT was calculated on grossed up values, significantly depleting the residue. The children varied their gifts with the aim that the whole estate would pass tax free to the deceased's wife, and she made lifetime gifts to the children. The variation was found to be ineffective for the purposes of writing back under s 142(1) because of the consideration received by the children.

Provided the beneficiary complies with all of these conditions, the variation is not a transfer of value by him and so no IHT will be payable (IHTA 1984, s 17(a)).

13.2.1.2 Capital gains tax

The conditions for CGT are similar to those for IHT: the variation must be in writing, made within two years of the deceased's death and must not be made for any consideration in money or money's worth. For variations made on or after 1 August 2002, there must be a statement in the instrument of variation, by the persons making it, that TCGA 1992, s 62(6) is to apply to the variation. No CGT is payable on the deceased's death in any event so that the substitution of new beneficiaries will not affect the CGT position on the death. However, electing for writing back means that the beneficiary making the variation does not make a disposal.

Where the variation creates a settlement for CGT purposes and the benefit of s 62(6) of TCGA 1992 is claimed, the variation itself is treated as being made by the deceased, so that the original beneficiary does not make a disposal. However, this beneficiary is regarded as the settlor of the settlement that comes into existence as a result of the variation (TCGA 1992, s 68C).

13.2.2 Whether or not to choose the writing back effect

The original beneficiary is the person who decides whether to make use of the writing back effect for either or both taxes.

13.2.2.1 If the original beneficiary makes no statement that IHTA 1984, s 142(1) is to apply to the variation

For IHT purposes the property is treated as passing to the original beneficiary. He is then treated as making a PET to the new beneficiary. If he survives for seven years, the transfer will become fully exempt; but if he dies within seven years, it will become chargeable.

13.2.2.2 If the original beneficiary states that IHTA 1984, s 142(1) is to apply to the variation

There will be no possibility of a charge to IHT so far as the original beneficiary is concerned. He is not treated as having made a transfer for IHT purposes. The property is treated as passing from the deceased to the new beneficiary direct.

The effect on the IHT liability of the deceased's estate will depend on several factors, for example whether the original or new beneficiaries are exempt. There may be no change, there may be a reduction in IHT or there may be an increase in IHT. If there would be an increase, this should be weighed against the benefit to the original beneficiary of avoiding making a PET.

> **Example**
>
> Dan dies having used all of his nil rate band, leaving his £500,000 estate to his wife, Shona. Shona decides to give this to their children.
>
> Without statement that s 142 is to apply:
>
> (a)   IHT on Dan's death is nil as the death estate is spouse exempt.
>
> (b)   Shona makes a PET. Provided she survives 7 years there will be no IHT on the transfer.
>
> With statement that s 142 is to apply:
>
> (a)   Recalculate IHT on Dan's estate of £500,000.
>
>   As there is no nil rate band available, the £500,000 is all charged at 40% = £200,000 tax. (The PRs would need to consent to this variation.)
>
> (b)   Shona avoids making a PET.

13.2.2.3   If the original beneficiary makes no statement that TCGA 1992, s 62(6) is to apply to the variation

The original beneficiary will make a disposal for CGT to the new beneficiary. There may be a gain or a loss if the asset has increased or decreased in value since the date of death. The new beneficiary will be treated as acquiring the asset at market value at the date of the disposal. If the gain is small it may be covered by the original beneficiary's annual exemption. If the original beneficiary has losses available, these will offset the gain. In neither case will any CGT be paid.

13.2.2.4   If the original beneficiary states that TCGA 1992, s 62(6) is to apply to the variation

There will be no disposal by the original beneficiary and, therefore, no question of any liability to CGT. The asset will be treated as passing from the estate of the deceased to the new beneficiary direct. The new beneficiary will be treated as acquiring it at market value at the date of death.

> **Example**
>
> (1)   Assume in the above example that the £500,000 includes quoted shares that have increased in value by £9,000 since death. Shona is not going to make any disposals in this year.
>
>   Without statement that s 62(6) is to apply:
>
>   (a)   CGT on Dan's death is nil.
>
>   (b)   Shona makes a disposal with chargeable gains of £9,000. This is covered by her annual exemption so Shona pays no CGT.
>
>   (c)   The children acquire the shares at the higher current value.
>
>   With statement that s 62(6) is to apply:
>
>   (a)   CGT on Dan's death is nil.
>
>   (b)   Shona makes no disposal and pays no CGT.
>
>   (c)   The children acquire the shares at the lower value at the date of death.
>
>   In this scenario, Shona should not make a variation for either IHT or CGT purposes.
>
> (2)   Assume in the above example that the £500,000 includes quoted shares that have increased in value by £20,000 since death. Shona has already made several disposals showing gains of £10,100 in this year.
>
>   Without statement that s 62(6) is to apply:
>
>   (a)   CGT on Dan's death is nil.
>
>   (b)   Shona makes a disposal with chargeable gains of £20,000. This is added to her other gains in the year, and the total exceeds her annual exemption, so she will pay CGT.

> (c)   The children acquire the shares at the higher current value.
>
> With statement that s 62(6) is to apply:
>
> (a)   CGT on Dan's death is nil.
>
> (b)   Shona makes no disposal and pays no CGT.
>
> (c)   The children acquire the shares at the lower value at the date of death.
>
> In this scenario, Shona should make a variation for CGT purposes but not for IHT purposes.

13.2.3   Capacity to make a variation

An original beneficiary under a will or an intestacy can make a variation in relation to his interest provided he has attained 18 years of age and has mental capacity. The beneficiary with an absolute interest may settle it on trusts for the benefit of others or make an outright gift.

> **Example**
>
> David by will leaves £325,000 to John, who wishes to provide for his own child, Carol, now aged 19 years. By post-death variation, David's will is varied, leaving £100,000 in trust for Carol contingently on her attaining 25 and the residue of £225,000 for John.

13.2.3.1   Consent of the court

In some cases, the consent of the court will be needed before a variation can be made. Under the Variation of Trusts Act (VTA) 1958, the court has power to consent on behalf of beneficiaries who are (inter alia) minors or mentally handicapped. The court's powers are wide enough to permit the variation of beneficial interests whether they are vested, contingent or discretionary, but it will exercise the powers only where the proposed arrangement is for the benefit of the beneficiary.

However, VTA 1958 applications to the court are expensive and time-consuming so that, to be justified, the tax saving to be achieved by estate planning should be substantial. HMRC indicates in its Inheritance Tax Manual that it may accept deeds unapproved by the court provided, of course, that they are beneficial to the minor or leave the minor's interest substantially unaffected.

Problems of lack of capacity to consent generally do not arise in the context of 'flexible' wills containing discretionary trusts or an overriding power of appointment. In these cases, any rearrangement of the deceased's estate after death occurs as a result of the decision of the trustees acting under the terms of the will. The lack of ability of a beneficiary to consent is not crucial to making the proposed arrangement. This feature of flexible wills tends to make them attractive in practice (see **12.4**).

13.2.3.2   Can the estate of a deceased beneficiary be varied?

> **Example**
>
> Veronica, who is unmarried and has made no lifetime gifts, dies leaving the whole of her estate valued at £325,000 to her brother, Arthur (a divorcee). He dies soon after his sister leaving his estate of £825,000 (£500,000 of his own plus £325,000 inherited from Veronica) to his child, Damon. Arthur's PRs can make a variation to redirect Veronica's estate to save IHT.
>
> Without variation:
>
> (a)   IHT on Veronica's death is nil
>
>   £325,000 is within her nil rate band
>
> (b)   IHT on Arthur's death
>
>   £325,000 @ 0% = Nil
>
>   £500,000 @ 40% = £200,000

Damon receives £625,000 as a result of the death of his aunt and father.

With variation:

The PRs make a variation of Veronica's estate to pass all her assets to Damon.

(a)   Recalculate IHT on Veronica's estate of £325,000

IHT is still nil as the estate value is within her nil rate band

(b)   Recalculate IHT on Arthur's estate of £500,000

£325,000 @ 0% = Nil

£175,000 @ 40% = £70,000

As a result of the variation, Damon's total entitlement from his aunt and father is £755,000.

The Revenue accepts that a variation by the PRs of the deceased beneficiary is permitted. Provided the PRs comply with the conditions, the variation will be written back into the will of the first testator to die for IHT purposes.

13.3   The scope of the statutory provisions for variations and disclaimers

It is possible to vary or disclaim 'any of the dispositions (whether effected by will, under the law relating to intestacy or otherwise) of the property comprised in the estate immediately before his death ...' (IHTA 1984, s 142).

In the application of this provision the following points should be noted.

13.3.1   Interests in joint property

An interest in property held as joint tenants is an asset of the 'estate' of a deceased person for IHT. Although an interest in property held in joint tenancy passes on death by survivorship to the surviving joint tenant, it is nevertheless within the IHT (and CGT) provisions permitting variations and disclaimers following a death. This is because these provisions apply where a disposition on death is effected 'or otherwise', ie, by survivorship.

Example

Alice and Bill inherited Rose Cottage as joint tenants many years ago. Since then they and their respective families have used the cottage for holidays.

Alice has just died leaving her estate by will to her only child, Clara, but her share of the cottage passes to Bill by survivorship. Bill feels Clara should have inherited her mother's interest in the cottage.

Bill can effect a variation so that Alice's estate is taxed as if her will had left her half of the cottage to Clara. This will be effective for tax purposes provided Bill makes the elections. To complete the gift Bill must convey the legal estate to himself and Clara by a separate deed.

13.3.2   Interests in property not capable of variation

The 'estate' of a deceased person includes, inter alia:

(a)   the property in which the deceased had an interest in possession immediately before death, for example a life tenant under an existing will trust; and

(b)   the property to which the deceased is treated as entitled by application of the 'reservation of benefit' rules (FA 1986, s 102 and see **4.6.5**).

Although both of these interests may attract IHT on death as part of the deceased's estate, it is not possible for either to be the subject of a variation (or disclaimer) for taxation purposes. This is because the definition of 'estate' within the meaning of s 142 of IHTA 1984 specifically excludes each of these interests. Any estate planning following the death must, therefore, proceed on the basis of excluding these interests from any calculations.

13.3.3 Do the reservation of benefit rules apply to variations?

Do the reservation of benefit rules apply if a beneficiary (the donor) makes a post-death variation but still continues to enjoy the property? If so, any advantage intended through the post-death variation would be lost.

The IHTA 1984 applies 'as if the variation had been effected by the deceased or, as the case may be, the disclaimed benefit never conferred'.

Thus, the effect for all IHT purposes of making use of the writing back effect is that the deceased is to be taken as making the variation and, therefore, is the donor of the gift. The original beneficiary under the will or the intestacy is not the donor. As a consequence, any benefit which is reserved by the variation to the beneficiary who made it cannot come within these provisions.

Example 1

Ellen died leaving a will containing a gift of her house to Rex. Rex occupies the house but subsequently redirects this gift by post-death variation to his only child Paula. The variation contains the relevant statement and Rex remains in occupation. This will not result in a reservation of benefit to him since the gift of the house is taken to be by Ellen for all IHT purposes. Rex's estate on his death will be taxed on this basis.

Example 2

Roger dies leaving a substantial cash legacy to Jo absolutely. Jo redirects this property into a discretionary trust by means of a variation containing the relevant statement. Jo is named as one of the beneficiaries of the discretionary trust. No reservation of benefit for IHT will result as the discretionary trust is taken to be made by Roger. However, there may be income tax consequences as there are no writing back provisions for income tax equivalent to those for IHT and CGT. Jo, not Roger, will be treated as the settlor for the purposes of the income tax avoidance rules (see **6.2.11.1**).

13.3.4 More than one variation?

Sometimes beneficiaries may want to make a number of variations in relation to the same will or intestacy. No difficulty will arise provided each variation deals with a separate part of the estate. Clearly, property given by a legacy in a will and the property in the residuary gift are separate parts each capable of being the subject of a variation. It is also accepted that two or more variations, each relating to separate items of property in residue, can be effective. For example, a residuary beneficiary can validly redirect by variation one half of the residuary property to new beneficiary A and the other half to new beneficiary B, and in each case achieve the writing back effect for IHT purposes (provided the variations contain the relevant statements).

However, the Revenue has stated (inter alia) that in its view 'an instrument will not fall within s 142 of IHTA 1984 if it further redirects any item or any part of an item that has already been redirected under an earlier instrument'. A second variation in relation *to the same property* will, therefore, not be effective for tax purposes.

13.3.5 Beneficiaries other than members of the family

Normally, the rearrangement will involve redistribution of the deceased's property among members of the family. However, there is no restriction in the legislation, whether for IHT or CGT, which restricts the introduction of a new beneficiary who is not a member of the family. This opens up the possibility of introducing as a beneficiary the following:

(a)   A claimant under the Inheritance (Provision for Family and Dependants) Act 1975. For example, a claim by a person 'maintained by the deceased' under s 1(1)(e) of the Act for reasonable financial provision may be compromised within two years of the death. If the conditions are satisfied, this may take the form of a variation which, provided it contains the relevant statement, will achieve the writing back effect of any other post-death variation and will be effective for both IHT and CGT.

(b)   A charity. A charitable donation, within the IHT exemption, can be made from the deceased's estate by introducing a charity as a legatee. If the conditions are satisfied, the terms of the will or of the intestacy law will then be read as if the deceased had made the donation himself to the named charity.

13.4   Income tax, tax avoidance and post-death arrangements

13.4.1   Income before a variation or disclaimer is made

There are no specific income tax provisions equivalent to the IHT and CGT provisions where a variation or disclaimer has been made. Thus, income received before the variation or disclaimer from the property concerned will be taxed as the income of the original beneficiary. This will apply even if the beneficiary has specifically given up all income from the property since the date of death. For example, if the original beneficiary by variation redirects a specific legacy of shares, he remains liable to pay any income tax on dividends paid before the variation.

13.4.2   Income after a variation or disclaimer is made

In most cases, once the rearrangement has been made, the original beneficiary ceases to be liable to pay income tax on income produced after the variation or disclaimer. The new beneficiary becomes liable for income tax on income produced by the property concerned. However, the position will be different where the new beneficiary is the minor child of the original beneficiary. In such cases the parent will remain liable for income tax on the income even though he does not enjoy it or own the property which produces it. The reason is the income tax anti-avoidance provisions discussed at **4.6.2** and **4.6.4**. These are of general application and can apply to pre- and to post-death arrangements.

13.4.2.1   How do the income tax avoidance rules apply to variations?

If the variation creates a settlement for income tax purposes from which the original beneficiary may continue to benefit, he will still be liable to pay income tax on all the settlement income (see **6.2.11.1**). To avoid this, the variation must be drafted so as to exclude the settlor and spouse from all enjoyment from the property which has been redirected, and from its income.

However, the original beneficiary may nevertheless be caught by the anti-avoidance rules and so still be liable to income tax on the income of the property subject to the variation. This will be the case if his minor unmarried children are constituted the new beneficiaries as a result of the variation, and the income is paid for the benefit of those beneficiaries and not accumulated. The same result will occur whether the variation gives the children absolute interests or an interest in new trusts which are created by the variation.

If the anti-avoidance provisions apply, they will cease to do so once the children have reached their majority or have married; from then onwards their parents will no longer be taxed on the settlement income.

> **Example 1**
> A variation by Hannah (of the estate she inherited from her father) redirects £325,000 absolutely to her adult children. The children will pay income tax on the income of the property.

> **Example 2**
>
> A similar post-death variation is made by Ania but her children (the new beneficiaries) are minors. Even though the children have an absolute (vested) entitlement to the £325,000, the income of the property is deemed to be Ania's for tax purposes.

13.4.2.2 Disclaimers distinguished

A variation is the positive redirection of benefit by the original beneficiary, whereas a disclaimer is merely the rejection of a benefit. The Revenue does not consider a disclaimer to be a 'settlement' and so to come within the income tax anti-avoidance provisions. The consequence is that income of property which is disclaimed by a parent is not taxed as though it is still his, even if his minor unmarried child inherits the property as a result of the disclaimer. Similarly, any capital gains made would not be taxed as the settlor's. Thus, parents who are considering post-death rearrangements for the benefit of their children should, where possible, use a disclaimer instead of a variation which might fall within the provisions.

13.5 Drafting a post-death variation and the election

13.5.1 Is a deed required?

Both IHTA 1984, s 142 and TCGA 1992, s 62 require only an instrument in writing, but as a post-death variation is a gratuitous promise to transfer property, it should be by deed to be enforceable. Further, unless it is by deed the deceased's personal representatives may not be prepared to act in accordance with its terms.

13.5.2 The date and opening words

Sample clause

> This deed of variation is made the [   ] day of [   ]
> Two thousand and …

13.5.3 Parties

Both IHTA 1984, s 142 and TCGA 1992, s 62 require only 'the persons who benefit or would benefit under the disposition … to make the written instrument'. However, often there will be three parties:

(a) the original beneficiaries (who give up the benefit);

(b) the new beneficiaries (who receive the property and thus will include trustees if the variation creates a trust); and

(c) the personal representatives of the deceased's estate (who must also join in any statement that s 142(1) IHT is to apply if additional IHT is payable as a result of the variation).

Sample clause

> BETWEEN
> (1) [name and address] ('the Original Beneficiary')
> (2) [name and address] ('the New Beneficiary')
> (3) [name and address] ('the Executors')

Personal representatives should be made parties for their own protection when they distribute property in accordance with the post-death variation rather than the will in its original form. It is not essential to join the new beneficiaries in receipt of property as parties, but many practitioners prefer to do so.

13.5.4   Supplemental to the will or intestacy

The deed of variation is made to relate expressly to the deceased's death.

Sample clause

> Supplemental to the will [with ... codicil(s)] ('the Will') of [name] ('the Deceased') and to the other documents and events specified in the Schedule

The Schedule will contain details of the will, date of death, grant of probate, etc.

13.5.5   Recitals

Recitals will always be used in the deed to explain the circumstances giving rise to the variation. Usually the recitals are restricted to statements relating to:

(a)   the entitlement of the original beneficiary under the will or the intestacy of the deceased; and

(b)   the wish of the original beneficiary to vary the provisions of the will or the intestacy in the manner stated in the operative part of the variation.

Sample clause

> WHEREAS
>
> (A) Under the Will the Original Beneficiary was given [   ] interest ('the Interest') in [all of the] [x% of the] residuary estate of the Deceased
>
> (B) The Original Beneficiary wishes to vary the dispositions effected by the Will in relation to the Interest in the following manner

The interest will be an 'absolute' interest or a 'life interest' and the clause should be completed accordingly, showing whether it relates to the whole or part of the residuary estate.

13.5.6   The operative part

It is often convenient when drafting the operative part of a post-death variation to consider how the will, or a codicil to it, might have been drafted for the testator before his death. This can often give valuable guidance on drafting the post-death variation. For example, in the context of a variation to create a nil rate band legacy for a child, only a short provision is required.

Sample clause

> Now this deed irrevocably witnesses as follows:
>
> By way of variation of the disposition made by the Will the Original Beneficiary declares that the Will shall have effect as if it contained a pecuniary legacy to the New Beneficiary of an amount on which no IHT is chargeable other than at the nil rate on the death of the Deceased such legacy to be discharged from the Interest.

An alternative approach is to draft replacement provisions in full, ensuring that the wording and definitions are consistent with the will.

Sample clause

> By way of variation of the disposition made by the Will the Original Beneficiary declares that the Will shall have effect as if clauses 3 and 4 were omitted and replaced by the following:
>
>> '3. I give £10,000 to The Landmark Trust (registered charity number 243312) for its general charitable purposes and I direct that the receipt of a person who appears to be a proper officer of The Landmark Trust shall be a sufficient discharge to my Executors.
>>
>> 4. I give £100,000 to each of my granddaughters, Bella Jones and Rebecca Brown, free of tax.'

If a legacy is being introduced into the will by the post-death variation, it should be considered whether it is to be a legacy 'subject to' or 'free of' IHT. In the former case, any IHT which does become payable is paid by the legatee. The payment of the legacy will be directed to be made from a particular part of the estate, which normally will be the residue.

If trusts, rather than outright gifts, are to be created by the variation, these may either be set out in a schedule to the deed or it may refer to trusts created by a separate instrument. For example, the original beneficiary may wish to direct that his interest be transferred to the trustees of a settlement created by the deceased during his lifetime for his grandchildren.

13.5.7   Achieving the writing back effect

To achieve the writing back effect for tax purposes, there must be a statement in the written variation by the beneficiaries making the variation that it is intended that IHTA 1984, s 142(1) and/or TCGA 1992, s 62(6) shall apply to the variation.

If the variation causes additional IHT to become payable, for example where a spouse gives up a benefit and the spouse exemption is lost, the PRs must join in the statement. Only if the PRs have no funds available to them for payment of any extra IHT may they refuse to join in the statement. This protects PRs who have already distributed the estate before they become liable to pay the extra IHT resulting from the written variation.

If there will be additional IHT payable as a result of a variation made on or after 1 August 2002, the persons making the variation and the PRs must supply a copy of the variation to the Revenue within six months of the variation being made (IHTA 1984, s 218A (inserted by FA 2002)) or be liable for a fine (IHTA 1984, s 245A (inserted by FA 2002)).

Sample clause

> The Parties hereto hereby declare pursuant to section 142(2) of the Inheritance Tax Act 1984 and section 62(7) of the Taxation of Chargeable Gains Act 1992 that section 142(1) of the Inheritance Tax Act 1984 and section 62(6) of the Taxation of Chargeable Gains Act 1992 shall apply to the variation made by this deed

Summary – Post-death Arrangements

Topic	Summary	Reference
Post death arrangements	The way in which an estate is left on death is not final. Beneficiaries can redirect property without tax implications for themselves if they comply with certain statutory requirements. It therefore allows a further opportunity for tax efficient lifetime giving.	Chapter 13
	A variation allows the beneficiary to redirect the property in whatever way he chooses. A disclaimer is a rejection by the beneficiary, and the property then passes in accordance with the terms of the will or testacy.	
	The beneficiary may elect that the variation or disclaimer be treated as 'written back', ie treated as if made by the deceased on death, for either or both IHT and CGT purposes. It depends on the particular circumstances as to whether it will be beneficial to make these elections. To achieve the writing back effect certain formalities must be followed.	13.2.2 and 13.3.3 13.2 and 13.5

Chapter 14
Trust Administration

14.1 Introduction

Many aspects of trust administration have been considered in the earlier chapters in this book. Most of these matters have related to the dispositive provisions of the trust instrument, ie, the provisions dealing with the beneficiaries and beneficial entitlement and include the following:

(a)   TA 1925, ss 31 and 32 in **Chapters 5** and **10**;

(b)   the powers of trustees in **Chapter 11**;

(c)   advances and appointments by trustees in favour of beneficiaries in **Chapters 9** and **10**;

(d)   capital tax implications of changes in beneficial entitlement arising from (a) and (b).

There are many other matters relevant to the proper administration of a trust the more important of which are discussed in this chapter. These include:

(a)   trustee investments;

(b)   the appointment of trustees;

(c)   vesting trust property in trustees and in beneficiaries;

(d)   taxation liability arising during the trust period, including CGT on sales by trustees on rearrangements of the investment portfolio and the income tax liabilities of the trustees and beneficiaries; and

(e)   accounting for the trust assets and income.

14.2 Management powers of trustees

When creating a settlement, particularly a discretionary settlement, the settlor will wish to incorporate wide-ranging powers for his trustees covering all aspects of the trust fund and its administration. He must bear in mind the present and future trust property, the wide-ranging nature of the trusts, and the wide class of beneficiaries. The trust may continue for many years so it is necessary to consider all the provisions which may be of assistance to the trustees in the future. The modern policy is to incorporate these wide powers by inserting them in a schedule to the trust instrument.

14.2.1 Other matters relating to the trustees

Apart from the appointment and retirement of the trustees referred to in **14.4**, express provision in relation to the following will normally be made.

14.2.1.1 Self-dealing

The fiduciary position of the trustees prevents them from purchasing the trust property or entering into any other transaction affecting the trust property where the trustees' duties and personal self-interest are in conflict. Express provision may permit self-dealing by the trustees.

14.2.1.2   Losses

To protect an honest trustee, the trust instrument will often contain a general indemnity against loss to the trust fund caused by the trustee or an agent (other than where there is wilful fraud or dishonesty of the trustee).

14.2.1.3   Delegation of powers

The TA 2000 allows trustees to delegate 'delegable functions' to an agent, who can be anyone except a beneficiary. Delegable functions do not include decisions on distributing trust property to beneficiaries, paying fees and appointing trustees. Having made the appointment, the trustee must continue to review it from time to time. It may be desirable expressly to exclude the limitation on a beneficiary being an agent. Section 25 of TA 1925 (as substituted by the Trustee Delegation Act 1999) permits the trustees to delegate by power of attorney any of their powers and discretions for up to 12 months. In addition, s 9 of TLATA 1996 permits trustees of land to delegate by power of attorney their functions in relation to the land, for example their power of sale, to beneficiaries of full age who are beneficially entitled to an interest in possession in the land.

14.3   Trustee investments

14.3.1   Retention of the original trust fund

For a settlement to be effective, it needs property to be subject to the trusts. When a settlement is created the initial trust fund may consist of cash, or assets (eg, shares or land), or a combination of cash and assets. The trustees must decide whether they are permitted to keep the initial trust fund as it is and, if so, whether in fact they should do so.

Most lifetime settlements and will trusts are drafted by professionals who will ensure that the settlement gives the trustees the widest possible powers of investment and enables them to keep any assets transferred to them by the settlor or from the estate.

The TA 2000 implies similar powers into trusts where there are no express powers, for example, where a statutory trust arises under the AEA 1925 on the death of someone intestate.

14.3.2   Suitable investments

In deciding whether to retain permitted assets, the trustees must consider the suitability of the assets for the aims of the settlement. This is also a governing factor when deciding how to invest any cash that may have been settled.

Example 1

A settlement is created for Donna for life with remainder to Nigel. The trustees are faced with competing needs: Donna requires an income from the trust fund whilst Nigel needs the real value of the capital to improve. As a general rule, assets producing a good income return, for example, a building society account, offer little or no capital growth, and vice versa.

The trustees need to invest the trust fund in a range of investments which provide overall income and capital growth; perhaps gilts and a National Savings Income Bond for income and quoted shares or unit trusts for growth.

Example 2

A settlement is created for Adam and Belinda, 6-year-old twins, contingent as to both capital and income on their attaining 25 years of age. They are unlikely to need any income for at least the first five years of the settlement, and any income accumulated in the settlement will suffer 50% income tax (see **14.5.2**).

As there is no need for income, the trustees can concentrate on improving the capital value of the trust fund, perhaps by investing in quoted shares.

Note: There may be circumstances where the settlor does not want the trustees to hold a balance. For example, a testator may leave his property to his elderly wife for life and the remainder to charity. His major concern may be that his wife should be well provided for and he may not be very concerned as to the amount the charity eventually takes. He can leave a statement of wishes, but the trustees will be at risk of an action for breach of trust from the remainderman. To protect them, he should include a direction in the trust stating that the trustees are not to be required to invest impartially.

14.3.3   Subsequent changes to the trust fund

Although with an express power of investment the bulk of the fund is likely to be invested in land and/or securities, most trustees should consider retaining a degree of liquidity by holding a small amount of cash in an interest-bearing instant access bank or building society account. This will provide the trustees with cash to meet expenses, such as solicitors' or accountants' fees, and their own out-of-pocket expenses. It will also provide them with the ability to make a new purchase for the trust fund if an opportunity suddenly arises. On occasion, they may also use such an account to retain the proceeds of sale of an investment where there is not to be an immediate reinvestment of the realised fund.

Once a settlement has been created, trustees need to review the trust fund regularly. Trustees can make many of the investments which an individual concerned with his personal estate planning might make (see **Appendix 2**). How often trustees review their investments depends on a number of factors but should not be less than once a year and may be more frequently. This is to ensure that the fund continues to provide for the aims of the settlement; to minimise the liability to CGT; and to protect the fund against economic forces.

Regular review is particularly important now that the TA 2000 has imposed a duty to review on trustees. Trustees should ensure that there are minutes of trustees' meetings confirming that review took place.

14.3.3.1   Changes to reflect the aims of the settlement

Settlements are designed to last for many years. An investment strategy that was appropriate at the outset may not be appropriate 10 years later; in particular, the beneficiaries needs may have changed or there may be about to be a change in the beneficial interests in the settlement. Trustees may need to alter the investments in the trust fund to reflect these changes.

> ### Example
> Twelve years ago, Damien settled £100,000 cash on discretionary trusts for his three grandchildren then aged 5, 4 and 2 years. The children had no immediate need for income and, as all income accumulated within the trust suffers income tax which is non-recoverable, the trustees invested the majority of the trust fund in low income, high-growth shares and unit trusts. The trust fund is now worth £180,000 and produces £3,500 per annum income. The eldest beneficiary intends to start medical school in three months' time, and the trustees have decided to exercise their discretion and pay her £5,000 per annum income from the trust fund.
>
> The trustees must, therefore, sell some of their investments and reinvest the proceeds to increase the income generated by the trust fund. As a known amount of income is required, the trustees might consider achieving this by investing in gilts or a guaranteed rate building society account.

14.3.3.2   Minimising CGT

A large proportion of a trust fund is likely to be invested in assets such as quoted shares which attract a charge to CGT on their disposal. As trustees have only an annual exemption of £5,050 and gains are charged at 28% in all settlements, it is sensible (where possible) to manage the fund to minimise the liability. For example, trustees may invest in land to be occupied by a beneficiary under a trust as his residence. If so, any gain on sale by the trustees would qualify for the principal private residence exemption. If such investment and occupation occur under the terms of a discretionary trust, this (at least in the view of the Revenue) may amount to giving the beneficiary an interest in possession in the part of the settled property represented by the private residence (see **4.7.3**).

A charge to CGT will arise on two occasions: on a deemed disposal when a beneficiary becomes absolutely entitled to trust property; and on an actual disposal when trust property is sold as a result of investment changes (see **14.5**). Trustees should always aim to utilise their annual exemption, as it cannot be carried forward to future tax years or transferred to beneficiaries.

In a year in which a deemed disposal will occur, trustees should consider carefully whether any investment changes need to be made or whether they can leave the changes to the next tax year, so keeping their annual exemption available to set against the charge on the deemed disposal.

14.3.3.3   General reviews

Most investors who invest in the stock market, whether through the direct purchase of shares or via unit trusts, do so to make money rather than as a desire to be part of a particular company. The stock market is divided into sectors with companies predominantly involved in particular activities being grouped together, for example, both WH Smith plc and Marks & Spencer plc are in the 'Retailers General' sector whilst Lloyds TSB plc is in the 'Banks' sector. Trustees, like most individual investors, are looking for a spread of investments, investing in companies from a number of sectors rather than concentrating on companies in one sector. This is because sectors of the economy perform differently depending on different economic factors and, if one sector is suffering, the value of the shares in the majority of companies in that sector is likely to fall. It is unusual, however, for all sectors to be depressed at the same time and the theory of investing in a number of sectors is that the gains and losses should be evened out.

Trustees may be advised to sell their shares in companies in a particular sector and invest the proceeds in a different sector for a while, or to change companies within a sector.

Example

The trustees of a discretionary settlement have invested one quarter of the trust fund in gilts and the remainder equally between A plc (an insurance company), B plc (a food manufacturer) and C plc (an oil company). Their stockbrokers advise that the insurance market is depressed and that the value of their shareholding is falling but that companies in the 'Water' sector look set to make large profits. The trustees decide to sell their shares in A plc and use the proceeds to buy shares in D plc, a water company.

14.4   Appointment of trustees

14.4.1   The original trustees

14.4.1.1   Choice of trustees

The choice of the original trustees of the settlement is made by the settlor at the time he makes a settlement. Their appointment as trustees takes effect immediately the trust instrument is executed. Once appointed, they are in a fiduciary position and so must act with good faith. Their duty is to administer the trust for the benefit of its beneficiaries.

14.4.1.2   Number of trustees

Although every trust must have at least one trustee, it is usual for the settlor to appoint between two and four individuals to act as trustees of his settlement. A maximum of four trustees can be appointed for trusts of land, but at least two trustees (or a trust corporation) are required to give a buyer a valid receipt for the proceeds of sale of land held in a settlement. There is no limit to the number of trustees who can be appointed for trusts of personalty, but the appointment of more than four can cause the trust administration to be unnecessarily cumbersome.

14.4.1.3   Selection of trustees

The settlor should take great care in choosing the original trustees. It is possible to appoint a trust corporation to act as trustee, but most settlors prefer to appoint individuals because of the personal involvement this will bring to the administration of the trusts. The settlor should consider the following.

A professional trustee

It is of advantage if a solicitor or other professional person is appointed to be a trustee (often together with member(s) of the settlor's own family). Where a professional is appointed, the administrative provisions of the trust should include a charging clause. Even if a professional is not appointed at the outset, it is a good idea to include a charging clause in case a professional is appointed as a trustee in the future (see **14.2.3**).

The settlor as trustee

The settlor may appoint himself to be the sole trustee or one of several trustees of his settlement. This allows him to retain an involvement in the settlement and have some influence over how it is administered, for example he will have a say in whether the trustees should exercise their discretion in favour of a particular beneficiary under a discretionary settlement. If he is appointed a trustee, the settlor must not allow his personal wishes to overshadow his duties as trustee.

Instead of being appointed a trustee, the settlor may prefer to exercise some influence over the trustees through the use of a 'letter of wishes' (or a side letter) addressed to the trustees. Clearly, such a letter will have no binding effect on the trustees but, by setting out how he wishes the settlement to be administered in the future, the settlor hopes the trustees will have some regard to his intentions.

A beneficiary as trustee

The settlor may appoint one or more of the beneficiaries to be a trustee of the settlement but this may cause difficulty, for example a conflict of interest may arise between the individual's position as trustee on the one hand and as beneficiary on the other. In view of this, a beneficiary should not be a sole trustee. Two or more trustees provide safeguards in that they must supervise one another, must be unanimous in the exercise of their powers (an important protection for the beneficiaries) and their appointment will ensure a continuing trustee if one were to die or to retire from the trusts.

14.4.2   Subsequent trustees

14.4.2.1   Appointment by the settlor

Once the original trustees have been appointed the settlor has no further power to appoint trustees. If a settlor (who is not also a trustee) wishes to control the selection of trustees during his lifetime, he can do so only if the trust instrument gives him the express power to appoint new trustees.

Sample clause

> During the lifetime of the Settlor the power of appointing new trustees shall be vested in the Settlor.

14.4.2.2   The statutory power of appointing new or additional trustees

If there is no person nominated in the trust instrument (eg, the settlor), s 36 of TA 1925 provides wide statutory powers for the appointment of new trustees.

Replacement trustees (TA 1925, s 36(1))

The appointment of a new trustee must be made in writing (but will normally be by deed, see **14.4.4**) by:

(a)   the surviving or continuing trustees, including any retiring or disclaiming trustee if he wishes to join in the appointment; or

(b)   the personal representatives of the last surviving trustee.

A new trustee can be appointed under s 36(1) to replace, inter alia, a trustee who has died, is incapable of acting, or who retires.

Additional trustees (TA 1925, s 36(6))

The appointment of additional trustees must be made in writing by the continuing trustee(s). The number of trustees after the new appointment is made must not exceed four.

Directions as to trustees (TLATA 1996, s 19)

If there is no person still alive nominated in the trust instrument to appoint new trustees, the beneficiaries of full age and capacity who together are entitled to the trust property can give written directions to the trustees for the retirement and appointment of a trustee. As it is possible for the trust instrument to exclude s 19, settlors should be invited to consider whether they prefer future control over the appointment and retirement of trustees to remain with the existing trustees or to pass instead to the beneficiaries.

14.4.3   Vesting the trust property in the trustees

14.4.3.1   On creation of the settlement

Once the original trustees have been appointed, the settlor must transfer to them the 'settled property', ie the assets mentioned in the trust instrument as being subject to the trusts of the settlement. It is a duty of the trustees to bring all the trust property under their control.

The settlor will transfer the settled property to the trustees by whatever means of transfer is appropriate to that property. For example, stock transfer forms will be used to transfer shares; a deed will be used to transfer the legal estate in land.

14.4.3.2   On the appointment of replacement or additional trustees

Following a change in the trustees, the trust property must be vested in the new trustee(s). If the appointment of the new trustee(s) is by deed, s 40(1) of TA 1925 provides that the vesting of the trust property will occur automatically. There are, however, circumstances where s 40(1) does not apply so that formal transfer of the trust property to the new trustee(s) will be required. In particular, there is no automatic vesting of stocks and shares. In these cases, a stock transfer form transferring the shares into the names of all the trustees must be signed by the 'old trustees' and registered with the company. Although the shares are held by the trustees as trust property, there is no reference to this on the company's membership register. Shares are shown as registered in the individual names of the trustees without reference to their capacity as trustees.

14.4.4 Drafting a deed of appointment of new trustees

14.4.4.1 Heading and date

Sample clause

> DEED OF APPOINTMENT AND RETIREMENT
> DATE: [   ]

14.4.4.2 Parties

Who the parties are will depend on the circumstances giving rise to the appointment of new trustees. The person(s) with the power to appoint will always be parties; so too will the new trustee(s) and any retiring trustee.

Sample clause

> BETWEEN
> (1)   [name and address] ('the Continuing Trustees')
> (2)   [name and address] ('the New Trustee')
> (3)   [name and address] ('the Retiring Trustee')

14.4.4.3 Recitals

Normally, there will be three or four separate provisions detailing the circumstances giving rise to the change of the trustees.

Sample clause

> RECITALS
> (A)   This Deed is supplemental to the settlement ('the Settlement') [and to the other documents and events] specified in the [First] Schedule.
> (B)   The statutory power of appointment applies to the Settlement and is exercisable by the Continuing Trustees and the Retiring Trustee.
> (C)   The Continuing Trustees and the Retiring Trustee are the present trustees of the Settlement.
> (D)   The Continuing Trustees and the Retiring Trustee wish to appoint the New Trustee to act as a trustee of the Settlement in place of the Retiring Trustee.
> (E)   It is intended that the property now in the Settlement [, details of which are set out in the Second Schedule,] shall be transferred to, or under the control of, the Continuing Trustees and the New Trustee

Such clauses allow for the retirement of the trustee. If no trustee is retiring, all references to 'the Retiring Trustee' should be deleted from the clauses as well as from 'the parties'.

Clause (E) is intended to enable the trust property to be detailed in the schedule to the deed of appointment. It is not an express declaration vesting property in the new trustee.

14.4.4.4 The operative part

By this clause, those with the power to do so make the appointment of the new trustee. If power to appoint new trustees has been retained by the settlor (see **14.4.2**), the settlor, defined as 'the Appointor', would be added as a 'party' and would make the appointment in the operative part. If the present trustees are to exercise the statutory power to appoint the new trustees, they will do so in this part of the deed.

If a trustee is retiring, it is usual to include a statement in the deed confirming that there is no intention for the residence status of the trust to change. Where a trust 'emigrates' (see **Chapter 15**) there is a CGT charge, and this can result in anyone who has been a trustee within the 12 months prior to the emigration of the trust being liable. The statement will help prevent a retired trustee being liable.

Sample clauses

> Appointment of New Trustee in place of Retiring Trustee
>
> In exercise of the power of appointment conferred by the Trustee Act 1925 and of all other powers (if any), the Continuing Trustees and the Retiring Trustee hereby appoint the New Trustee as a trustee of the Settlement to act jointly with the Continuing Trustees in place of the Retiring Trustee who hereby retires and is discharged from the trusts of the Settlement.
>
> Declaration as to residence
>
> It is hereby declared that, at the date hereof, there is no proposal that the Trustees of the Settlement might become neither resident nor ordinarily resident in the United Kingdom.

Again, if no trustee is to retire, the references to 'the Retiring Trustee' should be deleted and there is no need to refer to the residence of the trust. The appointment is then made by 'the Continuing Trustees', ie, they do so in exercise of the statutory power.

14.4.4.5 Schedules

It is usual to include in the schedules particulars of the settlement to which the deed of appointment is supplemental, as well as details of the trust property currently held by the trustees. This list of trust property is useful for the new trustee who must now exercise his duties as trustee in relation to it.

14.5 Taxation during the administration of a settlement

The settlor's liability to IHT and CGT on the creation of the settlement is considered in **Chapter 5**, and liability to the same taxes which arises on trust advances and appointments is considered in **Chapter 10**. Broadly, these earlier chapters covered the capital tax position on creation and termination of the settlement. The liability to CGT and income tax arising on the trust capital and its income during the administration of a settlement are considered below; any relevant IHT liabilities during the trust's existence are considered in the chapters referred to above.

14.5.1 Actual disposals: CGT

If the trustees of the settlement rearrange their portfolio of investments, CGT liability may arise on any sales. If so, the trustees are liable to pay the tax and will do so from the settled funds. Sales by the trustees are 'actual disposals' giving rise to CGT liability in a manner similar to disposals by an individual.

Example

Trustees are holding 5,000 XYZ plc shares as part of a trust fund. These shares are sold for £30,000 having been worth only £5,000 when they were acquired by the trustees.

	£
Disposal consideration	30,000
Less:	
Acquisition cost, ie, the value of the shares when they were acquired by the trustees	5,000
Chargeable gain	25,000

The calculation is the same as any CGT calculation. It is based on the trustees' disposal consideration and their acquisition cost, ie the value of the shares when transferred to them by the settlor at the time the settlement was created, or the price paid by the trustees when they bought the shares if they were acquired later.

14.5.1.1   Reliefs, exemption and rates of tax

Rates of CGT

The net gains made by trustees on all disposals in a tax year are aggregated, and the annual exemption is deducted. Since 23 June 2010 trustees pay tax at a flat rate of 28%. (The rate was 18% in the period 6 April 2008 to 22 June 2010.)

Exemptions

Trustees of any settlement are entitled to an annual exemption of £5,050, ie one half of the exemption for individuals. If the settlor has created a number of settlements, the exemption is divided between them with a minimum of £1,010 in each case.

Reliefs

In limited circumstances, Entrepreneurs' Relief may be available where there is an actual disposal of business assets held in the settlement and a number of conditions are met (see **4.4.5.3**).

Hold-over relief is not available on actual disposals. It is available only on deemed disposals by trustees.

14.5.1.2   Losses

> **Example**
>
> Trustees of a discretionary settlement sell the trust's holding of shares in A plc which are now worth £10,000, having been purchased three years ago for £25,000.
>
> | | £ |
> | --- | --- |
> | Disposal consideration | 10,000 |
> | *Less:* Acquisition cost | 25,000 |
> | Loss | (15,000) |
>
> As this loss is incurred by the trustees, they are entitled to claim loss relief. They do so by setting the loss against gains they make on other sales in the same tax year. If there are none, or if there are insufficient gains to absorb the loss, the trustees may carry the loss forward to set against gains made in future years.

14.5.2   Income tax

It is necessary to distinguish the liability of the settlement trustees from the beneficiary's liability.

14.5.2.1   Trustees' liability

The trustees must pay tax on all income produced by the trust assets. In many cases, the trustees will receive savings income, such as bank interest, or dividend income after tax has been paid or credited as paid. The 20% deduction at source on interest and the 10% credit attributable to dividends will satisfy their liability to pay at basic rate or dividend ordinary rate. On any untaxed income, the trustees pay at 20%. Whether the trustees have any further income tax liability depends on the type of settlement since the nature of the beneficial interests in the settlement governs the rate of tax for which the trustees are liable. The distinction is between settlements where beneficiaries have a right to the income and settlements where they do not.

Settlements where there is a right to income

Where beneficiaries have a right to income, the trustees are only liable for income tax at the basic rate (20%) and dividend ordinary rate (10%), depending on the type of income or the price paid by the trustees when they bought the shares if they were acquired later.

As, in the majority of cases, the trustees will receive 'net' income, no further liability to income will arise. Any 'gross' income receipt will be taxed in their hands at 20%.

Example

Trustees of a trust where B has a right to income receive the following income in the tax year 2010/11:

£4,500 dividends (net) (£5,000 gross)

£1,600 interest (net)   (£2,000 gross)

The trustees have no further income tax to pay as their liability has been satisfied by the 10% tax credit on the dividends and the 20% tax deducted from the interest. If they had also received £10,000 rent (gross) in that tax year, the trustees would be liable for tax at 20% on this, and would have to pay £2,000.

Settlements where there is no right to income

Trustees of trusts where the beneficiaries have no right to receive income must pay 'the trust rate' or 'the dividend trust rate' on income which is to be accumulated or which is payable at their discretion (ITA 2007, s 479). Income which is properly used to pay management expenses is deductible from the income before tax (ITA 2007, ss 484–486).

The trust rate (50%) is paid on non-dividend income and the dividend trust rate (42.5%) is paid on dividend income. The trustees have the benefit of any tax credit where the trust income is received net.

Since 6 April 2005, for trusts where the beneficiaries have no right to receive income, a basic rate band applies. For the tax year 2010/11 it applies to the first £1,000 of income as follows:

(a)   non-dividend income within this level that would have been charged at the trust rate of 50% will instead be charged at 20%.

(b)   dividend income that would have been charged at 42.5% will instead be charged at 10%.

This means that a number of trusts do not pay the trust rate on any of their income because their total income falls below the £1,000 threshold.

Example 1

Trustees of a discretionary trust receive the following income in the tax year 2010/11:

(a)   £150 rent income (gross);

(b)   £80 interest (net) (gross £100);

(c)   £360 dividends (net) (gross £400).

All the gross income falls within the £1,000 band so:

(a)   The gross rent (£150) is charged at 20% = £30.

(b)   The gross interest (£100) is charged at 20% = £20.

(c)   The gross dividend income (£400) is charged at 10% = £40.

Total tax is £90.

There is a credit of £20 on the interest and £40 on the dividends, leaving £30 to pay.

Where the trustees have annual income above £1,000, the excess will be chargeable at the trust rate, but the basic rate band will still apply to the first £1,000 slice of income. The basic rate band is allocated to income in the following order:

(a)   non-dividend income;

(b)   dividend income.

Example 2

Trustees of a discretionary trust receive the following income in the tax year 2010/11:

(a)   £300 rent income (gross);

(b)   £400 interest (net) (gross £500);

(c)   £900 dividends (net) (gross £1,000).

The gross income is £1,800. That part of the gross income that falls within the £1,000 band escapes the trust rate (50%) or dividend trust rate (42.5%) so:

(a)   The gross rent (£300) is charged at 20% = £60

(b)   The gross interest (£500) is charged at 20% = £100

This leaves only £200 of the basic rate band, so:

(a)   £200 of the gross dividend income is charged at 10% = £20

(b)   The remaining gross dividend income (£800) is charged at 42.5% = £340

(c)   Total tax is £520

There is a credit of £100 on the interest and £100 on the dividends, leaving £320 to pay.

For those trusts that consistently have income below £1,000 per annum, a self assessment tax return would be issued only periodically; the current proposal is once every five years. Trustees would still be under an obligation to notify the Revenue where they had a liability to tax, whether on income or chargeable gains.

14.5.2.2 The beneficiary's liability

It is necessary to distinguish the position of a beneficiary who has a right to the income of the settled property from other beneficiaries, for example, beneficiaries of a discretionary settlement.

Right to income

The beneficiary with a vested entitlement to the settlement income receives from the trustees the trust income after deduction of the relevant amount of tax. If it is non-dividend income it is received after tax at 20% has been paid. If it is dividend income it is received after tax at 10% has been paid on it. The beneficiary is liable to tax on this income in the same way as he pays tax on any other income he may have. As tax at 20% and 10% has been paid, the beneficiary's liability (if any) is confined to tax at 32.5% or 42.5% on dividends and 40% or 50% on any other income, depending on whether the beneficiary pays tax at the higher and/or the additional rate. To justify their payment of tax, the trustees provide the beneficiary with a tax deduction certificate in Form R185 which he will pass on to the Revenue.

Example

Trustees are holding a trust fund in which Tony has a right to income. The trustees' gross dividend income is £1,000 (£900 net). They pay £900 to Tony to whom they give Form R185 justifying the payment of tax at basic rate. Tony's gross income from the trust is £1,000, ie, £900 + £100.

Tony's tax position depends on the amount of his other income:

(a)   If he is an additional rate tax payer

gross trust dividend income £1,000 × 42.5% =	£425
Less tax @ 10% credited as paid by the trustees	£100
tax due	£325

(b)   If he is a higher rate tax payer

gross trust dividend income £1,000 × 32.5% =	£325
Less tax @ 10% credited as paid by the trustees	£100
tax due	£225

> (c)   If he is not a tax payer, he will not be able to reclaim the £100 tax credit.
>
> (d)   If he pays tax at basic rate, he has no further tax to pay.

No right to income

Where no beneficiary has the right to receive the income of the trust property, the trustees may exercise their discretion to pay it to a beneficiary, or they may accumulate the income. If they do pay out income to a beneficiary, they must provide the beneficiary with a Form R185. This states the amount of tax paid on the income by the trustees. The beneficiary will pass it on to the Revenue and will receive a tax credit for the tax paid by the trustees. All income received by the beneficiary is treated as income received net of the trust rate of tax (50%) (ITA 2007, s 494).

Example 1: income accumulated

The trustees of a discretionary settlement receive, after deduction of 20% tax at source, bank interest of £1,600. This £2,000 gross income is taxed as follows:

The first £1,000 is taxed at 20% = £200, and the remaining £1,000 is taxed at 50% = £500. There is a total tax liability of £700, of which £400 has already been deducted at source, leaving the trustees to pay an additional £300.

They have no expenses. None of the income is paid to beneficiaries. The trustees accumulate the remaining £1,300 by adding it to the capital of the trust. The £700 tax paid on the gross income of £2,000, ie, £400 (credit) plus the £300 additional tax, cannot be recovered from the Revenue.

Had the income come from dividends, the trustees would have received £1,800 net of 10% tax (£2,000 gross). They would have paid an additional 32.5% on the gross income above the first £1,000 income (ie, £325). As in the previous example, the tax paid would not have been recoverable from the Revenue.

Example 2: income applied

The facts are the same as in Example 1 but the trustees pay £300 of the remaining income to a discretionary beneficiary, Abdul. His income from the trustees is treated as the net amount from which 50% tax (the trust rate) has been deducted. Therefore the gross value of this £300 received by Abdul is £600.

Abdul's tax position depends on the amount of his other income:

(a)   If he is an additional rate tax payer

gross trust income £600 × 50%		£300
Less tax treated as paid by the trustees at 50%		£300
	no further tax due	£0

(b)   If he is a higher rate tax payer

tax treated as paid by the trustees at 50%	£300
tax at higher rate £600 × 40%	£240
refunded by the Revenue	£60

(c)   If he is a basic rate tax payer

tax treated as paid by the trustees at 50%	£300
tax at basic rate £600 × 20%	£120
refunded by the Revenue	£180

(d)   If he is not a tax payer (ie, he has no other income)

net income	£300
tax treated as paid by the trustees at 50% (refunded by the Revenue)	£300
gross income	£600

Where beneficiaries are not additional rate tax payers, the trustees should consider exercising their discretion over the income and pay it for the maintenance, education or benefit of the beneficiaries rather than accumulating it. The tax paid by the trustees can then be repaid to the beneficiaries (see Example 2). If the income is accumulated as in Example 1, the tax cannot be reclaimed.

Trustees of settlements who pay income to a beneficiary who has no right to receive it provide the beneficiary with a new source of income for his own tax purposes. The source of the income is the trustees, not the underlying companies which pay dividends or banks which pay interest to the trustees.

The current legislation requires trustees who exercise a discretion to pay income to a beneficiary to provide the beneficiary with a tax deduction certificate at the trust rate of tax (50%) even when, in fact, the trustees have paid at a lower rate (either because the income is within the £1,000 basic rate tax band or because it is dividend income on which the top rate of tax is only 42.5%). There have been proposals to alter this rule, but, as yet, these have not been implemented.

A beneficiary who is not an additional rate tax payer can, therefore, reclaim tax from the Revenue. Non-tax payers can reclaim the whole 50%; basic rate and higher rate tax payers can reclaim the difference between the 20% or 40% for which they are liable and the 50% tax credit.

This creates a difficulty for trustees. Any shortfall between tax due at the trust rate (50%) and the rate at which it is actually paid (20% or 10% for the first £1,000 income and 42.5% in the case of any other dividend income) will be assessed on the trustees (ITA 2007, s 496). Trustees must retain sufficient income to meet this extra liability unless they are willing to have recourse to capital to cover the additional tax due. (For further discussion of this see, for example, *Revenue Law: Principles and Practice*, 28th edn (Tottel, 2010).)

An alternative (and probably better) approach is for the trustees to give one or more beneficiaries a right to receive the trust income in the short term. They could give a beneficiary a right to receive the income arising in the next 12 months. The settlement will then be treated as one in which the beneficiary has a right to income; the trustees will be liable to basic rate income tax only and the beneficiaries will receive a tax credit for the tax actually paid.

14.6 Distributing the trust funds

14.6.1 Accounting to the beneficiaries

Trustees must prepare capital and income accounts when changes in the beneficial interests under the settlement occur. The most likely occasions of this happening are:

(a) when a beneficiary becomes entitled to receive settled property from the trustees, for example, following the exercise of a power of advancement under s 32 of TA 1925; or

(b) when the trustees exercise a power of appointment, for example, when they appoint property to or for a beneficiary.

The accounts will show the investments and any cash in the trust fund together with any income which the trustees hold in their income account. From these accounts the beneficiary can ascertain precisely what his entitlement amounts to. The task of producing these accounts will be considerably eased if the trustees have kept full and accurate records of all transactions affecting the trust during the period of its administration. These will include records of sales and purchases of investments, advances made to the beneficiaries and any tax liabilities discharged.

14.6.2 Form and content of accounts

There is no prescribed form for trust accounts. The aim is to present clear and concise accounts which can easily be understood by the beneficiaries. Normally, trust accounts are produced in a vertical format showing the trust fund, payments made from it, for example, IHT and solicitors' costs and a balance for the beneficiary. A separate income account will reveal the income available for distribution, less any expenses payable from it, for example, any income tax due to the Revenue. The form of trust account shown in **Appendix 6** adopts this more usual vertical format.

14.6.3 Vesting the trust property in beneficiaries

Once the trustees have paid any tax liabilities and have prepared their accounts, the trust fund (or the appropriate part of it) must be transferred to the beneficiary. The means of vesting property in the beneficiary will depend on the nature of the property. The legal estate in land can be vested in the beneficiary by means of a deed; a stock transfer form will be required to transfer shares. Chattels (if any) pass to the beneficiary by delivery and any remaining cash will be transferred by cheque drawn on the trustee's bank account.

Summary – Trust Administration

Topic	Summary	Reference
Trust administration	Whilst the trust is in existence trustees have a number of duties and powers in relation to the day to day administration of the trust. These include those relating to:	Chapter 14
	(a) investment; and	14.3
	(b) retirement and appointment of trustees. This must be done in accordance with any express provisions in the trust deed or, if none, in accordance with statutory powers. It is usual for the retirement and appointment of new trustees to be made by deed.	14.4
	Trustees must report and pay any CGT and income tax liability arising from the investment of the trust assets.	
	CGT Trustees may make actual disposals of trust assets. The trustees are liable at a flat rate of 28%, although they have the benefit of a trust annual exemption which is half that of an individual.	14.5.1
	Income tax Trustees receive income generated by trust investments. They must pay it to any beneficiary who has a right to it, but otherwise may have powers to accumulate or pay it out.	14.5.2
Trusts where a beneficiary has a right to income	The trustees are liable at basic rate or dividend ordinary rate. In the case of interest and dividends the liability is already satisfied. Trustees will pay at 20% on any income received gross.	
	This income is paid to the beneficiary who adds this income, in its original form, to his other income and is liable to income tax. The beneficiary has the benefit of any tax already deducted at source or paid by the trustees.	

Topic	Summary	Reference
Trusts where no beneficiary has a right to income	The trustees must pay at the dividend trust rate (42.5%) on dividends and the trust rate of 50% on all other income, except for the first £1,000 of gross income where they are only liable at basic and dividend ordinary rate. If trustees choose to pay this income to a beneficiary, the beneficiary receives a new source of income, treated as having suffered tax at 50%. If the beneficiary is a non-, basic or higher rate tax payer he may recover the difference between his rate of tax and the 50% deemed to have been paid. The trustees are liable for any shortfall between the 50% and the tax actually paid by them.	

Chapter 15
The Overseas Dimension

15.1 The foreign element

The previous chapters in this book assume that private clients are UK resident and are domiciled in the UK. It has also been assumed that the property owned by these private clients is situated in the UK. However, the affairs of many private clients have an overseas dimension, for example:

(a) a UK resident and domiciled client may be leaving the UK to work abroad, or may be leaving the UK to emigrate; or

(b) an individual, while remaining a UK resident, is buying property overseas; or

(c) a foreign national is proposing to come to the UK on a temporary or long-term basis, or intends to invest in the UK.

15.1.1 The issues involved

There are many practical and legal issues where a client's affairs take on an overseas dimension.

15.1.1.1 Practical issues

The solicitor in the private client department tends not to be involved with the many practical issues when a client intends to leave or come to the UK. These matters include visa applications, work permits and accommodation. Clearly, in these areas there are legal issues involved about which the solicitor may be asked to advise, but generally the client will be able to handle practical matters for himself.

15.1.1.2 Legal issues

The solicitor should be asked to advise and become involved as early as possible where legal issues arise. Two particular aspects may call for early consideration.

Ownership and devolution of property

The UK client may need advice in relation to a property he is proposing to buy in a foreign country. If, for example, he is purchasing a holiday cottage in France, he will need advice as to French succession law and the extent to which he can leave that property by a will made in England or in France.

As a minimum this advice should be given by a lawyer from, or specialising in the law of, the jurisdiction in which the property is situated, but ideally the lawyer should also be qualified in the law of England and Wales. Not only may the laws of the foreign country differ from those of the UK, but the law may vary from state to state within that country.

Taxation, and in particular the concepts of residence, ordinary residence and domicile

These concepts affect such matters as the basis of assessment, territorial scope and reliefs in relation to UK taxes. The private client will need to know the extent to which he becomes or remains liable to income tax, CGT and IHT following immigration to or emigration from the UK.

15.1.2 Scope of this chapter

Where a foreign element is involved, there are always many complex issues to be considered. Essentially, a solicitor is required to plan the client's affairs in relation to the international dimension to achieve the most favourable tax position for his client. There is often a considerable degree of urgency so that appropriate advice must be given quickly before the client changes his residential or domiciliary status. The remainder of this chapter is limited to introducing some basic tax concepts as a basis for further study.

15.2 Residence and domicile

Whether a client is an immigrant or an emigrant, or whether he intends to invest in the UK or overseas, the rules of income tax, CGT and IHT can apply to him, but frequently in a modified form depending on his particular circumstances. The keys to an understanding of a client's tax position are the concepts of residence and domicile.

15.2.1 Residence

In view of the importance of residence within the UK tax system, it is surprising that there is no statutory definition. There are statutory provisions in ITA 2007, Pt 14, Ch 2 entitled 'Residence'. These provisions merely adapt the concepts of residence and ordinary residence as developed by the courts in a series of cases over many years. The decisions have developed the criteria against which residence is assessed. In order to give practical guidance, the Revenue has produced some guidance in its booklet HMRC6 (2009) *Residence, Domicile and the Remittance Basis*. This replaces the previous guidance issued in booklet IR20 *Residents and non-residents – liability to tax in the UK*, which is relevant for the period before 6 April 2009. Although without statutory authority, and therefore capable of challenge, these booklets are generally accepted by practitioners as a basis from which to provide advice to immigrant and emigrant clients.

Residence as a concept is concerned with physical presence in the UK. If an individual is physically present in the UK at some time in a tax year, it is a question of fact whether he is resident for tax purposes for that year. The fact that an individual is in the UK involuntarily is not generally relevant to this question. Basically, an individual will be considered resident in the UK if, for the time he is in the UK, it can be said to be his 'home'. It is not necessary that he owns a property in the UK; he may be resident even if he is living in hotel accommodation.

Any of the following tests may determine whether an individual will be treated as resident in the UK.

15.2.1.1 183 days in the UK: temporary residence

An individual will be treated as resident in a tax year if he is present for, in aggregate, 183 days or more in the year of assessment. For periods prior to 6 April 2008, the usual rule was to ignore days of arrival and departure when counting days, although in *Gaines-Cooper v Revenue and Customs Commissioners* [2007] STC (SCD) 23, the Revenue Special Commissioners indicated that in some circumstances these days could be counted.

However, from 6 April 2008 onwards the HMRC guidance indicates that if a person is in the UK at the end of a day (taken as midnight), that day will count as a day of presence. This will not be so if a person arrives in the UK on one day, in transit to a destination outside the UK, and continues the journey the next day without taking part in any activity unrelated to the journey, such as attending a business meeting.

Visits to the UK for some temporary purpose only (eg a holiday), and which are for less than six months, will not usually give rise to tax. In determining whether the visit is for a 'temporary purpose', any available accommodation in the UK is disregarded.

In addition to being resident whenever a person is in the UK for at least 183 days in a tax year, there are a number of other circumstances described in HMRC6 in which a person may be regarded as resident. Two examples of this are mentioned below.

15.2.1.2   Short term visitors

Where a person makes visits to the UK over several years, but without any intention to remain for an extended period, he will be regarded as resident if his visits average 91 days per tax year over four years. In such a case, the visitor is usually treated as resident from the fifth year. Days spent in the UK because of exceptional circumstances beyond the individual's control may be ignored, for example an extended stay in the UK because of ill-health.

15.2.1.3   Longer term visitors

Where a person comes to the UK with a purpose, such as employment, that will mean remaining for at least two years, he will be regarded as resident from the day of arrival.

15.2.1.4   Ordinary residence

The phrase 'ordinary residence' is often used in the legislation, particularly in relation to CGT, but nowhere is it defined. The concept of ordinary residence is used to prevent an individual from avoiding liability to tax simply by ceasing to be resident in the UK.

The courts have considered the phrase on a number of occasions. It is best described in the following extract from the judgment in *Lysaght v Commissioners of the Inland Revenue* [1928] AC 234:

> ordinarily means … established custom or practice or a matter of regular practice or occurrence … to be contrasted with casual or occasional.

The Revenue's view as to the meaning of ordinary residence, contained in HMRC6, is that if a person is resident in the UK year after year, this indicates that he normally lives there and is therefore ordinarily resident. It is possible to be resident in the UK but not ordinarily resident here, for example where a person is present for at least 183 days in a year, but normally lives outside the UK. It is also possible to be ordinarily resident but not resident in a tax year, for example where a person who usually lives in the UK has a long holiday abroad that means that he does not set foot in the UK in that year.

There is guidance in HMRC6 indicating the range of circumstances in which HMRC will regard a person as ordinarily resident for a tax year.

15.2.2   Domicile

Unlike residence and ordinary residence, an individual's domicile is not confined to determining liability to taxation. It is relevant to many other matters, for example, when determining in private international law which system of law governs succession to property owned in a foreign jurisdiction. Like residence and ordinary residence, domicile is not defined in statute but its meaning has been established by the courts in a number of decisions. An individual can only be domiciled in a country which has its own system of law, for example, England and Wales.

An individual is usually domiciled in the country which he considers as 'home'. Thus, an individual who emigrates to the USA where he lives for 20 or 30 years will not necessarily cease to be domiciled in some part of the UK. Domicile is distinct from nationality or residence, although according to the guidance in HMRC6 both may have an impact on assessing domicile. It is not possible to be without a domicile, and a person can only have one domicile at a time.

15.2.2.1 Domicile of origin

Every individual must have a domicile. Normally, a domicile of origin will be determined at birth, ie, a child acquires as his domicile of origin his father's domicile at the date of his birth. This may not be the country in which the child is actually born; nor need it be a country which the child has visited.

15.2.2.2 Domicile of dependency

A child under 16 who derived his domicile of origin from his father will acquire a new domicile, ie, a domicile of dependency in place of his domicile of origin if his father acquires a new domicile (see below).

15.2.2.3 Domicile of choice

Domicile can change where an individual voluntarily acquires a new domicile, ie, a domicile of choice. There is a heavy burden of proof before an individual can show that a domicile of choice has been acquired. Domicile is a matter of intent but a mere intention to change domicile is insufficient. Many factors are relevant including abandoning an existing domicile. Unless all connections with the previous domicile are broken, it may be difficult (if not impossible) to show the acquisition of a domicile of choice.

A client who, at the time of emigrating from the UK, is considering acquiring a new domicile of choice should compile all available evidence of intention. Inter alia, the following should be considered:

(a)   he should take up residence in the country involved, preferably acquiring property in that country and selling all property in the UK; and

(b)   he must have a permanent intention to remain indefinitely in the new country in order to show a change in domicile. This requirement as to intention is often the most difficult obstacle for a client to overcome when endeavouring to change domicile. Ideally, he should make a written statement, or statutory declaration, before leaving the UK, setting out all personal circumstances giving rise to the decision to change domicile. Such a statement is not conclusive but will always be of assistance when attempting to convince third parties, particularly the Inland Revenue, of the change of domicile; and

(c)   in addition to purchasing a residence in the new country, he should forge as many associations with that country as possible while at the same time ending associations with the old country. He should consider a new business or employment, make a will valid under local law, open a new bank account, sell investments and reinvest in the new country, etc.

15.2.3 United Kingdom

The UK consists of England and Wales, Scotland and Northern Ireland. It does not include the Channel Islands or the Isle of Man, which, because of their relatively lower tax rates, are often termed 'tax havens'.

It is incorrect to link the concept of domicile with the UK. An individual has a domicile in a territory or a state which has its own legal system. Thus, an individual may be domiciled in Scotland or in England and Wales. For brevity, this chapter refers to a person domiciled in some part of the UK as UK domiciled.

15.3   Taxation of the individual and the foreign element

The effect of the rules as to residence and domicile on an individual's liability to tax depends upon the tax involved. Spouses are independent persons for tax purposes. Their residence and ordinary residence status, and their domicile, are determined by reference to their individual circumstances and so may not coincide with the status of their spouse.

Transfers of property between spouses both of whom are domiciled in the UK are free of IHT by virtue of the spouse exemption. However, transfers by a UK domiciled spouse to a non-UK domiciled spouse are exempt up to a cumulative limit of £55,000 (IHTA 1984, s 18(2)).

15.3.1   Income tax and CGT

15.3.1.1   Income tax

Very broadly, an individual who is UK resident is liable to income tax on his worldwide income, ie, he must pay income tax on all income whether its source is within the UK or elsewhere. Special rules apply in some situations; see **15.3.2.4**.

A non-UK resident is only liable to income tax on income arising from a source within the UK. The rules to determine whether a person is resident in the UK are considered at **15.2**.

Whether a source of income is within the UK depends on the type of income. For example, income from employment within the UK, rent from land within the UK and dividends from companies whose membership register is kept within the UK are all sources of income within the UK. If the duties of the employment, the situation of the land or the membership register are outside the UK, the income will have a non-UK source.

15.3.1.2   Capital gains tax

An individual who is UK resident or ordinarily resident is generally liable to pay CGT on gains made on disposals of assets wherever they are situated.

If an individual is neither resident nor ordinarily resident in the UK, he is not normally liable to CGT whether the gains arise on disposals of assets in the UK or elsewhere, although note **15.3.2.1** below.

15.3.2   Effect of ceasing to be resident and ordinarily resident for income tax and CGT

If an individual is resident in the UK for part of a tax year and absent for the remainder of it, the general rule is that income tax and CGT is charged for the whole tax year. By concession, the Revenue may split the tax year so that an individual is treated as resident in the UK for only part of the year. For example, where an individual leaves to live permanently outside the UK, the Revenue treats him as non-resident from the day after the day of departure.

Tax planning by emigrating from the UK is perhaps the ultimate form of tax avoidance. To be successful, the individual will need to convince the Revenue that he is no longer resident or ordinarily resident in the UK on the date on which the liability to tax arose.

The operative date will depend on the tax in question. For CGT purposes, liability arises on the date of disposal of the asset in question. This is generally the date on which a binding contract is made (and not the date of later completion). If an individual is still a UK resident when the terms of the contract were substantially agreed, the Revenue may argue that this should be taken as the date of disposal, even though a formal contract had not yet been made. For effective tax planning, therefore, a client may be best advised to become non-resident well before negotiations are concluded.

If emigration is for a relatively short period, even though technically it may meet the non-residence test, the Revenue may argue that absence from the UK was always intended as temporary and, therefore, the individual was never truly non-resident. Although there is nothing to stop an emigrant from subsequently returning to the UK and resuming resident status, it is usually advisable for the period of emigration to be for at least three tax years if non-residency is to be achieved.

15.3.2.1   Temporary non-residence – CGT

To prevent abuse by UK resident individuals leaving the UK on or after 17 March 1998, FA 1998, s 127 introduced a new anti-avoidance measure into TCGA 1992, s 10A. No longer can the individual, who is about to realise a large capital gain, avoid CGT by the simple expedient of making the relevant disposal in a tax year when he is neither resident nor ordinarily resident in the UK. To avoid CGT on such a gain, the individual must ensure non-UK residence or ordinary residence for a five-year period before returning to the UK. If return occurs within the five-year period, gains will be charged in the tax year of the return to the UK.

15.3.2.2   Employment overseas

Although an employee going overseas to work full time on a contract of employment may not consider he is emigrating, he is effectively doing so for income tax and CGT purposes. The employee will be treated as non-resident and not ordinarily resident from the day after leaving the UK to the day before returning if all the following conditions are satisfied (HMRC6, para 8.5).

The employee:

- is leaving to work abroad under a contract of employment for at least a whole tax year; and
- has actually physically left the UK to begin the employment and not, for example, to have a holiday until beginning the employment; and
- will be absent for at least a whole tax year; and
- will only have visits to the UK after leaving which total less than 183 days in any tax year and average less than 91 days a tax year. (This average is taken over a period of absence of up to a maximum of four years.)

Once in the overseas employment, the employee can dispose of assets within the UK without liability to CGT on gains realised. To achieve this, he should be advised to enter into contracts disposing of assets likely to realise substantial gains only after he has gone overseas and achieved non-resident status (see above).

Any income which the employee may have from sources within the UK remains subject to income tax.

15.3.2.3   Longer-term emigrants

Emigrants in circumstances where an overseas employment is not intended will need to convince the Revenue of change in their residential status. This evidence might include having taken steps to acquire accommodation abroad as a permanent home. If HMRC is satisfied that a person has left permanently, he will be treated as non-resident and non ordinarily resident from the day after the day of departure, provided the person has been absent from the UK during a whole tax year and visits back to the UK since leaving are less then 183 days in any tax year and average less than 91 days a tax year, taken over four years.

Emigration of itself does not give rise to a disposal of assets for CGT purposes so that assets showing large in-built gains should be sold after the individual is no longer ordinarily resident in the UK.

Emigration within six years of a gift

Hold-over relief on the disposal of assets by way of gift has been discussed at **4.4.5.2**. The relief is available only if an election is made by the donor and donee, and if the donee was resident or ordinarily resident in the UK at the time. If the donee emigrates within six years of the gift, an emigration charge arises whereby the heldover gain becomes immediately chargeable. Tax is payable by the donee but the Revenue can recover it from the donor if it remains unpaid 12 months after the due date. The charge does not apply if the donee is an employee who leaves to work abroad under a full-time contract of employment.

Example

In 2004, Dana gave her son her shareholding in ABC Ltd. The gain of £10,000 was held over. In 2007, her son emigrated from the UK and took up residence in France. The £10,000 is immediately chargeable, ie, at the rates of tax relevant in 2007. The actual value of the shareholding in 2007 is irrelevant.

15.3.2.4   Long-term immigrants – remittance basis

Prior to 6 April 2008, persons who retained their non-UK domicile enjoyed more relaxed rules. Broadly, persons who were resident but not domiciled in the UK were only taxed on their foreign income and gains to the extent that these were remitted to the UK.

The Finance Act 2008 introduced changes to the remittance basis, which came into effect on 6 April 2008.

A person who is resident but not domiciled in the UK will be taxed on all foreign income and gains wherever arising each year unless, for the tax year in question, the person has *claimed* the remittance basis of taxation. If this is claimed, the person will only pay tax on income and gains arising in the UK and on income and gains remitted to the UK. By claiming the remittance basis, the person will not be able to use the income tax personal allowance or CGT annual exemption. If the person is an adult and has been resident in seven out of the nine tax years prior to the tax year in question, he may only claim the remittance basis if he pays the 'Remittance Basis Charge', which is £30,000. Any period of residence prior to 6 April 2008 will be counted when assessing if a non-domiciled person has been resident for seven years. The person may choose each year whether to claim the remittance basis.

If a person who is resident but not domiciled in the UK has, in any tax year, less than £2,000 worth of income and gains which are not remitted to the UK then this person will be taxed on the remittance basis, without having to pay the Remittance Basis Charge, and he will have the income tax personal allowance and CGT annual exemption available.

15.3.3   Double taxation treaties

An individual may be liable to tax in the UK and in a foreign country at the same time. The client may be 'dual resident' because the residence criteria in the two countries where he has lived treat him as resident in each country. If there is a double taxation agreement between the countries, this will provide relief from double taxation of income and gains. If no double taxation agreement exists, unilateral relief may be granted by one of the countries. There are no special EU tax rules and the rules of individual Member States have not yet been harmonised, but there are various double taxation provisions and reliefs between EU countries.

15.3.4   Inheritance tax

Residence (or ordinary residence) is not relevant as a concept to determine liability to IHT. Instead, an individual's domicile governs liability to IHT.

An individual who is domiciled in (some part of) the UK is liable to IHT on a transfer of value of assets whether the assets are in the UK or elsewhere. If an individual is not domiciled in (some part of) the UK, liability arises only on the transfer of value of property situated in the UK, although there are some exceptions to this rule, for example, exempt gilts (government stock).

15.3.4.1   Deemed domicile for IHT (IHTA 1984, s 267)

Section 267 of IHTA 1984 contains provisions extending the meaning of domicile. An individual not domiciled (some part of) in the UK under the principles discussed at **15.2.3** may nevertheless be deemed to be domiciled there for IHT. This can happen in one of two circumstances.

The domicile test

An individual actually domiciled in (some part of) the UK within the three years immediately preceding a transfer of value will be deemed domiciled there at the time of the transfer. The aim of this provision is to stop an individual transferring his property from the UK and then emigrating in the hope of avoiding IHT on future transfers of his property.

Example

Alexis acquired a domicile of choice in California in January 2005 when she emigrated there from England. She died two years later. As Alexis had given up her English domicile within three years of her death (the transfer of value), her entire estate is chargeable to IHT.

The residence test

An individual who was resident in the UK for income tax purposes in not less than 17 of the 20 years of assessment ending with the year in which the transfer of value occurs is deemed to be domiciled in the UK. In determining whether an individual is resident in any year, the income tax tests discussed at **15.2** are used.

This provision is intended to bring long-term residents who have not become UK domiciliaries into the charge to IHT.

Example

Alexandra's employment in the UK since July 1985 has just ended following the failure of her employer's business. As a result, she plans to return home to Greece as soon as possible. Last year, she gave some land she owned outside Athens to her daughter. In view of Alexandra's residence in the UK for over 20 years, she will be deemed domiciled in the UK so that her death within seven years of the gift of the land would cause the gift to become subject to IHT.

15.3.4.2   Death of a UK domiciliary with foreign property

Succession

If the testator left two wills, one dealing with his foreign property, and an English will dealing with his other assets, a foreign lawyer should be instructed to prove the foreign will and to administer the foreign property in accordance with its terms.

If the testator left only an English will, this should be proved in the usual way and then a foreign lawyer instructed either to reseal the English grant in the foreign jurisdiction or to extract the appropriate grant in that jurisdiction using sealed and certified copies of the English grant and will. As a grant obtained in the UK contains a 'notation of domicile', ie the deceased's domicile at death is stated on the grant, the grant will be recognised in other parts of the UK without further formality (Administration of Estates Act 1971 (AEA 1971)). Thus, the English executors of a deceased client can prove title to property in Scotland or Northern Ireland without resealing their grant in either jurisdiction (and vice versa).

Devolution of foreign property, particularly land, is often subject to local succession taxes (or equivalent) and to local laws of entitlement which may override (to a given extent) the terms of an English will. For example, in Scotland, Spain and France a stated proportion of the testator's estate passes automatically (and not by will) to certain relatives; in the USA and Scandinavian countries there is 'community of property' provision for spouses. In view of these local succession laws, it is usually appropriate for the clients to be advised to make a will in the particular jurisdiction taking local law into account; any English will should in terms exclude the property in the foreign jurisdiction.

Inheritance tax

Worldwide assets are part of the estate of a client domiciled in the UK for IHT purposes (under either of the tests discussed above) and should be disclosed in Form IHT400. Subject to any relief under a double taxation agreement or convention, the English PRs are liable to pay any IHT which is due although their liability is limited to the extent of assets received or which might have been received but for their neglect or default (IHTA 1984, s 204). Unless the testator's will provides otherwise, the beneficiaries of the foreign property bear the burden of the IHT which that property attracts (IHTA 1984, s 211). Thus, the UK PRs, having paid the IHT to the Revenue, will need to recover an equivalent amount from the beneficiary of the property.

15.3.4.3 Death of a non-UK domiciliary with UK property

Succession

Foreign PRs may obtain title to the property in the UK by resealing their foreign grant in the appropriate court in the UK. Except in Scotland (where local laws apply), succession to the property is generally in accordance with the terms of the deceased's will.

Inheritance tax

Certain government stock and other property is exempt from IHT, even though situated in the UK, if owned by an individual who is neither domiciled nor ordinarily resident in the UK. Otherwise, property physically situated in the UK is subject to IHT. All such property should be disclosed in Form IHT401.

15.4 Trustees and the foreign element

The residence and ordinary residence of trustees is generally determined separately from the status of the settlor or the beneficiaries and without regard to the location of the trust assets.

Before 6 April 2007, the test for whether trustees were UK resident was different for income tax (FA 1989, s 110) and for CGT (TCGA 1992, s 69) purposes. Since 6 April 2007 the test is the same (ITA 2007, s 475 and TCGA 1992, s 69, as amended by FA 2006). Under these sections, for both income tax and CGT, trustees of a settlement are together treated as if they were a single person, and this deemed person is treated as resident and ordinarily resident in the UK whenever either:

(a)   all the trustees are resident in the UK; or

(b)   at least one trustee is resident in the UK and the settlor was resident, ordinarily resident or domiciled in the UK when the settlement was created.

The sections also provide that a trustee not resident in the UK is treated as if resident at any time when he acts as trustee in the course of a business which he carries on in the UK through a branch, agency or permanent establishment there.

15.4.1 Income tax

Non-resident trustees are not liable to UK income tax other than on income arising in the UK (see above). In such cases, basic rate tax (20%) is generally deducted at source so that the trustees receive income net of tax. Trustees of no interest in possession settlements are liable to tax at the 'trust rate' or 'dividend trust rate' (see **14.5.2**); in practice, the Revenue often cannot collect this extra tax from the non-resident trustees because there is no means of withholding it at source, nor can it enforce the liability in the overseas jurisdiction.

15.4.2   Capital gains tax

Non-resident settlements have been popular with clients and estate planners as providing a ready method of sheltering the trust's gains from CGT. Non-resident trustees are in the same position as individuals who are not resident in the UK. Thus they are not liable to pay CGT on their chargeable gains on disposal of trust assets, provided the settlement is a non-resident settlement for the entire tax year in question. If the trustees become non-resident part way through the year, the Revenue will not split the year for assessment purposes so allowing avoidance of CGT for the period when the trust is non-resident. Ideally a client should be advised to set up his non-resident trust, or export his existing trust (see **15.4.4.1** below), well before 6 April in the relevant year.

15.4.3   Anti-avoidance legislation

Ever since the introduction of CGT in 1965, estate planners have advised clients to use non-resident settlements (normally discretionary settlements) to shelter the trustees' gains from CGT. Over the same period, various legislative attempts have been made to counter loss of revenue through use of these settlements, but only recently has the large-scale use of non-resident settlements been substantially halted. Even now some opportunities remain for use of such settlements.

On the whole, clients were less concerned with avoidance of inheritance tax (or its predecessor capital transfer tax) or income tax in relation to their non-resident settlement, although sometimes this was the result even if not the overriding intention. Often clients wished for some continuing enjoyment from the settled property or its income. The real objective, therefore, was sheltering the non-resident gains from CGT while, so far as the legislation permitted, continuing to enjoy the property.

Anti-avoidance legislation is always complex even if the objective is reasonably certain. Whether the objective is achieved, is, of course, another matter. Apart from 1965 (with the introduction of CGT), there have been two principal occasions when anti-avoidance legislation has been introduced: the first by FA 1981, s 80, and the second 10 years later by FA 1991, Sch 16. Neither of these was entirely successful in that estate planners continued to find ways round the provisions and so defeat the intention of the legislation. Each of these provisions has been retained, and strengthened, and appear now as ss 86 and 87 of TCGA 1992. A further provision, TCGA 1992 s 80, has introduced an export charge. Section 80 is discussed below. Sections 86 and 87 are beyond the scope of this book and will not be considered further. However, for anyone involved in advising settlor clients seeking to avoid CGT, they must be fully understood.

15.4.4   Anti-avoidance legislation – the position now

The current position in relation to anti-avoidance legislation is set out below.

15.4.4.1   Migrant settlements – export charge (TCGA 1992, s 80(2))

Consider the following example.

> **Example**
>
> Derek Godfrey formed his electrical engineering company. He settled the shares on UK resident trustees to hold on family discretionary trusts. He continued to draw director's fees. Expecting imminent growth in value of the shares due to the success of the company, the UK trustees retired in favour of non-resident trustees. The company prospered. The non-resident trustees sold the shares realising a substantial capital profit.
>
> Derek Godfrey's tax position:
>
> (a)   deemed disposal on transfer of shares to the UK trustees: no significant capital gains realised and so covered by the indexation allowance and the annual exemption;

> (b)   appointment of non-resident trustees: no disposal, the trustees are a single continuing body of persons (TCGA 1992, s 69, see **15.4**).

The consequence of these transactions (before 1981) was that any increase in value of the shares by the time the appointment of the new trustees was not charged to CGT. The gain (often large) was free of CGT. To counter this, an 'export charge' was introduced to tax gains which had accrued but which had not been realised to the date of the appointment of the non-resident trustees by FA 1981, s 83 (now TCGA 1992, s 80).

Advice to clients contemplating the 'export' of their settlement covers two main aspects; legal and taxation issues.

Legal issues

What is at issue is the export of a UK trust to avoid CGT. Export of the trust is simply achieved by appointing persons who are resident abroad as trustees and ensuring that the administration of the trust is carried on outside the UK. But what considerations should the present trustees have in mind when faced with a proposal that the trust be exported? First, there is no absolute bar in English law preventing the appointment of non-resident trustees of a UK trust and, secondly, such an appointment should be made only in 'appropriate circumstances' because the result is to remove the trust from control by the English courts. The following extract is from the judgment of Pennycuick V-C in *Re Whitehead's Will Trusts; Burke v Burke and Others* [1971] 1 WLR 833:

> The law has been quite well established for upwards of a century that there is no absolute bar to the appointment of persons resident abroad as trustees of an English trust. I say 'no absolute bar', in the sense that such an appointment would be prohibited by law and would consequently be invalid. On the other hand, apart from exceptional circumstances, it is not proper to make such an appointment, that is to say, the court would not apart from exceptional circumstances, make such an appointment; nor would it be right for the donees of the power to make such an appointment out of court. If they did, presumably the court would be likely to interfere at the instance of the beneficiaries. There do, however, exist exceptional circumstances in which such an appointment can properly be made. The most obvious exceptional circumstances are those in which the beneficiaries have settled permanently in some country outside the United Kingdom and what is proposed to be done is to appoint new trustees in that country.

Clearly, if the court would appoint non-resident trustees, it will be proper for the trustees themselves to do so, for example where all the beneficiaries are resident in the country where the trust is to become resident following the appointment. If the trustees made an appointment where the court might not, there is unlikely to be any real concern if all the beneficiaries have approved the non-resident appointment. This will require all beneficiaries to be ascertained and to be *sui juris*. If the trustees are in doubt about a proposed appointment, it would be sensible to apply to the court first (as in *Re Whitehead*).

In many cases, there will be appropriate express provision in the trust instrument for the trustees to retire in favour of non-resident trustees. Such a power can be exercised without further consideration by the trustees, provided its exercise is in the best interests of the beneficiaries.

The choice of overseas jurisdiction requires some thought by the trustees. It is prudent to appoint the non-resident trustees in a jurisdiction which will, if necessary, enforce the trustees' duties; the concept of a trust and the division of legal and beneficial ownership is not known in many civil law jurisdictions. Care should also be taken to choose a country where tax laws are less stringent than the UK since, otherwise, the trustees may be taxed as heavily, if not more so, than in the UK. It is also sensible to choose a jurisdiction which is likely to be stable – the Channel Islands or the Isle of Man – and to select reputable trustees, for example a well-known trust company or a firm of lawyers practising within the jurisdiction.

Taxation issues

The export charge is levied under TCGA 1992, s 80 in a manner familiar to the CGT legislation. When the trustees become neither resident nor ordinarily resident in the UK, they are deemed to have disposed of the trust assets at market value and to have re-acquired them at the same value. The retiring trustees are primarily responsible for the tax due on the chargeable gain; if it is not paid by them within six months of the due date, the Revenue can recover the tax from any person who was a trustee in the 12 months before the export of the trust (unless, broadly, when he ceased to be a trustee there was then no proposal to export the trust). Because of their personal liability for the tax, the retiring trustees should retain sufficient assets under their control so that they can pay the tax due.

This export charge may not necessarily deter the use of a non-resident settlement by a settlor, particularly where the growth in the settled assets is expected to occur after the export rather than before it.

The charge is suspended in cases where an 'inadvertent' change in the residence status of the settlement occurs provided the UK resident status is resumed within six months. For example, the death of the only UK resident trustee leaving two non-resident trustees, would cause the settlement to become non-resident. If the trustee is replaced by another UK trustee within six months no charge is made under s 80.

None of the three final anti-avoidance provisions is considered further here:

(a)   non-resident settlements – attribution of gains to settlors (TCGA 1992, s 86 and Sch 5);

(b)   non-resident settlements – attribution of gains to beneficiaries (TCGA 1992, s 87);

(c)   non-resident settlements – the supplementary charge (TCGA 1992, s 91).

APPENDICES

Appendix 1 – Income Tax Rates and Allowances

Rates		2010/11	2009/10
Basic rate	20%	£0–£37,400	£0–£37,400
Higher rate	40%	£37,401– £150,000	Over £37,400
Additional rate	50%	Over £150,000	n/a
Savings income			
Starting rate for savings limit (applies only to the extent that income other than savings and dividends falls below this threshold)		£2,440	£2,440
at or under starting rate for savings limit		10%	10%
at or under basic rate limit		20%	20%
above basic rate limit		40%	40%
above additional rate limit		50%	n/a
Dividend income			
at or under basic rate limit		10%	10%
above basic rate limit		32.5%	32.5%
above additional rate limit		42.5%	n/a

Allowance	2010/11	2009/10	Reduction in tax	
			2010/11	2009/10
			10%	10%
	£	£	£	£
Personal	6,475	6,475		
aged 65–74	9,490	9,490		
aged 75 and over	9,640	9,640		
Married couple				
aged 74 and over	6,965	6,965	696.50	696.50
Blind person	1,890	1,890		
Income limit for age-related allowances	22,900	22,900		

Note:

(a) The 'Reduction in tax' columns show the amount of tax credit available where relief is restricted to 10%. It is given by reducing the individual's total liability by the amount of the credit.

(b) Age-related allowances:
   income limit: £22,900/£22,900.
   income below limit: allowance in full.
   income exceeds limit: allowance reduced by 50% of the excess.

(c) The personal allowance for individuals of any age is reduced if they have net income above £100,000. The allowance is reduced by £1 for every £2 of income over £100,000, so for example a person with £110,000 net income would lose £5,000 of personal allowance.

Appendix 2 – Investment and Financial Products

The purpose of this Appendix is to provide a brief introduction to some of the more popular types of investment and financial products currently available to individuals and trustees. It is not intended to be a definitive list. Where appropriate there is a brief summary indicating risk and showing income and capital growth potential for the investment, and suggestions as to the type of client for whom the investment might be suitable, though many factors will determine the actual choice of investment for a particular client. The tax rules are those for the client and not for the product.

The investments listed are:

(1) Bank accounts

The two most common accounts are the current account and the deposit account.

Current account

The current account is one where the saver's money is immediately available to him, and he may have a cheque book and a cash card to enable him to spend the money in or withdraw the money from the account at any time. Because the money is always available the bank is unlikely to pay interest to the saver on the amount in the account, and where it does, the interest rate will be very low.

Deposit account

A deposit account is an account which pays interest to the saver. The saver can withdraw money from the account on demand but will lose interest equivalent to that which would have been earned during the notice period. The bank will require notice (generally of seven days) of an intended withdrawal to release funds from the account. Amounts in accounts and transactions are shown by the bank on regular statements which are sent to the saver.

Tax

All interest paid by a bank on these accounts will be paid net of basic rate tax. If the saver is a non-tax payer, he may sign a declaration to this effect and hand it to the bank so enabling it to pay the interest gross. A tax repayment claim by the client can thus be avoided in appropriate cases.

Suitability

The majority of a solicitor's clients – both individuals and trustees – will have at least a current account in which a sufficient balance is maintained to enable regular expenditure (such as utility bills) to be met.

However, because of the lack of interest or comparatively poor interest rates, it is inadvisable for the majority of a client's savings to remain in such an account.

Banks and building societies encourage people to place their savings with them by offering interest on the money deposited. The bank or building society then uses this money to fund loans and mortgages to borrowers. The borrowers pay back not only the amount borrowed but also interest on the loan. This rate of interest is higher than that paid to the people saving with the bank or society. The difference covers the institution's running costs and provides a profit for the bank or society.

Example

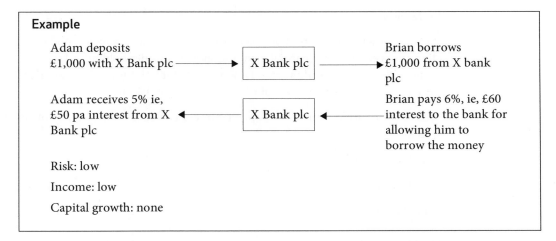

Adam deposits £1,000 with X Bank plc → X Bank plc → Brian borrows £1,000 from X bank plc

Adam receives 5% ie, £50 pa interest from X Bank plc ← X Bank plc ← Brian pays 6%, ie, £60 interest to the bank for allowing him to borrow the money

Risk: low

Income: low

Capital growth: none

(2) Building society accounts

Building societies offer deposit accounts and an array of share accounts. Ownership of an account is evidenced by a passbook held by the account holder in which the building society records all payments to and withdrawals from the account. Interest rates vary from time to time.

Deposit accounts

Money is repayable on demand and interest calculated on a daily basis is paid on the amount in the account. In the event of the building society ceasing to exist, deposit account holders will receive back their money in priority to all other savers. Hence, this is the safest type of building society account and, therefore, pays a lower rate of interest than a share account.

Share accounts

There are a wide variety of accounts offered by the various societies. For small sums or as an alternative to a current bank account, an ordinary share account offers a higher rate of interest than a deposit account and access to all money in the account on demand. Where immediate access is not required, higher rates of interest are paid on 'notice' accounts, for example, 28-day access account. The saver has to give the society a specified length of notice of his intention to withdraw his money. The longer the notice period, the higher the rate of interest paid on the account.

These accounts often also have a tiered interest system so that interest is paid at different rates on the amount in the account.

Example

Charly has £30,000 in a 60-day notice account. She is paid interest on:

(a)   the first £10,000 @ X% pa;

(b)   the next £15,000 @ X + ½% pa;

(c)   the balance @ X + ¾% pa.

The best rates for both bank and building society accounts are now paid on accounts which have internet-only access.

Tax

The tax treatment of building society accounts is exactly the same as for bank accounts.

Suitability

Building societies offer a relatively safe investment with a reasonably good rate of return. Most clients concerned with financial planning should consider holding at least one share account as they offer liquidity and interest. However, if the interest is required to supplement income, the underlying value of the capital will be eroded by inflation.

Trustees with wide express investment powers can invest in all types of building society account.

Risk: low.

Income: low.

Capital growth: none.

(3) TESSAs

Tax Exempt Special Savings Accounts (TESSAs) were introduced by the Government in January 1991, and were offered by most banks and building societies. They allowed a person to invest up to £9,000 gradually over five years, and to receive tax-free income. When a TESSA matured after five years, it was possible to reinvest all of the capital (but not the interest) in a 'follow up TESSA'.

It became impossible to start a new TESSA after 5 April 1999, when Individual Savings Accounts (ISAs) became available (see (**21**) below). When a TESSA matured after this date, it could be transferred into an ISA – a ' TESSA-only ISA', which can be held in addition to other ISAs.

From 6 April 2008, such accounts will be treated as ISA cash accounts.

(4) National Savings

National Savings are schemes offered by the Government which guarantee the security of the money invested with it. There are a number of National Savings products and some of the most common are identified below.

National Savings Bank accounts

This bank offers an investment account, which is operated with a passbook through the saver's local post office, and from 1 August 2004, an easy access savings account, which is operated via phone, post or post office.

Interest is paid annually on both accounts.

Easy access savings

The minimum amount for each payment into the account is £100 and the maximum holding in an individual account is £2 million.

Tax

The interest is taxable but is paid gross.

Suitability

It may be particularly useful for non-tax payers such as children and the elderly, providing easy and convenient access and a small amount of tax-free income. By receiving the income gross, non-tax payers do not have to worry about tax reclaims or filing tax returns. The low rate of interest is unlikely to make it an attractive account for others. The once a year interest payment makes it unattractive for those needing a regular income.

Risk, income and capital growth: low.

Investment account

The minimum investment at any time is £20 and the maximum that can be held in the account is £1 million. The rate of interest is competitive with banks and building societies.

Tax

All the interest is taxable but is paid gross.

Suitability

The convenience of withdrawing money at the post office and the receipt of gross interest appeal to the elderly. The annual interest payment can be a deterrent for those needing regular income.

Income bonds

Income bonds provide a regular monthly income. Ownership is evidenced by a bond or certificate. The minimum purchase is £500 and the maximum holding £1 million. Income is paid monthly to the investor. The interest rate may vary from time to time.

Tax

All the interest is taxable but paid gross.

Suitability

The bond provides an attractive rate of interest for non-tax payers and a regular income. It is, therefore, particularly suitable for elderly clients with limited savings. The main disadvantages are the need for tax payers to account for income tax on income received each year and the lack of protection of the capital against inflation.

Risk, income and capital growth: low.

Guaranteed Income Bonds and Guaranteed Growth Bonds

(These bonds were temporarily withdrawn from sale in July 2010.)

These are lump sum investments that earn a fixed rate of interest over a set term of one, two, three or five years.

The Guaranteed Income Bond pays out interest monthly.

The Guaranteed Growth Bond adds the interest to the sum invested each year over the term, and nothing is paid out until the end of the term.

For both types of bond, the minimum for each is £500 and the maximum for total holdings in both types of bond is £1 million. There is a penalty for accessing the investment before the end of the fixed term.

Tax

For both, the interest is taxable, and paid net.

Suitability

The Guaranteed Income Bond provides regular, guaranteed income, which means that it may suit someone who wants to be certain exactly how much monthly income he receives. As the income is paid net, this Bond is less suitable for non-tax payers, and it will not produce any capital growth.

The Guaranteed Growth Bond allows a saver a guaranteed return over the term of the investment, and does allow for capital growth. The non-payment of interest means that this Bond will not suit someone who needs regular income.

National Savings Certificates

(These were temporarily withdrawn from sale in July 2010.)

National Savings Certificates can be purchased from the Post Office and offer tax-free interest. In return for the purchase of Certificates the interest rate is guaranteed. The rate of interest increases each year the Certificates are held over a two-year or five-year period but averaged over the two years or five years is equivalent to the guaranteed annual rate. For example, a guaranteed average rate of 2.9% pa over five years will be achieved by paying 2% in year 1 increasing to 3.5% in year 5. The interest is added to the capital each year and only paid out when the Certificates are cashed. To achieve the maximum interest the Certificates must be held for the full five years. The minimum purchase is £100 and generally the maximum holding in any issue is £15,000.

Certificates should normally be cashed in after the two-year or five-year period as thereafter the annual rate of interest paid drops significantly.

Certificates can be repaid early, but this is penalised by interest being calculated at a lower rate for the period of ownership.

There are also index-linked savings certificates, which offer similar terms but a choice of a three-year or five-year term.

Tax

There is no income tax or CGT to pay.

Suitability

Because of their favourable tax treatment, National Savings Certificates offer an attractive investment to higher-rate tax payers. They are also suitable for parents or trustees wishing to invest money for minor children.

Because the interest is compounded and paid out only when the Certificates are redeemed, this is not a suitable investment for anybody requiring a regular income.

Risk and income: low.

Capital growth: medium (interest is added to the capital).

Pensioners Guaranteed Income Bonds

In 1994, Pensioners Guaranteed Income Bonds ('granny bonds') were introduced for people aged 65 (reduced to 60 for 1996/97) or over. These are no longer available (since 23 February 2008) but existing Bonds will continue until they mature. The minimum investment is £500; the maximum investment is £1 million. Income rates can be guaranteed for five years. Alternatively, a one- or two-year period can be chosen. After five years the money may be withdrawn without any penalty.

Tax

Income is taxable but is paid gross.

Suitability

These bonds are suitable for elderly people with modest amounts of cash to invest. There is little risk and no capital growth. Income rates should be compared to rates available from an equivalent investment elsewhere, for example in a building society.

Premium bonds

Premium bonds can be purchased from the Post Office and online. Bond holders are automatically entered for regular prize draws. Bonds are divided into £1 units and each unit has a separate chance in the draws, ie a £100-bond has 100 chances of winning a prize in every draw. Prizes range from £25 to £1 million. Bond holders can reclaim their money from the bonds at any time. The minimum holding is £100; the maximum holding is £30,000.

Tax

All prizes are totally tax free.

Suitability

Statistics suggest that holders of bonds to the maximum limit are likely to receive sufficient prizes to represent an acceptable return on the amount of prizes each year, making it a worthwhile purchase for wealthy higher-rate tax payers. For lower holdings, there is no income and no capital growth, merely the gamble that a bond will win one of the larger prizes.

Trustees whose investment powers come from TA 2000 cannot purchase premium bonds as they involve no income or capital growth, and they are unlikely to be suitable for most trusts.

Risk, income and capital growth: low.

(5) Local authority bonds

These bonds are a way of investing in local authorities. When a local authority needs to raise money, it may encourage investors to deposit money with the authority in return for a competitive rate of interest. The minimum investment is usually £1,000 with no maximum. The bond will last for between one and four years, and must be held to maturity. The local authority guarantees the rate of interest to be paid throughout the period.

Tax

There is no CGT on these bonds. The interest is paid net of basic rate tax.

Suitability

The guaranteed interest rate may be attractive at a time of falling interest rates and is usually competitive when compared to other forms of interest-only savings. The safety of the money invested depends upon the standing of the local authority. Because it is a fixed-term investment, these bonds are not suitable for people needing immediate access to their capital. The bonds may be suitable investments for some trustees.

Risk, income and capital growth: low.

(6) Gilts

'Gilts' is the popular name for government stocks otherwise known as 'gilt-edged' securities. They are issued by the UK Government as a way of raising money, and are a secure form of investment as interest and repayment are guaranteed by the Government.

The majority of gilts pay a fixed rate of interest ('the coupon') over the life of the stock and guarantee repayment of the nominal value of the stock (known as par value) on a given date (known as the redemption date). Interest is usually paid half yearly in two equal amounts.

Example
John purchases £100 nominal of 10% Treasury Stock 2012. He will receive an annual guaranteed income of £10 (10%) gross until 2012 when he will be paid £100.

Normally, when the Government issues the gilt, it does so at a discount to its par (nominal) value.

> **Example**
>
> Assume that in 2005 the Government issued 10% Treasury Stock 2017 at 94p. This means that for every 94p invested with it in 2005, the Government guarantees to pay £1 on redemption in 2017.
>
> So when John purchased £100 nominal in 2005, it actually cost him £94. If he holds the stock until the Government redeems it at par, he will receive £100, ie, a profit of £6.

Once a person has purchased a gilt, he does not have to continue holding it until its redemption date. He can sell his holding to another investor via the stock market. The stock market determines how much a stock is worth on any given day prior to its redemption date. The seller pays commission to the stockbroker for arranging the sale.

> **Example**
>
> Having bought £100 nominal 10% Treasury Stock 2017 in 2005, John needed some money to pay for his holiday in 2008. He therefore decided to sell his stock. The market price on the day of sale is 96p. John will receive £96 less commission.

Tax

The profit made from selling or redeeming a gilt is exempt from CGT. All interest payments are liable to income tax.

Gilts can be bought and sold through a stockbroker. Interest on all gilts is paid net of lower rate tax, meaning that non-tax payers have to reclaim the tax deducted.

Suitability

Higher-rate tax payers appreciate the CGT exemption but capital gains tend to be moderate and sales (as opposed to redemption) are subject to commission charges. A fixed rate of interest can be advantageous at times of falling interest rates but, conversely, unattractive if interest rates rise during the period of ownership for people on a limited income. A guaranteed rate of return can help budgeting. Gilts are often suitable investments for trustees where a beneficiary requires income.

Risk: low.

Income: medium/high.

Capital growth: if held to redemption, depends on whether bought for a premium or at a discount; otherwise prices vary according to the coupon and prevailing interest rates.

(7) Quoted shares

An investor may wish to invest money in a company listed (quoted) on the Stock Exchange. The aim is to receive an income and also real (net of inflation) capital growth from the investment. Income is received in the form of dividends paid by the company. The size of a dividend is decided by the company and is normally paid in two, not necessarily equal, instalments. The dividend can vary from year to year.

The capital value of the shares is determined by the market and is based on a number of factors including past and projected profits and takeover rumours.

Shares are, therefore, a speculative investment which may increase or decrease (sometimes spectacularly) in value, and whose value can change daily.

Example 1

In 2008, Taj bought 1,000 shares in A plc at £1 each (cost £1,000). In 2010 he received a dividend of £70 and in 2011 a dividend of £83 as the company made good profits, had good industrial relations and a secure market for its products.

Early in 2012, shares were listed as being worth £1.20 each. Taj sold his 1,000 shares for £1,200 less commission.

Example 2

In 2008, Victor bought 1,000 shares in B plc for £1 each (cost £1,000 plus commission and stamp duty). Soon afterwards the company suffered a strike by its workforce and introduced a new product, which incorporated a faulty design and had to be withdrawn and compensation paid to people who had already bought the product. In 2010 the company borrowed money to enable it to pay shareholders a dividend. Victor received £50. Shortly afterwards the company went into liquidation. Victor's 1,000 shares are now worth £20.

Tax

All profits on the disposal of shares are liable to CGT. Any losses made on disposal can be set against gains in the same tax year and any excess carried forward to set against gains in future years.

Dividends are treated as if income tax at 10% has been paid. This credit is irrecoverable. No further liability arises if the recipient is a basic rate tax payer, but higher and additional rate tax payers will have further tax to pay.

Suitability

Because of the financial risks, shares should be purchased only by those who can afford to lose the money invested. In return for that risk, shares offer both income and capital gains opportunities but fairly substantial sums need to be invested in a 'portfolio of shares' (ie, several shareholdings in different companies) to produce significant gains.

Shares are often purchased by trustees and may form the bulk of trust investments.

Risk: medium/high.

Income: low/medium.

Capital growth: medium/high.

(8) Investment trusts

Investment trusts are quoted companies whose assets consist solely of shares in other companies. The investment trust company may specialise in acquiring shares in companies in one particular sector of the market, or it may own shares in a wide variety of companies. The advantage for the investor holding shares in the investment trust is that he can have an indirect interest in a number of companies with the investment management handled by professional managers: the investment trust.

The investment trust pays dividends and the value of investment trust is determined by the stock market.

Tax

Dividends paid on shares in investment trusts are taxed in the same way as dividends on other quoted shares.

When an investor disposes of his shares in an investment trust, a liability to CGT can arise.

Suitability

Investment trusts are suitable for anybody, including trustees, who might reasonably consider investing in quoted shares, and also smaller investors who lack the expertise to manage their own portfolio or for whom transaction costs on shares are high compared to their amount of investment. The risk of loss as compared with investment in individual companies may be reduced due to the spread of investment by the trust, but an investment trust may have to be held for several years to realise much capital growth.

Risk: medium.

Income: medium.

Capital growth: medium/high.

(9) Unit trusts

Unit trusts provide a method of investing on the stock market for anybody who wishes to invest in a range of companies but lacks the time or expertise to manage his own share portfolio.

Unit trusts are offered by a number of banks and other institutions who employ investment managers. The managers charge an annual management fee for their expertise and there is also an initial 'setting-up' charge. The investor hands his investment money to the investment manager in return for a number of units. The value of the units is determined by the value of the shares in the companies in which the managers invest. The investment manager then uses the investor's money to buy shares in other companies. Different unit trusts invest in different types of company, for example, UK Gilt Unit Trust only invests in UK government securities; M&G Far Eastern Unit Trust invests only in companies quoted on stock exchanges of countries in the Far East (eg, Japan and Hong Kong).

An investor can sell his units back to the unit trust managers at any time. If the unit trust has performed well, the sale price should be greater than the price at which the investor purchased his units. Unit trusts have two prices: the bid price which is what an investor will receive if he sells his units, and the offer price which is the price at which the units can be purchased.

Example

Daisy decides to invest £1,100 in the Magic Unit Trust which invests in UK companies. On the day of her investment the bid price is £1 and the offer price £1.10. She receives 1,000 units.

Daisy must wait until the bid price of units in Magic Unit Trust increases to at least £1.10 before she sells in order to get back her full investment. The bid price must increase further for her to make a capital gain on her investment.

Unit trusts also pay dividends or interest to investors.

Tax

Dividends paid to unit holders are taxed in the same way as dividends on quoted shares. Interest is taxed in the same way as bank or building society interest. Since 6 April 2007, UK resident non-tax payers have been able to receive the interest gross.

Any profit made by an investor on the sale of his units is liable to CGT.

Suitability

Anybody, including trustees, wishing to invest in UK or overseas companies but without the time or expertise to manage their own portfolio, should consider unit trusts. However, the initial costs mean that unit trusts are not suitable for short-term investment.

Risk: medium.

Income: low/medium.

Capital growth: medium/high.

Note: Open-ended investment companies (OEICs) are a more modern version of the unit trust. An OEIC has all the characteristics of a unit trust but uses the structure of a corporation, as is commonly done in the rest of Europe and in the USA.

Like a unit trust, an OEIC is a collective investment pooling the resources of many investors. Both are open-ended and have to dispose of assets if there is a run on the fund.

Structurally OEICs are different from unit trusts. They are formed as limited liability companies. People invest in them through the purchase of shares, but these are traded in the same way as unit trusts. The shares have a single price for buying and selling. The tax treatment of OEIC funds and their investors' proceeds is identical to that for unit trusts.

(10) Personal equity plans (PEPs)

A personal equity plan (PEP) provided a way of making a tax-free investment in shares. The scheme was introduced by the Government in 1987 as a way of encouraging investment in UK companies. A maximum of £6,000 per annum per tax payer could be invested in a general PEP plus another £3,000 in a single company PEP (in the shares of a single company), making an overall limit of £9,000 per annum.

The income and capital gains generated by the investments held were not subject to income tax or CGT.

New PEPs could not be started after 5 April 1999 when ISAs (see (21)) became available. Existing PEPs continued after this date, but from 6 April 2008 all PEPs are treated as ISAs (stocks and shares accounts).

(11) Insurance bonds

Usually known as 'investment bonds' or 'single premium bonds', insurance bonds are single premium (one off capital payment, not the more usual regular insurance premiums) non-qualifying policies (ie, not satisfying ICTA 1988, s 267 and so attracting tax at maturity). The bonds are normally 'unit linked' with-profit policies, so that bonuses are added to the value of the units by the life company.

Income and capital are retained within the bond. Withdrawals up to 5% of the premiums paid can be taken tax free for the first 20 years of the bond.

Tax

No tax is payable by the investor during the life of the bond provided withdrawals do not exceed 5%. Gains arising on maturity of the bond are subject to higher-rate tax (as non-qualifying policies) but not to basic rate tax.

Suitability

These bonds are suitable for higher-rate tax payers with a lump sum to invest as there is no tax to pay during the life of the bond. The 5% tax free withdrawal represents the income entitlement from the investment. Ideally the bond should be planned to mature when the investor's tax rate has fallen below higher rate (so as to avoid income tax), for example, the bond could mature following retirement when income is less.

Risk: medium.

Income: low (max 5%). Capital growth: medium/high.

(12) Guaranteed bonds

These are single premium non-qualifying life policies which last for a fixed period. Guaranteed income bonds guarantee income at fixed rates, and guaranteed growth bonds guarantee a fixed return when the bond ends.

Tax

As non-qualifying life policies, there is no basic rate liability but higher rate tax may be payable.

Suitability

Both bonds may be suitable for basic rate tax payers (as only higher rate tax may be payable) with capital to invest.

Risk: low/medium.

Income: low/medium (none on guaranteed growth bonds). Capital growth: medium (income on guaranteed income bonds).

(13) Enterprise Investment Scheme (EIS relief)

A scheme introduced by the FA 1994 to replace the existing Business Expansion Scheme.

Individuals with capital to invest (maximum £500,000 in any tax year) obtain income tax relief at 20% of the amount invested provided various qualifications are met for the next three years. Capital gains made on disposal are free of CGT.

Qualifying investments are shares in unquoted trading companies carrying on trading activity in the UK. UK resident tax payers may obtain the relief but they are not eligible if they are 'connected with' the company, for example, as an employee or paid director. Further, combined shareholdings of the investor and his 'associates' must not exceed 30% of the share capital.

Example

£50,000 is invested in EIS shares in January 1998 (1997/98).

(a)   The initial investment – attracts 20% relief, so that the effective cost of the shares is £40,000.

(b)   If shares are sold more than three years later – any gain is free of CGT.

Because of the generous nature of the relief, and in an attempt to restrict its abuse, there are many detailed conditions in the FA 1994, Sch 15.

Suitability

Investors with substantial capital to invest in unquoted trading companies with which they are not connected. Although income tax relief at 20% is available on the investment, dividends received will attract income tax. Generally, it should be remembered the company's articles of association and questions of marketability of the shares may make it difficult to find a buyer for the shares. The danger is getting 'locked into' the investment – or perhaps only being able to sell at a reduced price.

Risk: medium/high.

Income: possibly none, depending on whether the company pays dividends.

Capital growth: medium/high (but marketability may make sale difficult).

(14) Offshore funds

These funds are managed by companies registered outside the UK tax and regulatory system under the Financial Services Act 1986 in places such as the Channel Islands and the Isle of Man.

Funds actively marketed in the UK (being approved by the Securities and Investments Board (now the Financial Services Authority)) are either Distributor Funds (ie, a fund which pays dividends equivalent to 85% of its income) or Accumulator Funds (where gross income is retained within the fund to increase its value).

Tax

Dividends from Distributor Funds are paid gross but are taxable on receipt into the UK. Income and capital gains of Accumulator Funds are subject to tax on sale of the investment and rates then prevailing.

Suitability

These funds are similar to UK unit and investment trusts and so are suitable for anyone with capital to invest. Distributor Funds (paid gross) may be particularly suited to non-tax payers. Accumulator Funds are more likely to be attractive to higher-rate tax payers who can afford to retain their investment offshore until after retirement when their tax rates are lower.

Risk: medium/high.

Income: medium/high.

Capital growth: medium/high.

(15) Pensions

Pension schemes are a way of saving for old age, so providing an income after retirement.

The main categories of scheme include State pensions, occupational pensions for employees, and personal pension schemes.

The State scheme

The State scheme is funded by the self-employed, employees and employers paying national insurance (NI) contributions. The scheme has two parts: a compulsory contribution and an additional voluntary State pension. Up to April 2002, the additional State pension was called the State Earnings-Related Pension Scheme (SERPS). This was based on the employee's record of NI contributions and level of earnings as an employee. It was possible for employers and employees to 'contract-out' and was not available to the self-employed.

All employers, employees and the self-employed must contribute to the compulsory part of the scheme. Provided a person has made sufficient contributions during his or her working life, he or she will currently receive the old age pension at 65 (though women born before 6 April 1955 will receive it at an age between 60 and 65). The Pensions Act 2007 provides for the State pension age for both men and women to rise from 65 to 68 in stages between 2024 and 2046, though on 20 October 2010 the Government announced that the retirement age will rise to 66 by 2020.

The additional SERPS pension is paid by the State if employer and employee have paid extra NI contributions. Contributions are based on the employee's annual earnings and there is no income tax relief for the employee's contributions. The pension will currently be paid at 65 (or between 60 and 65 for women born before 6 April 1955). It is possible to 'contract out' of SERPS. In this case, a lower level of NI contributions is payable but only the old age pension will be received after retirement. The Government has previously actively encouraged 'contracting out'; however, the Pensions Act 2007 will introduce some restrictions on the ability to contract out, by 2012.

On 6 April 2002, the Government reformed SERPS and replaced it with the State Second Pension. Any SERPS entitlement already built up is protected. The State Second Pension provides a more generous additional State pension for employees. It also assists certain carers and people with long-term illness or disability whose working lives have been interrupted or shortened.

Occupational pension schemes

These are often called company pension schemes but apply equally to those employed by partnerships and other non-corporate entities. The scheme must be offered by any employer who wishes to contract out of SERPS and may be contributory or non-contributory.

A non-contributory scheme is one where only the employer pays into the scheme to provide his employees with appropriate pension benefits on retirement. Such payments by the employer are not treated as an emolument of the employee for his income tax purposes and are based on a percentage of the employee's earnings.

In a contributory scheme, both the employer and employee contribute. Again, the employer's contributions are based on a percentage of the employee's annual earnings and do not count as emoluments. The employee's contributions are an agreed minimum percentage of earnings. He may also pay additional voluntary contributions (AVCs) into the scheme, or free-standing AVCs (FSAVCs) into a separately run scheme.

All contributions and AVCs are paid into a fund which is invested by the trustees of the pension scheme with the aim of increasing the value of the fund.

There are two main types of scheme:

(a) Salary related schemes (also known as 'defined benefit' schemes). The pension the employee gets is based on the number of years employed by the scheme provider and the level of earnings (usually at the date of retirement or the date when the employee leaves).

(b) Money purchase schemes (also known as 'defined contribution' schemes). The employee's contributions (together with any provided by the employer) are invested. The final pension is based on the amount invested and how well the investments have performed. The money is used to purchase an annuity.

Businesses are increasingly closing their salary schemes and turning to money purchase schemes which are cheaper to provide.

On retirement, an employee will receive either an annual pension based on the amount of his final salary, or a cash lump sum and a smaller annual pension.

Legislation controls the maximum amount of pension and lump sum which can be received.

Where an employee dies before retirement age, a lump sum based on contributions made to the scheme may be payable to the employee's dependants. Having started to receive a pension, all rights to it ceases on the employee's death. However, an employee can elect to receive a smaller pension than he would normally be entitled to with the guarantee that, on his death, the pension will continue to be paid to his widow for the remainder of her life.

Self-employed pension schemes

These schemes are available to the self-employed and to employees who either do not wish to join their employer's occupational pension scheme, or whose employers do not provide an occupational pension scheme.

An individual taking out a scheme for the first time is now limited to a personal pension, but until 1988 pension provision was made through retirement annuity contracts. Although it is no longer possible to buy new retirement annuity contracts, it is still possible for contributions to be made to contracts taken out before 1988, and most people who have existing retirement annuity contracts continue to pay into them in preference to acquiring a new personal pension because the various maximum limits are often more favourable.

Personal pensions

Contributions are paid to the pension fund company – usually one of the life assurance companies – which invests them to provide a cash lump sum and/or an annual income and annuity, for the individual when he reaches retirement age. The pension can start at any time between the ages of 50 and 75 years.

On retirement, the individual can choose to receive an annuity, ie a pension for life, or a reduced annuity plus a tax-free lump sum. This lump sum is calculated as a percentage of the total value of the fund available to the individual.

If the individual dies before retirement, the pension company will pay out a lump sum calculated in accordance with the scheme. To avoid this sum forming part of the individual's estate on death, and so chargeable to IHT, death benefits should be settled during the individual's life on, usually, discretionary trusts for the family and dependants.

Stakeholder pensions

In essence these are personal pension schemes which meet the following Government-imposed minimum standards:

(a)   annual management charges must not exceed 1.5% for the first 10 years, and thereafter must not exceed 1% (where a person joined a stakeholder pension scheme before 6 April 2005, the charges must not exceed 1% at any time);

(b)   there must be no initial charges or exit penalties;

(c)   the scheme must accept contributions of as little as £20 gross;

(d)   the rules must allow for contributions to be stopped, started and changed without penalties;

(e)   scheme managers must be authorised by the FSA or have trustees.

Many providers are offering charges which are substantially lower than 1% (sometimes as little as 0.4%).

As from October 2001, most employers will have to offer a stakeholder scheme unless:

(a)   they offer a group pension plan without exit charges, which employees who have been employed for three months can join, and the employer either pays a contribution of 3%, or will match an employee's contribution of 3%; or

(b)   the employer offers an occupational scheme which individuals can join within one year of starting employment.

Future reforms

The Pensions Act 2008 contains measures aiming to encourage more people to save in private pension schemes. Most of these measures are due to come into effect in 2012. They include the automatic enrolment of most employees not already in a qualifying pension scheme within either their employer's workplace scheme or a new savings vehicle (a 'personal account scheme'). Employers will be under a duty to contribute a minimum amount either into the workplace scheme or the personal account scheme.

Tax relief

Before 6 April 2006 there were a number of rules regulating the types of pension a person could have, how much a person could contribute to each type of pension and the tax relief available.

Since 6 April 2006 most of these rules have been replaced with a single regime. It is possible to save in more than one type of pension scheme at the same time, and there is no limit on the amount that may be saved, though there are limits on the tax relief available.

Tax relief is given on contributions made by a saver on the lesser of the value of that person's earnings or £255,000 (for the tax year 2010/11). This means that for every £1 paid in, the Government will pay an extra 25p (or more if the person is a higher rate tax payer). On 14 October 2010 the Government announced that from 6 April 2011 the annual maximum amount of contributions eligible for tax relief (at the highest rate of tax paid by the saver) will drop to £50,000.

Non-tax payers may also benefit from this but up to a limit of £3,600 gross, ie the non-tax payer pays in £2,880 in a tax year and the Government will add in a further £720.

When a person comes to take his or her pension, there may be a charge to tax if the total pension 'pot' at this point exceeds the 'Lifetime Allowance', which is set for the tax year 2010/11 at £1.8 million but is to drop to £1.5 million from 6 April 2012.

(16) Life assurance (insurance)

There are a number of life assurance products, only the most common types of which are dealt with below.

Whole life assurance (whole of life assurance)

In return for a regular monthly or annual premium an assurance company will contract to pay out an agreed fixed sum on the death of the life assured.

Most assurance companies refuse to insure the life of anybody over the age of 80 years and the older a person when they enter into a contract, the more expensive the premium. For example, a person aged 30 years might insure his life for a given sum for £50 per annum, while a person aged 60 years might pay £100 per annum for the same level of life cover.

Whole life policies can be written on single lives and also on joint lives. In the latter case, two lives are insured and the assurance company will either pay out on the first death or on the death of the survivor of the joint lives depending on the policy purchased. It is also possible for a person to insure a second person's life provided that he has an insurable interest in the second life. The fixed sum is paid out to the proposer on the death of the life assured.

If the policy is non-profit only a specified sum is payable on death. If it is with profit or unit linked there is an investment element. The sum assured will be paid with bonuses (with profit) or accumulated units (unit linked).

Tax

Premiums may be paid out of capital or income. No income tax relief is available for premiums paid.

On the death of the life assured, the assured sum forms part of his estate and will be liable to IHT unless the policy has been written in trust or assigned.

Suitability

Whole life assurance is suitable for anyone who wishes to provide a lump sum for his family or dependants on his death.

This may be to provide another asset, or to provide cash with which to meet debts such as an IHT bill or a mortgage or to provide funds to buy a deceased partner's share or the shares of a deceased shareholder/director whose shares might have to be sold to an outsider if the other members cannot afford to buy them.

It is not suitable for anybody wishing to save to provide a benefit for themselves.

Term assurance

In return for the payment of a regular premium the assurance company will pay out an agreed sum if the life assured dies within a fixed period of time from the purchase of the assurance policy. The term assurance provides protection only. There is no investment element.

If the proposer ceases to pay the premiums during the agreed term or the life assured survives the term, the policy comes to an end. It has no surrender value.

Tax

The tax treatment is the same as for whole life assurance.

Suitability

Term assurance is suitable for anyone, including trustees who needs to provide a lump sum with which to pay IHT which would become chargeable on a lifetime transfer if the transferor died within seven years of the transfer.

It may also be used by an individual to cover a fixed-term commitment such as a mortgage or school fees.

It is not suitable for anyone aiming to provide a benefit for himself.

Endowment assurance

In return for regular premiums, the assurance company contracts to pay the sum assured on the earlier of a given date or the death of the life assured. In these cases, there is clearly the possibility of personal enjoyment of the policy proceeds by the life assured.

The policy may be with profits or unit linked. It can be written on single or joint lives. There is an investment element.

Endowment policies provide protection as well as a sum payable on the maturity date for the policy or the earlier death of the life assured. These policies are frequently used in planning for the repayment of mortgages (where they are linked to the date for repayment of the mortgage) or school fees (where they are planned to mature at a time appropriate to payment of the fees).

Tax

Policies are normally for a minimum period of 10 years so that as 'qualifying policies' under ICTA 1988, s 267 the sum payable on maturity is tax free. If the life assured survives to the given date, he will receive the assured lump sum free of all taxes. If the payment is made on death, the sum forms part of the estate of the assured.

Suitability

Endowment assurance is suitable for any tax payer looking to build up a tax-free lump sum over a long period either for his own benefit or to meet commitments such as the repayment of a mortgage or the payment of school fees.

Keyman assurance

Where a person is a 'key' man or woman within an organisation, his or her premature death will affect the profitability of the company or partnership. The company or partnership may, therefore, insure that person's life so that the company or partnership receives a lump sum on the death of the 'key' man. The life assurance may be a whole life, term or endowment policy.

(17) Permanent health insurance (PHI)

A person who is in employment anticipates receiving a regular wage or salary or share of partnership profits in return for working. If that person becomes disabled and, therefore, unable to continue working, he will lose this source of income. He can, therefore, insure himself by paying an annual premium so that if he is no longer able to work, the insurance policy will provide him with regular sums of money for a stated period or up to a stated age. There is a limit on the annual amount which can be received from PHI.

Payment may not commence immediately after the disability arises as the policyholder can defer claiming benefit, for example, for three months. The longer the agreed period of deferral, the lower the annual premium.

An employer often provides PHI through group arrangements. Contributions paid are generally deductible as trading expenses.

Tax

An individual does not receive tax relief on the premiums paid.

Once benefits are claimed they are taxable as income.

Suitability

Permanent health insurance is suitable for anyone in work who has dependants, but cover may not be available for a person who is already in poor health when he applies to purchase the insurance cover. It is particularly suitable for the self-employed for whom replacement of income when permanently disabled will be essential. The effect on the business through absence of the 'owner' may cause it to fold.

(18) Annuities

In return for the investment of a capital lump sum, a life company will guarantee a regular amount of income (annuity) to the investor – purchased life annuity. The annuity can be paid annually, quarterly or monthly as the investor wishes. A good rate of return can be obtained if the annuity is purchased when interest rates are high. But the cost of the annuity depends partly on the age of the annuitant and may not be worthwhile until he reaches 70 years of age. On the death of the annuitant or expiry of the agreed term, usually no capital is returnable.

Tax

The Revenue regards purchased life annuity payments as being partly income and partly a return of the original capital invested (ICTA 1988, s 656). Only the income element is subject to income tax at the annuitant's income tax rates and is received net of lower rate tax. Some or all of this tax can be recovered by non and lower rate tax payers.

No tax is payable on the capital element.

Suitability

Annuities are suitable for anyone who needs a guaranteed income or income for life and who can afford to spend capital. The main disadvantages are that the real value of the income may be eroded by inflation and that once purchased there is no ability to surrender the annuity or recover the initial capital investment. Annuities may be suitable for elderly clients, or younger clients with children wishing to make provision for school fees.

Risk: low.

Income: medium/high (depending on age at purchase).

Capital growth: nil.

(19) School fee plans

There are a number of commercial plans available or parents can create their own provision. Those listed below are intended to give an indication of how some of these plans work. The deciding factor as to the type of plan is often whether the parent can afford a 'one off' lump sum payment out of capital, or whether the cost of the plan has to be met from income.

Funding from income

Life assurance schemes

Certain qualifying with profits or endowment life assurance policies enable the proceeds to be received completely tax free provided that premiums are payable for at least 10 years. The idea is that a series of such policies are purchased each maturing in consecutive years to provide annual funds for annual school fees.

Deferred annuities

Monthly premiums are paid to purchase an annuity equivalent to the level of fees whose payment is deferred until the fees are needed. The premium payments need not commence until shortly before school fees start to become due and continue until the last term for which fees are required.

The income element of the annuity will be subject to income tax at the parent's highest marginal rate.

Funding from capital

Compounding

Many schools offer their own fee plan. In return for a guaranteed level of fees parents pay a lump sum to the school in advance of the child starting at that school.

This can result in a substantial saving to the parents but care should be taken to check what happens to the lump sum if the child does not subsequently start at that school or leaves before the anticipated year.

There should be no tax consequences.

Educational trusts

There are a number of charitable educational trusts which, in return for an administration fee, invest the parents' lump sum in the purchase of an annuity payable termly to meet the fees. The annuity can start immediately or be deferred. The longer the deferral (eg, the plan is established on the birth of a child, to commence when he is 7 years old) the greater the value of the annuity. Any over-provision against the school fees can be paid to the parent.

Any annuity paid to the school is unlikely to be subject to income tax, but any surplus paid to the parent will suffer income tax at his rate(s) on the income element.

Gilt-edged securities

A lump sum can be invested in gilts with a range of redemption dates to mature over the school life of the child. If suitable redemption dates are not available, long-dated gifts can be purchased and holdings sold as and when school fees become due.

There is no CGT to pay on any gains made on the redemption or sale of gilts.

(20) Mortgages

Mortgages cannot be described as investments from the point of view of the borrower. Frequently, but not necessarily, they are linked to insurance policies which are investments. The insurance policy is designed to repay the mortgage debt at the end of the term or on the earlier death of the borrower so that the property on which it is secured can pass free of mortgage to the beneficiary under the borrower's will or intestacy.

There are many types of mortgage. The borrower must be advised to 'shop around' to find the type which best suits his particular circumstances. This is particularly true for the first-time buyer needing a large mortgage (or large as a proportion of the purchase price for the house).

In principle, there are two types of mortgage: the repayment mortgage and the interest only mortgage.

Repayment mortgages

Here, the monthly repayment is partly interest and partly a repayment of the capital sum outstanding. In the early years, the payments are largely of interest but include some capital repayment. As the capital is repaid, the proportion of interest in the monthly repayment reduces and the capital proportion increases.

To cover the possibility of the borrower dying before the capital is repaid at the end of the mortgage term, the lender will require a mortgage protection policy. A decreasing term assurance (with no investment element) is usual. It is decreasing in that the cover provided equates to the reducing capital sum due to the lender.

(Until April 2000, tax relief was available (within limits) on the interest paid to the lender in each year. The amount of this interest was certified to the Inland Revenue by the lender for tax relief purposes.)

Interest only mortgages

In these cases, the lender does not expect monthly repayment of capital but he will require interest on the amount borrowed. The capital remains due at the end of the mortgage term. Arrangements should be made by the borrower to fund this liability (sometimes the lender will lend only if adequate arrangements have been put in place). There are two main types of interest only mortgages.

The 'endowment mortgage'

This is a misleading phrase for a commonly met arrangement. There are two transactions – the mortgage and the endowment policy. The premiums on the policy attract no tax relief and represent a further outlay by the borrower but he is, at least, acquiring a valuable asset.

The policy is assigned to the lender. At the end of the mortgage the policy will mature. After the mortgage debt is discharged, any balance will be paid to the borrower. If the policy was a 'with profits' policy, there will often be a sizeable sum due to the borrower. In this way, the policy may prove to be a good investment.

Some 'with profit' policies assume that when bonuses are added at the end of the term, the sum assured will then be the equivalent of the sum borrowed. In such cases, the premium payable on the policy may be reduced because the sum assured is reduced. This will be attractive to many borrowers but increases the risk that the policy may not be sufficient to pay off the sum borrowed when it matures.

A 'pension mortgage'

This phrase is also misleading. Again there are two transactions – the mortgage and the pension. The assumption is that the repayment of the mortgage at the end of the term is funded from the 'tax free' lump sum payable from a personal pension (see (**15**)).

While superficially very attractive (bearing in mind the favourable tax position of a personal pension), it must be remembered that the real purpose of the pension is to provide an income for retirement (and not a lump sum to repay a mortgage debt).

(21) Individual Savings Accounts (ISAs)

Individual Savings Accounts (ISAs) become available from April 1999 to replace TESSAs (see (**3**) and PEPs (**10**)) from that date.

Cash ISAs and stocks and shares ISAs

From 6 April 2010, UK resident and ordinarily resident adult savers may subscribe a total of up to £10,200 each year in up to two different ISAs. They may invest up to £5,100 in a cash ISA and may invest the balance of their £10,200 allowance in a stocks and shares ISA. So, for example, in the 2010/11 tax year an adult may invest £4,200 in a cash ISA, and £6,000 in a stocks and shares ISA. The annual limit was £7,200 during the period 6 April 2008 and 5 April 2010.

A UK resident and ordinarily resident person who is aged between 16 and 18 may invest up to £5,100 in a cash ISA.

It is possible for savers to transfer existing cash savings held in ISAs (either from cash invested in the current tax year or in previous years) from a cash ISA to a stocks and shares ISA, up to the maximum for the year, but not vice versa. If a transfer is made, the saver may then 'top up' his cash ISA, up to the maximum for the year.

From 6 April 2011 the ISA subscription limit will be increased in line with the retail prices index each year, taking effect on 6 April. The new limit will be rounded to a convenient multiple of £120 to allow monthly savers to calculate their monthly payments more easily. The limit for 2011/12 has been announced as £10,680.

Income and capital gains arising from ISAs are exempt from income tax and CGT.

A husband and wife can each have their own investments in ISAs. There is no minimum investment, nor is there any overall lifetime limit.

Rules before 6 April 2008

Before 6 April 2008, the rules were slightly different. UK resident and ordinarily resident adult savers could subscribe to either a maxi-ISA or up to two mini-ISAs each tax year.

£7,000 could be invested annually in a maxi-ISA. Of this, up to £3,000 could be in cash (on deposit) and the rest in a mixture of investments (equities and certain life assurance policies). Alternatively, less (or none) could be in cash and the rest (or the whole) in investments. Instead of one maxi-ISA, investors could have up to one of each of two types of mini-ISAs: a cash mini-ISA of up to £3,000; and an investments mini-ISA of up to £4,000.

From 6 April 2008, all existing maxi- and mini-ISAs became either cash ISAs or stocks and shares ISAs. All existing PEPS became stocks and shares ISAs and all existing 'Tessa-only' ISAs became cash ISAs.

Appendix 3 – Discretionary Settlement

Table of contents

SETTLEMENT

DATE: [   ]

PARTIES:

(1)   [   ] (the 'Settlor'); and

(2)   [   ] (the 'Trustees').

RECITALS

(A)   The Settlor wishes to make this Settlement and has transferred or delivered to the Trustees or otherwise placed under their control the property specified in the Schedule. Further money, investments or other property may be paid or transferred to the Trustees by way of addition.

(B)   It is intended that this Settlement shall be irrevocable.

PART 1 – OPERATIVE PROVISIONS

1. Definitions and construction

In this Deed, where the context admits, the following definitions and rules of construction shall apply.

1.1   The 'Trust Fund' shall mean:

    (a)   the property specified in the Schedule;

    (b)   all money, investments or other property paid or transferred by

        any person to, or so as to be under the control of, and, in either case, accepted by the Trustees as additions;

    (c)   all accumulations (if any) of income added to the Trust Fund; and

    (d)   the money, investments and property from time to time representing the above.

1.2   The 'Trust Period' shall mean the period ending on the earlier of:

    (a)   the last day of the period of 125 years from the date of this Deed, which period, and no other, shall be the applicable perpetuity period; and

(b)   such date as the Trustees shall at any time specify by deed, not being a date earlier than the date of execution of such deed or later than a date previously specified.

1.3   The 'Beneficiaries' shall mean:

(a)   the Settlor's children and remoter issue;

(b)   the spouses, widows and widowers (whether or not such widows or widowers have remarried) of the Settlor's children and remoter issue;

(c)   [   ];

[(d)   Charities;] and

[(e)]   such other objects or persons as are added under clause 3.

1.4   'Charity' shall mean any trust, foundation, company or other organisation whatever established only for purposes regarded as charitable under the law of England and Wales.

1.5   The expression 'the Trustees' shall, where the context admits, include the trustees for the time being of this Trust.

1.6   References to the children, grandchildren and issue of any person shall include his children, grandchildren and remoter issue, whether legitimate, legitimated[, illegitimate] or adopted [but shall exclude any illegitimate person and his descendants].

1.7   Words denoting the singular shall include the plural and vice versa.

1.8   Words denoting any gender shall include both the other genders.

1.9   References to any statutory provision shall include any statutory modification to or re-enactment of such provision.

1.10   The table of contents and clause headings are included for reference only and shall not affect the interpretation of this Deed.

2. Power to receive additional property

The Trustees may, at any time during the Trust Period, accept additional money, investments or other property, of whatever nature and wherever situate, paid or transferred to them by the Settlor or any other person. Such additional money, investments or other property shall, subject to any contrary direction, be held upon the trusts and with and subject to the powers and provisions of this Deed.

3. Power to add Beneficiaries

3.1   The Settlor, or such person as the Settlor shall have nominated in writing, may, at any time during the Trust Period, add to the Beneficiaries such objects or persons or classes of objects or persons as the Settlor or such other person shall, subject to the application (if any) of the rule against perpetuities, determine.

3.2   Any such addition shall be made by deed:

(a)   naming or describing the objects or persons or classes of objects or persons to be added; and

(b)   specifying the date or event, not being earlier than the date of execution of the deed but before the end of the Trust Period, on the happening of which the addition shall take effect.

[3.3   This power shall not be exercised so as to add to the Beneficiaries either the Settlor or any person who shall previously have added property to the Trust Fund or the spouse for the time being of the Settlor or any such person.]

4. Discretionary trust of capital and income

4.1   The Trustees shall hold the capital and income of the Trust Fund upon trust for or for the benefit of such of the Beneficiaries, at such ages or times, in such shares, upon such trusts (which may include discretionary or protective powers or trusts) and in such manner generally as the Trustees shall in their discretion appoint. Any such appointment may include such powers and provisions for the maintenance, education or other benefit of the Beneficiaries or for the accumulation of income and such administrative powers and provisions as the Trustees think fit.

4.2   No exercise of the power conferred by sub-clause 4.1 shall invalidate any prior payment or application of all or any part of the capital or income of the Trust Fund under the trusts of this Deed or made under any other power conferred by this Deed or by law.

4.3   Any trusts and powers created by an appointment under sub-clause 4.1 may be delegated to any extent to any person, whether or not including the Trustees or any of them.

[4.4   Notwithstanding clause [   ], the Trustees may not release or restrict this power during the Settlor's lifetime without his written consent.]

4.5   The exercise of the power of appointment conferred by sub-clause 4.1 shall:

(a)   be subject to the application, if any, of the rule against perpetuities; [and]

(b)   be by deed, revocable during the Trust Period or irrevocable, executed during the Trust Period [; and

(c)   be subject to the written consent of the Settlor during his lifetime].

5. Income trusts in default of appointment

The provisions of this clause shall apply during the Trust Period until, subject to and in default of any appointment under sub-clause 4.1.

5.1   The Trustees shall pay or apply the income of the Trust Fund to or for the benefit of such of the Beneficiaries as shall for the time being be in existence, in such shares and in such manner generally as the Trustees shall in their discretion from time to time think fit.

5.2   Notwithstanding the provisions of sub-clause 5.1, the Trustees may at any time in their discretion accumulate the income by investing it in any investments authorised by this Deed or by law and, subject to sub-clause 5.3, shall hold such accumulations as an accretion to capital.

5.3   The Trustees may apply the whole or any part of the income accumulated under sub-clause 5.2 as if it were income arising in the then current year.

6. Power to apply capital for Beneficiaries

The provisions of this clause shall apply during the Trust Period notwithstanding the provisions of clause 5 but subject to any appointment made under sub-clause 4.1.

6.1   The Trustees may pay or apply the whole or any part of the capital of the Trust Fund to or for the benefit of all or such of the Beneficiaries, in such shares, and in such manner generally as the Trustees shall in their discretion think fit.

6.2   The Trustees may, subject to the application (if any) of the rule against perpetuities, pay or transfer any income or capital of the Trust Fund to the trustees of any other trust, wherever established or existing, under which any Beneficiary is interested (whether or not such Beneficiary is the only object or person interested or capable of benefiting under such other trust) if the Trustees in their discretion consider such payment or transfer to be for the benefit of such Beneficiary.

7. Trusts in default of appointment

From and after the expiration of the Trust Period, and subject to any appointment made under sub-clause 4.1, the Trustees shall hold the capital and income of the Trust Fund upon trust absolutely for such of [ ] as shall then be living and, if more than one, in equal shares per stirpes, provided that no issue shall take whose parent is alive and so capable of taking.

8. Ultimate default trusts

Subject as above and if and so far as not wholly disposed of for any reason whatever by the above provisions, the capital and income of the Trust Fund shall be held upon trust for [ ] absolutely.

9. Administrative powers

The Trustees shall, in addition and without prejudice to all statutory powers, have the powers and immunities set out in Part 2 of this Deed. No power conferred on the Trustees shall be exercised so as to conflict with the beneficial provisions of this Deed.

10. Extended power of maintenance

The statutory provisions for maintenance and education shall apply but so that the power of maintenance shall be exercisable in the discretion of the Trustees and free from the obligation to apply part only of the income for maintenance where other income is available.

11. Extended power of advancement

The statutory provisions for advancement shall apply but so that the power of advancement shall extend to the whole, rather than one half, of the share or interest of the person for whose benefit the advancement is made.

12. Appointment of new trustees

12.1   During the lifetime of the Settlor the power of appointing new trustees shall be vested in the Settlor.

12.2   A person may be appointed to be a trustee notwithstanding that such person is not resident in the United Kingdom. Remaining out of the United Kingdom for more than 12 months shall not be a ground for the removal of a trustee.

13. Proper law, forum and place of administration

13.1   The proper law of this Trust shall be that of England and Wales. All rights under this Deed and its construction and effect shall be subject to the jurisdiction of, and construed according to, the laws of England and Wales.

13.2   The courts of England and Wales shall be the forum for the administration of these trusts.

13.3   Notwithstanding the provisions of sub-clauses 13.1 and 13.2:

(a)   The Trustees shall have power, subject to the application (if any) of the rule against perpetuities, to carry on the general administration of these trusts in any jurisdiction in the world. This power shall be exercisable whether or not the law of such jurisdiction is for the time being the proper law of this Trust or the courts of such jurisdiction are for the time being the forum for the administration of these trusts, and whether or not the Trustees or any of them are for the time being resident or domiciled in, or otherwise connected with, such jurisdiction.

(b)   The Trustees may at any time declare in writing that, from the date of such declaration, the proper law of this Trust shall be that of any specified jurisdiction. No exercise of this power shall be effective unless the law of the jurisdiction specified is one under which this Trust remains irrevocable and all, or substantially all, of the trusts, powers and provisions contained in this Deed remain enforceable and capable of being exercised and so taking effect.

(c)   Following any exercise of the power contained in sub-clause 13.3(b), the Trustees shall, by deed, make such consequential alterations or additions to this Deed as they consider necessary or desirable to ensure that, so far as may be possible, the trusts, powers and provisions of this Deed shall be as valid and effective as they were immediately prior to such change.

(d)   The Trustees may, at any time, declare in writing that, from the date of such declaration, the forum for the administration of these trusts shall be the courts of any specified jurisdiction.]

14. Exclusion of Settlor and spouse

14.1   No discretion or power conferred on the Trustees or any other person by this Deed or by law shall be exercised, and no provision of this Deed shall operate directly or indirectly, so as to cause or permit any part of the capital or income of the Trust Fund to become in any way payable to or applicable for the benefit of the Settlor or any person who shall previously have added property to the Trust Fund or the spouse for the time being of the Settlor or any such person.

14.2   The provisions of sub-clause 14.1 shall not preclude the Settlor or any such person from exercising any statutory right to claim reimbursement from the Trustees for any income tax or capital gains tax paid by him in respect of income arising to the Trustees or capital gains realised or deemed or treated as realised by them.

14.3   Subject to sub-clause 14.2, the prohibition in this clause shall apply notwithstanding anything else contained or implied in this Deed.

15. Exclusion of Trusts of Land and Appointment of Trustees Act 1996, s 11(1)

Section 11 (trustees' duty to consult beneficiaries) of the Trusts of Land and Appointment of Trustees Act 1996 shall not apply to the trusts contained in this Deed.

PART 2 – ADMINISTRATIVE PROVISIONS

SCHEDULE
[The initial Trust Fund]

Signed as a deed and delivered   )
by [   ]   )
in the presence of:)

Appendix 4 – Settlement for Bereaved Young Persons

EXTRACT FROM WILL CREATING A SETTLEMENT FOR BEREAVED YOUNG PERSONS

1.   Definitions and construction

In this Will, where the context admits, the following definitions and rules of construction shall apply.

1.1   The 'Trust Fund' shall mean:

    (a)   the sum of [   ];

    (b)   all accumulations (if any) of income added to the Trust Fund; and

    (c)   the money, investments and property from time to time representing the above.

1.2   The 'Trust Period' shall mean the period ending on the earlier of:

    (a)   the last day of the period of 125 years from the date of my death, which period, and no other, shall be the applicable perpetuity period; and

    (b)   such date as the Trustees shall at any time specify by deed, not being a date earlier than the date of execution of such deed or later than a date previously specified.

1.3   'Primary Beneficiary' shall mean:

    my children, namely

    [   ] who was born on [   ];

    [   ] who was born on [   ];

    [   ] who was born on [   ]; and

    [   ] who was born on [   ].

1.4   'Beneficiary' shall mean any person actually or prospectively entitled to any share or interest in the capital or income of the Trust Fund.

1.5   The 'Closing Date' shall mean whichever shall be the earlier of:

    (a)   the date on which the first Primary Beneficiary to do so attains the age of 25; and

    (b)   the date on which the Trust Period shall determine.

1.6   The expression 'the Trustees' shall, where the context admits, include the trustees for the time being of this Trust.

1.7   References to the children, grandchildren and issue of any person shall include his children, grandchildren and remoter issue, whether legitimate, legitimated[, illegitimate] or adopted [, but shall exclude any illegitimate person and his descendants].

1.8   Words denoting the singular shall include the plural and vice versa.

1.9   Words denoting any gender shall include both the other genders.

1.10   References to any statutory provision shall include any statutory modification to or re-enactment of such provision.

1.11   The table of contents and clause headings are included for reference only and shall not affect the interpretation of this Will.

2. Gift to Trustees

I give the Trust Fund to the Trustees to hold on the trusts set out in clause 3.

3. Principal trusts

3.1   The Trust Fund shall be held upon trust for such of the Primary Beneficiaries as:

    (a)   attain the age of 25 before the end of the Trust Period; or

    (b)   are living and under that age at the end of the Trust Period

    and, if more than one, in equal shares absolutely.

3.2   The provisions of sub-clauses 3.3, 3.4 and clause 4 shall apply to the share of the Trust Fund to which any of the Primary Beneficiaries is or may become entitled under sub-clause 3.1. In those provisions, such share is called the 'Share' and that one of the Primary Beneficiaries who is primarily interested in the Share is called the 'Primary Beneficiary'.

3.3   If any Primary Beneficiary shall die during the Trust Period, under the age of 25 and leaving children who survive him, the Share of such Primary Beneficiary shall be held upon trust for such of the children of the Primary Beneficiary as attain the age of 25 before the end of the Trust Period, or are living and under that age at the end of the Trust Period, and, if more than one, in equal shares absolutely.[1]

3.4   No Primary Beneficiary shall be entitled to any share of the Trust Fund without bringing any assets or interest advanced to him or paid or applied for his benefit (in exercise of any of the powers conferred by sub-clause 4.2 or clause 9) into account in such manner as the Trustees shall in their discretion determine with a view to achieving an equitable division of the unadvanced part of the Trust Fund.

[1] If a child dies under the age of 25 and with children who survive, the portion of the settlement funds held for the substituted grandchildren will be held on relevant property trusts, not s 71D trusts. The substitution does not affect the status of the rest of the settlement. The settlement will, therefore, contain both relevant property and s 71D trusts.

Most settlors will want to provide for bereaved grandchildren and so will include a substitution provision, even though there will be anniversary and exit charges on the portion held for the grandchildren.

4. Trusts for Primary Beneficiaries under 25

This clause shall apply, during the Trust Period, in respect of the Share of any Primary Beneficiary who is living and under the age of 25.

4.1   The Trustees may pay or apply any income of the Share to or for the maintenance or education or otherwise for the benefit of the Primary Beneficiary, or any other Primary Beneficiaries who are for the time being living and under the age of 25.

4.2   Subject as above, the income of the Share shall be accumulated as an accretion to the capital of the Share. Any such accumulations may, at any time, be paid or applied in the manner set out in sub-clause 4.1 as if they were income of the Share arising in the then current year.

4.3   The Trustees may also pay or apply any capital of the Share to or for the maintenance, education, advancement or otherwise for the benefit of the Primary Beneficiary. No capital may be applied in such a way that the income of it might meanwhile be dealt with except by being applied for the maintenance, education or otherwise for the benefit of one or more of the Primary Beneficiaries for the time being living and under the age of 25 or by being accumulated.[2]

[2] The trustees can use this power to advance capital to beneficiaries early. If they do it before the beneficiary reaches 18 there will be no exit charge; if the beneficiary has already reached 18 at the time of the advance, there will be a charge based on the period that has elapsed since the beneficiary's 18th birthday.

The power is wide enough to allow the trustees to settle funds on further trusts if they think that a beneficiary is insufficiently mature to deal with an absolute advance. Settling the funds will be an exit from the original s 71D settlement, and the new settlement produced will be a relevant property settlement subject to both anniversary and exit charges.

The powers conferred by this clause are limited to the share of each primary beneficiary who is under 25.

5. Trust to accumulate

Subject as above, so long as no Primary Beneficiary has attained the age of 25 and further Primary Beneficiaries may come into existence, the income of the Trust Fund shall be accumulated.

6. Ultimate default trusts

In the event of the failure or determination of the above trusts, the capital and income of the Trust Fund shall be held upon trust for [such of the Primary Beneficiaries as are living at the date of this Will, and if more than one, in equal shares] absolutely.

7. Administrative powers

The Trustees shall, in addition and without prejudice to all statutory powers, have the powers and impunities set out in Part 2 of this Will. No power conferred on the Trustees shall be exercised so as to conflict with the beneficial provisions of this Will.

8. Extended power of maintenance

The statutory provisions for maintenance and education shall apply, but so that the power of maintenance shall be exercisable in the discretion of the Trustees and free from the obligation to apply part only of the income for maintenance where other income is available.

9. Extended power of advancement

The statutory provisions for advancement shall apply, but so that the power of advancement shall extend to the whole, rather than one half, of the share or interest of the person for whose benefit that advancement is made.

Appendix 5 – Will – Outline Structure

Opening	Name, address, occupation and date (unless at end of will)
Revocation	Previous wills and codicils
Executors and trustees	Individuals (lay, professional); trust corporation
Specific bequests/devises	Particular items owned
Pecuniary legacies	Money
Residuary gift	Absolute or contingent gifts to individuals or class of individuals
	Substitution provision in case prior gift fails
Powers of executors and/or trustees	Implied by statute Express provision
Attestation	Signed by the testator in the presence of two independent witnesses
	Witnesses sign in the presence of the testator

Appendix 6 – Trust Distribution Account

John Bale Trust

(a) Tom Bale set up an accumulation and maintenance trust for his nephew John under which John became entitled to the trust capital on his 18th birthday on 10 February 200–.

(b) The trustees being satisfied that no capital tax liability arises (no IHT since the trust is an accumulation and maintenance trust; no CGT because their annual exemption covers the gain on their deemed disposal caused by John's absolute entitlement) have transferred the investment in ABC plc to John.

(c) The dividend shown in the income account was received on 25 March 200– and it, together with the remaining cash has been transferred to John.

Capital account

	£
Assets held on 10 February 200–	
ABC plc ordinary shares	10,000.00
Cash	50.00
	10,050.00
Less: Lowe, Snow & Co's costs, disbursements and VAT on distribution of the funds	30.00
Balance held for John Bale	10,020.00

Income account

Income tax year 200–/200–	
Dividend	
ABC plc ordinary shares	10.00
Balance held for John Bale	10.00

Beneficiary's account

Capital, per capital account	10,020.00
Income, per income account	10.00
Total due	10,030.00
Represented by	
ABC plc ordinary shares	10,000.00
Balance of cash, now due	30.00
	10,030.00

Index